# LEFT OF THE LEFT

★

## MY MEMORIES OF
# SAM DOLGOFF

## ANATOLE DOLGOFF

**INTRODUCTION BY ANDREW CORNELL**

**Praise for Anatole Dolgoff's *Left of the Left*:**

"The American left in its classical age used to celebrate an ideal, which was the worker-intellectual—someone who toils with his hands all his life and meanwhile develops his mind and deepens his knowledge and contributes mightily to progress and decency in the society around him. Sam Dolgoff was a mythic figure in a certain corner of the radical left, and that is because he conformed to that ideal in every particular. He was a first-rate Wobbly. He was a great man. And his son, Anatole Dolgoff, has written a wise and beautiful book about him."

—Paul Berman, author of *A Tale of Two Utopias*,
*Power and the Idealists*, and other books

"If you want to read the god-honest and god-awful truth about being a radical in twentieth-century America, drop whatever you're doing, pick up this book, and read it. Pronto! If you're not crying within five pages, you might want to check whether you've got a heart and a pulse. Anatole Dolgoff's love, admiration, and memories of his father saturate the pages, making it required reading for folks interested in Wobblies, anarchists, workers, unionists, New Yorkers, Americans, non-Americans, un-Americans, and every other human being, for that matter. Make no mistake, the seventy-nine-year old Dolgoff's one helluva a brilliant story-teller."

—Peter Cole, author of *Wobblies on the Waterfront: Interracial
Unionism in Progressive-Era Philadelphia* and
*Ben Fletcher: The Life and Times of a Black Wobbly*

*Left of the Left: My Memories of Sam Dolgoff*

© 2016 Anatole Dolgoff
This edition © 2016 AK Press (Chico, Oakland, Edinburgh, Baltimore)

ISBN: 978-1-84935-248-2
E-ISBN: 978-1-84935-249-9
Library of Congress Control Number: 2015959328

AK Press
370 Ryan Ave. #100
Chico, CA 95973
USA
www.akpress.org
akpress@akpress.org

AK Press
PO Box 12766
Edinburgh EH8 9YE
Scotland
www.akuk.com
ak@akedin.demon.co.uk

The above addresses would be delighted to provide you with the latest AK Press distribution catalog, which features books, pamphlets, zines, and stylish apparel published and/or distributed by AK Press. Alternatively, visit our websites for the complete catalog, latest news, and secure ordering.

Cover design by John Yates | stealworks.com
Printed in the USA on acid-free, recycled paper

To my friend Herbert Miller.

"Now, he has departed from this strange world a little ahead of me. That means nothing. People like us, who believe in physics, know that the distinction between past, present, and future is only a stubbornly persistent illusion." —Albert Einstein

# TABLE OF CONTENTS

# INTRODUCTION

## BY ANDREW CORNELL

Until very recently, the history of anarchism in the middle part of the twentieth century has remained frustratingly opaque. Anatole Dolgoff's memoir of his father, Sam, and the worlds of work and activism Sam inhabited, is a unique gift in that it sheds both light and warmth on this period. Readers learn not only who knew whom and how anarchists reacted to major historical events, but also gain real insight into the emotional and family lives, the motivations and coping strategies, of a network of stalwart radicals confronting the highs and lows of the American Century.

Sam Dolgoff was a house painter, a loving husband and father, a militant labor organizer, a powerful orator, and a self-taught public intellectual. He was not, perhaps, as daring and globetrotting a figure as Emma Goldman or the subjects of some other radical biographies. To hilarious and heart-breaking effect, Anatole describes the way Carlo Tresca and other mentors talked Sam out of joining street fights with Italian-American fascists or shipping out to fight in the Spanish Revolution, owing to his poor eyesight and family responsibilities. But Sam Dolgoff was heroic in a least one respect, and that was his tenacity.

Sam stuck to his bedrock beliefs that humans were capable of cooperating with one another, managing their own affairs, and sharing earth's wealth equitably. For seven decades he continued to express these ideas in print and speech. And he continued to show up—to demonstrations, to lightly attended forums, and to tedious meetings—even when many of his former collaborators had given up. In doing so he served as a connecting thread that stitched together generations of people invested in the project of human liberation. His willingness and ability to play this bridging role is powerfully exemplified in the story Anatole tells of Sam taking members of the countercultural Up Against the Wall/Motherfuckers group to beg financial assistance from octogenarian friends of Sacco and Vanzetti in the late 1960s.

It also becomes readily apparent that Sam and his wife Esther truly lived the communal ethos they espoused. Hardly a chapter of this memoir passes without an account of old Wobblies camped out on the Dolgoffs' living room sofa, or Sam giving away prized possessions to a new acquaintance. This spirit of selflessness is mirrored in the structure of the book, for Anatole's portrait of his father soon spins off to recount the stories of his mother (herself a dedicated anarchist organizer), other family members, and more than a dozen fascinating revolutionaries, such as Russell Blackwell, Ben Fletcher, Dorothy Day, and Federico Arcos, whose own stories and contributions are in danger of being lost to history. The book, then, serves as the collective biography of an entire milieu, echoing the fashion in which Goldman studded her own autobiography, *Living My Life*, with biographical sketches of comrades and lovers.

These stories are not always rousing. We meet aging seafarers and longshoremen grown cynical and lonely following the cascading catastrophes of the Red Scare, the repressive turn in world communism, and the defeat of the Spanish Revolution. But that is part of what makes this book so fascinating; where else can one glimpse the interior life of old Wobblies still devoted to class war as they watch fellow workers embrace middle-class identities and the anarchist movement become overrun with college students? As these sections unfurled, I recognized the double entendre tucked into the book's title; this is not only the story of a man who was more radical than many other rabble-rousers, but also an account of what remained—what was left—of the Left during the years that Anatole was growing up. That the book is, at other turns, incredibly funny testifies to the author's skills as a writer and raconteur—especially his ear for dialogue.

Since Anatole's narrative jumps forward and backwards in order to emphasize points and personalities, it may be useful to briefly review some context and chronology. Social anarchism emerged as a distinct tendency within the labor and socialist movements of the United States in the early 1880s, appealing primarily to immigrant laborers from eastern and southern Europe. The movement reached a peak of influence in the first two decades of the twentieth century, during Sam's childhood and adolescence. In these years, anarchist newspapers published in English, Yiddish, Russian, Italian, and Spanish reached tens of thousands of people each month. Socialists, anarchists, and other labor militants launched the Industrial Workers of the World (IWW)—the organization that would long serve as Sam's political home—in 1905, three years after he was born. It grew in size and reputation over the next decade by leading a series of historic strikes in textile, mining, and other basic industries.

Anarchism was fertile enough during the Progressive Era to encompass competing strategic tendencies. Anarcho-syndicalists saw the IWW and other radical unions as vehicles to help workers win immediate improvements while preparing for a general strike that would usher in revolution. Another group, sometimes referred to as insurrectionary anarchists, believed that unions and anarchist federations would actually hinder the process of social conflict needed for change to occur. They promoted assassination and other forms of "propaganda of the deed" that they believed would spark off mass uprisings of the oppressed. Italian anarchists influenced by Luigi Galleani proved to be the most consistent advocates of the insurrectionary strategy in the United States between 1910 and the 1940s. (Though Anatole describes these anarchists as "individualists," I consider the clunky term *anti-organizationalist* more precise, since adherents advocated for a communal future.) A third group of anarchists began attracting larger numbers of native born and middle-class supporters as they turned their attention to gender equality, free speech, progressive methods of education, and art—the "transient" issues Sam and Esther debate in Chapter 19.

Most U.S. anarchists and Wobblies opposed the First World War, and faced an avalanche of repression as a result. Government officials deported leaders, suppressed newspapers, and severely curtailed immigration, drying up an important pool of working people from which the movements had historically drawn recruits. A variety of foreign language anarchist journals survived this Red Scare (or quickly reconstituted themselves in its wake), but spoke to aging constituencies as assimilation and the use of English became increasingly common for the younger generation. Small groups that conducted meetings in English emerged in a few large cities by the mid-1920s. During these years, East Coast anarchists also developed the Stelton and Mohegan colonies—intentional communities of radicals centered on "modern schools"—in which the Dolgoffs lived for a few years. Residents of the Stelton Colony launched *The Road to Freedom*, the first English-language anarchist newspaper of national scope to appear in the United States since the war. Sam's first contributions to the anarchist press appeared in *The Road to Freedom* later in the decade.

As the boom years of the 1920s gave way to the Great Depression, anarchists found themselves losing ground to the Communist Party-USA in struggles to win large numbers over to their social vision and strategy for change. When *The Road to Freedom* ceased publication in 1932, it was replaced by two new English-language periodicals. The first was *Vanguard*, the anarcho-syndicalist-oriented journal that Sam cofounded and contributed to regularly. As Anatole explains, the Vanguard Group allied with Carlo Tresca and his circle of Italian-American anarchists. The other major English-language periodical of the decade, *Man!*, was published in Oakland, California, by Marcus Graham—the man Anatole reveals (in Chapter 13) to have competed with Sam for Esther's affection. *Man!* aligned itself with the anti-organizational, insurrectionary anarchists who published the newspaper *L'Adunata dei Refretarri* (loosely, *The Summoning of the Unruly*).

Anatole describes Marcus Graham as belonging to the "individualist-vegetarian-anti-technology school" of anarchism. In the 1930s, this was a school of one; in refusing to eat meat and critiquing the dangers of "machine society" Graham's ideas anticipated core themes of 1990s anarchism, but placed him at odds with nearly all of his contemporaries. Despite personal rivalries and strategic disagreements, both camps spent the decade battling American fascists and building support for the Spanish anarchists, who attempted to implement a social revolution in the midst of that country's 1936–1939 civil war.

The Second World War proved to be another turning point for the anarchist movement in the United States. After *Vanguard* and *Man!* ran aground in 1939, the Dolgoffs helped to launch the journal *Why?* in 1942, but withdrew from the project when the editors—some of whom had been mentored by the Vanguard Group while still in high school—took an anti-war position. As the decade progressed, anarchists associated with *Why?* (the title was changed to *Resistance* in 1947) formed alliances with radical pacifists, poets, and playwrights, including Dorothy Day's Catholic Worker group and members of the avant-garde Living Theatre troop.

This younger cohort, which included Paul Goodman and David Wieck, attempted to adapt anarchism to the rapidly changing post-war world, shifting focus from class exploitation to authoritarian social conditioning, sexual repression, racism, consumerism, and the destruction of the natural environment. Sam saw their attempts to address psychological aspects of power and to "live differently" as a self-absorbed abandonment of mass struggle; they saw him as living in the past, clinging to failed strategies. Neither approach made immediate headway in a period marked by the incorporation of the mainstream unions into the power structure, rising living standards for white workers, and intense Cold War anti-radicalism.

The Libertarian League, which the Dolgoffs founded with Russell Blackwell in 1954, kept the shaky flame of class-struggle anarchism burning in the United States. With the IWW flagging, it functioned as something of an international clearinghouse, providing U.S. Americans with translated news about the struggles of workers in South America and other places where revolutionary union federations remained mass phenomena. And it was there, able to serve as a point of connection to past struggles, when a new generation of civil rights and anti-war activists started becoming radicalized in the early 1960s.

The artist Ben Morea attended Libertarian League meetings before going on to launch the journal *Black Mask* in 1964 and Up Against the Wall/Motherfuckers, a "street gang with an analysis," in 1967. Through their early connections with the Situationist International, the Dutch Provos, and other countercultural militants in the United States and abroad, Morea and company served as an essential point of reference for the vast anarcho-punk culture that took shape in the 1970s. League meetings also provided stepping-stones for Murray Bookchin as he crossed over from Trotskyism to anarchism. Later in the decade, Bookchin formed the Anarchos Group, which published a journal and organized small discussion groups, as the Libertarian League had, but threw its chips in with the burgeoning ecology movement and the youth counter culture, while the Dolgoffs served as mentors to 1960s radicals eager to reinvigorate the IWW. These three tendencies, along with a distinct anarcha-feminist current that emerged in the early 1970s, shaped the complex terrain of contemporary anarchism as it developed in the final decades of the twentieth century. It is not an overstatement to say that Sam and Esther Dolgoff were crucial, directly and indirectly, to the revival of anarchism as a major vector of egalitarian struggle in the world today.

The later chapters of *Left of the Left* discuss Sam's contributions to anarchist scholarship, such as his important books on Bakunin's thought and the Spanish and Cuban revolutions. Sam taught himself to read multiple foreign languages to better understand international events and keep abreast of anarchist and labor struggles throughout the world. He penned prescient analyses of postcolonial governments, technological change, and the shortcomings of centrist labor unions, while providing crucial information to the historian Paul Avrich, to whom we owe much of what is known about pre-WWI U.S. anarchism. This production and preservation of fugitive knowledge, outside the university and other official channels, should be seen as another important form of activism, from which we, as readers, can learn and take inspiration. I am grateful that Anatole Dolgoff chose to follow in his parents' footsteps, in this regard—to collect and protect the stories and the hard-won knowledge of earlier generations of radicals, knowing there would be a time, like now, when many people would be ready and eager to hear them.

# 1

# PROLOGUE: A LONG WALK, 1944

I'm seventy-nine years old and remember clearly the joy I felt as a small boy when my father, having decided "to give the old woman a rest," announced it was "time to visit the Five-Ten Hall." When the three of us—my father, my brother Abraham, and I—survived Mother's loving last-minute attentions, and escaped onto the still Sunday-morning street.

The Five-Ten Hall was at 134 Broad Street, a short block to Battery Park and South Ferry. We lived across town on the Lower East Side, in whichever tenement was cheapest, but as close as possible to the water; mother insisted on light and air. So, poor as we were, from our high bedroom window on Cherry Street, just a few hundred yards from the antiaircraft gun battery that commandeered a chunk of park along the East River, Abe and I could see clear across the flat water to the mysterious Brooklyn Navy Yard, where ant-like men labored over mountainous battleships.

Mother's restrictions ensured that the straightest route to the Five-Ten Hall, the one we always followed, was west along South Street. Those Sunday mornings we were the only things moving. South Street belonged to us. At times Abe and I would forage ahead independently, secure as puppies on a long leash, only to fall back to our father's side. If we listened carefully we could hear a soft melody exhale from deep within his chest: over and over, private, in step with his stride. There was no FDR overpass to divide us from the water then, and no thump of overhead traffic. The timber piers groaned and creaked in the waves.

We had our rituals. We never crossed extra wide, cobbled Pike Slip without paying homage to the raised stone vat in the center of the street. Too large for a bath tub, too small for a swimming pool, it was filled with the clearest, most bubbling water I had ever seen. I can still feel the delicious shock of that water as I dipped my face into it, eyes open.

"Why?" I asked the first time we stopped there.

"For the horses," father said. "This is where the horses drink."

But I did not see many horses, mostly cars and trucks.

"Think about Moishe's horse!" Abe said.

And he was right. Moishe, the last true teamster, delivered massive blocks of ice from a horse-drawn cart to economic laggards like us who lacked refrigerators. At this late date of my life I can still see the steam rising from the exhausted animal's hide as it drew to a slow halt in front of our building. I'd bolt down the stairs in time to catch Moishe lifting the ice block from the back of the cart onto his burlap-covered shoulder, using huge tongs, and then I'd follow him as he trudged the five flights to our kitchen, where, grunting, he fitted the block into the back of our ice box. The effort required skill and no small grace. Mother always had a few kind words in Yiddish for Moishe, and a glass of homebrewed tea, so he could catch his breath.

"The ice is heavy," I said on Pike Slip to my father, who knew what I meant.

"You get used to it if you start young."

Eight years old is young enough, which is the age my father began *his* working life, a few blocks from where we presently lived, delivering milk in the pre-dawn from a horse-drawn cart like Moishe's. The driver needed a nimble kid to lug the full bottles into the dark hallways before the customers woke up and to haul back the empties of the previous day. That was 1910. Child labor was the norm. There were five children. The oldest son had to work.

A few years later grandfather Max delivered my father to his friend and fellow house painter with the following instructions, in Yiddish.

"This is my son Sam. Make him a painter. If he gives you trouble, kick him in the ass."

My father told this story many times, never neglecting to add the little coda, "That was my life adjustment." He had a deep voice that wheezed around the edges from emphysema—Paul Berman in his tribute to him upon his death called it a "broken cello"—and the ironic shading he gave it never failed to get a laugh.

He was eighty-six years old the last time I heard him tell that story. "He jokes about it!" I exclaimed to Mother.

"Yes, he's eighty-six years old and he still jokes about it!" She understood him completely and had that way of cutting to the bone.

Early on he rebelled against the life arranged for him. When he was thirteen he left for work one day and simply vanished. Searching turned up nothing and the family was forced to assume him dead, lost to the Calcutta streets of the Lower East Side. Until the following postcard arrived months later: "Dear Ma, I'm in China, Shmuel." China! Family lore has it she fainted on the spot. Turns out he had hopped freight trains across the country to San Francisco, got a job shoveling coal on a ship to Shanghai. How he survived he never told us; the hobo jungles of the time were filled with runaways.

"Came back the sensation of the neighborhood!" Father would recall with a wry smile. "Wore a money belt!" His celebrity lasted about a week, about as long as his cash. But he was not proud of the escapade in the telling. The grief he caused my grandmother, who died three months before I was born, stayed with him.

Weaned on oil-based paint, turpentine, thick brushes, and dust, he remained a house painter fifty-five years until hernias laid him low and he rasped for breath. He had a special way of running his fingertips appraisingly across the wall of any room that was new to him. Yet he was fundamentally untamed.

I knew none of these stories of my father's early life those Sunday mornings on the way to the Five-Ten Hall, nor would it have occurred to me he was my age when he worked the milk carts. What held me in awe was the immensity of the Manhattan and Brooklyn bridges as we passed under them, and in a different way, the stench of the oncoming Fulton Fish Market. The main pier was closed for the day, as were the stalls of the wholesalers on our side of the street. But the rotting fish stained the air.

"It smells! Are we there yet?" I would whine in small-boy disgust. Secretly I liked the smell.

My complaint was ignored. This too was part of our ritual.

Recently I took the old walk down South Street and found the mood, the sense of place, completely transformed. The FDR Drive traffic pounds over head. The Fulton Fish Market is closed for good. The red-brick eighteenth-century buildings—home to the warehouses, the workshops, the converted stables, the flea bag hotels, the twenty-five cent haircuts, the secondhand trouser and boot shops, the cheap eateries with the salt and pepper in one shaker and the steamed-over windows—they are all gone, gone with the merchant ships and tug boats that plied the harbor. Gone, as well, are the clattering, clanking overhead train lines, the "els" that branched from South Ferry like the tentacles of a gigantic iron squid, shedding rust and dust to the far reaches of Manhattan and the Bronx. Except for the faux South Street Seaport, which preserves a few of the old buildings as a stage set, the route is lined with monolithic housing projects and the cold towers of the financial district.

134 Broad Street, home of the Five-Ten Hall, was one of those ancient brick buildings in the permanent shadow of the "el" that has long since been demolished. I remember my sense of triumph as I turned right on the intersection of Broad and South, and let my tired legs propel me the last short block. I loved to climb the rickety stairs to the second floor loft ahead of Abe and my father. Climbing the rickety stairs of ancient lofts would turn out to be a staple of my childhood.

The loft was a simple spare rectangle, colored white. A polished timber floor creaked like the piers when you walked across it. Above your head loomed a dark, pressed-tin ceiling. At the far end, close to the naked windows, were two round poker tables of the kind you might encounter in the saloon of a Hollywood western—although the preferred game was pinochle. There was a leather couch along the wall opposite the door, some chairs, a table with literature arranged in scrupulously neat stacks, and behind it an equally neat, full bookcase. There were scrupulously detailed miniature ships— architects models, not toys—and all kinds of nautical things, knotted ropes and stuff: manly things that went straight to a boy's heart.

What gave the place distinction, though, and what burns in my memory still, was the single decoration that hung flat against the long wall to your right as you entered. It was a ship's steering wheel in solid mahogany red, nearly the size of the wall itself, gleaming in the morning light. Solid mahogany cylinders, spaced at regular intervals, radiated from its perfect rim. The center of the wheel challenged you with the following blunt message:

Industrial Workers of the World
I\*W\*W\*
Marine Transport Workers
IU 510

These words, this hand-stenciled challenge, arose in shining red splendor above a simplified black globe: one world, the IWW logo.

This was the place our father walked us across town for—to 134 Broad St, the home of the IWW—the *Wobbly Hall*. It was also known as the *Five-Ten Hall*, after Industrial Union (IU) 510, the Wobbly name for its merchant seamen's branch.

The IWW was a revolutionary labor union dedicated without apology, without obfuscation to the overthrow of capitalism, to the abolition of the wage system, to the world-wide solidarity of all labor, to the complete democracy of its internal affairs, to the building through the institutions of labor "the new society within the shell of the old." It is the only such union in the history of the United States. The IWW, the Wobblies! This was the place— and now I am not speaking of 134 Broad Street, that had my father's heart. To quote a song he sang in good moods, he "wore that button, the Wobblies' red button and carried their red, red card." Proudly. From 1922 until his last breathe in 1990.

The IWW was formed by revolutionary unionists and progressive activists who convened in Chicago in 1905. The pejorative "red"—as in despicable-flag-hating-revolutionist-less-deserving-of-life-than-a-cockroach—was originally directed at its members, the Wobblies, and not at members of the Communist Party, which did not exist until more than a decade later. No, the Wobblies were born of the American experience: Big Bill Haywood of the Western Federation of Miners; Mother Jones of the Pennsylvania soft coal fields; Eugene V. Debs, leader of the Pullman railroad strikers and later of the Socialist Party; Father Haggerty, the defrocked priest and union organizer; Lucy Parsons, a black woman and the widow of Albert Parsons, the anarchist—and before that Confederate Civil War veteran—who was lynched by the State of Illinois following the Chicago Haymarket bombing of 1886.

The aim of the Wobblies was to "fan the flames of discontent," to organize the poor, the oppressed, the people of no account in society into an effective fighting force. That many of the strikes they led were successful in the teeth of the entrenched power of mine owners, lumber barons, and textile manufacturers, who had at their disposal the goons, the police, the state militia, the press, the clergy, and the Federal Government is a tribute to their skill and bravery. You must not confuse a typical Wobbly-led strike of a century or so ago with today's tepid union affair, top heavy with lawyers and professional bargainers. A Wobbly strike was a localized revolution. The old-time Wobblies I knew as a boy would tell of these struggles that raged across the American landscape—in the mines, lumber camps, factories, wheat fields, and waterfronts of a tooth-and-claw nation. The recitation of these forgotten battles, unadorned and at random, can bring a lump to the throat in the manner of a Whitman poem.

I go into this history because the Wobbly glories were a distant thunder by the time the three of us entered the Five-Ten Hall those sleepy Sunday mornings when I was a boy. Outright murder, state sponsored persecution and imprisonment, induced mass hysteria, internal dissension, mistaken tactics, the rise of the Communist Party, the Roosevelt New Deal with its social programs and favored treatment of "responsible" unions, and, above all, WWII and the general modernization of American life—these things conspired to bring the Wobblies low. The Five-Ten Hall was little more than a social club: a place for seaman who shared each other's values to spend time together, to play silent games of pinochle, to gossip, to discuss the latest outrage, to speak of the past as if it were still happening. All this while waiting to "ship out." The sea was their true home.

They were lonely men for the most part, childless, so they made a fuss over Abe and me. Huge shiny packages labeled Baby Ruth and Hershey would magically appear to my delight. Abe, who has four years on me, would immediately make a bee line for an empty card table, where waiting for him was Nick the Greek: a thick, powerful, middle-aged man in a turtle-neck sweater, with a skull bald as a turtle's. They would lay out the chess board without exchanging a word and play for hours in silence.

Abe had another game going with a seafaring Wobbly named J. B. Chiles. Chiles made it a point to send him a postcard from every port he visited. Each morning Abe would race down stairs to the front of our building and wait for the mailman to deliver his card.

Ah, Abe, you are lucky. One arrived today, and Abe clutches it to him. On the back of the card: "Dear Abe, Here I am in Valparaiso, J. B. Chiles" On the front: a grainy black-and-white photograph of the harbor of Valparaiso, Chile.

The cards did not arrive on a regular basis. But Abe stuck with it and in time he filled a shoe box with cards from all the exotic places of the world: cards that were sent to him alone in an age devoid of TV, computer, and iPod. It was a collection he prized beyond value. He had a large map of the world taped to the wall beside his bed. Valparaiso, Chile? There it is! Abe stabs Valparaiso with a pin, like an insect, and stands back to admire all the pins scattered across his map.

I had my game, too—checkers, with a short, wiry ex-prize fighter known, perhaps insensitively but nevertheless accurately, as Punch Drunk Morse. His mashed in face fascinated me: flattened nose, unnaturally thick brow, scar tissue, pinned back ears, tight curly hair. It was hard to tell how old he was. But he was obviously an adult and I was able to beat him every time! Probably that was the best Morse could do, although now that I am old it pleases me to think he let me win because he enjoyed seeing a small boy happy, for he was a kind and gentle man.

Though Morse wouldn't swat a fly in anger and certainly not a "civilian," his face was an advertisement for trouble. Everywhere the poor fellow went he encountered an ass spoiling to prove his "manhood" in public by punching him out. There was the night my father loved telling about when a drunk they encountered in a bar gave Morse no peace. He taunted him, interrupted him when he was in conversation with other people, shoved him on the shoulder. Finally it became intolerable. So Morse stepped to the center of the saw-dust floor.

"You want to hit me? Here, hit me," he says to the guy, sticking out his chin. The bar grows silent as a church.

Morse weighs maybe 140lbs. His tormentor is a lumbering water buffalo with a huge gut. He proceeds to swing a round house right at Morse, then a round house left, a right again, and so on, huffing and puffing. All of them fan the air, of course, as Morse stands in one spot with his hands in his pockets and weaves side to side, at times crowding and nudging the drunk off balance with his shoulder.

"Here I am. Hit me. Hit me. Get it out of your system."

The drunk swings himself to exhaustion, red faced, gasping. Morse leaves him stationary as a confused bull amid-the sawdust. It is a Buster Keaton farce come to life.

"Remember Sammy Weinstein?" my father would call out to Morse across the silent Five-Ten Hall.

Weinstein, I learned later, was a small-time "club fighter," a lightweight from the early 1930s, when a Jewish boxer was not an oddity. He was also a Wobbly and proud of it, so he had "IWW" sewn in red letters onto the back of his black trunks. The crowd would roar when they saw it.

"In the long run it wasn't good propaganda" was my father's growled appraisal. "Poor Sammy spent too much time on his ass." Morse would nod in sad agreement.

That was how I remember talk went at the Five-Ten Hall. Spare. Ironic. Things heated up, however, if the talk turned to political philosophy, literature, history; seafaring Wobblies were generally far better educated than mainstream college folk. They took advantage of their years of confinement on the high seas to read, read, read. They would not parrot what a literature professor might *say* about Dickens, for example; most never saw the inside of a college classroom nor benefited from the guidance of the learned man up front. Instead they actually *read* Dickens, maybe five of his novels, and formed their own opinions. I can remember more than one Wobbly quote verbatim long passages of Marx, of Shakespeare, of Whitman, of the Old Testament. There was a savage quality to their learning.

The Wobblies would not let the expectations of others define them. A migratory farm worker was called a "bindle stiff" because he carried his bed on his back. He rode freight trains, dodging the brutal railroad "bulls" and murderous "hijackers," to get to the vast grain fields, where he and his fellow stiffs harvested the nation's bread for a pittance. Decades before the world heard of Cesar Chavez—before he was born—the Wobblies led thousands of these homeless men in a series of violent strikes that raged across the American West. Many were imprisoned. Around our dinner table I heard stories of how their jailers observed them conduct disciplined meetings inside their crowded cells, according to *Robert's Rules of Order*—and from then on treated them with respect.

I loved the Five-Ten Hall for reasons that ran deeper than a boy can express. It was there that my father introduced me to the adult world of *men*, and that I began to learn the importance of honor and bravery in this world. I also learned as I grew older that the Wobblies had their share of bad actors. But, taken as a whole, they were men who sacrificed in the just cause of others without expectation of reward or fame, which meets my definition of nobility. With the passage of time, I have come to realize how privileged I was to know these men, albeit from a boy's perspective. There was a certain dignity to the best of them, a certain grace. Their speech, their bearing, carried echoes of a lost nineteenth-century America. All of them were poor, long forgotten, if ever known. They were the best of America, although America largely spat upon them.

> In the broader sense, there is no such thing as a foreigner. We are all native born members of this planet, and for the members of it to be divided into groups or units and to be taught that each nation is better than the other leads to clashes and the world war. We ought to have in place of national patriotism—the idea that one people is better than another—a broader conception, that of international solidarity.... The IWW believes that in order to do away with wars we should remove the cause of wars; we should establish industrial democracy instead of commercialism and capitalism and the struggles that come from them. We are trying to make America a better land, a land without child slaves, a land without poverty, and so also with the world, a world without a master and without a slave.

James P. Thompson, a big, square-shouldered man and a co-founder of the IWW said this at a trial in the run-up to World

War One. For this and similar statements he was sentenced to ten years in Leavenworth Federal Penitentiary—his wife and two small children left destitute. I would come to know many such men—aged men who had paid a hard, heavy price.

Indeed, the reward for many a Wobbly was a tragic life. I think of J. B. Chiles, the lonely man who sent Abe postcards from around the world when he was a boy. He was Secretary of the Five-Ten Hall, which in reality meant he slept there in return for managing things and keeping the place clean. Chiles's skull had been cracked open in the 1920s by California prison guards in whose loving care he had spent five years for fomenting strikes. Slowly, gradually, Chiles went mad and as he grew old found himself committed to an upstate "nut house." Abe would take the long train ride to visit him there, until one day he was told that his old friend had wandered off the grounds. He was never heard from again.

There is an old Wobbly song that comes to mind as I write this: *My Wandering Boy (A Mother's Lament)*, to the tune of the famous Offenbach aria. The author of the lyric is unknown, which seems altogether fitting. The elderly men I remember at reunions sang it sardonically, with a cruel edge, perhaps to ward off messy emotions. But I never took it that way.

> Where is my wandering boy tonight?
> The boy of his mother's pride?
> He's counting the ties with his bed on his back,
> Or else he is bumming a ride.
>
> Oh, where is my boy tonight?
> Oh, where is my boy tonight?
> He's on the head end of an overland train,
> That's where your boy is tonight.
>
> Oh, where is my boy tonight?
> Oh, where is my boy tonight?
> The chilly wind blows, to the lock-up he goes,
> That's where your boy is tonight

As a child I was of course unaware of the sad, glorious history of the Wobblies. In truth, with no one remotely my age, time dragged at the Five-Ten Hall after an hour or two. What rescued the afternoon was lunch at the Bean Pot Cafeteria around the corner, which faced South Ferry, Battery Park, and the Statue of Liberty which was the size of a toy far out in the harbor. Grease all over the place, dirty plates—the decrepit Bean Pot catered to seamen, floor moppers, and various others who sweated for their money. A nice contrast to this description would be that the food was hearty workingman's fare. In fact it was terrible. What did I know or care? The chunky soiled man behind the counter ladled me a bowl of split pea soup and white bread. For dessert—always dessert!—there was lemon meringue pie so gritty you spat out the sugar grains.

Nevertheless, I stood at the side of my father, my older brother Abe, and the Wobblies at the Bean Pot. It was as if I had been initiated into an exclusive club. After the Bean Pot, tired now, came the long walk back to Cherry Street in the fading light.

# 2
## DURRUTI AND ME

I was born April 8, 1937. On November 11 of that year, my father, Sam Dolgoff, addressed an open-air meeting held at Waldheim Cemetery in Chicago. Directly behind him stood the stone monument to Albert Parsons and three other anarchists falsely accused of planting a bomb that killed a number of policemen at a rally for the Eight-Hour Day in Haymarket Square. They were hanged for the crime in 1887 despite their innocence, in what has become known as the Haymarket Tragedy. My father shared the platform at this fiftieth anniversary of their martyrdom with Lucy Parsons, who had been a cofounder of the IWW. She was still beautiful, but frail and nearly blind by then, and she called out to my father, her old friend, "Sammy, Sammy!" and clung to his arm.

I have a photograph of him facing that small crowd, the monument behind him, wearing an overcoat against the Chicago wind: young, wild black hair swept back as best he could. It is the proudest moment of his life—the proof being he is wearing a suit and tie for the occasion. My father considered himself the direct spiritual descendant of the Haymarket anarchists and all who knew him well had no doubt that he was.

April 8, 1937, followed the death of Buenaventura Durruti by a few months. The leader of an anarchist column defending Spain against Francisco Franco's fascist army, he took a bullet through the brain in the Battle of Madrid. Durruti held no rank and answered only to his unadorned name. He refused to be saluted. He slept amongst his comrades, in the field. My father was moved to tears by his death, and that is how I became the only person in the world named Anatole Durruti Dolgoff.

As you can see, I was born into a revolutionary family—and a revolutionary tradition.

Durruti: the son of a railway worker, short, stocky, and very strong; a kind man, "with a Herculean body, the eyes of a child in a half-savage face."

Durruti: a man who "laughed like a child and wept before the human tragedy."

Durruti: his coffin carried aloft by comrades through the streets of Barcelona, his path attended by over five hundred thousand mourners.

Durruti: whose "Column," noted a comrade, "is neither militarily nor bureaucratically organized. It has grown organically. It is a social revolutionary movement.... The foundation of the Column is voluntary self-discipline. At the end its activity is nothing less than libertarian communism."

Durruti: who said, "We carry a new world here, in our hearts."

That was the essence of my father. He carried a new world in his heart—in the words of James P. Thompson "a world without a master and without a slave." Call it foolish, call it hopelessly naive, call it visionary: that was the cause to which he dedicated his life.

Lofty stuff. The reality is I hated my name as a child. Bad enough Anatole—and with it the god-forbid connotation of femininity on the Lower East Side, reinforced by Danny Kaye's swishy "I'm Anatole of Paris" routine in the hit film of the time, *The Secret Life of Walter Mitty*. Bad enough, Anatole. But, Durruti? Such a strange name out of nowhere, I was never quite sure of the spelling. The neighborhood Johnnies and Jimmies laughed at me when the teacher read it off in class, and my shameful secret was exposed.

"I hate my name," I would announce dramatically to Mother, who took these things seriously: which is partly why I brought the subject up, to mischievously see her get ruffled.

"Sam, the boy hates his name," she would announce, in hurt, baffled tones.

And my father would say simply, "The day will come when you will appreciate your name. It is a name of nobility and honor."

Who needed that?

But the years have passed. And yes I have come to appreciate my name, deeply so. I have come to embrace it as a way of "coming home," to do right by my heritage in my old age. How to do this? I will never be the man Buenaventura Durruti was, nor, frankly, the man my father was—warts and all. I am also not a professional historian. What I can do is tell stories: of my parents and their world, which spans seventy years of revolutionary activity; of the Wobblies and anarchists of my childhood—a colorful lot; of what it was like to grow up in a family whose ethics and politics ran against the grain. Hopefully it will add up to a history of sorts—one you will enjoy. Do not look for "objectivity." To hell with it. I have read many such "objective" accounts of the anarchists and Wobblies, and few of them bear any resemblance to the flesh-and-blood human beings who broke bread with us or snored on our sagging couch. I've opted for the truth instead.

# 3

# SAM'S PERSONALITY - EARLY LIFE - OTHER THINGS

Sensitivity to the world's great anguish and its wrongs were at the core of my father's character; he had an organic identification with the abused and exploited of this world. I remember sitting on the living room couch with him one evening in the last months of his life, following Mother's death. The year was 1990 and the TV news was filled with the economic collapse of the Soviet Union. The camera lingered on the care-worn face of an impoverished old woman, draped in black, symbolic of the desperate plight of the Russian people. My eighty-eight-year-old father sobbed.

"Who is to feed her?" he asked.

Sympathy for those who suffer is, fortunately, a thoroughly human trait. What made my father become an anarchist was his hatred of those institutions that perpetuated and profited from the suffering of others, namely the State, the Capitalist system, and organized, entrenched religion. In his reading of the world they were the embodiment of arbitrary authority and his hatred of arbitrary, hierarchal authority had no bottom. Nor was there a bottom to his contempt for those who held power within these institutions. He took it all *personally*.

His scorn could reach operatic proportions.

There was the time he flung a chair across the living room at the grainy TV image of Secretary of State Dean Rusk calmly explaining in his composed manner the necessity of the Vietnam War. "Go ahead, that will do a lot of good," Mother taunted him. My father despised diplomats.

Then there was the quiet Sunday afternoon he rose from his chair upon reading Kipling and threw his complete works, book after book, out our fifth-floor window. It was an action he later regretted, because he actually admired Kipling's work, but the man's war-lust and racism infuriated him.

His comments concerning the "greats" of this world came marinated in lye; he was most defiantly *not* a subscriber to the Great Man Theory of History.

Of Stalin, the Man of Steel: "That evil sonofabitch is lower than whale shit!" And the *sonofabitch* had a special twist to it.

Nothing pleased him more than deflating an inflated reputation. He mocked Lenin ("that Mongolian conniver") and Trotsky ("you mean Brownstein, the tailor?") as much for the cultish worship they inspired in their followers as for their betrayal of the Russian Revolution. He relished the tidbit that came down from Emma Goldman, who was a close friend of Lenin's wife during the early years of Bolshevik rule ("Seems the Hero of the Revolution was less than a hero of the bedroom").

The Founding Fathers fared no better. The thought of them curled his lip. "A bunch of slave owners, autocrats, smugglers. Tom Paine was the only one any damn good—and they got rid of him. Read the Constitution they came up with. See if you like it."

As an adult I enjoyed playing the foil to his hyperbole; I might say, "President Johnson wants to leave his mark on history."

To which the answer might come, after a caustic pause: "You mean, he wants to drop his turd on the sands of time!" He was fond of Shelley's "Ozymandias."

Mother said many times my father wore his crusty shell as protection against the pain of the world; the vituperation he used often was not for comic effect. He was in fact the gentlest of men. He never referred to Mother as his "wife"; he felt the term demeaned her. Rather she was his "life companion" and he meant it—although he was not above calling her "my ball and chain" in front of visitors for the naughty pleasure of watching them squirm. He preferred that Abe and I call him by his first name; he did not like the authoritarian implications of "father." Nor did he demand that we respect him because we lived under his roof. "Respect me if you feel I've earned it," he often said to us. You could argue with Sam, tell him to shut up as we did regularly, and he would do so, meekly. He was delighted when my six-year-old daughter Stephanie talked back to him. "I like a fresh kid! A rebellious child!" he'd say, and hand her a quarter.

Then, for no apparent reason, the broken baritone would burst through the crusty shell. He would start to sing: at home, on the street, wherever the spirit moved him, in and out of tune at the same time. He loved the great IWW songs printed in its *Little Red Song Book*. "Hallelujah I'm a Bum," was a favorite, though there were any number of others.

> Be cheerful and gay, for the spring time has come.
> You can throw down your shovels and go on the bum
> Hallelujah, I'm a bum
> Hallelujah, bum again,
> Hallelujah, give us a handout
> to revive us again!

Beyond the obvious mockery and irreverence, Sam saw pathos in the lyric.

I suppose you could trace Sam's rebellious personality in part to Grandfather Max and to his roots in a *shtetl* (that is, a tiny secure Jewish community) near Vitebsk, a city just inside the eastern border of Belarus. "Do not go back. Nothing is left," a friend from that part of the world advised me recently. "The Lithuanian Fascists wiped out everything and everybody in 1941: thirty-five-thousand Jews in mass graves, at least. Anyone tells you he can trace your family is just taking your money." But in the late 1890s Vitebsk was home to a vibrant Jewish culture that spawned Marc Chagall and so many others.

Grandpa Max was a contrarian from the start. He scandalized the *shtetl* by smoking cigarettes on the Sabbath and enraged my great grandfather, a rabbi, by renouncing religion altogether. He was an atheist during his waking hours. When he slept, though, between snores you could hear him recite the ancient Hebrew prayers in a clear voice.

Around 1900, Grandpa Max worked as a commissary clerk on the Trans-Siberian Railroad.

They had a bunch of railroad cars where the track and train men slept and another car where Grandpa Max supplied them with cigarettes, tobacco, underwear, and different things. He also had charge of their feeding, and pinch hit as their timekeeper. So he got to know how exploited the men were and he bonded with them. When they struck for better pay and conditions, his supervisor, in the spirit of the times, called for the Cossacks, who clubbed them from horseback. "How can you do that?" Max asked. "These men slave for you every day. You know they are desperate."

"You are management," his boss said, "You have a good job for a Jew. You must decide whose side you're on. That's the way it is."

"Nobody owns me," Max told him and he was fired. At about the same time the Tsar wanted him as cannon fodder for the upcoming Russo-Japanese War. So Max skipped to America, where he learned to be a house painter, and sent for grandmother Anna and three-year-old Sam in 1905. Along the way he simplified the family name from Dolgopolski to Dolgoff.

Max was basically a kindly man, who accepted the world as it is and not as it should be. The true revolutionist of the family was Max's brother, Tsudik, who remained behind. I'll let Sam tell his story:

> Through the many years spanning the 1905 Russian Revolution to my father's death in 1945, we had no news about what happened to Tsudik and doubted strongly that he was still living. But (much later)... I was given a copy of the Russian Communist Jewish periodical *Soviet Homeland* which, to my great surprise, (contained) a photo and an obituary article about my uncle. It read, in part: "Tsudik Dolgopolski was born in the village of Haradok, not far from the Vitebsk. At 13 years of age he began work in a brush factory. In 1909 after many difficulties he became an elementary school teacher. In 1926, his novel *Open Doors* was published in which the great events of the October Revolution were graphically described. In 1928 his book *On Soviet Land* was published. Later, two volumes of memoirs, *Beginnings* and *This Was Long Ago*, appeared. Dolgopolski's writing graphically described the awakening of Jewish life thanks to the achievements of the October Revolution."

Sam continues, "This sketch omits the fact that Tsudik was sent to Siberia for fomenting strikes and demonstrations against the Tsar, that extracts from his *Sketches of Village Life* were printed in the New York *Jewish Daily Forward*, and that my uncle declined the *Forward*'s invitation to come to New York as a staff writer. More importantly, a full report from a reliable source revealed that my uncle (was) condemned to hard labor in Stalin's concentration camps where he died." I have since learned that Sam's belief about his uncle's demise. was incorrect. It seems that Tsudik managed to survive both Stalin's camps and the subsequent Nazi invasion. He died in 1959.

Imprisoned by two tyrants, Uncle Tsudik was a man for many a season. The only family anecdote about Tsudik that comes down to me through the years was from Sam's brother, Louie. Seems Tsudik knew Stalin's NKVD were coming for him, late at night, as was their way. So he left the door open and waited for them to thump up the stairs in their winter boots. "Pigs, can't you see she has just polished the floor! Respect my wife," he snapped at them as they burst in. And so they stood at the door, abashed, as Tsudik rose from his chair. The tale may well be apocryphal, but it moves me to this day.

There is another story that may well be apocryphal that also moves me. It arrives from that far away place in the mind where what you think was told to you merges with what you would like to imagine was told to you. Yet the image is indelible. I "see"—or do I feel?—my future father, the four- or five-year-old *Shmuel*, in the knickers children wore in those days. There is the carcass of a dead horse abandoned in a vacant garbage strewn lot, a feast for the flies and rats. And, in a metaphor of his life to be, my father-to-be is astride it, crying, imploring it back to life, while several adults, Grandpa Max among them, are yanking him off the fetid thing.

The diaspora of Eastern European Jews to New York's Lower East Side has acquired a polyurethane coating of nostalgia as it recedes ever further in time. The upper-middle-class descendants of this Diaspora are taken on tours of a meticulously preserved nineteenth-century tenement and to colorful relics of the old days: Gus's Pickles, Yana Shimmel's Kinnishery, Katz Deli, and so on. *Fiddler on the Roof* makes for a good cry at a safe distance and allows for more than a bit of smug self-satisfaction. Not many people have read Michael Gold's *Jews Without Money*, which presents a bitter, astringent picture of immigrant life—in other words, the way things were.

This is what Sam had to say as an old man, looking back:

Upon our arrival in New York we lived in a typical Lower East Side slum on Rutgers Slip, a block or two from the East River Docks, in overcrowded quarters. The two toilet seats for the six families on each floor were located in the common hallway. There was no bathroom. A large washtub in the kitchen also served as a bathtub. When another immigrant in need of shelter came, a metal cover over the washtub also served as a bed. There was no central heating, no hot water, and no electricity. Gas for illumination and for hot water in summer was supplied only by depositing a quarter in the meter. Neither the electric trolley nor the auto were in general use and both commercial and passenger traffic was horse drawn.

Nevertheless there was richness to life; the seeds of his anarchist philosophy were planted in the hard dirt of poverty.

Despite the horrible economic conditions, there was, at least in our neighborhood, far less crime than now. We could walk the streets at all hours of the night unmolested, sleep outside on hot summer nights and leave our quarters unlocked and feel perfectly safe. To a great extent this can be accounted for by the character of the new immigrants. The new immigrants, fortunately, had not yet become fully integrated into the American "melting pot." The very local neighborhood communities, which enabled the immigrants to survive under oppressive conditions in their native homes, sustained them in the deplorable new environment.

The new arrivals lived in the same neighborhoods as did their friends and countrymen, who shared their cramped lodgings and meager food supplies, found employment for them where they learned a new trade. They helped the new arrivals in every possible way, at great sacrifice, to adjust to the unfamiliar conditions in their new homes. Thus, upon arrival, as already noted, my father was taught the painting trade by his fellow countrymen, who lodged and sustained him until he could establish himself.

My father became a member of the Vitebsker Benevolent Society, which provided sickness and death benefits, small loans, and other essential services at cost. Fraternal and other local associations actually constituted a vast integrated family. Neighbors in need received the widest possible assistance and encouragement, and the associations promoted the fullest educational and cultural development.

Social scientists, state "welfarists" and state socialists, busily engaged in mapping out newer and greater areas for state control, should take note of the fact that long before social security, unemployment insurance, and other social service laws were enacted by the State, the immigrants helped themselves by helping each other. They created a vast network of cooperative fraternities and associations of all kinds to meet expanding needs—summer camps for children and adults, educational projects, cultural and health centers, care for the aged, etc. I am still impressed by the insight of the great anarchist thinker Proudhon who in the following words outlined a cardinal principle of anarchism: "Through the complexity of interests and the progress of ideas, society is forced to abjure the state.... Beneath the apparatus of government, under the shadow of political institutions, society was closely producing its organization, making for itself a new order which expressed its vitality and autonomy. (*General Idea of the Revolution in the Nineteenth Century* [London: Freedom Press, 1923], 80.)

When Grandpa Max pieced together the money to move his family to the less crowded "wilds of the south Bronx," their meager possessions were loaded onto a horse-drawn cart. Grandma Anna wept and embraced the other wives as if she were crossing the Atlantic again. It might as well have been. The trip took nine hours through congested streets and the virtually impassable Willis Avenue Draw Bridge. Can you imagine the pile up of loaded down carts, teamsters, horses, horseshit, flies, and stink?

Sam loved the common horses that did the world's hard work. He would approach them on the street and pat their sweating hides. Though it is hard to imagine a more unsuitable soldier than my father, he was, along with cousin Izzy, enlisted in the U.S. Cavalry and sent to hot, faraway, hostile New Mexico: two underage Yiddish kids circa 1916. They served as grooms, mucking out stables and swabbing and feeding the animals. Sam liked that part of it, and—contrary to what you might expect—he liked his sergeant, too, who counseled him in a kindly way on how best to adjust to the disciplines of Army life. That did not prevent Izzy and Sam from deserting at the first opportunity.

It is clear to me Sam was a restless, sensitive boy condemned to hard labor and poverty, searching to know the world, searching for a way out. School certainly did not provide that way out. It was instead his introduction to hierarchal authority, and a profoundly unhappy one. He often described grade school as a hell hole of neo-Victorian child abuse.

> You'd walk through the halls and hear the bedlam coming from the rooms. "Ouch! Leave me alone you bastard." Whoop! You could hear the rod come down. Children would run out the rooms screaming and their teachers—who were like prison guards—would drag them back in by the ear. You sat on benches and recited things by rote. The teacher would walk behind you with the rod. You had to look straight ahead. You never knew when the rod would come down on you or if you had to open your hands for it in front of the room. The object was to break the child's spirit, make an obedient citizen.

Eight-year-old Sam faced the added obstacle of having to help his father support a family of five children. That is when he took to delivering milk and bread from a horse-drawn wagon, seven days a week: school days, six to eight each morning and four to six in the afternoon; Saturdays and Sundays all day. It paid three dollars a week. Under those circumstances, he found it difficult to pay attention in class and, worse yet, he was plagued with poor eyesight. And he was rebellious. So he was left back, and surrounded by younger boys in class. They ridiculed him because he could not see well, called him "dummy," and did to him all the nasty things oppressed children can do.

He graduated elementary school, then found work ten to

twelve hours a day on the factory floor of the Continental Can Company. But he was rebellious. Finally, Grandpa Max felt it best to leave his obstreperous son with his friend, who was a small-time contractor: "Stay on top of him, because he don't like to listen." He did learn to be a painter, but he also learned that his salvation lay in escape: San Francisco, Shanghai, the U.S. Cavalry, the Open Road, and ultimately, himself.

Sam's "formal education" ended at the eighth grade, but not his education. These are among my strongest boyhood memories of him: He would arrive home from work with the smell of sweat and turpentine about him, paint encrusting his nails and glasses: exhausted, haggard. After eating, he soaked in the bathtub for an hour; he had a tight, muscled body in those days, not the bloated, emphysema-distorted one that many who knew him in later life remember. Then his education began. He would lie in his bed surrounded by books and obscure radical publications piled as high as the mattress. And he would read. Not just political theory. Everything. Night after night, every weekend, each spare moment, he would lie on his back in a haze of cigarette smoke, reading.

He took his learning seriously but not his learned self. Years beyond these childhood memories, in 1971, Angus Cameron, the distinguished editor at Alfred Knopf, prepared to publish Sam's ground breaking *Bakunin on Anarchy*. It was—is—a scholarly treatise on the towering nineteenth-century Russian revolutionist. Sam had translated Bakunin's writings from various languages into English; the manuscript was replete with footnotes and references, which in some respects are the most important part of the book.

"Your credentials?" Cameron asked.

"Doctor of Shmearology, New York University, with a concentration in shit houses and boiler rooms," Sam answered with mock pomposity, describing what he had painted there. It was the closest he had ever come to a college degree.

Cameron, a man of humor, appreciated the answer. "Bet you never expected to be in this office," he exclaimed.

"As a matter of fact, I am well acquainted with your office!" Cameron was astonished to learn that by astounding coincidence Sam had painted his office several years earlier.

In fact, Sam's knowledge of history, social movements, philosophy, psychology, and literature was vast and deep on many fronts. It started when he was a young man, taken under the wing of many leading anarchist and socialist intellectuals of the time. *"They* were my university," he said.

He would take no job that required him to hire or fire another worker; he considered it immoral to exercise the power of bread over a fellow human being. Nor would he follow the career path of many an ex-radical and take the cushy jobs in the union bureaucracy he was offered. He wanted no part of union corruption and the betrayal of its members.

*"Sam! Sam, it's great to have you back!"* It is Martin Rarback, the all-powerful Secretary Treasurer of the all-powerful District Council 9 of the Painter's Union. Council 9 had all the large-scale work in Manhattan and the Bronx—basically NYC—tied up. Every office building, apartment project, public space, old and new, had to go through Council 9.

Sam had left the union years earlier when it was under communist domination, preferring to work for peanuts on his own. But now it was the 1950s and he wanted back in. So there he is in the large office of Rarback, who is facing him behind his large desk. He is genuinely delighted to see my father. They remember each other from the old days when Rarback was a burly young rebel who served as Leon Trotsky's bodyguard during his brief stay in NY—before Trotsky headed to Mexico, where Stalin's ice-pick awaited him. He eyes my father with a combination of warmth and veiled contempt. But the nostalgia wins out.

"Still at it, eh Sam? The Wobblies, the old days! I know what you think, seeing me here 'taking Pie.' Big office, good money, soft." He grows passionate now, leans forward. "But Sam, let me tell you, I'm the same man. *When those barricades go up, you'll see me there!"*

In the course of waiting for those barricades to go up, Martin Rarback came under criminal indictment for being neck deep in corruption. The inexcusable part to Sam was that Trotsky's former bodyguard, who now lived at a lofty twin towers Central Park West address, took kickbacks for having his men work under substandard, dangerous conditions. He considered him a depraved person.

This is as good a time as any to mention that Sam had *guts*—a quality of his that I discovered in a strange way when I burst home from school one ordinary day to find him in bed, in fetal position, wrapped in blankets, shivering violently, and Mother draped over him, cradling him in her arms. Sun streamed in through their bedroom windows. It was broad daylight. Sam was never home at this time and never in bed. I was eleven years old.

He had been brought home by two of the men on the job. Seems he had cleaned his arms and neck with a rag soaked in benzene; that is how you removed the oil-based paint. But he had neglected to dry himself thoroughly and lit a cigarette, which ignited his right arm in flames. It was a revolting scene and as his flesh started to roast, some of the men started to gag and vomit from the odor. And in those seconds when he could have burned to death he extended his flaming arm outward—horizontal to the ground—and walked calmly to the other end of the large room, some thirty feet, and thrust it into a pile of sand. The men said they had never seen anything like it.

Sam went into shock; he could not stop shivering. Then he caught the flu and it took him ten days to get back to work. Not once did he mention the incident to us.

Old-fashioned guts: intestinal fortitude. The second time I was surprised to find him home in the afternoon involved high scaffold work—which he was wary of, and took only when there was nothing else to feed us. Far above the pavement, some ten stories up, he discovered the hard way that his partner, a new man, did not know how to tie the security knots. The scaffold turned into a lever, which rotated in a vicious arc, and threw the man off. Desperately, he hung on to the scaffold, torso and feet dangling, rigid with fear. As happens in New York, a crowd materialized in an instant to stare upward at the unfolding horror. Sam was at the pivot point twenty feet or so above the new man. He, too, had been knocked off balance and clung to the vertical cable. Somehow, he got to the new man, spoke to him gently, and holding him firmly, guiding him, managed to slide the two of them down the cable to the ground. The audience clapped, which was nice, then dispersed.

I remember his hands that day. The cables had sheared off a lifetime of calluses, and left them red, smooth, and painful. But the interesting thing to me now, as I write this, was his response: he got on the scaffold the next morning. And he took the new man, a Dominican immigrant, up with him after a stern talking to, and taught him the ropes. The man explained he was desperate for the work and had lied about his experience, thinking he could pick up what to do by watching Sam. All Sam had to hear was that the man was desperate for the work.

I think it is self-evident that Sam's life strategy was not designed for economic advancement. You can add to that his refusal to take unemployment insurance for many years because he thought it charity from an institution he opposed: the State. Nor would he accept a tip or bonus, which he thought demeaned him. He put food on the table with back-breaking labor. Mostly he painted the decrepit apartments of the crumbling nineteenth-century tenements in our neighborhood. He was a superb old-fashioned craftsman: able, in the age before hi-tech, to match colors perfectly; even those that have faded from exposure over the years. He knew how to plaster, spackle, provide primer coating, and otherwise prepare a wall before actually applying the finishing paint that you see. It was incredible the way he could cover one-quarter of a wall with a single dip of the brush and long seemingly effortless strokes of his right arm—all to the rhythm of a Wobbly tune that he exhaled faintly, as unconscious to him as the Hebrew prayers were to his sleeping father.

I have often asked myself why a man able to destroy a trained trial lawyer in public debate was no match for a slumlord who wanted him on the cheap. Sam was incapable of bargaining effectively on his own behalf. They sensed his need. He always gave in, consistently underestimating the time element, especially in the winter months when pickings were lean. "Boys, go help your father," Mother would say to us as he toiled late into the night. Abe and I would find him on the top floor of a forsaken tenement somewhere, a naked light bulb revealing him in coveralls on a rickety ladder, long shadows dancing across the walls. The wide open windows and the piercing cold did not hide the oily paint smell, which triggered my gag reflex, nor did it prevent choking from the fucking dust everywhere. I hated being in the room. But I can still sense my father's simple pleasure at having his two boys, his sons, by his side in the night.

This lasted about three minutes. He did not want us anywhere near what he had to do. "Go home, boys," he'd say. "Tell your mother, 'Soon, not to worry.'"

"Soon" stretched to the incipient morning light.

In 1948, Sam painted the home of a Mrs. Harris, which required an interminable subway and bus journey "to the country"—that is, to far away Jamaica, Queens. I was dumbfounded that she and her family occupied an entire house, and that grass and trees grew in front and in back of the house! Every Saturday morning, for months after the agreed-upon work was completed, there came the dreaded Harris phone call in a whining, wheedling accent that grated like chalk on a blackboard:

"Sammy, pleees, one more thing…"

The woman was insatiable—a tapeworm of demands. Like shit on my poor father's shoe, there was no shaking her off! Mother loathed her. Still, Mrs. Harris kept calling to extract every ounce of advantage from my father's hide. She smelled his essential decency, his good heart, his inability to say "no."

The Harris Job passed into family lore. Abe shared Sam's mordant wit and it became a running joke, a bond of affection between them.

"Finish the Harris Job yet, Sam?" he'd ask whenever he came to town. (He lived first in Houston, Texas and then Chicago.)

"Just a few things, here and there," Sam would answer, deadpan.

The joke went on like that forty years. Abe asked Sam about the Harris Job for the last time in the final weekend of Sam's life, beside his hospital bed. Sam smiled "Just a bit here and there," he answered, deadpan.

That is how he was. He and Abe spent their final Sunday afternoon together singing the old Wobbly songs. They are piercingly beautiful sung in the right spirit. I came the next morning to take him home by ambulance in a stretcher with oxygen tank. He was not supposed to die just then. Dr Inkles predicted he had a month or two. Sam knew better. "It's getting dark. Turn on the lights," he said as I eased him into bed.

"It is broad daylight," I snapped.

"Give me the phone! I want to call Federico!"

Federico Arcos was an old and unrepentant anarchist, an autoworker in Windsor, Ontario. As a boy he had fought on the barricades of Barcelona with a rifle from the Crimean War that was taller than he was. My father loved Federico. I handed him the black rotary phone with the long cord. He insisted on dialing the number himself. I do not know where he got the breath to speak without panting.

"Hello Federico! Listen, I'm going to go soon. I wish you farewell. Keep up the fight, good comrade. Salud!" And he hung up.

He died that night.

# 4
## SAM BECOMES A SOCIALIST

The Soapbox: you can say it transformed Sam's life. Seventy years after the event, he recalled to me that moment when a man he never knew, speaking plainly and eloquently up on the box, set him on the revolutionary path. He spoke of Spartacus and the Slave Revolts that shook ancient Rome to its foundations. Sam, returning from work, stood transfixed. Naive fourteen-year-old that he was, he could not see where the basic power relations between Master and Slave, between Employer and Worker had changed at all. At the same time, he also saw that there existed a tradition of revolt.

The soapboxer recommended a book that had served as the basis of his speech: *The Ancient Lowly*, by Cyrenus Osborne Ward, with the lengthy subtitle: *A History of the Ancient Working People from the Earliest Known Period to the Adoption of Christianity By Constantine*. Sam devoured it. Surely he was not the first to be inspired by this nineteenth-century classic. "I was, by reason of harsh economic conditions, my bitter life as a low paid, exploited wage slave, and above all by my rebellious temperament, most receptive to the socialist message," he said.

He took to attending—"haunting" was his word—Socialist Party meetings after work and on weekends, especially those of their youth branch, The Young People's Socialist League (or YPSLs). He came early, before the audience: swept the floors; swabbed the toilet; arranged the chairs; cranked the mimeograph; distributed the leaflets; hung the signs; set the table, water pitcher, and lectern up on the small stage for the speakers and chairmen; circulated the cigar box to take up collections. For outdoor meetings, he lugged the portable platform. When, at times, the chairman failed to show, he stood up on the box and conducted the meeting, too. The Wobblies called all this "Jimmy Higgins work," after the hard-working character in an Upton Sinclair novel: the unsung labor without which nothing gets done. Sam liked this work. He learned from it. It gave him purpose and confidence, and in any case—an awkward boy with poor eyesight and rudimentary schooling—he felt that was his station.

He also learned he was not a socialist, at least not in the sense of the socialism advocated by the Socialist Party. He came to this conclusion for political as well as personal reasons, and he made the crucial observation that the two were inseparable. Again, to simplify matters, there were two socialist parties living under the same roof. Each believed in using the electoral process and the machinery of government to abolish Capitalism. But for one group, which I call the reformers—others might say collaborationists—the abolition of Capitalism was a far away goal, receding ever into the distance, having about as much impact on their daily behavior as the "In God We Trust" motto on the dollar bill. They believed in specific, immediate demands designed to improve the lives of the poor: Better housing, milk for babies, job safety, medical care, a reformed Civil Service, improved education. Their unions, electoral politics, alliances were designed to reform the system respectfully, peacefully.

Let me say right now as the son of an anarchist and Wobbly that the things the reform-minded socialists advocated were all for the good. I live in a cooperative housing complex built by the old-time Social Democratic unionists and I am grateful to them for that. My young neighbors have little idea of how their nice apartments got built. They regard the faded mural of an industrial America in our lobby to be as quaint and irrelevant as a statue in the park grown green and coated with pigeon shit. Not me. But all this "good" also brought the "bad" for politics—the capture of state power—became the sole reason for the existence of the collaborative wing of the Socialist Party. Certain kinds of people were attracted to leadership roles within the party, which did not sit well with Sam: "The hair-splitting quarrels...about how the *pronunciamentos* of the high priests of the socialist church should be interpreted and the lust for power between sectarian political connivers repelled me. Thousands of sincere, intelligent young militants...left the movement altogether.... My estrangement from the Socialist Party came not from contact with leftist factions but from my disappointing experiences and observations. I joined the YPSL because I believed it

fought for the overthrow of capitalism and the revolutionary trans-
formation of society. But this was not the case."

Sam began to notice other things, trivial things: That the lawyers and young college students of the YPSL inner circle never
picked up a broom or arranged a chair. Such tasks were presumably
left to the *goyim* but since there were no *goyim*, they fell to lesser
types such as my father. He took a good look at them, took the
measure of them, and what he saw were young men in search of a
career. They regarded the Socialist Party as a vehicle of opportunity
that enabled them to run for office, to find sinecures in govern-
mental agencies and union bureaucracies, and only incidentally to
improve the lives of those who voted for them. The entire lot of
them, taken together, began to repel Sam, though he found many
of them decent on a personal basis.

What most repelled him, however, was the moral collapse of the
reformist wing of the Socialist Party in the run-up to World War I:

> The anti-war World War I declaration of the Socialist Party in
> 1917 aroused hundreds of thousands of citizens to elect social-
> ists; some to the New York State Assembly, others to the post of
> New York City aldermen. The prominent socialist Jacob Pan-
> ken made it to the Municipal Court, and, a signal triumph, the
> voters sent socialist Meyer London to the United States House
> of Representatives. I still remember when the newly elected
> assemblymen chartered a special railway coach to Albany, the
> state capital. The coach was flamboyantly decorated with red
> flags and banners, while a brass band blared out the proletarian
> hymns *International* and *The Marseilles*. Jacob Panken and the
> other dignitaries hailed this event as the beginning of the long
> awaited social revolution.

"I did not at the time grasp the significance of the fact that
these duly elected socialists were expelled and not allowed to take
their seats on a legal pretext a few months later," Sam noted. Being
who they were, the expelled lawyers wrangled and compromised.
In the general euphoria, my seventeen-year-old father-to-be joined
the YPSL in 1919.

In the run-up to World War I and immediately thereafter the United States became a fascist country. It was the time of the orchestrated Red Scare and as with every fascist country the pressure came not only from government persecution, but from the entire machinery of the dominant society: the press, the clergy, the entertainment industry, the military. It was open season on radicals, unionists, and other nonconformists. And they came down hard. My parents knew many men imprisoned during the Red Scare, and Abe and I met more than a few of them growing up. Our adroit socialist "reformers," however, like cats sensing the warmest spot in the room, managed to find their personal comfort zones.

"A few months after its St. Louis anti-war declaration," Sam pointed out, "members of the party were beginning to shy away from the anti-war position; Jewish socialistic unions like the powerful United Hebrew Trades supported the pro-war policies of the government and insisted that the St Louis antiwar stand must be reversed and repudiated. Meyer London, twice elected to the House of Representatives, who from the beginning reluctantly accepted the party's antiwar position, now urged the party to support the war efforts of the government. He refused to introduce a bill for the repeal of conscription into the armed forces." London even sent a telegram to the head of the Provisional Government following the overthrow of the Tsar, urging Russia to continue fighting the Germans, the revolution be damned.

Nationalism, laced with fear, trumped socialism. *The Jewish Daily Forward* at the time had a circulation in the hundreds of thousands and was the largest Jewish newspaper in the world. The editor, Abraham Cahan, served notice that, "Now that war has been declared, opposition to the war must be given up and we, loyal citizens, must faithfully carry out all decisions of our government." The Jewish socialistic labor unions—the garment and allied workers, shoe, bakery, and furniture trades, the great national fraternal association the Workingmen's Circle—all knuckled under.

So did the far more powerful German socialists, who proclaimed their everlasting support of the Kaiser's military ambitions. Never mind that these beacons of working-class solidarity on both sides of the Atlantic now advocated killing one another. Never mind thirty-seven million dead and maimed. After the war men such as Abraham Cahan of the long-declining *Forward*, and David Dubinsky of the International Ladies Garment Workers' Union (ILGWU), found lifetime warm spots in the unions and front organizations associated with the emasculated Socialist Party. With time, these men came to be hailed as "statesmen" in *New York Times* editorials, their offices decorated with plaques and honorary degrees.

There were a few reform leaders, brave men, who never wavered in their opposition to the war. And a more militant wing of the Socialist Party, to its everlasting lasting good name, refused to knuckle under, and faced the force of the government head-on. In 1917, Charles Schenck, Secretary of the Socialist Party, was sentenced to prison for six months in violation of the newly passed Espionage Act. His crime had nothing to do with espionage as that word is commonly understood. Rather it was for speech previously protected under the First Amendment. The Party had mailed out leaflets urging opposition to compulsory military conscription on the grounds that it constituted involuntary servitude, which is prohibited under the 13th Amendment. Such speech violated a weasel-worded sedition clause tucked into the Espionage Act. The clause was clearly unconstitutional; nothing in the Constitution says you are not allowed to speak out against war during war time, or Capitalism, or the United States government. But the Supreme Court knuckled under, too, and upheld Schenck's conviction.

"Free speech would not protect a man in falsely shouting fire in a theatre and causing a panic," wrote Oliver Wendell Holmes Jr. in his Jesuitical opinion that introduced the "clear and present danger" justification. In 1918, the Sedition clause was strengthened to include "any disloyal, profane, scurrilous or abusive language about the form of government of the United States—or the flag of the United States, or the uniform of the Army and Navy."

My teenage father at the time knew little of the Wobblies, who, like the militant Socialists, were imprisoned and otherwise abused under the Espionage Act for antiwar speech. Still a Socialist, his attention was focused on a man he would revere his entire life—and whom he was privileged to meet briefly when that man was aged and bent: Eugene V. Debs. I tried over the years to get my father to explain exactly what it was that so attracted him to Debs and he would give me nothing specific. You had to be in his presence, you had to see him, was all he would say. "He brought out the better part of you."

At Debs's funeral in 1926, a leading journalist of the day, Heywood Broun, repeated this quote from a cynical admirer: "That old man with the burning eyes actually believes that there can be such a thing as the brotherhood of man. And that's not the funniest part of it. As long as he's around I believe it myself."

The "old man" was surely one of the great orators of American history. He was brave and he was honest. In 1906, less than a year after playing an instrumental role in the founding of the IWW, Debs told an audience of working men: "I am not a Labor Leader.... I would not lead you into the promised land if I could, because if I led you in, someone else would lead you out. You must use your heads as well as your hands, and get yourself out of your present condition." He left the IWW with the conviction that electoral politics rather than strikes and industrial agitation was the best path toward a just society. He ran for President on the Socialist Party ticket in 1912 and received 900,000 votes: not bad for a revolutionist. He would not back down as the U.S. geared for war, and the patriotic fervor began to mount.

"When I say I am opposed to war I mean ruling-class war, for the ruling class is the only class that makes war. It matters not to me whether the war is offensive or defensive, or what lying excuse may be invented for it. I am opposed to it, and I would be shot for treason before I would enter such a war." Debs was eventually convicted of Sedition under the Espionage Act. At his trial he said, "Your Honor, I have stated in this court that I am opposed to the form of our present government, that I am opposed to the social system in which we live, that I believed in change of both, but by perfectly orderly and peaceable means.... I ask no mercy, I plead no immunity." And he received none. He was sentenced to ten years in Atlanta Penitentiary. At his sentencing hearing on November 18, a week after Armistice Day, Debs told the Court. "Years ago I recognized my kinship with all living beings, and I made up my mind I was not one bit better than the meanest on earth. I said then and I say now, that while there is a lower class I am in it, and while there is a criminal element I am of it, and while there is a soul in prison I am not free."

In 1894, in response to his leadership of the Pullman Railroad Car Strike, the *New York Times* labeled Debs "a lawbreaker at large, an enemy of the human race."

Years later, Woodrow Wilson agreed. He called Debs "a traitor" and refused to commute his sentence in 1920, although Debs—disenfranchised for life, and behind bars—nevertheless received over 900,000 votes for president that year. Leading citizens of the day—historians, lawyers, journalists, philosophers—appealed to Wilson as a scholar as well as president to show some humanity; they mentioned historical precedents where men of high principle were treated differently by those in high power. Even Attorney General Palmer, of Palmer Raids notoriety, urged leniency for Debs on the grounds of the man's failing health. But Wilson was too small a man for that, and said no to that specific request, apparently preferring that Debs die in jail. It took Warren Harding to finally commute his sentence in 1921. Upon his release his fellow inmates sent him off "with a roar of cheers." Harding invited Debs, old and sick, to the White House. "I've always wanted to meet you," he said, "and shake your hand."

# 5

## SAM IS BOUNCED FROM THE SOCIALIST PARTY

Sam's disillusioning experience with the Socialist Party and its response to the Red Scare led him to question the basic premise for the existence of the Party—and beyond that, the basic premises of "capitalist democracy" itself. His critique was intuitive and expressed in the unpolished fashion of an unlearned working-class kid. Nevertheless it had a powerful internal logic.

How can one expect those who have spent a lifetime trying to gain power within an unjust system—with all the compromises, connivances, and betrayals that takes—to fundamentally change it? Far from opposing the capitalist system, the Socialist Party reinforced capitalism by siphoning off discontent into the same harmless channels advocated by the Democratic Party: cheaper subway fares, lower prices, workplace reforms, etc. In fact, the Democratic Party was more effective at these things. Eschewing its revolutionary ideals, the Socialist Party had become capitalist democracy's poor relation.

And what of this vaunted "democracy"? You elect a president who, like Wilson, campaigns for peace and turns on a dime to declare war—what's more passes laws that compel you to fight whether you agree or not, and other laws that suspend the Bill of Rights to imprison you if you object. He can keep you vindictively in prison or pardon you magnanimously as he chooses. He can bestow privileges on one segment of the population and pursue policies that punish others. He holds in his person dominion over a hundred-million human beings. In what sense, the young Sam asked, does a president differ from a king?

Ah, you say, the president is not a king because he cannot do these things without consent of Congress. But what is a Congressman, after all? How few of them there really are! Can one individual truly represent the interests of five-hundred-thousand people—or in the case of a senator, an entire State? Obviously not; he represents himself alone. Yes, Congress as an institution may oppose a president's policies and act as a brake on his ambitions, but only to further its own interests; it constitutes a class unto itself. To paraphrase Pierre-Joseph Proudhon, Congress is, with the president, "a king with six-hundred heads."

But surely, you may say, this is a gross caricature; these people are elected. You can turn them out if they do not represent you. Yes, Sam would say, you—or, more accurately, an electorate involving vast numbers of people who may or may not share your views—have the right to bring in a fresh pack of kings every few years (and how few of them are really exchanged, and how minimal are the policy changes!). But ruled you are, make no mistake about that. Why, he asked, should one support a system that rules over you? Electoral politics is a fraud—and worse than that pernicious, because by fostering the illusion of freedom it seduces people into participating in their own enslavement.

What of civil liberties, you counter? Surely freedom of speech and other guarantors of human rights differentiate democracy from tyranny, one might say, by definition. Surely that makes our government—and similar democracies—worthy of support. However, Sam would insist, this line of thinking confuses matters by equating Government and freedom. After all, aren't all these cherished rights protections *against* the power of Government, or as he called it the State? These rights are not granted by the State. They were—are— won by struggle against the State, as they were against kings, and they are in constant danger of being usurped—as indeed they are whenever the State feels itself threatened. The difference between a democracy and tyranny is that, in a democracy, the State does not have the power to completely impose its will.

There is an old counter to Sam's critique: One may call it "the human nature" ploy. Human beings are by nature selfish, predatory, and often violent. Government is needed to keep the various factions from one another's throats. It is needed, despite flaws and imperfections, to prevent descent into chaos and barbarism; it is necessary for the proper functioning of civilized society. This justification Sam held in contempt; because, he said, if human beings cannot be trusted to settle their own affairs rationally and peacefully, then certainly they cannot be trusted to elect others to do these things for them. The only solution is absolute tyranny imposed upon them, for the more freedom granted the greater the chaos and barbarism. However, a State-directed tyranny turns out in fact to be no solution to violence and chaos; for, far from preventing violence, the State monopolizes it in the form of police and the military, with disastrous results too numerous to mention. How can one deny this, Sam asked, when millions of WWI dead serve as a fresh example? Indeed, the authority of the State rests on violence. Threaten that authority and see how peacefully it responds! The young Sam, having knocked around more than most adults in a lifetime, having seen the best and the worst, did not take a simplistic view of human nature.

Economists, philosophers, and political scientists have made much of the differences between Capitalism—the private ownership of the means of production and distribution of goods and services motivated by profit—and the State. Sam chose to concentrate on their similarities. For arbitrary authority is at the core of each system. The typical capitalistic enterprise is an economic tyranny. The employee serves at the pleasure of the employer under his conditions and can be hired or fired at will. The worker has no say in the management of the enterprise or the dispersing of profit, which usually goes to absent shareholders who have not put in a day's labor and have nothing to do with the enterprise. The entire business can be sold or closed down from under him without a whisper of consultation or even notice. If he doesn't like the set-up he can quit—his sole "liberty"—and seek work elsewhere. If he has the wherewithal or good luck, he may better his lot, while the job he has left is filled by another slave. And a slave the worker remains, for he must submit to economic tyranny whether he stays or leaves.

"The essence of all slavery consists in taking another man's labor by force. It is immaterial whether this force be founded upon ownership of the slave or ownership of the money that he must get to live." These words are not Sam's, but those of Leo Tolstoy. And Tolstoy was not alone in this view; it is why the radicals of his day referred to Capitalism as wage slavery. Sam came to view the whole of dominant society—the whole of centralized authority, be it the State, the Capitalist System, or organized hierarchal Religion—as a vast moral crime. And it is this moral crime that the dispossessed of the world must oppose.

These were not the beliefs of a good Socialist Party member, but Sam expressed them with accelerating vehemence and force, to the extent that the officers of the Party, and not a few rank-and-file members, accused him of disrupting the functioning of the organization. The upshot of Sam's sojourn through the Party was that he was put on trial for insubordination and expelled. Decades later he would exclaim with a droll smile that the Party was right to do so—though not so much for his being insubordinate as for asking inconvenient questions. Hardly Galileo facing the hooded Inquisition, he welcomed the trial, because it gave him the opportunity to expound his views. "After the trial, one of the judges came up to me and said, 'You know, you are not too bad. In fact you put up a pretty good defense, as far as things go, although your case is hopeless. I am going to give you a tip. You are not a socialist. You are an anarchist. You belong with the crazies.' So I asked him, 'What is their address?'"

I doubt the judge gave Sam an actual address, but he and a number of other failed YPSLs found their way to "a dingy little loft on Eighteenth Street and Broadway near Union Square," headquarters of the anarchist periodical *Road to Freedom*. "We were heartily welcomed and without membership qualifications invited to attend group meetings and participate in all activities. I was overwhelmed to learn that there existed a different, anti-statist international…movement diametrically opposed to authoritarian Marxism."

Sam had found his home.

# 6

## AN INTERLUDE: I TAKE SAM TO SEE *REDS*

*Road to Freedom* had a nominal co-editor who seldom showed up, and never worked. His name was Hippolyte Havel. Sam did not know him "at the height of his career as a militant anarchist writer, editor, close friend of Emma Goldman, and well-known member of the Greenwich Village Bohemian community." When Sam knew him he was pretty much incapable of doing anything, was entirely supported by comrades and what he could cadge from gullible strangers passing through. Sam remembered him as "an ill tempered, abusive alcoholic, a paranoiac who regarded even the slightest difference of opinion as a personal affront. Nor could he carry on a discussion on any subject for more than a few minutes without constant interruptions, abruptly launching into a tirade on totally unrelated matters. It was most painful to witness the deterioration of a once vibrant personality."

Many years later, in the 1940s, Sam attended *The Iceman Cometh*, Eugene O'Neill's bitter commentary on lost illusions, cowardice, and betrayal. One of the characters spends the entire play sprawled across a table in Harry Hope's funereal bar, drunk; every now and then he rises to spout something vehemently incomprehensible before collapsing again. "That's Hippolyte Havel!" Sam exclaimed. There was no doubt!

Hippolyte Havel, flesh and blood human being, morphed into a character in an O'Neill play! That provides me the solution to a problem I have had. How to make accessible to people who were born after Sam died the breadth of his experience and the myriad people he knew so many years ago? Simple chronology—you know, first Sam did this, and then he said that—cannot convey to you the richness of Sam's lifetime journey in the anarchist movement, which he embarked upon when he joined *Road to Freedom*. But we do have the movies, and a special one at that.

*Reds* was the film I dragged Sam to so many years later, in 1982, for he disliked going to the movies. The film was finishing a fairly long run and the only theater showing it was at a mall in Northern New Jersey. I had to drive him there. He insisted on paying for his own small paper cup of Coca-Cola in the lobby. "A buck fifty? Why you can't be serious man! Maybe you should wear a mask and gun?" Sam growled. The young fellow behind the counter, probably a suburban high school kid born into an entirely different world, caught the glint of humor in Sam's eyes and smiled indulgently. That was the last bit of indulgence he received as he proceeded to wreck the film for the sparse audience scattered throughout the dark cavernous space that mid-week afternoon.

*Reds* is a three-hour long, romanticized but fundamentally accurate depiction of the life and times of the brilliant American journalist John Reed (played by Warren Beatty). The man cut quite a figure. He rode with the Mexican bandit/revolutionary Pancho Villa. He was closely associated with the Wobblies and good friends with Big Bill Haywood. He was active in the rich New York radical/bohemian scene, knew everybody, was in on everything. He witnessed the Russian Revolution first hand; his *Ten Days That Shook the World* remains a classic account of that momentous event. He became a committed Bolshevik and was instrumental in founding the American Communist Party. He died young of a terrible illness, typhus, in Moscow where his remains were interred in the Kremlin Wall. Numerous old-time radicals and writers—themselves, not actors—appear throughout *Reds* and comment on the characters depicted in the film. I thought Sam would enjoy *Reds* and on the whole he did. ("Who ever thought Hollywood would make such a film?")

The problem was in the details. Sam was nearly deaf at this stage so I had to trundle him up front, where, with his swollen belly, he sat on the edge of his too small seat, leaning forward on his wooden cane, breathing noisily, trying to catch the dialog. He knew personally or was familiar with nearly every character in *Reds*. This included many of the aged witnesses, who were, after all, his contemporaries. As the film got going, Sam became involved and growled comments on the proceedings, his gravel baritone blasting into the darkness. There followed from the audience, like a Greek Chorus, a call and response session.

Sam, viewing one of the old-timers on screen, blares: "Henry Miller! The man was a bohemian in Paris. He knows nothing about these things."

*Response*: "*Shhh!*"

An aged lady I do not remember appears on screen.

Sam: "Her!"

*Response*: "*Quiet!*"

The scene shifts to Roger Baldwin, founder of the American Civil Liberties Union.

Sam: "Him I can respect. That's more like it."

*Response*: An intolerant "*HISSS!*"

Big Bill Haywood shows up in little more than a bit part for a line or two. Sam waves his hand in disgust at the actor. "Nothing like him! The man has no stature. Haywood had stature! Haywood had one eye, but he never wore a patch like this fella!"

*Response*: "*Shut the fuck up! Call the manager!*"

Later on, an appealing scene, in which after a fight Warren Beatty brings flowers, a box of chocolate, AND a puppy to Diane Keaton (who plays Louise Bryant, Reed's lover).

Sam chuckles to himself, whispers loudly to me: "Reed was a hard drinker, rode with Pancho Villa. Flowers? The back of his hand!"

*Response: "Jesus Christ!!"*

Then, toward the end, there is the touching if slightly absurd montage of the devoted Diane Keaton, in the attempt to reach the dying Beatty, hiking through the Soviet snow in a blizzard. Apparently, she is not allowed to enter Moscow directly.

Sam: "Now that is ridiculous. Those days anyone could get in! The regime was looking for support. Did you know that Bryant married the American Ambassador after Reed died?"

The audience response ends here; instead a flash light skips through the darkness and two young ushers find us up front. "Sir, we must ask you to leave!"

"Why? What did we do?"

"Come on, it is almost over anyway," I say.

Outside, in the bright sunlight of the parking lot, some of the film's patrons can barely contain spitting at us; seeing an old man in suspenders with white socks showing beneath the cuffs of his pants made them angrier. Their fury was directed at a character that could have walked directly out of the film.

On the way home, in the car, I search for something about which Sam and I can agree. "How did you like the guy who plays Eugene O'Neill?" It was Jack Nicholson, who has an affair with Bryant in the film. I enjoyed his performance.

"No good!"

"No good? I thought he was very good. Why?"

"Too gloomy."

"Well, O'Neill must have been a gloomy guy, right? Look at his plays!"

"But he was not gloomy in that way." Sam insisted, "He was a good fella to have a drink with. He had that Irish wit. He didn't wear his troubles in public like a hair shirt, going around depressing everybody!"

Their paths had intersected in the radical, artistic, bohemian circles of the time. Early on O'Neill had shipped-out—that is, worked as a merchant seaman—and had been a Wobbly, and hung out with anarchists. He was not yet *Eugene O'Neill*.

Sam's off-hand comment surprised me. "You know that? You knew Eugene O'Neill? You drank with him? Why didn't you tell me?" I felt not hurt, but put-out.

"Why should I tell you? What earthly difference does it make if I knew Eugene O'Neill?"

I suppose he was right in the scheme of things.

Sam was always pulling surprises like that. He did not think that knowing famous people was important. Sometime later, I mentioned a PBS documentary on Diego Rivera. Sam smiled and said simply, "Diego was a good guy. You couldn't help but like him." They had met several times in the early '30s at radical meeting halls on lower Broadway and at a Union Square diner so infested with communists it was called The Kremlin.

As I've mentioned, the purpose of my autobiographical, cinematic diversion is to make accessible the richness of Sam's life nearly a century ago. He came to know personally virtually everyone who mattered in the radical movement of his day or he came to know of them intimately through their friends and enemies. Not that he thought his life was rich; it was simply his life.

# 7

# BACK TO *ROAD TO FREEDOM*

At *Road to Freedom* Sam was taken under-wing by Walter Starrett Van Valkenburgh, universally known as "Van"—the first of his many colorful mentors. He was a close friend of Emma Goldman, and had come to New York City via upstate Schenectady where, years earlier, he had lost a leg in a railroad accident. Normally Van got around on a crutch, but before a street demonstration—picture this—he would strap on his wooden leg and use the crutch to flail away at the cops, communists, and other enemies. What impressed Sam most, however, was the man's almost infinite tolerance, and his kindness. He would publish almost anything of an anarchistic flavor, no matter how outrageous, with perhaps a single line at the bottom saying it was not necessarily the view of the editor. There were no qualifications for membership; all were welcome. Total strangers passing through had voice equal to "old-timers." Impossible, you say? And yet the little group somehow functioned by mysterious consensus and put out the paper—although Van worked full time elsewhere and came in evenings and weekends.

Not that *Road to Freedom* at all times resembled the Peaceable Kingdom. Archie Turner was an Englishman of no trade or special talent save as a ladies man—an anarchist Don Juan. He had a way of getting under one's skin. Van detested him. The two were fire and water until Van boiled up one day and theatrically pulled a gun on him. Sam calmly took it away.

Theatrics aside, "Van" did a great thing for my father. He watched him, each night and weekends month after month, carry out the same menial tasks he had performed for the Socialist Party. Then, from nowhere, one day he said to him firmly: "You are writing an article for the paper. Next issue!" It was as close to a command as this gentle man was capable of generating.

"Me?" Sam asked, shocked.

"You can do this," Van said, and that was that. He insisted Sam sign his name to it, and he did, calling himself "Sam Weiner," a pen name he used for many years for inexplicable reasons; surely he was not fooling anyone.

"How do you like seeing your name in print?" Van asked after the paper came out.

It was a sense of pride Sam never forgot, although he did not remember the article too well maybe sixty years later. "I think I called Gandhi a bourgeois reformer," he said with characteristic self-mocking smile. Van's kindness had recast his self-image.

I suppose this is as good a time as any to define anarchism for it has bearing on the next stage of Sam's life. The word stems directly from the ancient Greek: *an*—without, and *arche*—realm or sovereignty. You can also substitute *arkhos*—leader or ruler. A society without a Ruler be it an individual or an institution, such as the State: that is what anarchists advocate, at least those who take the trouble to advocate. They do not believe in disorder, merely the type of "order" or rule imposed from above, the so-called hierarchal order one is forced to obey. Voluntary organization, voluntary association, the freedom to join or leave, mutual obligation free of coercion—this is anarchist order.

Anarchism is a wide tent; all kinds of people come in from the rain: from individualists who regard any conversation between three or more people as an authoritarian conspiracy to tightly organized communalists; from lifestyle anarchists who believe no restrictions should be placed on their behavior to traditionalists whose personal behavior is a model of Calvinist rectitude. *Road to Freedom* attracted anarchists of all kinds and not a few plain, old-fashioned nut-cases— the categories being not mutually exclusive.

I remember some of the people from Sam's early years; they still came to anarchist meetings in the 1950s—older, balder, but according to Sam spouting the same stuff. One fellow, Sid Wright, offered a singular solution to the world's problems. It was self-evident to him that all evil, aggression, and drive for power and domination exhibited by the human race stemmed from the same root cause: children are conceived clandestinely, in the dark, clothed in guilt. Children should be made in the open, in the fields, in the park, in sunlight, man and woman fucking naked for all to see. Then they would be born devoid of shame, full of hope and possibility, and free of the crippling neuroses that shackles the world. A return to the Garden of Eden, although you better not mention that corrupt document, the Bible, to him. He advanced his theory in an impeccable, scholarly English accent, with his wife, a most dowdy and respectable lady, looking on approvingly. There was a certain cock-eyed logic to it if you forgot all about genetics and embraced idiocy.

*Road to Freedom* attracted far too many people like that for Sam to hang around long—though he enjoyed the company of many of these eccentrics and remained friends with them throughout life. Those anarchists in *Road to Freedom* who were not crazy (and to be fair that was most of them) were difficult to organize—like herding cats. Sam had the idea of a regional anarchist convention so that groups of whatever stripe would have an opportunity to express their views and know each other. "Not possible," said one comrade who liked the idea in the abstract. "The Italians do not believe in conventions and the two Jews are not on speaking terms."

*Road to Freedom* was a debating society made impotent by its lack of structure. The place was not for him. He wanted to put his energy into things that matter, such as the fight against Capitalism and the domination of the State. These institutions he felt in his bones. He had no illusions he would be successful, but the struggle was what mattered to him. That struggle was best accomplished through revolutionary unions that had economic impact, that organized workers at the point of production, that had the power to demand changes in the System. Van agreed that Sam was not a *Road to Freedom* type. "You are an anarcho-syndicalist. You are an IWW, a Wobbly!"

"What's their address?"

# 8

## WITH THE WOBBLIES - ON THE BUM - CHICAGO

So Sam became a Wobbly—an anarchist Wobbly—the rest of his life. He joined and founded other groups as well, but his sense of belonging, his deepest affection, his love for the IWW never abated—even as the One Big Union faded to a few old-timers such as himself. The reasons were social as well as ideological. He joined as a young man, a "working stiff" in Wobbly terms, sometime in the early- to mid-1920s—his early membership probably overlapping with his time at *Road to Freedom*. The Wobbly greeting, their term of respect was "fellow worker," and he found fellowship there indeed. It was his passage into true adulthood and his time of personal liberation.

His early days with the Wobblies coincided with a return to his life on the bum, to the way he had lived when he skipped out as a boy to San Francisco on his way to Shanghai. "I became a migratory worker—a working hobo." These men worked on "railroads and waterfronts, in lumber camps, canneries, steel mills, factories, farms, construction camps, hospitals, hotels, restaurants." At the time automobiles were not within reach of poor men, and roads had not evolved into an efficient nationwide network. These men had but a single means of getting from job to job: to hit the rails. They led a hard, lonely life. They were the foot soldiers in the vast army of manual labor that made America run during a time when technology had not fully revolutionized modern life and abject wage slavery was not yet exported to China. Disdained by the American Federation of Labor (AFL), they were prime candidates for IWW recruitment.

Sam explains, "There is a world of difference between a *working* hobo as a migratory worker and a derelict, a hobo as a non-working vagrant, an aimless wanderer sleeping in box cars, abandoned shacks near railroad freight yards, a panhandler, subsisting on handouts begged from passing people, leftovers scrounged from restaurants and markets"—though at times Sam did some of that, short of panhandling. "But the *working* migratory hobo is a rebellious cuss.… The lumberjacks, the 'harvest stiffs,' the 'gandy dancers,' the itenerant laborers and so many other migratory workers who have fought for 'a place in the sun' have surely earned a heroic place in the American labor movement." They were Sam's kind of men, which explains why skid-row held no disgrace or terror for him.

Neither were the hobo "jungles" a jungle, if by that we mean a lawless place of fear, brutality, and tooth and claw predation. They were simply more or less established campsites near freight train terminals where the men congregated around fires that burned into the night in order to share food, blankets, and human company.

Throughout my years growing up, his hobo life having faded into his retreating youth, Sam would recite/sing this little ditty, with an impish expression:

> They flopped in the jungle together,
> The Hosier, the Wise Guy, and John,
> The Wino, the Dino, the Ding Bat,
> The Gazuni was also around…

I forget the rest and never knew who these guys were, only that Sam relished this long-forgotten bit of doggerel.

"People cooperated and helped one another," Sam always said, and there were unwritten but strict rules of etiquette and behavior concerning privacy, belongings, and food portions. People organized themselves. A good example is the Fraser River railway strike in Canada that began in March 1912, about which Wobbly poet and martyr Joe Hill wrote several songs, including "Where the Fraser River Flows." By April 2, eight-thousand men were on strike and work had ceased on 397 miles of construction line. The unskilled immigrant workers were demanding strict enforcement of the Provincial Health Act, a nine-hour day, and a minimum wage of $3 per day. The Wobblies who organized the strike were migrant workers. It was natural that the camps they and their fellow strikers constructed to feed and shelter themselves were a more tightly organized version of the hobo jungles. In his definitive book about Joe Hill, William Adler quotes an eye-witness journalist who called the isolated camps, strung over four-hundred miles of Canadian forest, "socialistic, egalitarian societies in miniature."

Also, remarkable for their time, the hobo jungles run by the Wobblies were free of racism. In *The Messenger* (a black radical publication) of July 1923, George S. Schuyler claimed that, "There was no discrimination in the 'jungles' of the I.W.W. The writer has seen a white hobo, despised by society, share his last loaf with a black fellow-hobo."

Sam made his way, he said, "by stealing rides on railway box cars, and 'shipping out' as a gandy dancer (or track maintenance man, a pick and shovel guy). The railroad provided free transportation to the job site, sleeping quarters, dining facilities, meals and bedding." Not a bad deal considering the times. But Sam was sometimes a bad boy. "I remember shipping out from New York City to Hornell, New York, near Buffalo, on the Erie Railroad. When we arrived we were given a 'nose bag' (lunch to be eaten on the job)...practically all of us would-be employees, ignoring the pleas of the foreman to return, took our nose bags and simply disappeared."

Work was not usually a scam. The job he most hated was at the Montgomery Ward depot in Rochester, New York. Ward at the time was the world's largest mail order house. Packages and crates of all sizes were piled high as a small hill in the center of a wide warehouse floor. Radiating from the pile, like the spokes of a gigantic wheel, were lanes labeled for the States of the Union. Sam's job was to load packages onto a huge wheel barrel, push it to the end of a lane, unload, and return to the pile to reload. A foreman drove him and the other men like horses.

Working when he had to, drifting here and there, Sam immersed himself in the IWW, which has been described by many historians as an organization in irrevocable decline at the time he joined, its back broken by Red Scare persecution—most especially the imprisonments and crackdowns of the Espionage Act (1917) and Sedition Act (1918). Hundreds of men were given long terms in Federal prisons: Leavenworth Penitentiary—"hells 100 acres"—being especially notorious. We must add to that outrage the forced deportations of radical immigrants under the auspices of Attorney General Palmer and his protégé, J. Edgar Hoover. And then there were the "patriotic" initiatives of private citizens: the lynchings and other forms of abuse orchestrated by those with vested interest in seeing Wobblies dead. The McCarthy witch hunts of the post-World War II era pale in comparison to what the Wobblies, radical Socialists, and religious nonconformists were put through.

There is no denying the impact of these actions, and, later, the "criminal syndicalism laws" passed by many states to protect the citizenry against the menace of the IWW. But most of the men imprisoned were rebels to the core and came right back. I think the reasons for the Wobbly decline were more complex. How else are we to explain that the IWW reached its maximum membership of 100,000 in 1923? And all historians would agree the Wobbly influence reached much further than formal membership. The union churned and discarded members like a threshing machine does wheat, but many of the ex members did not fall far. "Once a Wobbly, always a Wobbly," said the poet Ralph Chaplin who wrote "Solidarity Forever." He was speaking of himself as an old man near death, but the remark applies as well to thousands of others.

I think the decline of the IWW had as much to do with a disastrous internal split in 1924—over an issue never resolved. Where should ultimate authority rest, with local branches or with the General Executive Board (GEB) in Chicago? The centralizers versus the decentralizers; it is an issue that goes to the core of anarchism— indeed of all organizations. This lofty conflict hid nasty personal ones and opened the door to enough procedural wrangling to cross the eyes of a Philadelphia lawyer. Who would suspect that of Wobblies, of all people?

Then there was the rise of the Communist Party, which did more than siphon off members. The IWW was the first target of opportunity of its boring-from-within, rule-or-ruin strategy repeated on large and small scale in the United States and throughout the world. The Party was disciplined. When it could not capture the IWW it did all in its power to destroy the IWW—relatively easy to do because of the Wobblies' open democratic tradition and fluid structure. The subject is worthy of a PhD thesis and I will not go into details. Fred Thompson and Jon Bekken offer numerous examples in *The IWW: Its First 100 Years*. This passage summarizes matters:

Of the 46 on bond (while waiting appeal on the 1918 espionage conviction), Bill Haywood and eight others did not show up; they had been spirited away to Russia. The communists said they would make good on the bond losses, but never did, though publicly announcing that Haywood went to Russia on orders of the Communist Party. It soon became plain that the communists in the IWW were operating under instructions to wreck it.

They did help clarify IWW thinking. It became recognized that putches and insurrections cannot achieve industrial democracy....The chief damage done by the Communists to the IWW was the cultivation of the notion of a militant minority, priding itself on its revolutionary consciousness and holding in contempt...the majority of its members.

There were other reasons for the decline, the most important, I think, being the modernization of American life—which played out to the disadvantage of the IWW in many ways. On the most direct level, it is clearly harder to organize a timber wolf who drives to work and sleeps at home, than one who sleeps in a camp. Modernization included, later, the reforms of the New Deal and the rise of government favored unions—such as the Congress of Industrial Organizations (CIO) and the United Mine Workers of America (UMWA). The CIO had an industry-wide organization plan similar to the IWW, and many Wobblies crossed over. They kept dual membership in the beginning, but in time let the Red Card slip.

Whatever the causes, IWW membership declined to ten thousand by 1930, and in 1932 Sam, who was on close terms with the Chicago fellow workers of the General Executive Board, learned that the organization's treasury consisted of the grand total of twenty-nine dollars. Nevertheless, it is a mistake to judge the vitality of an anarchistic organization solely on membership, which can fluctuate wildly, or on money, which comes and goes. The Wobblies kept kicking, and they organized and led many significant strikes through the rest of the 1920s and 1930s and into the 1940s:

- The state-wide, Colorado coal miners' strike of 1927–1928, involving thousands of men. It was highly successful, despite the Columbine Massacre, during which state police shot and killed six striking miners, and injured many others.

- The North Idaho IWW lumber strike in 1936, also successful, despite the killing of three strikers and the wounding of a dozen—and threats by the Idaho governor to deport Wobblies from the state en masse.

- The major IWW activity during the construction of the massive Boulder Dam. The men shunned the radical Wobblies because they were fearful of losing their jobs in the pit of the Great Depression, and the employers scorned and ridiculed them, but in the end all the Wobbly demands were instituted—without credit or thanks, of course.

- The major presence of the IWW among the longshoremen and seamen of the West, East, and Gulf Coasts. Harry Bridges, an ex-Wobbly, led the militant West Coast longshoreman's union, which kept the old IWW slogan: "An injury to one is an injury to all."

- The significant job activity among the machinists in the industrial plants of Ohio; the IWW represented a number of locals, especially in the Cleveland area, very effectively, into the early 1950s. (More on this later.)

I leave for last the Wobbly organizing drive in 1929 among the soft coal miners of southern Illinois. The organization, out-manned and out-gunned, pitifully lacking in resources in comparison to the dictatorial and corrupt United Mine Workers of America, nevertheless made inroads. The first-generation Italian miners, a rebellious lot who fought to remain independent, formed their own union, The Progressive Mine Workers Union, which was closely affiliated with the IWW. But the Communist Party, sensing fertile ground, sent in teams of disciplined, well-financed Bolsheviks from New York to sway the miners toward their outfit, the National Miners Union (NMU). They were experts at strong-arming, taking over public meetings, silencing opposition, and manipulating policy.

The Wobblies fielded a particularly effective organizer by the name Sam Weiner: that is, Sam Dolgoff. If a man is known by his enemies, Sam figured he drew blood. The Communist Party official mouth-piece, *The Daily Worker*, published a libelous article charging that Sam Weiner was a paid agent of the mine owners. The mine owners posted notices warning miners to beware of that communist agitator, Sam Weiner. Although he downplayed the threat, we can read between the lines: "Upon my arrival, I was assured that the rank-and-file defense committee was well able to insure order at meetings, silence hecklers, repulse attempts to throw me off the platform and protect me against threatened physical assaults. In this, the comrades were entirely successful."

Sam had developed into a first-rate speaker at forums and street meetings by his trip to the soft coal fields. He knew how to handle hostile crowds and he knew how to handle himself in debate—an art form, as he called it. There was the night he annihilated the well-dressed, sarcastically devastating trial lawyer Max Shachtman before an audience of several-hundred people. The debate concerned the nature of the Soviet State, whether it was heading toward true communism. To a present-day audience this might seem nonsensical, like a debate over whether the Pope is Catholic. But "communism" meant something else to a leftist audience of the late 1920s and early 1930s; the issue was whether the Soviet Union would ever become a free and truly socialistic society under Bolshevik rule. Shachtman fervently thought so; he was an ardent supporter of Lenin's right hand man, Trotsky, who referred to the Soviet Union as a degenerate worker's state but a worker's state nonetheless. Sam answered to the contrary, and Shachtman, after calling Sam a political imbecile, proceeded to demolish his argument eloquently. Unbeknownst to him, Sam had quoted his answer verbatim from a revealing passage by Trotsky.

Sam, facing the audience, shrugged off the Shachtman's contempt, and said pleasantly, "I happen to agree with you. Argue with Trotsky! He wrote it!"

"Prove it!"

As Sam proceeded with theatrical flourish to open the passage from Trotsky he had memorized, the lawyer, stung, lunged across the stage for the book. The audience roared. Sam moved away, shielding the book. "You can see it in a minute, but let me first read some more!" The man had been reduced to a clown. Nothing he said after that escaped without deflating chuckles coming from the audience.

If it seems I am concentrating on the light side of things you are correct. That is how Sam recounted his youth: a man in his twenties during the '20s, on the loose, with nobody to feed or satisfy but himself. I think the escapade that tickled him most began as he ran across a soapbox orator while on the bum in Kansas City Missouri, around 1925 or so. The fellow stood on the "tailboard of a big hearse mounted on a Ford chassis flamboyantly marked: JUSTICE IS DEAD IN CALIFORNIA! FREE TOM MOONEY."

Mooney and Warren Billings were socialists framed for planting a bomb that killed ten people in the Embarcadero of San Francisco in 1916. The trial was conducted in a hysterical atmosphere; the convictions were based on perjured testimony; the prosecution suppressed exculpatory evidence; a Presidential Commission concluded there was no evidence to bring a case—and yet Mooney spent twenty-two years in prison before his pardon in 1939. The case was an international *cause célèbre*, one of a long line of labor/civil rights frame ups.

After the meeting Sam introduced himself and made a fast friend, Harry Meyers. "Are you loose?" Harry asked. "I need help."

Sam had one problem. How were they to get along selling and "spouting this stuff" in the reactionary small towns of the heartland? The police often as not partook of the disconcerting practice of making a man chew and swallow his Red Card—which was not a card at all, rather a dues booklet—before pounding the piss out of him.

"No trouble!" Harry assured him. "The cops in these towns, every last one of them, are Irish! They'll never arrest us for trying to free a guy named Mooney!"

And Meyers was right. Sam sold the literature and acted as chairman; Harry spouted-off and drove the hearse from town to town. At night, to his lifelong delight in the telling, Sam climbed into the coffin.

When they finally got to Chicago, Harry parked his beloved hearse in the garage across the street from Wobbly headquarters, at "three nickels," that is 555 West Lake Street.

Chicago became Sam's home base for the next six or seven years. He worked for a small-time painting contractor, slept at his house, and hung with the skid-row Wobblies and the anarchists. In keeping with his communal-anarchistic philosophy, and also because he had many friends there, he became active in the IWW Unemployed Union. We are skipping ahead to the pit of the depression, 1931 or so, before the New Deal reforms, when the capitalist economy teetered on collapse. Millions were living on the street and lining up for bread. You must be made of stone not to admire what the IWW did.

As Sam described it, "The Unemployed Union at 2005 West Harrison Street collected food from markets and large wholesalers to sustain unemployed members. If an unemployed worker found himself and family on the street for non-payment of rent, Union members would pack up their belongings and go right back into their home with them; let the land-lord think twice before throwing them out again." The food gathering procedure was equally direct. "An unemployed worker joining the Union was welcomed to free lodging and food, no questions asked. After two or three days he was given an empty sack after breakfast and told he would get no more help if he did not collect food before supper." The Unemployed Union distributed thousands of their popular leaflet *Bread Lines or Picket Lines*, which reminded those with jobs that all workers were in the same leaky boat. It urged them to help their unemployed brothers: not to work overtime, not to scab, to strike for shorter hours, to join with the unemployed in demanding cash allotments and unemployed benefits, to stage demonstrations outside plants and picket to publicize demands.

It is interesting from the perspective of our "individualistic"—synonym for selfish?—age that thousands of people with jobs helped the Unemployed Union.

# 9

# THE CLAP DOCTOR FROM CHI

Sam was fortunate to form close friendships with a number of colorful characters in his Chicago days. Some served as mentors; others he simply palled around with. He hit it off especially well with a tall, rugged-looking fellow of bad complexion, dirty knuckles, and greasy shoulder-length hair by the name of Dr. Ben Reitman—celebrated in Wobbly circles as "the clap doctor from Chi." They often met at the forums conducted by "hobo college," a fraternal organization that provided food, lodging, and education to the down-and-out on skid-row—West Madison Street—and less often at more dignified forums run by the anarchist Free Society group. The two men had more in common than poor personal hygiene. Each was the product of poverty-stricken Jewish immigrants. Each went on the bum early; Reitman was riding boxcars at age ten. Though Reitman was able to get training, and became a doctor, each man was restless, rebellious, difficult, and tenderhearted.

Reitman has been excoriated by feminist historians as a perfect son of a bitch, a cad, for what they deem his shabby treatment of Emma Goldman in the course of their torrid love affair of 1908 thru 1917. Not that Sam disagreed. Emma summed up Reitman's faults succinctly: his vulgarity, "his bombast, his braggadocio, his promiscuity, which lacked the least sense of selection." Sam once told his close friend, the historian Paul Avrich, that "it was impossible to have too low an opinion of him."

On the other hand, he liked the guy. Reitman earned his "clap doctor" appellation because he treated street prostitutes for VD at a time when no "respectable" doctor would touch them. This, long before penicillin was discovered. His "practice," consisted of whores, skid-row bums, thieves, destitute immigrants, and low-lives difficult to categorize. These were the people he grew up with and with whom he lived. He was a pioneer of public health, setting up free clinics for the most wretched of the poor, and with Goldman he toured the country advocating birth control, women's rights, and other disreputable causes. Hard to hate a man locked up at night for dispensing birth control advice in public, but let out during the day to treat imprisoned prostitutes and work in the hospital laboratory. And, not least in those Prohibition days, you could count on him for a prescription to buy legal booze.

Certainly, Sam thought, his good deeds deserved some positive mention from Emma's bitter defenders. But my father was in many ways an old-fashioned man. "Is the poor woman entitled to no privacy, no peace?" he pleaded when Emma's intimate love letters to Reitman were published in the 1980s. To which the answer is "no." She belongs to history now, and history loves scandal, revelation.

Reitman was kidnapped in San Diego while on a speaking tour with Emma in 1912. They had come to lend support to the Wobblies caught up in a free speech fight so vicious it drew national attention. While Emma was detained forcibly by authorities in another part of town, eight bastards pushed their way into his hotel room, drove him into the desert night, stripped him naked, beat him, burned IWW into his buttocks with a glowing cigar, poured hot tar over him head first, and rolled him. Then they wrenched his balls and shoved a club up his anal cavity. He nearly died.

That was all long before Sam knew Ben. So was Ben's affair with Emma, whom he last saw in 1919, the year she was deported. It was an intense episode in a full life. He placed flowers on her grave the day of her burial next to the Haymarket martyrs in Waldheim Cemetery. Ben died three years later, in 1943. Sam missed him, would always speak of him with affection. "Reitman never turned down anyone seeking help," he said.

It was rumored he left $1,500 in his will—a small fortune—for the bums on West Madison Street to drink to his memory. Sam had no doubt this was true.

# 10

# THE RUSSIAN ANARCHISTS - MAXIMOFF

The man who most influenced Sam's adult life was of an entirely different sort: self-disciplined, ascetic, scientific, deeply intellectual, prolific scholar, writer; a person of impeccable ethical behavior, and courageous beyond imagination. His name was Gregorii Petrovich Maximoff: one of the great figures in the history of twentieth-century Russian anarchism. They met in 1926, two years after Maximoff's arrival in Chicago and four years after he was expelled from the Soviet Union with the stipulation of summary execution should he return. He taught Sam many things, most importantly how to live.

We need historical context to appreciate this remark.

Maximoff was born in 1893 in the village of Matyushenko, Smolensk Province. His parents sent him to Seminary to study for the priesthood, but he renounced religion the year before his ordination and switched to the study of science instead. He graduated Petrograd Agricultural Academy as a qualified agronomist in 1915. That same year he was required to fulfill his military obligation; educated and privileged, he was of course to be sent to officer's training school. But Maximoff turned that down, preferring to serve as a common soldier.

The Tsarist regime was crumbling, the German's were invading on the western front, conditions in the countryside and the cities were deteriorating rapidly, the nation was in turmoil, there was general agreement that something had to be done. Maximoff applied his rational self to the problem. He delved deeply into the radical literature of the period, trying to determine which ideas best applied to the Russian situation. He was urgently concerned with the kind of society that would emerge after the fall of the Tsar. The ideas that most impressed him were expressed by two Russian anarchists of markedly different temperaments: Michael Bakunin and Peter Kropotkin—the latter was a prince, who hated that title, and threw it all away for a stay in the Tsar's dungeon, the same residence Bakunin had occupied a generation earlier, chained to a wall. Maximoff became an anarcho-communist (or *communalist*, as he sometimes described his credo).

To simplify a complex relationship, the Bolsheviks and anarchists were genetic enemies. The Bolsheviks, from their first moment, were dedicated to establishing a totalitarian State. The anarchists for their part did not believe in the State, certainly not in the exercise of centralized State power by the Communist Party, itself centralized into the authority of one individual—namely Lenin. They believed power should rest in freely associating committees of workers, peasants, and soldiers: naturally evolved societal units, such as on-the-job unions and farm cooperatives, whose representatives are freely elected, rotated, and given no special privileges. These grass-roots structures, which grew organically in the course of the Revolution, were the Soviets.

"All power to the Soviets!" That was the rallying cry of the Revolution, which was a spontaneous event, engineered by no single party or group, and certainly not the Bolsheviks, who in those early days dared not make that claim. They were in fact a distinct minority. But once in power they immediately set about to crush, capture, and emasculate the Soviets—to keep them in name only, and reduce them to organs of the State. They did this through a combination of state-induced terror (the Cheka, grandfather of the KGB), relentless propaganda, and dedicated Bolshevik worms "boring from within." Revolts were put down by military force, often with troops imported from far away and lied to, because those familiar with the issues could not be trusted to turn against their people. The anarchists fought the Bolsheviks, and their fate was slander, exile, imprisonment, and murder.

Sam writes in the introduction to *The Guillotine at Work* that Maximoff coordinated the anarchist resistance to the domination of the labor movement by the Bolshevik state, organizing the All-Russian Conference of Factory Committees (October 1917) and before that the Petrograd Factory Committees (June 1917). He was active not only in student and workers' circles, but also among the peasants, where his agricultural knowledge and understanding of their problems proved most effective.

Maximoff was an editor of the Golos Truda (Voice of Labor) printing collective, which, along with its bookshops in Moscow and Petrograd, circulated anarcho-syndicalist books and pamphlets throughout Russia: most importantly the works of Bakunin, Kropotkin, and others. Golos Truda was soon suppressed and—in an act of courage—Maximoff and comrades promptly proceeded to publish *Volny Golos Truda* (Free Voice of Labor).

Sam later wrote that "Maximoff's pre-eminent place in this history of Russian anarchism rests upon his ability to adjust theory to the practical needs of the workers. He formulated workable, constructive libertarian alternatives to Bolshevism: free Soviets; grassroots housing and neighborhood committees; self-management of industry through federations of factory committees; industrial unions; agricultural collectives and communes; networks of non-interest, non-profit co-operative agencies for credit and exchange. He envisioned a vast network of voluntary organizations embracing the myriad operations of a complex society."

In the spring of 1919 Maximoff went to Kharkov (a major center of steel production and heavy industry—you might call it the Pittsburgh of the Ukraine ) to work in the statistics department of the Northern Bureau of the All-Russian Union of Metal Workers. When the Bolsheviks conscripted him into the Red Army for propaganda work, he refused. Instead, he volunteered for something far more dangerous: frontline combat against the advancing White Guards, who had invaded Russia seeking to install the old regime… but on the condition that Lenin abolish the Cheka, stop breaking strikes and terrorizing the peasants, and restore civil liberties and power to the Soviets. Fat chance! Maximoff was arrested and summarily sentenced to death. He was saved from "the wall" by the Kharkov Steel Workers, who threatened a general strike; such was the standing of the man.

He remained in prison, however. He described that delightful experience in "One Day in the Cheka's Cellars," a chapter in his masterful *The Guillotine at Work*. Think of it as precursor to Solzhenitsyn's *A Day in the Life of Ivan Denisovich*, as Lenin was precursor to Stalin.

Maximoff's imprisonment was part of a larger pattern: the subjugation of the entire society to Bolshevik rule. In those early days

Lenin's regime was shaky and he saw the biggest threat came not from the right, but from the left—from those instrumental in forging the Revolution. He cracked down hard on all elements, and especially the anarchists. Thousands were imprisoned, thousands murdered, their fates lost to history. Yet the anarchists had strong support in the still to be tamed unions, and most importantly they had military power in the Ukraine. There, Nestor Makhno led an informal, shifting, but in its own way disciplined army of guerrilla fighters—massing at its peak to thirty-thousand men. Makhno has been called a bandit, an anti-Semite, a rapist, a plunderer—and much more—by apologists for the Bolshevik and the feudal regimes alike. None of that is true. In fact, independent historians have verified the opposite. I see a rough analogy between Makhno and the anarchist insurrectionary peasant leader Emiliano Zapata, who fought in Mexico during the same period. Like Zapata, Makhno was a brilliant strategist and the Red Army needed him to blunt the advance of the Whites across the Ukraine and into Russia. So Lenin and Trotsky agreed to Makhno's demand: That all anarchists be released from prison and from the control of the Cheka. And so Maximoff was released.

His "freedom" was brief. With the Makhno partisans playing a key role, the Whites were driven from the Ukraine, and were in retreat on other fronts as well. Confident now, Lenin and Trotsky turned against Makhno, treating previous agreements as so much toilet paper. They brought overwhelming Red Army force to the Ukraine, and also luck; a typhus epidemic had decimated half of Makhno's men before a shot was fired. Makhno and the remnants of his followers crossed the border into Romania, and I will leave their sad story to others, saying only that Makhno died in Paris as he was born in the Ukraine: in poverty and obscurity. He was forty-five years old. Not all was lost, however. While in Paris he befriended a young Spaniard, on the run, by the name of Buenaventura Durruti.

The Bolshevik ascendancy was successful on other fronts as well. Independent unions were abolished. The revolt—or more accurately the protest—of the Kronstadt sailors, who demanded that the regime restore civil liberties and the free elections of the Soviets, was drowned in the blood of the same eighteen-thousand men Trotsky had exalted as "the flower of the revolution" a few years earlier. Widespread strikes and peasant rebellions were put down with a ruthlessness that would have shocked the Tsar. Pitched battles in the streets—among other actions, the anarchists raided prisons to free all political prisoners—were doomed. The back of the resistance was broken.

*The Guillotine at Work: Twenty Years of Terror in Russia* is Maximoff's masterpiece. Over six-hundred pages, in two volumes, it stands after all these years as a searing indictment of Bolshevik rule, of Marxism, of the dangers of the concentration of state power. He lays the origin of that vast crime, the Soviet State, at the doorstep of Lenin, and not at his demented successor, Stalin, as apologists have done. These passages are from Bill Nowlin's excellent preface to the 1979 edition (rearranged slightly for our purposes).

Lenin, according to Maximoff, "followed in the footsteps of the French Jacobins." He believed in the necessity and even desirability of terror to implement his programme.... and the legitimacy of his authority. Maximoff presents scores of quotations from Lenin's published works in which Lenin urged shootings of political opponents, urged against sentimentality in the waging of political struggle and urged his fellow Bolsheviks to adopt unashamedly a policy of red terror. Maximoff charges that Lenin deliberately chose to provoke civil war in the countryside, to terrorize the peasantry and force their compliance with the forced grain requisitions, to subject them to state regimentation: "That we brought civil war to the village is something that we hold up as a *merit*," wrote Lenin.

The use of the death penalty was very rare in Tsarist Russia. When the Bolsheviks came to power one of the first things they did (in Lenin's absence) was to abolish the death penalty. Lenin reacted furiously, "beside himself with indignation" in Trotsky's description. "How," he demanded to know, "can a revolution be made without executions?" Maximoff compiles, from official Bolshevik sources, statistical summaries of the number of executions in each year of Lenin's rule. Estimates based on these figures range from 200,000 to over 1,500,000 shootings during

Lenin's period of leadership. Maximoff is willing to settle for the most conservative of all figures.

There is no question but that the Russian Revolution was a bloody affair. It would be unfair for anyone to attribute all of the deaths to Lenin's policies, all 10,000,000 to 12,000,000 lives. Any revolution takes lives. The white guardist counter-revolutionaries were certainly responsible for many deaths. The point is that many, if not most, of these millions of lives were shed not just because of the inevitable cost of revolutionary struggle but because Lenin insisted on implementing his own view of how that struggle should develop.... [Maximoff's] book stands as one of the most comprehensive documentations of the terror of the early Soviet state, which began under Lenin and was not just a Stalinist development. The principal lesson Maximoff wished to communicate, though, was that Marxism/ Leninism was a theory which, despite its revolutionary style, was in essence counter-revolutionary.

Sam for his part said many times that he knew the Bolsheviks were no good from the moment they slaughtered the Tsar and his wife and children, which he considered a profoundly immoral act.

In 1921, Maximoff and a number of other anarchists were remanded by the Cheka to the notorious Taganka Prison in Moscow. This was tantamount to a death sentence, either by the firing squad, torture, or more slowly by rot in a labor camp. The imprisoned anarchists launched a desperate gamble to save their lives and call attention to Bolshevik tyranny.

They owed the success of that gamble to three people on the outside whose moral and physical courage matched theirs. I speak first of Olga Freydlin. The Tsar had originally sentenced her to eight years hard labor in 1909 for smuggling subversive literature, but because she was barely a teenager, he relented and sent her to lifetime banishment in Yenesink Province, Siberia. She returned to her native Ukraine with the release of political prisoners following the February 1917 revolution and promptly resumed her anarchist activities. A year later she met an earnest young man named

Gregorii Petrovich Maximoff, and became his wife/life partner. (Sam spoke of her tenderly many years later: "Loyal, tough, courageous—you can't imagine!"). The others involved in the gamble are familiar to American radicals. Emma Goldman, deported by that indomitable G-man, J. Edgar Hoover, found herself a destitute guest of Lenin's regime. How easy it would have been for a lesser woman than Goldman to rationalize, to keep her head down, to stay comfortable. Instead, she and her dearest life-long friend, Alexander Berkman, also deported, rose in opposition, and in support of the imprisoned anarchists.

The three of them were well aware of how short was the distance between their freedom and the Taganka cellar.

The gamble: thirteen anarchists, including Maximoff, declared a hunger strike. The strike was timed to coincide with a prestigious conference in Moscow, that of the International Red Trade Unions (or Profintern). Though it was orchestrated by the Bolsheviks, many of the unions in attendance were independent, and even anarchistic. Olga, Emma, and Alexander—and others—fell upon the delegates and explained the situation. The delegates demanded the prisoners' release. The tension built. The conference threatened to blow-up in the face of the regime. The hunger strike stretched to ten days.

Lenin and Trotsky were clever men and not without charm. They claimed that there were no anarchists in prison. All of them are free, they said, offering addresses as proof. And sure enough, there was a print shop in a basement somewhere, free to publish. When the delegates arrived they found a harmless crack-pot cranking a crude mimeograph machine. But the charm-offensive backfired. The delegates were leaders of thousands, and in some cases, hundreds of thousands of men. Certainly, they were not fools and not pleased to be taken as such. The basement incident did not sit well. It was the origin of a remark I overheard an elderly man make to my father, some thirty years later: "And I told Lenin, the son of a beetch, I am leaving!" He was Armando Borghi, a leader at that time of the Italian syndicalists.

"Lenin?" I asked Sam, when we are alone. "The Russian guy? He knew Lenin?" I was, maybe, fifteen years old.

"Yeah, Lenin! Who was he? He was a man, flesh and blood, like any man."

So, finally, Lenin and Trotsky did the expedient thing. They released the anarchists, under the condition of lifetime exile, with the understanding they would be shot should they return. Having no other choice, the anarchists took the "compromise," and escaped with their lives, Berkman and Goldman among them, first to Berlin. Some remained there, others moved on to Paris, London, and the United States. In 1924, Olga and Gregorii, arrived in Chicago. They wasted no time in joining the IWW—not a symbolic act. Gregorii promptly founded *Golus Trushenika* (Worker's Voice) the Russian-language newspaper of the IWW that, at its peak, circulated among perhaps ten thousand exiles throughout North America.

# 11

## MAXIMOFF EDUCATES SAM

In time, Sam came to know many of the anarchists imprisoned with Maximoff during the Taganka hunger strike.

He came to know men who fought at the side of Nestor Makhno.

He came to know at least three men who I know knew Lenin personally and, as delegates to the International, demanded the anarchists' release.

He came to know I. N. Steinberg, the Minister of Social Justice in Lenin's first and only coalition government, a man who conferred face to face with Lenin in that room in the Kremlin where he ruled.

He came to know the surviving sister of Fanny Baron, executed by the Cheka.

He came to know the daughter of Peter Kropotkin, Princess Alexandra, who loved to regale Mother with tales of her London childhood in the home of her exiled parents.

He came to know Kropotkin's disciple, Rudolf Rocker, a powerful intellect and the author of the classic, *Nationalism and Culture*—in fact, he painted Rocker's house.

He came to know, with a special affection, Donuluk, the elderly impoverished anarchist who lived among his Ukrainian countrymen in the slums of New York's Alphabet City—a solitary little guy with a deeply creased face, bald head and rough clothes. In this country fifty years, he barely spoke English and never smiled; he'd come before meetings, prepare the room, and then leave with a nod to Sam.

And most of all Sam came to know Gregorii Maximoff.

When I check the birth dates of the two men it brings me up short that Maximoff was a mere nine years older than Sam. That is because Sam spoke of him with the respect one affords a much older man; he was in a sense his spiritual father. The gap in life experience, knowledge, and poise brushed aside years. Here was a man who had faced down the power of Lenin; had come within hours of a firing squad; had conducted a successful hunger strike in the

Cheka dungeons; had organized steel mills and peasant collectives; had served as an editor of important journals and, while in Berlin, helped found an international anarchist organization comprising— it may surprise you—several million people.

Sam first met Maximoff in Chicago, 1926. Yet I witnessed the esteem in which Sam held the man first hand in New York, 1949 or so. Notice I say that I witnessed the esteem rather than the man himself. I remember Sam rising from the kitchen table, waving the just-opened letter excitedly, calling out to Mother, "Esther! Maximoff and Olga! They are coming in three weeks!" I have never seen him react in such a strange way to visitors before or since. At all times he was a warm host, but a decidedly casual one. He thought nothing of greeting guests, male or female, in his undershirt, or if he knew them a little better in his *vakokta* undershorts. The guests ate what we ate: good, but no special fuss. And if Mother attempted to clean the house a bit, he would take the broom from her and throw it in the closet. All part of his casual, communal self.

But not this time. I had never seen my father actually wash the windows and polish the floor. If he had time he would have painted the place. He went shopping for the best Russian stuff: herrings, smoked salmon, etc., although as it turned out the Maximoffs ate little. No *vakokta* underwear for the Maximoffs! It was imperative to my father that they see him as a responsible adult worthy of their respect.

As to the man himself, all I remember is this frail, pale individual of uncertain step, accompanied by a concerned Olga. He was obviously a warm man, a sweet man, but not well and they did not stay long. Maximoff died in his mid-fifties a few months later after suffering a massive heart attack. It was the second time I had seen my father weep, the first being the death of his biological father, Grandfather Max.

I have read some accounts calling Maximoff a "designer of wall displays" or some such euphemism. A misguided attempt to preserve his status? The man hung wall paper. It was a trade he was taught by his close friend Boris Yelensky, an earlier arrived exile. Yelensky was the main reason he settled in Chicago, long a magnet for Slavic immigrants. Olga found work in a Loop department store, and that is how they lived. Physically. Spiritually, emotionally, intellectually it did not matter where or how they lived once they were expelled from Russia. Their life was anarchism, revolutionary syndicalism, social justice, history. They were a couple of immense erudition; spoke English fluently despite having arrived but a short time ago. The year was 1926 when Sam met him, as I have mentioned, a foot-loose twenty-four-year-old kid, leading a raffish semi-skid-row existence. Maximoff saw potential there, took him under wing. As Sam put it, "He taught me to read and write." Before long, Sam found himself the irascible pet of Maximoff, Yelensky—"a man born with boxing gloves on"—and a handful of other Russian anarchist exiles: "They were my university!" Sam recalled fondly.

Sam thought he was hot stuff when he met Maximoff. He had written a few articles, made some speeches, ran with the anarchists and Wobblies. Maximoff saw things differently. "You are bright, but you do not know anything. You lack an education. What have you read?"

So, he and the other Russian comrades proceeded to tutor him. They had him read the classical anarchists: Bakunin, Kropotkin, Proudhon, Reclus, Malatesta, and Rocker, of course. But they did not stop there. They had Sam read Marx, Engels, Lenin, Trotsky ("How do you know if you agree or disagree if you do not know what they said?"). They had him read Adam Smith, of all people, for whom he acquired a lifelong respect. ("Most of the things they claim he said, he never said or they've twisted. Modern capitalism would make him turn over in his grave.") They also had him read authors you would not expect. ("You need to be a rounded person. What do you know of poetry? Here, take this!") And it could be Shakespeare's sonnets, or Pushkin, or the novels of Tolstoy, or Mark Twain. You get the idea.

Maximoff—and comrades—did not let him off the hook by simply giving him things to read. They proceeded to grill him like a rabbi working over a lazy student of the *Talmud*.

"The 'Communist Manifesto' is at heart a reactionary document—never mind the rhetoric. Am I an idiot to say this? Where is the evidence?"

"What do you think of Marx's use of Hegel's categories? Was capitalism inevitable?"

It was never a question of indoctrination. Maximoff NEVER asked him to change an opinion, merely to defend it. He was a great teacher.

From Maximoff Sam acquired the life-long habit of devouring books. You would find his greasy thumbprints all over the pages; he had no respect for books as aesthetic objects, only for their print. Wherever he was, whenever he was not slinging a brush he would read—although it is plain to me that Maximoff's influence on Sam went deeper than books.

"You are twenty-five years old," he would say to him, with feeling. "What kind of man are you? How do you live? Is this the man you intend to be?" Sam came to see that, like Maximoff, it was necessary to lead a life that you, yourself, can respect. And Sam sincerely attempted to live that way, especially in his later years. But—then—there was the irrepressible, irreverent side to him. He loved to run with the Ben Reitmans and Harry Meyers of the world. He never lost that sly humor, that sense of the human.

I remember discussing the Cuban Revolution with him in the 1980s. He had written an important book on the subject years earlier, a critique of the Castro regime from the anarchist perspective. The conversation drifted to Batista's Havana: of the gambling, prostitution, and corruption that existed there, pre-Castro. Sam readily agreed. "It was awful," he said, very serious. Then his voice dropped and he added with a mischievous wink, "But, you know, people had a hell of a good time!"

# 12

# THE FATE OF *THE GUILLOTINE*

Maximoff went on to write a number of books and articles, all of them at night and weekends after hard manual work. I think we underestimate how difficult this is. Roger Baldwin, Harvard graduate, briefly a Wobbly, and founder of the American Civil Liberties Union (ACLU), was fond of quoting Clearance Darrow to the effect that "it was a lot easier being a friend of labor than a laborer." In this, as in many things, Sam was to follow Maximoff's example, working and writing.

The preface and title page of *The Guillotine* provide an interesting sub-plot to Maximoff's book. The title page lists the Alexander Berkman Fund as publisher—in memory of the courageous anarchist who, suffering from depression and incurable cancer, had recently committed suicide. No mainline publisher would touch the book. Who cared to hear what an obscure anarchist had to say about Bolshevik rule? The sycophancy of the Stalin lovers, so influential in publishing circles, bordered on the erotic. Funding of the book came from the meager contributions of thousands of working-class comrades the world over, funneled through their unions and cultural organizations. It was the middle of the Depression. No grants or fellowships for Maximoff, who continued to hang wallpaper.

The address listed on the opening page of the book was in fact the national headquarters of the IWW: 2422 North Halsted Street, Chicago, Illinois. There follows an item listed in the publisher's preface: "The Berkman Fund acknowledges its special gratitude to Ralph Chaplin, proletarian poet, (and to) Carl Keller, editor of the *Industrial Worker*, the weekly organ of the IWW." The Fund does not mention Chaplin was a Wobbly; it was a fact deemed obvious at the time. In other words, the IWW was instrumental in publishing *The Guillotine*, and thus at an early date exposing the nature of the Soviet state.

I know little of Carl Keller and have no doubt he was a fine, able man. But Sam spoke often and with feeling of Chaplin. His great anthem of labor, "Solidarity Forever," is sung at union halls, protest meetings, and picket lines around the country, and the world over. Was it coincidence that the Gdansk shipyard workers of the 1980s, who rose up in revolt against Soviet rule, called their movement Solidarity? Yet Chaplin remains one of the unsung heroes of American Labor, if you will grant me the pun. As American to the bone as Maximoff was Russian, the two men were nevertheless brothers under the skin, revolutionists to the core.

Chaplin became a rebel at the age of seven after seeing a worker shot to death during the Pullman strike of 1893. Later, having moved to Mexico he became a supporter of Emiliano Zapata. Back in the U.S. he worked with Mother Jones for two years and served with her during the bloody West Virginia coal mine strikes of 1912–13. It was in the name of the miners that he wrote poems, one of which, set to the tune of "John Brown's Body," became "Solidarity Forever."

Chaplin then joined the IWW and became a Wobbly through and through. A talented illustrator, he was responsible for the distinctive style of Wobbly art: the heroic figure of a laborer, his sleeves rolled to reveal brawny arms, leaning forward as if rising from the very earth; the strong face peering at you from behind prison bars, his hands gripping the bars, looking much like a self-portrait of Chaplin himself; the arched black cat in the night, hair raised stiff, to this day the anarcho-syndicalist symbol of revolt. The man was also a talented journalist and essayist; for years he was editor of the IWW paper *Solidarity*, and later the *Industrial Worker*.

He knew the great Wobblies and socialists close up and personal; indeed he was one of them: Mother Jones, Eugene V. Debs, Big Bill Haywood, Vincent St. John, James P. Thompson, Father Haggerty. And last but certainly not least, there was his closest friend, Frank Little; some would say he was the toughest Wobbly of them all. Born 1879 in the Indian Territory that was to become Oklahoma, the son of a white Quaker father and a Cherokee Indian mother, he was a slight man, had but one eye, and was crippled from beatings incurred during strikes and demonstrations. Yet the man was fearless; his body meant nothing to him. No law, no threat, no person could stop him until his luck ran out in 1917, and he was hanged from a railroad trestle in the dead of night while on a trip to organize the copper miners of Butte, Montana. Chaplin had begged Little not to go there, alone, unprotected, and vulnerable.

Chaplin saw the inside of many a prison, most severely when he was sentenced to twenty years hard labor for violation of the Espionage Act and was sent to Leavenworth Penitentiary along with one hundred other Wobblies in the wake of the disgraceful Chicago show trial of 1917. He served four years until he was released. The experience was wrenching, traumatic. What kept him sane, what kept him human was his art and poetry (see *Bars and Shadows: The Prison Poems*).

So we have two men from opposite ends of the earth whose experiences of life were not so different after all. In the vein of the Russian anarchists, Chaplin distrusted the Bolsheviks' centralized organizational structure from the start. He observed first hand the havoc they caused the Wobblies and the labor movement in general, and he knew them to be unprincipled and dangerous. As an experienced editor, he appreciated the quality of Maximoff's manuscript—and he admired the man. Chaplin slaved over the book, shaped the translations into readable English, and sent the work on its way in publishable form.

All this I see in the preface and title page, reading between the lines. But one more item in the preface needs attention, a simple footnote: "As our book goes to press, war is raging in Europe and Stalin and Hitler have come to an amicable understanding. Poland has been divided, the territory of Russian terror enlarged, and the plight of the Russian political prisoners have become worse than tragic."

Maximoff's book did not see the light of day until 1940. Soon Stalin was to become our temporary friend, never mind his pact with Hitler. Seventy million people were to die. *The Guillotine* was ignored.

# 13
## SAM FALLS IN LOVE

From our discourse on socialism, anarchism, the Wobblies, migratory labor, the Bolshevik betrayal of the Russian Revolution, the horrors of two World Wars, we turn to Sam's sex life. You'd think this would be a subject of importance to Sam, but in contrast to the myriad things he talked to me about, he never spoke of the sexual side of his wild youth—assuming one could describe his adventures and knock-about travels as wild, rather than sad and searching.

I received no tales of cozying face to face with a rebel girl in Harry Meyers's cozy coffin. No tales of youthful love lost. No free-love orgies on the April Farm, the disastrous experimental commune supposedly free of coercion and based on voluntary labor, where he lived for a year or two. Sam hung with skid-row Ben Reitman whose reputation as an undisciplined cock-smith was deserved, but no tales were forthcoming.

I suspect Sam left me with no direct knowledge of his youthful sex-life because there was little of it. His was a masculine world: Wobbly union halls, anarchist forums, skid row, hobo jungles. Women were a scarce commodity. In the main, however, I suspect Sam's problem— and I am convinced there was a problem—was a feeling of personal unattractiveness that lay embedded in the core of his personality. I have seen photos of him as a young man and remember how he appeared to me when I was growing up and he was in his forties. He was wiry and well-muscled with powerful arms and shoulders and a flat stomach: "ripped" is the current word. That's what hard labor and good genetics can do for you. He was not conventionally handsome, but he had a strong face, a rugged Russian Jewish face, wild black hair swept back, acute black eyes behind the glasses, a prominent nose. An interesting face. Another man, regarding himself in the mirror, might say "not a movie star, but not bad." Throughout his life he would stare into that mirror and distort his features into grotesque shapes and say to his image with contempt, "A puss ugly enough to stop a clock!" One did not feel comfortable watching this display.

I would say the young Sam was exiled to the state of the perpetually horny—his need stronger than his technique, socially maladroit in the company of women, overly aggressive. Although, who knows? He had a certain charm.

The clearest image of Sam as a young man, say 1930 or so, comes from a delegate to the Anarchist Forum who volunteered to meet a speaker from the IWW on the steps of the Cleveland Public Library one afternoon. The speaker was over an hour late and apparently not showing up, and so the delegate began walking down the library steps to leave.

"But there was this homeless-looking fellow, filthy, who had been pacing up and down in front of the steps for about an hour. That couldn't be him, I said to myself, but it was!"

Of course, the filthy "homeless" guy was my future father, who had ridden an overnight freight from Detroit to get there. The delegate was Esther Judith Miller, my mother-to-be. Esther was a proper young lady from a striving, high-achieving, first-generation immigrant family—well mannered, well spoken, and immaculately dressed. She took one look at filthy Sam and that was it. Something about him touched her heart.

Mother's respectable siblings were scandalized that she—an educated young lady with an MA in English literature, and one of the first women to be admitted to her medical school—should run off with a Wobbly, a filthy hobo house painter! To live in poverty? It was perverse! When she had a violinist of the Cleveland Symphony, and a prominent rabbi, and a guy who owned seven drug stores interested in her? They never got over it completely, though Ida, my grandmother, had a different take. Old, and sick with heart trouble, she fell into deep conversation with Sam, in Yiddish.

That evening she told Mother, as they sat alone, in the kitchen: "You're choosing a hard road for yourself, but you've chosen a Man."

My parents remained together fifty-eight years until death did them part. She never once complained about money, our semi-poverty.

Not that Sam lacked rivals in those early days. For the forty-five years that I remember, he never missed the opportunity to mock

Marcus Graham (real name Schmuel Marcus), a long dead anarchist of the individualist-vegetarian-anti-technology school. A lifestyle anarchist, and, as I learned later, a not inconsequential writer and thinker, Graham occupied a corner of the anarchist tent far from my syndicalist father. But why the vehemence, the sarcasm, and why bring him up all the time? It was only after Mother's death in 1989 that Sam mentioned with his confidential wink, "You know, he was after your mother. It's a good thing I fucked better!"

There is no doubt they were passionately in love and that it lasted an entire lifetime—though in the spirit of their generation nary a whisper of sexual matters between them ever reached Abe and me. Mother was not a woman! She was Mother! Never had I seen her in anything more revealing than a slip. Nevertheless, long after they were dead, just recently, with each of us in our seventies, Abe mentioned a few things. "Remember Saturdays?" he reminded me, wearing Sam's confidential wink. "Remember, how she hustled us both out of the house after breakfast?"

Yes, I do remember: Abe off to his clarinet lesson on the Upper Westside and me to the local theater, The Palestine, which showed fifty cartoons and cliff-hangers. She even gave me fifty cents for lunch after at the local kosher deli on the corner of Henry and Clinton Streets in a store still there, but now a bodega owned by Pakistanis. It was enough for two hot-dogs; crisp hand-cut french fries; a Dr. Brown's Celery Soda, and thirteen cents change. They were the best lunches I ever had!

"What do you think they were doing while we were out?" Abe asked in a tone that needed no answer. "Remember the flush in her face, the light step, the mood when she served the dinner? The old man 'resting'?" he added with a chuckle.

Yes I do.

Though they never discussed their sex life in front of Abe or me, my sense is that they were totally and completely frank with one another in private, as they seemed to be in all other things. Yet Mother had no sense of the off-color or vulgar. She was impervious to sexual innuendo. Example: two or three rough Wobbly seamen are "over the house," as Sam would say. Mother shows off her sons.

"This is my oldest" she says proudly, her arm around Abe, who is about eleven.

"Nice looking kid," says one of them. "If he behaves, we can set him up as a Cabin Boy on a Greek Ship." The "comrades" snigger.

Mother *kvells*—one of those untranslatable Yiddish expressions, insufficiently expressed in English as "coos like a bird with pride —"You hear that Abraham? These comrades will get you a job on a ship when you are older!"

Had she the faintest inkling of the "job" that the "comrades" had in mind, she'd have thrown them down the stairs.

In 1932, Sam and Esther hitch-hiked from Cleveland to Washington D.C. to observe the Bonus March. Forty-five-thousand marchers—veterans of World War I and their wives and children— had camped out in the swampy field that was Washington's Anacostia district. They demanded that the bonuses promised them in 1945, $1.00 for each day served in the States or $1.25 for each day served overseas, be moved up to the present instead. It was the pit of the depression. The men were facing destitution. Army Chief of Staff Douglas MacArthur and his aides, Dwight Eisenhower and George Patton, crushed the peaceful assemblage with cavalry and tanks, clubbing the families from horseback and flattening and setting to flames their plywood shanty towns. For years MacArthur was known in radical circles as "the hero of Anacostia flats."

How is that for a honeymoon? It was a sight Mother never forgot, though observed from a distance.

She cut to the moral center of the thing. She said of MacArthur, "The man clubbed the men who had fought at his side; he had them clubbed when they asked for bread."

# 14

## MOTHER - CHILDHOOD - OTHER THINGS

April 8, 1937 is the day I entered this world. True to my heritage I came out kicking and screaming and tore Mother's womb to shreds. Another pregnancy was dangerous and out of the question, the doctors told her: she should be thankful she had two strong, healthy boys, and that settled her quest for a girl. Her womb had dropped and in a few years she would suffer through a difficult partial hysterectomy.

Abe has recently reminded me of some things I was in no position to remember: that I was born 11:45 pm at Lincoln Hospital in the South Bronx; that after Sam carried me up the stairs in his arms to our tiny apartment on Trinity Avenue, he nestled me into my first home, swaddled in soft sheets and blankets: a dresser drawer.

"This is your brother," he said to Abe, who was not yet four years old. "He is part of our family."

We need to back up a bit before I go on with my life. We need context. We need to understand Mother: her anarchism, which she came upon before she met Sam; her integrity; her compassion; and, yes, her compulsion to control and dominate her sons through a love that was conditional upon our moral behavior as defined by her. Abe and I have thought a great deal about these things. He reminded me not long ago of an incident in Mother's young life that I think is key to the development of her character.

# 15

# IN THE HOUSE OF FATHER ABRAHAM

A good place to start is the photograph of Father Abraham and his young family circa 1909. They are stiffly posed and formally dressed in the manner of the day. Father Abraham is seated, his back straight, balancing Mother's sister, the infant Sarah, swaddled in white linen on his lap. Grandmother Ida, a pretty woman, stands to his right proudly, if slightly recessed, her hand resting on his shoulder. Mother, little Esther, stands in front of Ida and at Father Abraham's side. He clasps her hand gently. He is indeed a handsome man, and I can still discern Mother in that tiny face staring out at me from over a century ago.

Mother mentioned many times Father Abraham's straight back and military bearing, which he came upon honestly. That is, he served several stints in the Tsar's Army. Her fondest, most loving memory of him was creeping down to the bathroom of their Cleveland home in Garfield Heights, then a gracious suburb, to watch the ritual of his morning shave. He'd appear shirtless, suspenders over his long underwear, facing the small, round mirror. No shaving cream, stuff like that: instead soap, cold water, and straight-edge razor, which he stroked expertly on a long leather strap at his side, grown shiny with use. She loved the delicious sound of the blade against his cheeks, chin, and neck, and the way he got the blade around his mustache—all this while standing ramrod straight, as if at attention. He was of course aware of her as he shaved but said nothing; he'd smile, and she'd smile back, their little secret. Mother adored Father Abraham.

He came from a long line of bricklayers and construction tradesman. She was fond of telling us the stories Abraham told her of the pace of 1880s life in the small White Russian village of his birth. Here's one: Seems the village priest sent for him one evening. Could he do some brick restoration work on the local church? A portion of the wall was crumbling. "I'd be glad to," Abraham says, "but I am off to the Army tomorrow for at least two years." The

Tsar required one male from each family. Generally it was the oldest son, but since Abraham's brother was getting married, Abraham was going instead. The old priest shrugs, "So? When you get back!"

As usual, Mother saw beyond the superficial to the moral center of the story. "You see, the priest knew that was Father's work. He would not think of giving that work to another man. And the priest knew he was a Jew. That didn't matter. They respected each other."

That tolerance did not extend to the barracks of the Tsar's Army. He had a hard go, but, typical of him, he said nothing about it. There was one incident that he savored, however, and Mother recounted it to us with relish growing up: Father Abraham was assigned to the detail that stood guard and paraded at important ceremonies. The men were picked for their looks and bearing, for the impression they made. One Easter service found Abraham deployed front row in full dress uniform and full mustache on the steps of the St. Petersburg Cathedral. Out comes the priest in full regalia. Deliberately and in stately fashion he sprinkles holy water from a golden pail at the troops, first to one side, and then the other. Now, it is good luck and a blessing to be sprayed with as much as a drop, but a full blast catches Abraham's cheek. The water is cold and unexpected and he flinches. "Had to be a Jew!" the men behind him growl.

Once in the clutches of the Tsar's Army it was hard as hell to get out; they'd keep you for as long as they wanted. For that and the other familiar reasons, Abraham and his young wife made their way to the U.S., and eventually to Cleveland, where they were fruitful and multiplied. They had six children who made it to adulthood. Mother was the oldest by a few years; she was brought to America six months of age. There followed Sarah, Martin, Joseph, Sid, and Daniel, who was much younger, a change of life baby.

By all accounts Abraham was a wonderful father from a bygone age, as honest and direct as his back was straight. Though he knew Hebrew well he'd read passages from the Torah to the children in his accented English, tell them the stories of Daniel and the Lion, of King Saul, of David and Goliath (though never David and Bathsheba), of Noah; Mother grew up with the Old Testament in her bones. As an adult, she loved to read from it. She loved the poetry, the purity of the language, and the wisdom. She called it a remarkable document of an ancient people and that was enough for her. There was no need of a god to worship.

And Abraham was skilled in many things. He could do carpentry, metal work, masonry, bricklaying, and farming. He built the home they lived in with his bare hands. He kept a garden with fruit trees on to which he grafted the branches of other trees. And a proud man, proud of his work. He'd take the family, the whole brood, into the city proper to admire the brick bakery ovens he built with his bare hands, his labor. I wonder if any of them are still there? In use?

He made his own tools, kept them in a large storage shed that he built in the back yard. He took the wood from fruit crates and made pirate chests for the children, with curved tops that he painted and shellacked to look old. He used his forge to make iron hinges and ornamental metal of different design for each chest. He gave them secret locks, so that the chests could not be opened even if the padlocks were removed. He put a set of wheels on Daniel's chest to use as a scooter if he desired. He took some small tree branches and showed Daniel how to make a toy house by weaving the material together and anchoring it in the ground. The house had a roof and walls and it was still standing in the weather for some years after Father Abraham died.

They were not an observant family, vaguely socialistic, ardent Zionists. My great grandfather on my grandmother's side, the Hollanders, died in Austria, trying to get permission from the Turks to immigrate to Palestine. His son made it there in 1909 and there is a branch of the Hollander family I have little knowledge of. Apparently they did well; every now and then a basket of fruit would arrive to Garfield Heights. But by 1925 we find Grandmother Ida sending a letter in Yiddish to Uncle Hollander, asking sarcastically if ink and paper were expensive in Palestine, since he had not been writing. Separated by oceans and worlds, the families were drifting apart.

By Esther's account her mother was a stern and demanding woman—superficially the family disciplinarian, at least in everyday affairs. She was feisty, the rebel among the neighborhood wives. She got a group of them to lie to their husbands that they were having a "girl's night out at the theater." Instead, they stole off to downtown Cleveland to hear Emma Goldman or Margaret Sanger lecture on birth control. It was a defiant act for their time and class, though a bit like locking the barn door after the horse escaped if you figure Mother's six kids were the norm.

Caring for those kids, who were dropping out one after the other was a daunting, exhausting task. She needed help. So she enlisted Esther, her oldest by four or five years, as a sort of surrogate. "I was never allowed to be a child," Mother would complain bitterly to Abe and me when we were adults. "I couldn't simply play, get into mischief, and have friends. 'You are the oldest,' she'd say, 'I need you not to be silly. I need you to take care of your brothers!'" Which she did, before and after school every waking day of her childhood. Along the way she developed a fierce attachment to her brothers that was almost unnatural—not in the sexual sense but in its loyalty and love.

All this brings me to what I believe is the central traumatic incident in Mother's young life. You see, that shiny leather strap Father Abraham sharpened his razor on had another use. By all accounts— Mother's, my Uncles', and Aunt Sarah's—he was remembered as the kind, affectionate man I have described. Nevertheless, there was that strap and the boys knew it. The incident concerns Uncle Sid. I do not know what he did exactly to provoke punishment, but it was something dare-devil and dangerous—the kind of prank a fourteen-year-old full of testosterone and boyish defiance might try. I think it had to do with stunts at the railyard in company with a crowd Father Abraham considered unwholesome.

Time and again Abraham warned Sid to stop. Finally, he had enough. He called the entire family together in the living room: Mother, Esther, Sarah, Martin, Joseph, and, of course, Sid.

"Take off your clothes!" He had him strip naked, his genitals in full view of the family, including the women.

"If you are going to hurt yourself I might as well do it first! Bend over! You are going to say you are sorry! You are going to say you will never go there again! You are going to say please don't hit me anymore!"

"I'll never say that."

Father Abraham brought down the strap. And again. Mother said the sound of it striking Sid's flesh made her sick. "Stop! Stop!"

she cried, Sarah cried, her mother cried. The boys were silent. But Father Abraham was demonic, possessed. He had passed beyond punishment into another realm. Sid started to bleed. He held out for as long as he could, but the pain became too great.

"I am sorry. Never do it again. No more, please!" he cried. Father Abraham had broken his son.

The nub of it Mother would recount years later was not the strapping, which was bad enough, but the humiliation. That, to her, was her father's purpose, to have her dear brother stripped naked in front of his sisters, to leave him no dignity at all. For that she could not forgive her father. But she adored her father! That would never change. She took to temporizing, rationalizing her dilemma.

"Father warned Sid again and again," she would plead to a nonexistent jury. In other words, it was Sid's fault. But for what? Misbehaving? Crossing Father's authority? How is that relevant, for her father was on trial for sadism in her eyes. And what, finally, was Father Abraham's motivation in beating Sid? Sid's safety? Or maintaining his authority? If the latter, upon what did that authority rest? Love or force?

To Mother, Sid's punishment took on the force of biblical parable. She never resolved her feelings. Yet, there were such things as right and wrong. And if there is wrong in this world someone must be to blame and must be held to account. Not through physical brutality, which she abhorred, but there are other ways to punish. For example, it was unacceptable to Mother that my son Gregory was born brain damaged, afflicted with autism, and organic schizophrenia. Jessica, my ex, was to blame. She did not breastfeed him at birth, she rejected him, did not love him enough; it was her fault, in Mother's eyes. Never mind the diagnosis of a dozen neurologists, psychiatrists, psychotherapists, social workers—or the cruelty such an opinion visited upon Jessica. Someone had to be blamed.

The story of Abraham and his sons does not end there. Let me tell you about Uncle Joseph, whom Abe and I never met because he died before we were born. He was a strong, adventurous kid, played halfback on the high school football team when it was a very different game. That was a time when you played both offense and defense and a player could be substituted for only once a half. You played with virtually no padding and there was no medical coverage. When Joseph broke his collarbone, no one stepped in to take his place and the games were canceled for the remainder of the season. Joseph was not a particularly big kid, but he was strong and he took no shit. He once threw the neighborhood bully through a plate-glass store window. Father Abraham said that he did not mind paying for it.

My grandfather—the ex-soldier in the Tsar's Army, the kindly man of moral probity and military bearing and fierce temper—was constantly matching wills with Joseph. They'd argue up and down the house until Joseph stormed out in a huff. Hours later the two would be seen speaking quietly to each other, out front in the dark. The next day Joseph would help his father lay bricks. It was plain that Joseph was special to my grandfather, the favorite of his six.

There was scant demand for a skilled bricklayer in the Depression; the family fell on hard times. Joseph left college where he was studying to be an architect. He found work picking potatoes in Maine, and then rode the rails through Ontario and across Canada to the Northwest, working as a farm hand, harvesting crops. He finished the season there and traveled south into the States. He wrote regularly. At first his letters were cheerful, optimistic, bragging that he would make his tuition. Then they turned darker. Boy, this is hard work! Some of these fellows are real tough, scary; he needed to get away from them. He had had enough; he was glad to be coming home. My grandparents, everyone, was worried sick. But he was coming home! Sent them the date, the time, just a few more days. Aunt Sarah helped Grandmother cook a huge meal. The family waited, Father Abraham with suppressed joy.

Joseph never showed. He vanished from the face of the earth. The Royal Canadian Mounted Police traced him to a Canadian farm where he had worked and had sent a letter to the farmer. He told the farmer he wasn't coming back; he was going to try the mines instead. He said he was getting a gun because of all the hijacking going on. No police reports after that. Nothing. Private detectives. Years and years of investigation. Nothing. It broke my Grandfather. He spun into depression. What purpose was there to life for a man who defined his life by his work, but could not find any? What purpose was there to life for a patriarch who could not feed his family? What purpose to life was there for a father who had a beautiful son, Joseph, but could not protect him? Father Abraham committed suicide. Mother never spoke of this. The truth leaked out gradually over the years.

Seventy years later, at the dawn of a new century, Uncle Daniel was poking through his storage room and came upon a dusty, decayed carton. Inside were several of Joseph's textbooks.

Grandmother Ida died soon after Father Abraham. The siblings dispersed. All were either college graduates or well on their way, except Daniel. What to do with Daniel, still a boy? My parents offered to adopt him, move to Cleveland and live there with him. Aunt Sarah recoiled in revulsion at the very thought. No, she would become Daniel's legal guardian, his surrogate mother. No need to marry. She could play the martyr and at the same time blame Mother for abandoning her responsibilities. It was an effective club to drive Mother from her family. The sisters were oil and water; their relationship poisonous. Sarah—petite, red-haired, impeccable, tightly controlled, the very model of the old-maid school teacher, virginal to her ninety-sixth year—dripped disapproval of Mother. Mother—larger, wide-boned, gray-haired, open and generous, her emotions gushing to the surface—spent a lifetime trying to win Sarah's respect for reasons known only to the sisters.

Sarah had her good points. She was an A student in math, but decided to go into teaching when her Prof told her, "I'll recommend you to Graduate School, but I'll have to be honest and tell them you are a Jew!" By all accounts she was a terrific teacher, but strict as a straitjacket. On the other hand she spoke out against racism in the schools, even wrote a pledge that Cleveland teachers took to treat each child equally. And she was a one-woman crusade against child-abuse. She stayed with us a week in NY once on the rare occasion that the sisters called a truce. Abe recalls walking with his aunt, this tiny, precisely spoken woman with the flaming mop of red hair. They came upon a father at a street corner spanking his small son briskly in the behind for an unknown infraction.

"If that child were six-feet two-inches tall you'd find another way to communicate with him!" Sarah says to him firmly. The man is shocked at this little woman speaking to him that way. Then he recoils in shame.

Aunt Sarah followed the rules. She was sensible.

Dan in his teenage years pitched for the local American Legion baseball team. Tall, wiry, nay skinny, he had a surprising fastball and a curveball that kept hitters off balance. He once threw three scoreless innings against the legendary Birmingham Black Barons—the great barnstorming team filled with players kept out of the Major Leagues because of their color; indeed some were posthumously elected to the Hall of Fame.

"I was lucky; they were rapping me all over the park," Dan said to me with characteristic modesty. But he was eighty years old and he had not forgotten.

"What was it like facing them?" I asked. Dan made a gesture; no words could describe it.

Major League scouts took notice and he was offered a Minor League contract: Class D or something lowly like that. This is the late 1930s. Baseball is the only American sport. To play pro ball is every American boy's dream, his fantasy. But Dan needed Sarah's signature.

Sarah's response? "Town to town with a bunch of bums in the back of a bus, drinking beer! Smoking cigarettes! No Daniel, you are not playing baseball! You are going to summer school. You are taking calculus. You are going to be an engineer!" And an engineer he became after seeing combat in North Africa and France.

Mother followed a trajectory that differed from Sarah's. No money for medical school, she worked in a home for orphaned Jewish teenage girls and was reprimanded for unprofessional conduct: being too soft, too comforting, identifying too closely. She visited the girls at night after lights were out, listened to their sad tales, brought them treats. She scandalized the head rabbi when she warned him that a male member of the staff had trouble controlling his "member" or "staff." That is, he was "taking advantage" of the girls. "I won't hear this filth!" the rabbi said, and fired her.

Somehow, someway, Mother kept Father Abraham's rectitude, but rejected the authoritarian root. She came to despise arbitrary power, no matter how well intended, whether it be exercised by a father, a rabbi, or a government. It was all the same to her. And she came to identify with the victims of this world, be it a brother beaten with a strap, a poor man who picked potatoes to survive, or an unloved orphan girl. She gravitated toward the anarchists.

Sam was proud to the point of boasting that Mother had been an active member of the Anarchist Forum since 1928 and had come to anarchism on her own, well before she had met him on the steps of the Cleveland Public Library in 1930. At times he would wax exuberant that there were mystical ties that bound Mother to her birthplace in Volynia, Russia, and to Father Abraham's cousin—an anarchist who "went to the people."

# 16
## CHILDHOOD MEMORIES WITH MOTHER AND SAM

Mother had a religion. Not Judaism: breastfeeding. She was a fanatic. Beyond promoting infant health, it secured the mother-child bond. All good character traits stemmed from it—security, confidence, honesty, integrity, creativity, add your own—and conversely all evil, bad karma, and weakness, stemmed from the lack of it. She was suspicious and disdainful of women who did not breastfeed, implying they were selfish, that they resented their children, sometimes more than that. "Was Hitler breastfed?" I would ask her teasingly as a young adult to no reply.

So, boy, was I breastfed! I was not fully off the tit until three or four when every now and then mother would "let me have a nip," as she put it. Though I do not remember suckling her, I can still sense the warmth of her body, her smell, her embrace, her love.

We lived so many places during my infancy and boyhood that Abe had to remind me of them for purposes of writing this book. In a few instances he had to inform me, because I have no memory of them:

Avenue D between Third and Fourth Street, to which we moved the year I was born. So much for Sam's upward mobility in these United States. There were two toilet seats in the hall for six families; a bathtub in the kitchen; no central heating; and a wood burning stove. Abe remembers hunting for wood in the streets.

Cherry Street, across from Jackson St Park: One of two or three inhabited tenements in a block of abandoned ones, it had that East River view of the Brooklyn Navy Yard.

Madison Street facing Scammel, a street so narrow it reminded Mother of medieval Europe.

66 Montgomery Street, a dark building that violated Mother's insistence on light and air.

Finally, 250 Clinton St, where we stayed from 1944 to 1954—a converted Civil War facility of some kind or another.

Each of these distinguished residences, subsequent to our tenure, was promptly leveled and replaced with a low-income housing project. A paranoid might say the Government was hounding my anarchist parents from slum to slum.

A boy's life was on the streets those days and it was there I had my introduction to unsupervised society—no mother, no teacher, I was on my own. And it was there, age seven or so, that I learned that I—we—were not like other people. It was a lesson taught to me by "The Drunken Polish Lady," as she was known in my hermetic little world, my Jewish Catfish Row. She was a neighborhood fixture, the neighborhood drunk, a Christian, fitting a nasty stereotype in a closed society where public drunkenness is a disgrace.

She is still vivid to me after seventy years. She staggers around the corner of Clinton and Monroe, falls down, retches, shouts incomprehensible Polish. She is trying to make it to the front of her apartment house in the middle of the block, but she falls again. Something inside me draws me to her, though I can sense the entire block—children and adults—are watching the spectacle from street level and open windows. I try to help her up, but I am too small, and we lurch together in a grotesque waltz on the sidewalk. Her stockings are rolled down to her ankles, her blond hair wild, her face crimson. I lose balance and fall. A roar of laughter erupts from our audience and there is that shock of recognition that their hilarity is directed at me. An unhealthy self-hatred flushes over me, my first brush with shame. But I am in too deep now. So I continue to tug her down the block, and finally, finally pull her nearly deadweight up the four of five steps to the hall door of her building. I notice urine flooding down her legs. She speaks Polish to me and although I do not understand it, I understand her tone is not grateful.

I rush home, shivering from the ridicule. I collapse on my bed and curl up facing the wall, the door slammed. I cannot expel that shame from my body. Mother comes in what seems much later. She stretches out next to me, enfolds me in her arms, presses my face to her chest, kisses my forehead tenderly. I cling to her.

"Yes, I heard the story. They couldn't wait to tell me," she remarks, dripping contempt. She then grips my shoulders firmly in each of her hands and locks my eyes in hers. "I will never be as proud of you as I am today," she says slowly, so that it sinks in. "You tried to help another human being, a sick lady. Let them laugh. My boy has a heart! For that you should never feel ashamed."

That night Sam said to me: "Don't worry about being popular." And he said "popular" with that special twist he reserved for sonofabitch. "Worry about what's in here," and he gave my chest a thump.

Mother certainly felt no need to be popular when it came to her convictions. She took me to the movies one day. It was the midst of World War II and patriotic fervor is running high. The *News of the Week* features American soldiers in combat applying a flame-thrower—that is, a napalm device—to a Japanese bunker on a distant hillside in Iwo Jima. A Japanese soldier bursts out, tiny in long-view. He is literally on fire. He runs wildly like a demented cockroach for a few seconds, his arms waving in agony, before he dies smoldering, face down. I have seen this very clip replayed in war documentaries over the years and it has lost the ability to shock—either through repetition or the coarsening of my sensibility. But seeing it for the first time that afternoon triggers my vomit reflex, which I suppress. The audience has an entirely different reaction. It bursts into full-throated cheers.

"Kill the Jap bastard! Roast them all!" an otherwise normal looking man in front of us shouts.

Mother is appalled. With me in hand, she follows him out into the lobby. "You have just seen one human being burn another human being to death," she says to him. "Why are you cheering?"

The man regards her as if she were some kind of crackpot. "Go fuck yourself." And he turns away.

The War Years: I experienced them in safety as a boy who never ventured far from Mother's arms. Just the same, the memories remain sharp.

I remember the patrician voice of Franklin Roosevelt crackling through the radio static.

I remember the single antiaircraft gun battery set up in the park along the East River just a few hundred yards from my bedroom window—and the neighborhood kids running cigarettes for the soldiers confined behind the chain-link fence.

I remember the daily bulletins, always positive: General Patton's Army advancing four miles amid-heavy fighting along a broad front. The Nazi's giving ground in Poland to the heroic Red Army. The marines "mopping up" a Pacific island. (How do you mop up an island, what do you mop, I wondered?)

I remember the ENEMY straight from the comic books: robotic Nazis who talked the way dogs barked; yellow-skinned, bucktoothed "Japs," sadists all.

I remember the blackouts, the tinfoil and scrap metal collections, the rationing cards.

I remember the soldiers on leave: neighborhood boys in uniforms too big for them, looking anything but heroic.

I remember the Mothers clustered in a small group, speaking softly of the death of a neighbor's son. ("Judy Cohen's boy? Little Shelly? My God.")

I remember the grief of these women at the news of Roosevelt's death.

I remember the joy in the streets when the thing was finally over.

Above all, I remember a trip Mother insisted I take with her. She held my hand firmly the entire way, although by that time I was nearly nine years old and embarrassed by her grip. Why only me, and not Abe, too, I do not recall. Where it was, I am not sure, probably Staten Island: the trip by subway and ferry took a long time. What I do remember was a hospital of some sort and the sight of a man laid out on a bed in a brightly lit room. There was no bulk to him, no muscle, no fat, no flesh. Every bone of his skeleton protruded beneath his skin. His skull was too large for his shoulders and he had trouble raising it above the pillows. I had never seen anyone like him; he looked like an old child. He smiled eagerly, warmly at Mother and then at me. I could not turn away from his black, shining eyes. Mother spoke to him in Yiddish, and he nodded and laughed, then grew tired, and we left.

I was shaken. Outside the hospital Mother no longer took my hand, but spoke to me firmly and slowly, as an adult: the man we had just visited had been rescued from a death camp. Yes, there were such things as death camps.

"I want you never to forget this," she said. "I want you to remember what one human being is capable of doing to another."

The woman had a bad case of integrity. It made her glorious and impossible at the same time—which being which depended on one's perspective. What do you make of this incident? PS 147, I'm in the sixth grade. Wednesday is assembly day. Our class is scheduled to put on a show for the parents seated in the school auditorium. All the boys must wear a white shirt and tie, the girls a dress of a certain type and length, the hair combed a certain way. It is a bit of a big deal and Mother dresses me carefully, makes sure my hair is parted, my nails clean.

We march on stage singing "God Bless America" to the accompaniment of Mrs. Addlebaum, the piano teacher. Two huge American flags hang stage left and right. We take our places between the flags—me at the end of the third row. The auditorium is filled with smiling parents, their smiles merged in one huge smile of welcome. I pick out Mother seated prominently in the center of the curving rows, beaming.

Tap, tap from Mrs. Addelbaum. All rise for the "Pledge of Allegiance." The entire auditorium stands as one, hands over hearts. All except Mother. She simply sits, beaming, a lone seated figure in conspicuous contrast.

"What's wrong with your mother? She sick? Why won't she stand up?" my classmates whisper.

I stare ahead in silent humiliation as Mother sits through the whole pledge. She seems oblivious to the quiet sneers of several hundred people and to the position in which she has placed her son.

"Why didn't you stand?" I asked imploringly on the way home.

"Your mother does not salute flags."

"Then why did you come?"

"To see my son. I didn't know they were going to do that."

"But they always do. Couldn't you just stand and pretend?"

"I do not pretend. I do not salute flags." And that was that.

She would not pretend. She refused to dress up during the "Jewish Holidays"—most of which are not "holidays" but that is what they were called—when the women of the entire Lower East Side turned out in their working-class or lower-middle-class finery—fur coats and all—for just such occasions. Mother had no fur coat, would not have one if she could afford one, and certainly would not wear one on the "holidays." She was not religious. Our neighbors scorned her for that, called her *traif*—non-Kosher meat—behind her back. They went even further when she allowed my eleven-year-old friends to listen to the Yankee game in our apartment on Saturday afternoons—a clear violation of the Shabbat.

"You are corrupting my child! Don't let him in. Send him home," Mrs. Goldman demands.

"If you don't want him to listen to the ballgame that is between you and him. But this is my house and in my house he has done nothing wrong, so I will not throw him out. It is unjust!"

The Sabbath incident can serve as a template for a more serious event. Eugene Worth and Dorothy (I forget her last name) lived around the corner from us on Cherry Street in the middle of the block. I do not know exactly how my parents knew them, probably from the fringes of the radical circles my parents belonged to at the time. They were a bohemian couple: artistic, well educated, very young, though Eugene was a maybe five or eight years older than her. Abe remembers them more clearly than I, and to this day he remains charmed that whenever they visited us, which was two or three times a week, Dorothy would sit at our out of tune piano and play the first movement of Mozart's Concerto in A Major. Very well, indeed.

We grew close. Abe remembers bursting into their Cherry Street flat—the door was unlocked—to find Dorothy rising like Venus naked from the bath tub. Without the least embarrassment she reached for the towel; she regarded him as a little boy, though he was eleven and shocked. This was 1944 and he had never seen a woman naked, including Mother. Abe was fond of Eugene who took him places, showed him things he didn't know; his family owned real estate in the Greenpoint section of Brooklyn.

The template plate part comes in because Eugene was black and Dorothy white—although "black" is used here as a racial/cultural designation. In reality, Eugene was milky tan. He wore horn rimmed glasses, a trim, nice-looking fellow. Remember this was 1944. The poor couple encountered hostility wherever they went. Soldiers in uniform hassled them on the street, attempted to feel her up. People spat at them in the subway. They had trouble getting served in restaurants. Our home served as a refuge.

Abe remembers that Dorothy's mother was a communist. She was all for racial integration but not for the sexual integration of her daughter. "Why do you encourage her?" she berated Mother over the telephone. "It's the sex. That's what she sees in him!" She took to visiting us unannounced. She tried imploring Mother to help break them up; she cried; when all else failed she threatened a lawsuit. Mother had sympathy for the woman in the sense that she felt her anguish, and so she put up with her abuse. Finally she said something both characteristic and uncharacteristic: "I will not throw your daughter out of my house, but I will throw YOU out. Get out of my house!"

Things did not end there. Eugene and Dorothy split up. We can blame her mother's hysterical devotion to that cause combined with pressure from the outside world. But from my present perspective I suspect other factors were also at work. In any event Eugene took the break-up catastrophically. He committed suicide by jumping off the George Washington Bridge. My parents and Abe were devastated; I was too young to grasp the thing whole. Years later I learned that James Baldwin and Eugene were close friends—that indeed Baldwin professed his love for him. He immortalized Eugene as the central character of his novel *Another Country*.

Devout neighbors and irate mothers were not the only Jews who found Mother's behavior corrupting and unacceptable. My parents had a friend—I forget his name—who taught English, social studies, secular subjects in a Yeshiva (Jewish parochial school), somewhere near Avenue B and Eighth Street, I think. He had to undergo a serious operation and would be out for the term. Would Mother like to substitute? And she said yes. As you probably realize by now, Mother loved her sons' company and so I went with her one morning to see her teach. She carried a long pole wrapped in canvas under her arm. I took it to be a window shade of some sort. Her stride was determined.

It is an early spring morning. We enter an ancient stone building and into a large classroom that could double as a small auditorium. Mother stands on a wide stage a step or two above floor level. I am proud of her. She looks impressive. I have never seen her in this light, as an authority figure. She faces a full room of children spread out in benches and movable chairs. Toward the back they sit on levels higher than Mother. The wood floors create pandemonium under their feet. And that pandemonium cannot match the din created by the students themselves. They are several years younger than me, tiny, thin. They wear skull caps (yarmulkes) and sideburn curls (paius) that run down to their cheeks; white shirts; black pants held up by tiny suspenders; black shoes. They are the children of the ultra orthodox. The air crackles with the static electricity of their intelligence, their energy, their joy.

Mother gives a small tap and the pandemonium evolves into a noisy order. "Do you know what day it is?" she asks.

"Israel! Israel!" they shout, their happiness a palpable object in the room. It is the day of the creation of the State of Israel or very soon thereafter—I do not remember.

Now Mother unfurls the rolled up "window shade" she has been carrying and hangs it on a hook on the wall behind her. It turns out not to be a window shade after all but a large map of the world, the countries delineated in bright reds, greens, yellows, etc.

"Who can show me Israel?" she calls out to the boys. Technically Israel is not yet shown on the map, but there is Palestine to point to.

No one volunteers. Then one little boy strides from the back of the room, lopes onto the stage and points boldly to China. "No, no," another shouts, runs up and points to Brazil. Large countries. Impressive looking countries. Mother lets it go on like that several minutes, lets them argue amongst themselves. Then, when they quiet down in anticipation, she points to where Israel really is, the Israel of Partition: before the 1948 War of Independence; before the Six-Day War of 1967; before the occupation of the West Bank. With her finger she encircles a dot not much larger than a period on the world map. Within that dot lived a branch of her family that settled in Palestine in 1909 when it was under Turkish rule, the branch that tilled the soil in friendship with its Muslim neighbors and helped found a kibbutz.

"This is Israel," she announces with finality.

A moment of shock and then the eruption.

"You're crazy."

"What does she know? She's a woman!"

They would not accept it. This was not the Israel of their prayers, of their parents' hopes and dreams; the Israel that formed the imaginative fabric of their lives. The indignation subsides into a sullen silence. When Mother speaks of Israel's minute size, it is not to warn them of its enemies, which one might expect her to do. Instead, "You love Israel, yes. But it is such a big world! So much to learn, so much to experience."

Mother's lesson did not meet the approval of the head rabbi. He called her into his office.

"Why did you have to show them Israel on the map?"

"Because it is the truth."

"Your 'truth!'" The rabbi pounds the desk not so much in anger as in sadness. "If not for God, these children would have been reduced to ashes! That is also a truth. They are precious. Leave them their illusions. Leave them their joy. It will be time enough for them to learn your 'truth.'"

Mother did not last the term.

I am apprehensive as I recount these stories that Mother comes across as an unworldly, uncompromising moral prig. What I intend is to describe her honesty, courage, and humanity. She could act with sophistication, tact, and charm when the occasion arose, especially if she felt that Abe or I were under threat—and I must admit I gave her many such occasions when I was twelve years old or so. The modern psycho/medical interpretation of my behavior might be that I suffered from attention deficit disorder, that I was hyperactive. The interpretation that held sway at the time was that I was an unruly brat. I go with that one.

One occasion that forced Mother to step in to save my ass arose one wintry afternoon following a snowfall—a heavy wet snowfall perfect for snowballs. Classes have ended at Corlears Junior High

School. I am free and do not want to go home just yet. I'd rather pack snowballs and get into a fun-fight with my released fellow inmates. But I notice a short well-dressed lady in an overcoat and a large elaborate hat in front of the school. She is waiting for the bus, back turned. The target is irresistible. I loft a snowball packed extra tight. I watch in delight as it traces a parabola to warm Galileo's heart across Madison Street and plunks down on the lady's hat. She wheels around in a rage and there I am, nailed. How was I to know the hat belonged to Miss Halinan, the principal?

She sends for Mother. Mother enters her inner office. She recounts the snowball incident and then proceeds to read to Mother my misbehaviors recorded by all the teachers with whom I have come in contact the past year. It is an impressive rap sheet. There is no doubt I was a miserable kid to teach. I would have hated to have me seated in my class: disruptive, chaotic, "fresh," rebellious— though, in my defense, not violent. Miss Halinan is not joking. She has had enough of me. She is recommending that I be transferred to dreaded PS 75. It is a disciplinary institution rumored to be staffed by ex-cops; next stop a reformatory.

Mother listens quietly for Miss Halinan to release her anger. Then she says, respectfully,

"Miss Halinan, he's a boy! He threw a snowball! Of course he shouldn't have, but you know he didn't mean to hurt you. And he is unruly and I take some blame for that. Are you really going to throw him out of the school for these things, give him a criminal record, and scar him for life?" Somehow, through the magic of her voice my bad deeds have vaporized and scattered.

The dreaded Miss Halinan softens; after all, she has not spent her life as a teacher to punish a child. The women get to speak to each other humanly. Miss Halinan finds she has found a sympathetic soul. She recounts to Mother her unhappy love life and other disappoint-ments. Mother listens for as long as it takes. You see, she likes Miss Halinan. She had the empathetic connection that drew people in.

She spoke to me firmly when we got home: "You have got to behave yourself. You are not going to make me go through that again!"

I managed to stay out of PS 75.

My parents dreaded being the cause of another person's pain. Actions you and I might judge necessary, if unpleasant, tortured them. I am thinking of the time Sam violated his prohibition against firing people and confronted Abe's clarinet teacher. My brother had a gift for the instrument and Mother did everything possible, and impossible, to nurture it. She laid out hard money for a good clarinet, took him here, took him there, all over the city to youth orchestras, auditions, whatever, dragging me along with them. Above all, she found a wonderful teacher, James Collis, a graduate of the Curtis Institute of Philadelphia, who played for various orchestras and opera companies. Abe thrived and, as he matured, formed a lifelong friendship with Collis.

The problem arose in 1944 after Collis left New York for Hollywood where there was plentiful work for film-studio musicians. Before he left he found a suitable substitute, not an easy task during war time: the elderly Pasquale Acito, who pronounced his name "I-cheato" in a thick Italian accent. I can still hear the man's heavy tread and heaving breath, as he struggled to our top floor apartment. The firm knock on the door, Mother dashing to open it, and there stood the unsmiling Pasquale: a formal and formidable man in the August heat. Wide waist. Wide straw hat. Grey mustache. Steel wool grey hair that defeated the comb. Tinted glasses. Neat open-toed sandals, with socks. Well-pressed pants and a long-sleeved shirt. Impeccable. No visible sweat, save a damp forehead, which he dabbed with a folded handkerchief.

Our windows were wide open to catch a breeze, but it did not help.

Did he want some water? To rest before the lesson began? Mother would ask, concerned.

No, No! He was not for small talk. Let the lesson begin.

The lesson took place in the living room, where Abe had set up his metal stand, upon which he had placed the music he had practiced all week, two hours a day. Without ceremony Acito stood to the side of Abe as he began to play. The three of us—Mother, Father, and I—watched from the open kitchen behind them. His playing sounded beautiful. My parents beamed with pride. Until Acito cut it short. He turned to us.

"Mama like it? Poppa like it? Pasquale no like it!" Tap-tap. "Again!"

Abe's torture had begun. Tap-tap. "Paya attention to the beat!"

Tap! "Watcha you tonguing!"

Tap! "See how you breath give out? Itsa becauz you don't taka your breath BEFORE da trill."

Tap! "You behinda the beat."

Tap, tap! "Such a sloppy finger work!"

Again! Again! Again! Week after week. Gradually, Abe, who would run home to practice, did not feel like practicing. Close to lesson day he became nervous, did not sleep well. Lesson day his fingers tensed up. Finally he told Mother he did not want to play clarinet anymore. He was, after all, an eleven-year-old boy. Something had to be done. My father bit the bullet.

"We decided we don't want you to give the boy more lessons," he says to Pasquale. My father had to squeeze the words from his chest.

Pasquale is shocked, astounded. "Why you no like?"

"You don't think the boy has talent."

"Why you say that?" The man is truly wounded. Tears fill his eyes.

"You never praise him. All you do is scold him. Correct him all the time."

"I am da teacher. You wanta me not to correct him? He plays beautiful."

"Why don't you tell him that?"

"No! No! Never! You spoil da child. Then impossible to teach him!"

My father ends an indeterminate pause by speaking pleadingly to Pasquale, almost begging him for his understanding, but also with finality. "The boy gets nervous before you come. He can't eat. He doesn't want to practice." Then he makes the fatal mistake of reaching out his hand to Pasquale with the final payment.

Pasquale gathers himself up into his full state of dignity and from that fortress lets loose the dogs of scorn. "Do you know I played for Arturo Toscanini? You know I have bad heart? Seventy-five years old? You think I come down to this place in da heat, in the stink, and walka the stairs 'cause I need your five dollars? I don't need your five dollars. I come here because the boy has talent! It is my duty."

My poor father is crushed. "But the boy does not want to play for you."

Pasquale looks at Abe in front of the music stand, his clarinet half assembled. He cannot meet his stare. Pasquale says no more. He leaves the door for Mother to close as he moves slowly down the hall. To the day he died, my father believed that he had acted badly.

My father had an exasperating inability to protect himself from predatory people. It extended to every aspect of his existence. So-called comrades sponged off him, slept on our sagging couch, ate Mother's meals, and contributed nothing—all this for months at a time. They mocked him for the impractical way he lived; spread tales of his alleged faults far and wide; belittled him in front of his wife and children; stiffed him on payment for painting their flats; and he took it all. No matter how hurtful or outrageous the provocation, he shrugged it off with "they are comrades." He was not given to introspection.

I, on the other hand, could not understand how a man who dedicated his life to the struggle against exploitation could allow himself to be so obviously exploited. I often probed him on that point—unmindful that picking at the scabs of his life made him deeply uncomfortable. Finally, in his old age, he said plaintively, in a tone that almost begged me to go no further: "You see, I could never do to them the things they could do to me!" I did not raise the subject again.

Certain things friends said, or did, infuriated him, however, and when he was thoroughly pissed-off, his response could turn visceral and brutal. He drew no distinction between a challenge to his personal integrity and a challenge to the integrity of the Wobblies and anarchists, both of whom I am convinced he would have died for if necessary. Criticize their tactics, the character of certain individuals, even the fundamental tenets of the IWW and the anarchists—all that was fine with Sam, and he did so often himself. But never deny their sincerity, their intentions, their bravery. I sound melodramatic about all this, but my father knew of too many men imprisoned, too many men tortured and lynched, too many men whose blood had seeped into the soil of Spain, Castro's Cuba, the Ukraine, and, yes, the soil of these United States, to take insult lightly. He would have none of it. He lived in history; it was not an academic pursuit.

This brings me to the amputation of his long friendship with Mark Schmidt.

"Renegades? You call us Renegades? Get out of my house you *sonofabitch*!"

It was a shocking command. Schmidt—a short, round man, with a round face and owl-like, steel-rimmed glasses, grey-hair, impeccably groomed in suit and tie, courtly in the European manner—stared stunned and speechless at my father. Humiliated, he attempted to sputter something apologetic, conciliatory. But my father had turned his back to him. A pause. Twenty-five years had come to this. Schmidt silently gathered his coat and left. His footsteps faded down the hall.

I had never seen my father behave this savagely before or after. Schmidt had genuine affection for us, was a living-room fixture. As regular as the passage of a celestial constellation, he arrived the third Sunday of each month with the *Sunday Times* under one arm, and something exotic under the other: smoked whitefish and bialys, strange tasting sausages, halvah, and Turkish Delights, you never knew. We were his surrogate family. My father, for his part, admired Schmidt for his intellect, and there is no doubt in my mind that he was indeed a highly cultured and learned man. I say this even though I was a mere eight to thirteen years of age at the time, and in no position to evaluate what he had to say on any given subject. But I remember the kind of discussions he generated, and the special, wonderful relationship he forged with Abe.

Abe had a stratospherically high IQ, so high that his elementary school principal begged Mother not to transfer him when we moved out of his district, and offered to chauffeur him back and forth each day. I agree an IQ exam is an imperfect measure, especially one taken so many years ago, but just the same it is not every twelve-year-old boy who has read—I kid you not—Gibbons's *Decline and Fall of the Roman Empire*, followed by the complete works of Dickens a year later, and *War and Peace* after that. It was Schmidt who put him on to these books. The two of them would discuss the finer points for hours in long walks under the Williamsburg Bridge to Fourteenth Street and back—the East River and far away Brooklyn on their flank.

There was nothing Schmidt seemed not to know about, from Hollywood westerns to my math homework—and his knowledge blended well with Abe's. Mother had Abe enrolled in every youth orchestra possible up and down the city, and he read avidly the lives of the great composers. He loved music, could not wait to get home from school and practice his two hours a day. His atrocious eyesight—prelude to his blindness later in life—cut him off from baseball and the park and the usual things kids do; music was his release, his fulfillment. Schmidt was a man fully capable of dissecting a Beethoven, Schubert, or Stravinsky score with Abe as they listened to WQXR for hours on end. Afterward, they would take their long walks together. And I feel I must add in our suspicious age that Schmidt was not a pedophile. According to Sam, he was a bit of a hound, the kind of fellow you did not want to leave alone with your girlfriend—or wife.

Schmidt was the older man and Sam looked up to him in his youthful days of the 1930s. I do not know anything about his early life other than he was born in Russia and came to the U.S. as a very young man, nor do I know of his life away from us other than that he made a good living as a textile designer or salesman or some such thing. Prior to that and in contradiction to his cultivated appearance, he toiled as a laborer on the docks. He was a hard guy to get into focus. Sam mentioned often that Schmidt had sailed back to Russia in 1917 on the same ship as Leon Trotsky and took an active part in the Russian Revolution—perhaps as a journalist of some kind. While there he became a blood enemy of the Bolsheviks because of their murderous methods and their assassination of the spirit of the Revolution. He returned to the U.S. a committed anarchist. He became a founding member, with my father, of the Vanguard group in the early 1930s and wrote many erudite, if convoluted, articles for their publication, mostly under the pen-name Senex.

But over the years Schmidt came full circle and had morphed into a Communist and Stalin-lover. The induced famines? The purges? The Gulags? The Hitler-Stalin pact? The anti-Semitism? The tyranny? The personality cult? The general butchery and degrading of society? Schmidt had answers for all of it. Sam did not appreciate the recalcitrant nature of the Soviet peasantry; Sam did not appreciate that Stalin was merely stalling for time with Hitler, never mind he was completely unprepared for the double-cross; Sam did not appreciate the special circumstances that forced Stalin to take measures concerning civil liberties that, while deplorable in a Western democracy under normal times, were perfectly logical and necessary given the external pressures facing the Soviet state. The anti-Semitism? Exaggerated by the Zionists, and do not all societies have things of this sort? What about the Negroes in the South?

All of this Sam put up with in the course of their long friendship, but in recent months Schmidt had taken to snide remarks about the Russian anarchists: how impractical they were, how obstructionist, how "they belonged in the dust bin of history." And at last the final show of contempt: "A bunch of renegades." It is likely Schmidt let the remark go in the heat of argument and had not meant personal insult. Nonetheless my father had too much respect for the uses of language, too much respect for Schmidt as a man who meant exactly what he said, to let "renegade" go by. The word is somewhat archaic. Traitor. Turncoat. Betrayer. Defector. Deserter. Rat. These are in current use.

You see, Sam knew many of the anarchists that Schmidt called renegades: Maximoff, Yelensky, Donuluk, Mratchny, and I. N. Steinberg—not to mention men of the caliber of Nester Makhno, Alexander Berkman, and the anarchists knifed in the back by the Stalinists in Spain. They were men of high principle and courage. Schmidt, who knew these men too, knew this well, although he called them renegades. So Sam's reaction sprung from his gut. But their split, at its core, was not about personalities. It reached back to bloody events played out in the aftermath of the Russian Revolution—long ago and far away from our Sunday living room, circa 1950.

Sometime after their break, Schmidt moved to San Francisco. He did not speak directly to Sam for many years, but he always asked after him, and after Mother, and Abe, and me. At last, Sam and Schmidt spoke by phone. They had so much in common, Sam said, so many years. It was silly to let a moment of anger ruin a friendship. Schmidt readily agreed. Come over to the house when you get to New York, Sam urged. No. No. I will not do that, Schmidt said, and that was the end of it.

I return now to Mother. You may notice that I recount childhood memories of her and that all of them involve her response to pressures from the outside world. You may not agree with these responses, but there was a moral clarity to them—and they were invariably humane. I can say with pride that she was an admirable woman. There is another side to mothering, however, the intimate, emotional side, and in this regard she was often difficult. (What mother isn't, I can hear you say.)

The woman recognized no mental or emotional or even social boundaries. There was no such thing as space, emotional independence. It was as if the two of us—mother and child—were Siamese twins; she was inside your head. I am not good at "psychologizing"; neither are most psychologists, I suspect. She behaved the same way toward her younger brothers, though she seldom saw them as adults, which leads me to guess her emotional imperialism was related to her role as oldest sister/surrogate mother to them growing up. Perhaps, also, she responded to Abe and me out of deep insecurity and fear of rejection; therefore the need to dominate and control, to smother rebellion before it starts.

Ellen is a pretty girl, Abe's first girlfriend, classmates at the High School of Music and Art. They are inseparable for quite some time. Then they break up for reasons I don't know—remember I am four years younger than Abe—and both of them take it hard. What I do remember is Mother talking incessantly, indignantly, and dramatically about it: what she said to Helen's parents, what Helen's parents said to her. It was all about Mother, how she suffered on behalf of her son. There seemed to be no awareness of what the hell was she doing thrashing about in the middle of her son's high school love affair.

She could be just as impossible when it came to me. I'm sure it comes as no shock to you that teenage boys flock together in packs. So half dozen of us are in my room—by this time the family had graduated to an apartment in the Bushwick/Williamsburg section of Brooklyn and I, for the first time, to my own bedroom. What do teenage boys talk about? We talk dirty about girls. The bold ones smoke cigarettes, lounge on my bed; we listen to socially disapproved-of music—in those days rock and roll. We are boys! In walks Mother with a chair. She plunks down right in the center of my bedroom. She recognizes absolutely no distance between her and the hormone-soaked bunch of us, begins talking about Franz Schubert, Shelley's poems, civil rights, the Spanish Revolution. What is there to say? We are back in school.

The watershed moment for me—the incident that crystallized to me that it was imperative that I break from her control—took place when I was about fifteen years old. I am home sick with the flu. Mother is worried. She accompanies me to the doctor's office. The inner door opens and I am surprised it is a female doctor. She ushers me in to the inner room where she treats people. Mother muscles in behind me.

"Lower your pants," the doctor, a middle-aged lady, orders. I am to receive a shot of antibiotic in the buttocks.

Mother stands directly behind the doctor, peering worriedly over her shoulder. Now, Mother has seen me without pants my entire life—but somehow this is different. I feel something is wrong. I hesitate indecisively.

"For God's sake woman," the doctor says firmly. "Leave the room. Leave your son his dignity."

A trivial incident, and I saw it as such at the time, so why has it stuck with me through the years? I can only say that from that day forward my attitude toward Mother changed. I realized, dimly at first, that emotional separation was a matter of survival.

I find it interesting in thinking about myself that while I sought emotional separation from Mother I craved closeness to Sam. I cannot say exactly why. There was a gruffness and roughness about him that was appealing. He was a man and I wanted to be one! Yes he was a loving father, you can say a tender one—but not in an easy way. How to convey the texture of our relationship? I'll let this incident speak for itself: the day Sam took me to the movies.

This simple act brings back a bittersweet childhood memory because Sam hated going to them for the most part. He held an especially low opinion of Hollywood films, which to him were so artificial he could not willingly suspend his disbelief. Though he loved women in the flesh, the hyper-glamorized female movie stars were of no interest to him: so lacquered, so remote, so untouchable. Pretty leading men in action-adventure films—such as Douglas Fairbanks Jr., of the tidy mustache in the old Kipling classic *Gunga Din*—he found hilarious.

But I loved the movies (still do). I wanted him to take me to the movies. I nagged him about it incessantly, launched a campaign. He kept putting me off until the day I overheard Mother say to him sternly, "Can't you see the boy craves your company? Take him to the movies!" So he took me to the movies. But which movie? The typical theater of the time resembled an enormous palace, a huge vaulted space, a fantasy of faux-oriental splendor. The program was as predictable as a religious service: an "A" feature in Technicolor with big name stars; a "B" picture in black and white with lesser actors, perhaps a Ronald Reagan; a preview of coming attractions, very important, sometimes better than the feature; and a short bit of entertaining propaganda, the *News of the World*. That is what I wanted. I suppose, looking back, it was my symbolic way of saying I wanted to be like other people, to do like they did. To have a father who took me to the movies.

Sam had other things in mind. He took me to the Movietone on the Bowery. A grungy skid-row dump! An inside so cramped that noise seeped in from the street. A bathroom floor coated with pasty piss. Continuous all day features for a quarter. None of this I had in mind. But the movies were the crusher. They were ancient, in brownish sepia tone. The actors in a gangster movie wore old-looking suits and cabbie hats; the kids wore knickers! Knickers! The cars were square, real old-fashioned, not like the sleek models of 1948. Sam handed me an oversized Hershey bar, sat down next to me for a few minutes, and then slipped outside for a smoke, though he could have smoked inside. I watched for awhile, and then joined him, bitterly disappointed.

"Why? So what if they're old? Movies don't change! You get all the movies you want here!"

Sam said this defensively, because he knew he had behaved badly; I was forcing back tears. He gave me a short hug, which was not like him and then bought me lunch at a stand-up bar. The hot dogs with mustard and sauerkraut washed down with root beer helped superficially. Sam threw back a "shot" followed by a real beer "chaser."

# 17
## THE THIRTIES

The 1930s was, of course, a decade of worldwide economic collapse—not that the Roaring Twenties, a most overrated decade, roared for the working class. In New York, emblematic of conditions in American cities, the suicide rate tripled. More than half of formerly employed people in the city were out of work. Those working clung to their jobs after huge wage cuts. The homeless littered the streets while the landlord practically begged you to take an apartment provided you could pay the reduced rent. Across the nation, crops were burned to support farm prices while millions of the hungry lined up for bread. Never had the contradictions of capitalism appeared more blatant. From the perspective of young radicals "looking up," capitalism was staggering like a boxer waiting for the knockout punch. Meanwhile, partially as a result of the collapse, fascism was on the rise throughout the world and on American streets as well. In times like these, the stance one took on the issues of the day seemed critically important. There was the general feeling that one's actions, properly channeled, had impact, and beyond that, there were questions of conscience. Could one simply stand by? There was no such thing as feeling marginalized, as so many people of good will seem to feel today. One had to act.

My parents were typical of many of the Jewish anarchists that formed the core of a lively movement in the 1930s: first generation, born of anarchist parents or into a radical family tradition. Many, perhaps most—like Sam—lacked the opportunity to attend college and worked with their hands as tradesman or laborers. Nevertheless, they were well educated—incredibly so—and creative. *Working class intellectual* is, I believe, the sociological category, and a most ignored or underrated one in our increasingly bureaucratic and snobbish society. These first generation anarchists were supplemented by a flood of anarchist refugees from the Bolshevik regime, fascist Italy, Nazi Germany, and other places, who knew first hand, perhaps better than the mainstream press, what was really happening in the world. Sprinkle in a generous seasoning of Wobblies, some of whom did time and participated in major strikes. Add to that playwrights, novelists, and artists on the fringes—John dos Passos, James T. Farrell, Paul Goodman, Dwight Macdonald, Kenneth Rexroth, and the like. Stir in close proximity—for many years, the anarchists and Wobblies occupied the same headquarters, 94 Fifth Avenue—and you had the recipe for a small, but potent radical/intellectual tendency in American life.

One question intrigues me as I look back to Sam's life of the 1930s: Where did he get the energy to live as he did? To feed us, he painted apartments for slumlords and conniving contractors. He carried out organizational work and soapbox duties for the Wobblies. He worked closely with Carlo Tresca and other Italian anarchists in fighting fascists in the streets. He was instrumental in founding a sequence of anarchist publications, *Vanguard* being the most notable among them in the early to mid-1930s. He worked with the Jewish anarchists of *Freie Arbeiter Stimme*. Later came *Spanish Revolution*; the name of that publication speaks for itself. And of course there was World War II; our home became a port of call for itinerate Wobblies, anarchists, and socialist refugees.

It is not possible for me to follow all these trends and tendencies. The comrades who lived through the events of that time give a better account than I can in Paul Avrich's *Anarchist Voices*. I am interested in describing what mattered most to Sam, what affected him emotionally, the things that touched his heart: his attempts at communal life in various anarchist colonies; his close ties to Carlo Tresca; his work on behalf of the Spanish Revolution; the carnage of World War II; and the Wobblies, always the Wobblies.

# 18
## COLONIES

In 1933, Sam and Esther, my future parents, moved to Stelton, New Jersey. Stelton was a largely anarchistic colony (the modern term is commune), although not everyone who lived there was an anarchist by any means. Mother gave birth to brother Abe that August at the county hospital in New Brunswick, the closest town, some miles away. Sam had a soft spot for colonies in those days; it was quite the fashion among Jewish anarchists, indeed anarchists of all immigrant communities. The dominant culture was not welcoming. Perhaps this was Sam's way of repaying Mother for leaving her middle-class exurban home to cast her lot with him. Perhaps it was his need to settle down to something that seemed solid after years of hobo jungles and flop houses and blankets on the floor of Wobbly halls. Perhaps it was to supply Abraham and, later, me with grass and earth under our feet rather than city pavement and asphalt. Perhaps it was his need to demonstrate that anarchist ideals put into practice can indeed work. Whatever the reason, Sam settled us in to a barely winterized summer shack, and relocated our urban poverty to a semi-rural setting. Stelton was indeed a poor, working-class community. Many of the men worked in New York City or nearby towns. The shacks were laid out in a simple grid; the roads and sidewalks were unpaved; miles of farmland in all directions isolated the place.

The family did two stints at Stelton: The first was 1933 to 1936. Then Sam, Esther, and infant Abe moved to the Bronx to be close to Sam's dying mother, Anna, who passed three months before I was born, in 1937. Mother had a deep attachment to Anna and she nursed her to the end. She said Sam's compassionate "soul" was Anna's and the grandmother I was unable to know became the core of my name Anatole. The family stayed in the Bronx until I popped out of the oven at Lincoln Hospital, April 8th, 1937. We moved back to Stelton a few months later and stayed about a year.

Given this timeline, you might think my parents liked it there. But as events worked out, their relationship to the place grew increasingly combative. The Colony revolved around the Modern School, dedicated, at least in lip service to the teachings of Francisco Ferrer, who was executed early in the twentieth century by the Spanish monarchy for his opposition to the Catholic Church and his support of working-class revolts. Ferrer was indeed a martyr and a pioneer of modern education. The Modern School movement in his name attracted leading educators and a lively following for the first twenty-five years or so. But things were different by the time Abe attended the Stelton Modern School.

The Modern School supposedly followed the Ferrer principles of kindness to children and the encouragement of their creativity. In fact, it had degenerated under the directorship of "Uncle" and "Auntie" Ferm—a strange, unlikable couple—to a sorry state. According to one former student, "Auntie was strong willed, cranky…sexually very prudish with ingrained prejudices…she once washed a boy's mouth with soap for using foul language…, she hit another boy for peeping in the girl's outhouse toilet…named premarital sex an unhealthy indulgence and condemned masturbation as self-abuse." Indeed she once caught a boy masturbating and sewed up his fly! "[Even admirers] admitted that Auntie had a dictatorial streak." Sounds like old-fashioned Catholic school to me, the kind Ferrer opposed, except that Catholic schools emphasize the basic skills, whereas the Ferms "did not even consider reading and writing of prime importance."

I must add, in a rare show of fairness, that the account of the Modern School given here is Sam's version. The version of Sam's close friend, Abe Bluestein—a lifelong anarchist who fought in Spain—differed 180 degrees from Sam's. He remembered the Ferms fondly and had good things to say about the Modern School. He did recall a telling incident, however. The students were not compelled to attend class. So one day thirteen-year-old Abe and classmates decided to play hooky and see a silent movie in town. They were shocked and humiliated to discover they could not read the subtitles! Abe returned with a burning desire to read. This tells me something about the isolation of the place.

We can interpret the incident two ways. What kind of school is it that does not focus on teaching children to read and write?! On the other hand, all of the children eventually learned, and very well indeed. Abe grew up to report on Spain for the Canadian Broadcasting Corporation and handled English-language matters for the anarchist CNT/FAI. And a high proportion of Modern School kids went on to distinguished academic and scientific careers. So who can tell? A possible reason for the difference of perception between Abe Bluestein and Sam is that Abe attended the Modern School a decade before Sam got there.

My parents began to question the supposedly progressive education of the Modern School. Many of its adherents became increasingly nasty, especially after my parents enrolled Abe in the local public school across the highway. Sam called the Modern School clique a cult within a cult, and he came to view it as a symptom of the whole community. In time the bickering, the back-biting, the crackpot behavior, and the dictatorial hypocrisy of many of these Harbingers of a Harmonious World began to sicken him. Here he is, his caustic self, on his old rival for Mother's affection, the individualist, ox-cart anarchist Marcus Graham: "Marcus Graham always went barefoot, ate raw food, mostly nuts and raisins, and refused to use a tractor, being opposed to machinery; and he didn't want to exploit horses, so he dug the earth himself."

Sam also had misgivings about the local public school; he remembered his own sad childhood. But my parents gave it a try. Every day they took little Abe across the highway to the sturdy two-classroom, red-brick building in the middle of rural nowhere. Abe remembers his teacher's name to this day: Miss Fleming. She had flaming red hair and was *very* strict but not abusive; she ran a tight ship. You had to dress a certain way, almost in uniform. Once Abe scratched his varnished desk and Miss Fleming sent a curt note to Sam. He answered with an apology: "To err is human/to forgive divine." Miss Fleming was not impressed by Sam's knowledge of Alexander Pope. She forced Sam to take off work and attend her class. The scratch vanished miraculously with application of some spit.

Nevertheless, Abe did learn to read and write in Miss Fleming's class. And he learned something else. There was a cup next to the water fountain. Beneath it was the small sign: "For colored." One day a large black man burst into the classroom and ground the cup beneath his boot, in front of Miss Fleming. "My little girl is going to drink from that fountain like the other children. Do you understand that?" And from that day on the little girl did.

I leave my last comment on the Stelton Colony to older brother Abe, "From the perspective of my eighty-second year, and looking back to my childhood there, I still hate the place. I feel no nostalgia. Do you remember what they made us feel like? Outsiders? Contemptible!"

No, I do not remember, but after reading Joseph Cohen's comments on the failure of Sunrise colony in his interesting *In Search of Heaven*, I cannot shake the feeling that these utopian projects filled with idealistic, well-meaning people were permeated with a whiff of the cult, and I for one am not "into" cults. This, not withstanding that I attended several warm reunions of the Stelton colony with my parents and Paul Avrich a generation later.

My parents had their bellyful of the communal life before I was old enough to remember any of it. As Sam put the matter, "Numerous attempts conclusively demonstrate that the Stelton Modern School Colony and all other colonies are essentially self-isolationist forms of escapism. I came to realize more and more that freedom will be attained not in isolation, but only in association with the rest of humanity."

Agree with Sam or not, the communes were replete with fantastic people. Take your pick! Sam spoke fondly of Dora Keyser, a most beautiful soul. She raised her sister's orphaned children after she and her husband were murdered in Russia by the Bolsheviks. With the decline of the Modern School she settled in Los Angeles. There she devoted her life to raising funds for political prisoners and assisting hard-pressed workers on strike. These funds, by the way, included her own money of which she had little. When this gentle Jewish lady passed away at the age of eighty-five the delegate representing the United Farm Workers—Mexican laborers—wept openly at her funeral.

Sam's best buddy while at the Stelton Colony was Louis Raymond. "A fellow house painter, he worked in nearby New Brunswick and at odd jobs in the Stelton area. At times I used to help him and we got along very well indeed, except for his home-made beer. I could hardly swallow his awful tasting concoction. I was tempted to complain but refrained because I did not want to mar our harmonious relationship."

Raymond had a backstory of which Sam was well aware. His real name was Manuel Rey, a Spaniard who had spent years organizing longshoreman on the Philadelphia waterfront, shoulder to shoulder with the great black Wobbly, Ben Fletcher—of whom I will have a great deal more to say later. Together with Jack Walsh, Walter Nef, E. F. Doree, and other Wobblies, they forged a fully integrated, democratic union of up to ten-thousand black and white men: this before Martin Luther King was born and in the teeth of massive opposition. For their efforts they drew ten- to twenty-year sentences in Leavenworth Federal Penitentiary under the Espionage Act of World War I—never mind that there was no espionage. Manuel was released after a few years on the condition he was deported to Spain and never returned to the United States.

At this point *romance* enters the story. According to Sam, "Lilly Sarnoff was one of the young anarchists who carried on extensive correspondence with anti-World War I, IWW, and anarchist 'subversives' jailed during the notorious anti-red campaigns. Her extensive correspondence with the Mexican anarchist revolutionist, Enrique Flores Magón, (also) imprisoned in Leavenworth, where he died in 1922 has been published in English and translated into Spanish. Lily also corresponded with Manuel Rey. Upon his release, they met, fell in love, and began their long life together in Stelton Colony." You can understand why Manuel changed his name.

Harry Gordon is my favorite among the myriad "colonists" that Sam mentioned over the years. Lydia Miller, Harry's daughter, described her father this way: "Harry Gordon was born in Vilna in 1866 of a prosperous Jewish family. He was a man of few words and strong principles. He was a machinist by trade but refused to make machinery related to the military during the First World War. He instilled in me a great deal of his idealism. When he talked I was always impressed. He was almost a saint."

Harry was aged and feeble when Sam knew him. He lived with his wife (also named Lydia and a remarkable person in her own right) and daughters in a small house built on a piece of ground that they owned in Mohegan Colony, where they operated a gasoline station out front. Lydia added to the family income by selling her home-baked bread and pies to customers and neighbors. The Mohegan Colony, about fifty miles north of NYC, was richer and more successful than the Stelton Colony; many of descendants of the original anarchists live there to the present day, along with all kinds of people attracted to the place. Sam and Esther visited comrades there often, stayed on as houseguests of Rudolf Rocker and others.

Back in 1892, Harry is not old and feeble and is living in Pittsburgh. It is the time of the Homestead Steel Strike of western Pennsylvania, a titanic event in labor history. The two future philanthropists Henry Clay Frick and Andrew Carnegie set out to crush the steel workers union, to force the strikers to their knees, and have them grovel for a job. It is classic late-nineteenth-century industrial warfare. Frick has hired a private army of three-hundred Pinkerton thugs; there is rifle and cannon fire. Men and women are slaughtered—by the way, the Pinkertons are compelled to surrender, waving a white flag—the works! Finally, Frick calls on a favor from the Governor and 8,500 National Guard troops are sent to "restore order" to Homestead, that is, to protect the interests of Frick and Carnegie, for there is no disorder in Homestead. The town is under martial law for months. The strike is lost and the two sonofabitches have realized their goals.

It is a story told many times from many angles. As is the story of the most sensational incident in the entire Homestead tragedy: the attempted assassination of Frick by Alexander Berkman. Berkman is twenty-two years old, a Russian Jewish immigrant and an anarchist. He is also the lover, and later, intimate lifetime friend of Emma Goldman. Berkman—his emotional life and understanding of the world wrought in Tsarist Russia—imagines his dramatic deed will ignite the strikers to revolution, but his plans backfire in nearly all respects. Frick survives, indeed goes back to work that very day a "hero." The strikers are furious as public sympathy flows from them to Frick, of all people. The bullet Berkman aimed at Frick went right through the heart of the strike, as one union official put it. Who the hell is this guy, they ask, who asked him to "help" us?

Anti-immigrant, anti-Semitic, anti-anarchist sentiment is stirred up throughout the nation.

Foolishly acting as his own lawyer, Berkman is sentenced to twenty-two years hard time in Western Penitentiary of Pennsylvania, though most experts surmise that with competent defense his crime was worth, maybe, seven-and-a-half years. It is 1892. At this juncture we bring Harry Gordon into the story. He is among the first comrades to visit Berkman while he is held in a Pittsburgh jail immediately after his attempt on Frick. Berkman is then transferred to Western. Nine buried-alive years pass during which Berkman is straitjacketed to a bed and left to rot in his own excrement, is given a year's dose of solitary confinement, and is subject to other abuse. At last, he is allowed a visitor. That person is Harry Gordon. "I was so overcome by the sight of the dear friend I could hardly speak," Berkman wrote later. "You can realize with what feelings I beheld the first comrade to come to see me and with what emotions I pressed his hand."

Gordon's activities on behalf of Berkman transcended visits, however. He was in on the plot to spring him by digging a tunnel beneath the prison. The tunnel started at the basement of a rented house across the street from the eastern wall and ended at a court-yard close to the stable inside the prison—the product of a back breaking, dangerous, three-hundred feet of toil undertaken by sympathetic Italian miners. All Berkman had to do was get to the stable, rip up the wooden flooring, and crawl through the tunnel to the house, where money, clothing, and directions to a safe place were waiting for him. Destination? Canada, or Mexico, finally Paris. The tunnel was dug and all systems were "go" until Berkman ran into horrendous luck. The entrance to the tunnel in the stable had been covered at the last minute by tons of brick and stone dumped from a prison construction project! The tunnel was abandoned and not discovered until some time later by a child at play outside the prison walls. The startled authorities were embarrassed, of course. They had their suspicions but not enough evidence to build a case and so no one was ever prosecuted.

Sam, Esther, and little Abraham spent a summer with Lydia and Harry at their modest Mohegan home. And it was there, in

Mohegan Colony, that Harry told Sam of his exploits on behalf of Berkman and what a deeply humane person Berkman was. He was far more than a mere appendage to Emma Goldman's life, as he seems so often portrayed. The man served fourteen years. His *Prison Memoirs of an Anarchist*, written upon his release at Emma's insistence and encouragement, is the spiritual journey of an arrogant young fanatic who enters Frick's office dedicated to Mankind only in the abstract, and leaves prison a true human being after years of suffering, one capable of experiencing love and tenderness and compassion toward his fellow man. It is among the best books of prison life ever written. I think it is superior to Fyodor Dostoyevsky's *House of the Dead*, which is similar in theme. Berkman grips you, despite some didactic passages and the awkward present-tense phrasing; Russian, not English was his first language.

You may notice that I dwell on Berkman far more than necessary to describe Sam's colonial adventures. There is a reason for the digression. It concerns an anecdote told to me by my dear friend Paul Avrich over a plate of General Tso's chicken in a Chinese restaurant near Columbia University one afternoon in 2000. He grabbed the check, as he was notorious for doing; it was impossible to pay for your food in his presence. Paul died in 2006 before he was able to finish *Sasha and Emma*, his dual biography of Berkman and Goldman; he had a long way to go. The book is lovingly co-authored and the project carried to completion by his daughter, the writer and editor, Karen Avrich. I do not know where Paul's anecdote belongs, but I feel compelled to pass it along to you.

Paul visited Western Penitentiary, which is still there, and was granted permission to visit Berkman's cell. He was escorted to the cell by a strapping prison guard, a formidable looking fellow, who was given only the cell number and not Paul's purpose. Why this particular cell, the guard asks. Paul explains that he is an historian and writing a book on Alexander Berkman who was sent to this prison for trying to murder Frick during the Homestead strike. "Do you know of the incident?" Paul asks. The guard says nothing. Paul feels a chill as he is shown the empty cell; a century has not changed it much. Then the guard says something strange: "I get off work soon. I have some things that may interest you." So

Paul joins the guard off duty, and follows him by car to his modest home in a suburb of a suburb somewhere. There in the basement or garage—I do not know which—he shows Paul a veritable museum of documents and memorabilia dealing with Berkman, Frick, and the Homestead strike. Incredible stuff! The prison guard had spent a lifetime amassing this material and with serious intention. He was a scholar, not a stamp collector.

Throughout Paul's visit the guard's demeanor is courteous, formal, and impassive. He does not smile until the two of them shake hands and Paul is ready to leave.

"You see, I come from a long line of union men, back to the days of the Homestead Strike," he says. "A lot of us don't think Berkman was so bad. We think his heart was in the right place."

# 19

# SAM AND EMMA

About Emma Goldman, we are fortunate to have Sam speak for himself.

**Interviewer (I)**: Did you know Emma Goldman?
**Sam (S)**: Yes, I met her once or twice.
**I**: What was she like?
**S**: Well, I met her once in the house of her niece, Stella Ballantine, I think. And the Ballatines, that's the same family of the Ballantine Books, paperback books. In the Village. And I knew that she wasn't no big husky but I took a look at her; she was a little half pint. How in the hell a little half pint like that could make so much noise! And raise such a dickens of hell, you know.
**I**: She didn't have much to do with the IWW, did she?
**S**: Well, I had the feeling that it was a rather ambiguous relationship.

Either she or her sweetheart, the clap doctor from Chi we used to call him, Ben Reitman, they would help out or soapbox, you know; but I don't think they were really very enthusiastic about the IWW. Because they considered that the IWW was far too centralized, for one thing. Secondly, there were an awful lot of people in her circle who didn't believe in organization altogether. You said organization to them, that was like showing a red rag to a bull. They were inclined to be very individual-istically minded, and besides that (I know I wander here and there but that's alright), I always had the impression that she didn't represent the movement. See, with her, all her prestige and what have you, rested upon her personal contacts. And she was an enormously courageous and heroic figure in that sense. She was absolutely fearless for that matter. She happened to get in very solid, with all her revolutionary phraseology and the hyperbole. Basically, she was not really asking for much more than what today would be considered a liberal program. Birth control, equal rights for women, a better education, and so forth. There weren't many things that she asked for that the system couldn't withstand; in fact, they would help it. Of course I'm not talking about (her) socialism, but her appeal was not on that basis. Her appeal rested on these transient issues.

Emma and Sam met in 1934 during the three months she was allowed back into the U.S. following her deportation to Russia in 1919. She was sixty-four years old at the time, he thirty-two. Old-timers of the *Freie Arbeiter Stimme* have said to me that Emma, who enjoyed other people's babies, bounced my infant brother Abe on her knee, though I do not recall Mother mentioning the incident and it may be apocryphal. Emma was aware that Sam was a protégé of Gregorii Maximoff and the other Russian anarchists she and Alexander Berkman fought to rescue from the Bolshevik dungeons. So she was cordial and warm toward my parents. But there was no personal relationship; they were not friends. A bit more than acquaintances, young comrades, is a better way to describe it.

But a naked fact is often misleading. Sam knew perhaps a score of people who knew Emma well: from her ex-lover Ben Reitman to Hippolyte Havel to Alexandra Kropotkin (who loathed Emma's alleged bad manners and self-importance during her visit to her dying father in Russia) to Dorothy Rogers (who devoted her life to Emma—nursed her as she lay gravely ill in Toronto, and accompanied her funeral cortège to Waldheim Cemetery in Chicago). The small anarchist movement in America was an extended family in many ways, especially among its Jewish wing. Everybody more or less knew everyone else, almost certainly at one remove, and there were many who, like Sam, knew—or thought they knew—all about Emma's life. An illusion, no doubt.

You are correct if you sensed a degree of ambivalence toward Emma in Sam's remarks. Part of it stemmed from Sam's distrust of the celebrity she attained among people he instinctively distrusted. And he suspected her of self-promotion. He preferred the purer oratory and writing style of Voltairine de Cleyre, that other great anarchist-feminist of the twentieth century, who died in 1912. And

Sam was a Wobbly to his dying breath and had little use for the anti-organizational anarchists in her circle.

But I would not make too much of the latter ambivalence. Emma and her group supported the Wobblies and the class struggle "a-plenty," in my opinion. Alexander Berkman, Emma's dearest friend, was sent to prison for trying to assassinate Frick during the Homestead steel strike. Ben Reitman was brutalized and Emma held captive during the Wobblies' San Diego free speech fight of 1912. Sam's coolness toward Emma was an in-the-family thing. And ambivalence has its favorable side: He looked up to Emma, sought her approval. Eighty-eight years old and he still bragged to me that Emma had high praise for *Vanguard*.

Mother laid into Sam for his remark that Emma's appeal was over "transient" issues of feminism. "Has it occurred to you that women are half the human race?" she snapped at him, and Sam would hunch his shoulders and lower his head as if expecting a flying brick, but it was only Mother's verbal wrath that flew at his head.

I see a rough analogy between Emma Goldman and Carlo Tresca in one respect. They were strong personalities with the need to plunge into the life around them, to remain relevant. So during ordinary times, they became involved in "transient" issues, and—sin that it is—enjoyed their celebrity. But during the Spanish Revolution Carlo and Emma threw all that aside and returned to their anarchist roots. Sam was moved by the photos of Emma standing at the side of Durruti in Spain.

# 20
## WITH TRESCA AND THE ITALIANS

My parents did not have what might may politely be called "decorating sense." If they liked something for whatever reason they pasted or nailed it to the wall: an atrocious portrait of Sam, because a good friend painted it; a low quality reproduction of a Currier and Ives print cut from a magazine, because Mother thought the ice skating scene charming; a humorous Japanese scroll of an armless Buddha scowling at a fly disturbing his contemplation, because it was given to them by a Wobbly seaman. All kinds of stuff, amid a forest of green plants and baby pictures.

They had a curious attitude toward possessions, as if they did not deserve nice things, as if owning them was a form of corruption. Wobbly seamen would bring them exquisite ivory carvings from equatorial Africa, or lovely, delicate clay pottery from Peru, and it would end up in the closet, or as a gift to Aunt Elaine, Sam's sister, who did not need or appreciate it. This infuriated the seamen who explained to Mother that they climbed hills and visited remote villages to get these things. Remember, this was the 1930s, before mass air transportation and the tourism industry. My parents simply did not care or understand. A black, hand-carved African dagger lay around the living room for years, neglected until it lost its feathers and bead work.

In later years Sam decided he needed more room for his books. So he nailed shelves of crude lumber planking, floor to ceiling, on all of the bedroom walls. There was room for an equally crude desk and on it an ancient typewriter given to him by a friend, upon which he hunt-and-pecked his articles and books. On the foyer leading to the bedroom, pasted to the walls, were the quotes from Sam's heroes, for he had them despite his protestations. My favorite, from Michael Bakunin: "I shall continue to be an impossible person for as long as those who are possible remain possible!"

Sam's favorite, also from Michael Bakunin: "There is no horror, no cruelty, sacrilege, or perjury, no imposture, no infamous transaction, no cynical robbery, no bold plunder or shabby betrayal that has not been or is not daily being perpetrated by the representatives of the states, under no other pretext than those elastic words, so convenient and yet so terrible: 'for reasons of state.'"

"National security" is the preferred euphemism in our time.

On the walls above Sam's desk were excellent hand-drawn prints of anarchist brigades in combat during the Spanish Revolution, and ancient photographs and sketches of the bearded men who meant so much to him: a heavy, sloppy Bakunin, in unkempt beard; a neat, prim, balding Peter Kropotkin at his desk in long red beard; Leo Tolstoy in overcoat, walking stick, and white beard; a dignified, bespectacled Errico Malatesta in broad-brimmed black hat and very short gray beard, almost a goatee; finally, a stout Rudolf Rocker (I am not sure if he wore a beard).

At last we come to two photographs in simple frames next to Sam's typewriter. They are of the two men that he knew, and loved, above all others. One photograph is of gray-haired Gregorii Petrovich Maximoff, impeccably dressed and barbered, a dignified man in the old European style. The other is of Carlo Tresca in his wiry youth, perhaps his thirties: string tie, long face, prominent nose, goatee, dangerous dark eyes, charismatic. Carlo! Sam always referred to him like that, his voice upturned in an exclamation point. There would follow a low private chuckle of the deepest affection, infinitely sad.

There is another photograph of Tresca, taken by the celebrated crime photographer Weegee in 1943. It is of an overweight old man, gray haired, on his back in the night, a puddle of blood from his head staining the pavement: the victim of a classic Mafia "hit." It is hard to believe the two photographs—the one on Sam's desk and the one taken by Weegee for a New York tabloid—are of the same man. Tresca was celebrated in many circles, and the murder took place early in the evening on the corner of Fifth Avenue and Fifteenth Street. A sensational crime, front page news: investigations were demanded, but interest faded and no one was prosecuted. War was blazing, men dying on two fronts. Tresca remained a forgotten figure for half a century save for the dwindling few, who, like Sam, knew and loved him, and now there are none who knew him left.

It is not possible to describe what Tresca meant to Sam without recounting, at least briefly, the incredible arc of the man's life. For this I rely on two fine biographies, supplemented by the many things Sam told me about Tresca. The first is Nunzio Pernicone's *Carlo Tresca: Portrait of a Rebel*. An apt title indeed. "Carlo was a born rebel. No amount of pyschologizing will get to the bottom of it," Sam often said.

He was born 1879 to faded landed gentry in Sulmona, Abruzzi Province, Italy. (While yet a boy, the peasants referred to him as Don Carlo.) A troublemaker from the start, he was an incorrigible youth and the condition lasted a lifetime. As a teenager, he organized demonstrations against Catholic school seminarians, whom he considered parasites; it was the first manifestation of an active lifetime hatred of the Catholic Church. (Though, in a compromise I find endearing, he married his wife Helga in church secretively, under cover of night, solely to please his mother.)

Tresca became a socialist organizer soon enough. In 1902 he gave "his first speech at a May Day demonstration. His heartfelt, humorous, and impassioned speech earns him applause from the peasants. Tresca would always remember this speech as the time when he became a man." Tresca stood for everything his father rejected, so it is moving to me that his father, after seeing Tresca on the platform that day, said to his son that it was the first time he respected him.

A month later we come to another landmark in Tresca's career: "he is arrested for the first time for shouting a 'subversive' remark in a police captain's face. He is sentenced to thirty days in jail." Scores of arrests were to follow in years to come on charges more serious than that—and those thirty days in prison were the first of many such days.

Shortly thereafter Tresca became editor of the Socialist paper *Il Germe*—the start of his long career as a muckraking journalist and revolutionary propagandist—and in 1904, having outstayed his welcome in the land of his birth, found himself on the lam to the United States to avoid prison. On a stopover in Lausanne, Switzerland, Tresca met and briefly roomed with another young socialist in exile by the name of Benito Mussolini.

I like the way Nunzio Pernicone describes their relationship: "Neither is impressed with the other."

Sam recounts this conversation: "Tresca recalls that Mussolini boasted that 'He was a very radical man and an extreme socialist, while I, Tresca, was not radical enough. Can you imagine? I am an anarchist now. And what is Mussolini? A traitor, of course.'"

In short, the two men despised each other. Tresca, who spent the better part of his adult life in violent opposition to Mussolini and his regime, never forgot to taunt *il Duce* by sending him a birthday card each year. ("Greetings from Carlo!") Mussolini reciprocated by placing Tresca on his assassination list and having the Italian consulate beseech U.S. authorities to deport him.

Tresca's relationship with Mussolini—or shall I say nonrelationship?—illustrates why I also find Dorothy Gallagher's *All the Right Enemies: The Life and Murder of Carlo Tresca* aptly titled. All the right enemies, indeed! He dedicated his life to physical, moral, and intellectual combat against people and institutions far more powerful than he. He was on all the lists. The following is but a partial summary of his political enemies—and I exclude for the sake of brevity, and with tongue partially in cheek, deflowered virgins, betrayed lovers, cuckolded husbands, personal vendettas.

- the Italian fascists, who on occasions too numerous to count clubbed him, slashed him, shot at him, and attempted to blow him up;
- the politically connected and influential fascist/opportunist Generoso Pope, the publisher of an Italian-language newspaper empire, whose hatred of Tresca bordered on the religious;
- the *camorra colonia*, the complex of Italian business, diplomatic, and church interests that exploited and brutalized the impoverished miners, ditch diggers, and factory workers they imported from Italy as slave labor;
- the Black Hand (i.e. Mafia)—one of whose representatives slashed at Tresca's throat from behind with a razor on a Pittsburgh street, in broad daylight, in 1909. Tresca sensed the attack and grappled with the assailant. The razor snapped

against his jawbone, thus sparing the jugular. Still, Tresca nearly bled to death, and received twenty-six roughly sewn stitches from a hostile doctor. The signature goatee was to hide the scar;

- the New York City police, who, beyond the standard beatings and arrests, on one public occasion placed the barrel of a revolver to the back of his head—and on another between his shoulder blades—in order to disperse crowds of angry strikers;

- the New Jersey police who arrested him eleven times for incitement to riot and similar charges during the IWW-led Patterson, New Jersey silk strike;

- the Oliver Mining Company, a subsidiary of US Steel, which, in 1916, organized a "lynching party" for Tresca during the IWW-led strike of the Mesabi iron mines of northern Minnesota. The Company recruited thugs armed with rifles; they were deployed on both sides of the small truck Tresca and two other Wobbly organizers were riding in as they entered town. The rifles were pointed at Tresca. Behind the truck, preventing escape, were two cars of armed deputies. Tresca got out of the truck without hesitation and walked confidently among the gauntlet of armed men. None of them had the courage to pull the trigger. I remember telling Sam that, in Gallagher's book, Tresca called his get-out-of-the-car move a tactic: the best way to deal with intimidation was to confront it head-on. "Tactic! You call that a tactic?" Sam exclaimed. "I call it guts. Old-fashioned guts. Carlo was like that."

- the State of Minnesota authorities who arrest him for the murder of a miner even though he was a hundred miles away at the time of the incident. Standard Operating Procedure, the way to neutralize strike leaders;

- the Red Squads of every city and town he trod in;

- the Federal Government, on numerous occasions and pretexts. It indicted him and 167 other Wobblies in 1917 for "conspiracy to impede the war effort"; it convicted him on obscenity charges because he ran an advertisement in

*IL Martello* for a pamphlet that gave practical birth control advise (turns out the ad was placed by a government plant); it attempted to deport him at the urging of the Italian government for articles calling for the overthrow of the Italian Monarchy (H. L. Mencken, among other prominent people, defended Tresca in this case);

- the FBI, which devoted fourteen-hundred pages to his every hiccup and fart;
- the Stalinists, for many, many reasons.

He was sued and sent to prison for libel innumerable times. Misbehaving priests were his specialty. In one such trial, initiated by an aggrieved Rev. Di Sabato, Tresca produced "a photograph of the handsome young priest reclining on a sofa with his head nestled comfortably against the breast of his lovely 'housekeeper' whose left arm embraced him around the neck while her right arm balanced a perched parrot." That was too much even for the stacked jury. They acquitted Tresca. But, fear not, they found him guilty of libeling the priest's mistress instead. At the close of another lost trial involving a misbehaving priest, Tresca "hastened to assure 'the crew in cassocks' that their 'sacred and furious joy' would be short lived. Even if obliged to serve nine months, 'I shall return to the same post of combat and I shall empty other churches for you.'"

There was another side to the man, which Sam insisted, was the true Tresca. Pernicone describes how this aristocrat, born to privilege, began organizing among the Italian coal miners of Pennsylvania, West Virginia, Ohio, and Illinois: on his own, freelance, and unaffiliated.

Typically, after a long day on the lecture circuit he would enjoy himself thoroughly when invited by his hosts to share a simple meal of pasta and homemade wine and spending the evening playing cards, smoking, and telling tales. He enjoyed the conviviality without evidencing a trace of discomfort, for it was his cardinal rule never to make workers self-conscious for their poverty. Once, when his young daughter Beatrice accompanied him, she complained that the bed in which she was to sleep lacked sheets. He reproached her gently in private, explaining that the people were too poor to own such items. Thus he never balked when obliged to share a bed with a miner during a propaganda tour: "To sleep two in a bed, in the same room is not comfortable. But it is a blow to your imagination when on entering the sleeping room, you find four kids. You can't refuse such hospitality. It is all the miners can offer you."

Not every father in 1910 would take his daughter on a trip like that. You can sense the tenderness of the man, and that is how my parents remembered him. Sam said compassion, and passion, were keys to his personality. That and the compulsion to get involved, to assert himself, which ultimately led to his death. He was in the thick of it in the coal mines of Westmoreland, Pennsylvania; the textile and silk mills of Lawrence, Massachusetts, and Patterson, New Jersey; the iron mines of Mesabi Range, Minnesota; and other places where the going got tough.

Carlo's days as a key Wobbly organizer of these great strikes and localized, short-lived social revolutions were long gone when he and Sam met in 1933 and immediately became fast friends. So, too, was Carlo's key role in defense of Sacco and Vanzetti, whom he knew well and struggled to save. But he was still battling the fascists when Sam met him; he hadn't given an inch since the early 1920s when Mussolini came to power. "With his comrades…he held antifascist street meetings in communities dominated by the Fascists, he raided Fascist headquarters, dispersed Fascist meetings and assemblies, and in the streets fought the Blackshirts in hand-to-hand combat." The fascists were fond of canes and umbrellas with razors attached to their tips and they would swing the damn things at your face and neck. A lifetime of encounters with all the right enemies had left their mark on Tresca and I am not speaking metaphorically. Sam said the man's body was a canvas of cuts, broken bones, and bullet holes.

But Carlo was protective of Sam. He discouraged his participation in these scary affairs. "Sammy, we don't need you here with you glasses, you can't see nothing! We need you for other things," he'd say in his impossible to transpose speech—described by Max Eastman as Italian spoken with English words.

Not that Sam was an armchair antifascist. There was plenty of work to go around. Besides the Blackshirts, you had the pro-Hitler German-American Bund, which held rallies in their strongholds, the Yorkville section of Manhattan and in parts of New Jersey. Then you had the native, homegrown fascists led by an awful individual named Art Smith. And there were others. Indeed, Mussolini was popular from the early 1920s up to the late 1930s; Cole Porter wrote a flattering lyric to him in his "You're the Top," which was cut on second thought. Many sympathetic Americans thought that fascists were efficient, they got things done. Hitler was the strong leader Germany needed. He put people to work and tough measures were needed to handle the pushy Jews. Mussolini, Hitler these guys knew how to take care of the Commies, most of whom were Jews anyway! Sentiments like that were strong in big Eastern cities in the 1930s and the fascists sought to dominate the street corners and parks where rallies were held.

Sam did most of his antifascist street work in collaboration with the IWW. It is a lost chapter in the history of that heroic organization. There were not many Wobblies in NY at that time—perhaps several hundred or so if you took into account the Finns, and other ethnic groups—and most were not active at the same times. Some belonged to MTW (the seafarer's local, from the Five-Ten Hall) and some, like Sam, did other work. But they joined forces to hold open-air rallies—rallies designed to take back the streets from the fascists. They were not genteel affairs.

Mother spoke often of the time Sam faced down a potential lynch mob. He was on the soapbox one muggy summer night, addressing a large crowd at a street corner rally in Greenwich Village—Eighth and MacDougal streets, to be precise. Remember, this was the 1930s, the pit of the Depression. In those primitive days people would stop and give you a minute or two before moving on. It was up to the speaker to capture the crowd, to hold it. Sam—"the old man," as Abe and I took to calling him in later years—was a first-rate Wobbly rabble-rouser; he was proud of that. He spoke without a microphone. The purpose of the meeting was to enforce the Wobblies' right of free speech, to take back Eighth and MacDougal and other sites around the city from the fascists who thought of themselves as super-patriots; many of them—I repeat—were Hitler and Mussolini supporters.

That night Sam is entirely vulnerable. He is encircled, stands head and shoulders above everyone else, and is saying unpopular things. A red! The crowd moves in uncomfortably close. There follows an exchange that does not improve safety:

"Would you fight for the flag?" someone shouts.

"I fight for no flag! There are better things to fight for, like the solidarity of the human race," Sam answers, and a hissing sound passes through the crowd like a hot wind.

"Throw him off the platform!" And it looks like the crowd is preparing to do just that.

The finishing touch comes when a furious patriot calls out that his son was killed in combat in World War I and the crowd responds to his sacrifice with an air of hushed reverence. No such reverence is forthcoming from Sam. It is not the man's grief that he questions, rather the moral superiority that he wears like a breast plate, burnished by decades of rationalization and guilt. He speaks directly to him:

"You stand here and tell us you're proud you sent your son off to die? Even a rat will fight to defend its young!"

The crowd by this time is foaming at the mouth. Somehow they get hold of my father's name, which they turn into a nasty, Yiddish-accented, "Sammy, Sammy, go back to where you came from! Sammy, Sammy, go back to where you came from!"

The chant grows deafening, reverberates, each "Sammy" the force of a blow. Some malevolent-looking young goons have moved up front. The police do nothing. Mother is terrified; she sounded terrified recounting the story a generation later. She is sure the crowd has turned into a mob and is going to stomp him to death.

There follows a moment that I can only describe as transformative.

Sam stands perfectly still until the crowd begins to catch its collective breath and the "Sammys" die down. Now it is his turn. His demeanor is plaintive, his attitude that of a man apologizing for an event beyond his control. At the same time his voice assumes a mock pompous tone. "A number among you have vociferously raised the suggestion that I go back to where I have come from. Don't you think under these circumstances, and in consideration of the reception you have afforded me on this august occasion, that I too would prefer to go back to where I've come from? I've inquired of the eminent physician Dr Rudolph Shmuckleheimer about it, and he has informed me that it is a biological and physiological impossibility."

A pause—"did we hear him right?"—is followed by a collective chuckle, and then an eruption of appreciative laughter spreads from the toughs encircling Sam to the far reaches of the crowd. The tension is broken and the point made; he is not going anywhere. In the relative quiet and good will that follows, Sam suggests that, "Despite our differences there is one point upon which we can agree, and that is we respect fair play. Leave if you want to, but if you stay, then let the next man have his say!" That man was his good friend, Franz Fleigler.

Franz was a rugged Wobbly seaman and a close observer of human nature, which he didn't admire much. The man had the stature of a fire-hydrant and his every word seemed to escape clenched teeth. Nevertheless he did his best to ingratiate himself to the crowd. When the spontaneous chant, "I am an American, I am an American," rung out defiantly, Franz answered in his true Yiddish accent, "So you're American! Does that mean your shit don't stink?"

A most tactful remark. However, by this time the testosterone had drained from the crowd. I'll let Sam describe how things ended: "After the meeting one of the hostile listeners said my talk reminded him that his grandfather was a Wobbly. Another patriot suddenly discovered that there were a few Wobblies in his family tree. To my surprise, I was even invited by vociferous opponents to join them in a nearby tavern for the 'drop that cheers.'"

He needed no coaxing in that regard.

Back in the early- to mid-1930s, the anti-communist left was considerate of the FBI and the Red Squad. That is, they all nested down and cohabitated at the same address, 94 Fifth Avenue. Sam remembered the place fondly. "The whole building was occupied by the IWW, the studio of the artist Carlson, the anarchist-communist [i.e., communalist] Vanguard group, and Carlo Tresca's *Il*

*Martello* group. Members and sympathizers of these organizations in close contact with each other created a comradely atmosphere, an 'espirit de corps' which actually constituted a libertarian fraternal community." Tresca printed an English-language page written by Vanguard in *Il Martello* and he gave Sam's close friend, the anarchist editor Sid Solomon, space in his office. (Sid chatted with Tresca there on the afternoon he was murdered.)

The place generated a constructive synergy. A prime example was the case of Athos Terzani, a gutsy young follower of Tresca, who penetrated a Fascist rally at its stronghold in Astoria, Queens. There was gunfire. Terzani's close friend and comrade, Antonio Fierro, a twenty-one-year-old City College student was shot dead. Terzani was indicted for the murder on the supposed eyewitness testimony of Art Smith and another fascist. It looked bad for Terzani, especially since the Queens DA, courting the fascist vote, refused to consider other alternatives. Here is where the synergy kicked in.

A united-front defense committee was formed that included Norman Thomas of the Socialist Party, Roger Baldwin of the ACLU, and other notables. And Tresca and Sam, of course. That was how they met. It also included Herbert Mahler, a terrific old-time Wobbly, a self-taught legal genius with the instincts and guts of a bloodhound reporter. It was Mahler who cracked the case. He followed up on a letter the others thought was the work of a crackpot; traveled to Philadelphia and interviewed a key witness. Not only did the testimony of this witness prove Terzani innocent, but it led to the arrest of the actual murderer, a fascist, and the perjury conviction of Smith and another bastard. Smith's organization collapsed after that. A rare victory at the time. Pernicone largely credits Tresca, but Sam understood Tresca knew better. Tresca and Mahler were old friends.

Mahler had been Secretary of the Seattle, Washington local of the IWW during the Everett Massacre of 1915—when at least seven Wobblies and two deputies were killed during an exchange of gunfire on the Everett docks about twenty-five miles to the north. Preposterously, seventy-nine Wobblies were indicted for murder, but not one of the drunken "deputies," who opened fire on the Wobblies trapped in the ferry as it attempted to land. Mahler observed closely how the defense lawyers exploded the prosecution's case and got the first man off; the charges against the other Wobblies were then dropped. Mahler had found his calling. Soon afterward, he founded the General Defense Committee (GDC) of the IWW. Its purpose was to provide legal aid and money to Wobblies framed by the government. Ironically, the GDC, short on resources, did Mahler no good; he was sent to Leavenworth for five years under the Espionage Act. Nevertheless, the GDC served as a template for the American Civil Liberties Union (ACLU). Roger Baldwin, the founder of the latter, was a member of the IWW, if for a short time, and ACLU's first publication, a well-written brief, was titled "In Defense of the IWW."

Sam fondly remembers other characters who populated 94 Fifth Avenue. "Ninety-four was also a cultural center with classes in the arts, journalism and other subjects. The well-known socialist Samuel H. Friedman (various times Socialist Party candidate for the U.S. vice presidency and other posts) taught the public speaking class." This part I love: "The graduate exercises were held at an open-air street corner meeting. Friedman was the chairman. The speeches of the graduates were rated according to the applause of the audience."

Friedman was a classy man. He carried himself well, had a beautiful speaking voice, and without arrogance, he drew respect. He had been editor of the *New Leader* and the socialist *Call*, a champion of progressive education, and a friend of John Dewey. He was a militant fellow as well, arrested many times in civil rights demonstrations, and was set to join the soon to be martyred Michael Schwerner, and others, on the Mississippi Freedom Ride until forced to withdraw for some reason: this despite being in his sixties at the time. I think Mother had a platonic crush on him. He was the well dressed, courtly gentlemen of whom her middle class, respectable family would approve. I mention all this because of an incident Friedman recounted to Mother in our living room in my presence. It was the mid-1960s, I believe. By that time he was elderly, gray haired, a bit stout.

Friedman had been a strong supporter of the Cuban Revolution, a Fidel enthusiast, and was invited to visit Cuba as part of a delegation of sympathetic educators. The delegation was escorted to a model classroom, of which the Cubans were proud. Friedman was struck by the archaic, rigid teaching methods: silent students, sitting in rows; lessons recited by rote; uniformity of dress; the teacher as demigod; and so forth. And stunts like the distribution of treats. The teacher asked, "Who gives you this candy?" and the students replied in unison, "Fidel gives us this candy!"

So Friedman asked questions in what he considered a tactful, respectful manner. Have you heard of this method? That method? Experiments have shown that children react well to this or that, and so forth. The delegates and officials listened silently, courteously. That evening Friedman heard a knock on his hotel room door. Two no-nonsense guys in plain clothes entered. Politely but firmly, they insisted he pack. They escorted him to the airport with no explanation beyond that it was better for all that he should leave. Friedman was furious, humiliated. It was wounding to be singled out and extracted from a tightly knit group. He was a friend of the Revolution, he insisted, an admirer of Fidel. The escorts were impassive until he was about to board the plane. Then one of them said, in accented English, "Be thankful. You can leave."

But let's return to Tresca.

Mother remembered him with deep affection and equally deep exasperation: the affection because his charm was irresistible, the exasperation because he'd steal her husband without warning. Any time, any day, no matter if Sam was working, or had other obligations, there came that dreaded blast of an automobile horn from the street below. No need for Sam to look out the window, he would simply stop whatever he was doing and vanish for an evening, or days on end. Mother never knew, because Sam never knew; at least that is what he said racing out the door. Carlo would come up to the apartment to recruit Sam on occasion, especially if it involved an extended absence, probably as a put-up job initiated by Sam.

"Don't worry, Mother," he'd say, "I bring him home!" And Mother was left with the babies.

Their destination: Philadelphia, Boston, the mining towns of the Lehigh valley of Pennsylvania, the factory towns of Connecticut and Massachusetts—wherever there were knots of working-class

Italians waiting for Carlo. Forty years later Sam would shake his head in admiration of Carlo. "He didn't have a pot to piss in or a window to throw it out of. But he had this car and this half crazy chauffeur; Carlo couldn't drive."

These journeys often acquired an Odyssean quality. You got to Boston, for example, on Highway 1, the old single lane Boston Post Road that ran through every town and village along the way. There were no superhighways and Interstates then. And, of course, Carlo knew a comrade in every one of these towns and villages. Or so it seemed. "We pass Ruggiero (or whomever)! If he find out we don't say hello, you make him insulted!"

And so it was wine and pasta with Ruggiero (or whomever) in every town and village from NY to Boston. It was amazing. The comrades never seemed to know he was coming but were always ready for him. Warm, wonderful people! The problem was a five-hour drive turned into a fifteen-hour fiasco, with Sam and Carlo and the chauffeur—who was more friend than chauffeur—arriving soaked in wine and stuffed to the gills, and the meeting long dispersed. No harm; his hosts seemed to be used to it, and the audience returned.

The size of the audience never fazed him. He told Sam of a winter night in a southern Illinois coal town. The hall he was scheduled to speak in turned up empty, save for three or four miners. Carlo starts his speech, by rote, mechanically. Three of the men promptly fall asleep, a trio of snores at different pitch. The hall is drafty, the wind is howling outside, a blizzard is starting up. Carlo wants to go home. But his audience of one gestures he should go on. At length, Carlo says in Italian, "Son of a bitch, its cold. Let me go home!" "Not yet," the lone miner says. "What you say is interesting!" And so Carlo proceeds for another hour to expound on the principles of anarcho-syndicalism and the need for the IWW. Finally, the miner shakes Carlo's hand and says simply, "You will hear from me."

"Turns out he was my best man," Carlo said to Sam.

That man became a key organizer of the militant Progressive Mine Workers Union, an affiliate of the IWW. He single-handedly lined-up hundreds of men. The PMWU supported the Spanish Revolution. They assessed their members thousands of dollars, which they sent to the Spanish anarchists. Carlo's moral, which he passed on to Sam: The success of a meeting depends not on the size of the audience, but on the few that are impressed with your message.

Of charismatic people, my old friend Herb Miller cautioned, "Charm is suspect. It is seduction." Carlo was seductive and, at times insensitive and a bit ruthless when it served his purpose. I am thinking of a minor incident Sam never forgave him for until after his death, upon which he forgave him everything. They were scheduled at a large meeting in Philadelphia: perhaps 150 people in attendance, all Italians. On the drive down, Carlo asks Sam what he's going to say. The event is an important occasion for Sam and he has devoted time and energy to his address. He takes his outline from his shirt pocket and proceeds in detail to give Carlo his hour long meditation: on the rise of fascism, on Stalinism, on the conniving and jockeying of the United States, France, and England, on the impotence of the labor movement—and, finally, on what should be the anarchist response to all this in the face of the oncoming war. Carlo listens intently. "That's a good speech, Sammy. Good!"

Up on the platform, Carlo proceeds to give Sam's speech. In Italian. To thunderous applause! Sam follows. Undercut, he has nothing substantive to say, and settles for ten minutes of clichés to polite clapping. Sam is hurt by what he considers Carlo's betrayal. Carlo understands this and speaks to Sam on the drive back to NY.

"Sam, you see me? The glasses, the goatee, the black string tie, the black suit, the big black hat? I know these people! I am the *professore*! They come to see me! To me they listen. They don't listen to you. American speaks English. They know you, good anarchist, Carlo's friend, fight for Sacco, Vanzetti. But they come for Carlo."

Sam had to admit Carlo was correct. His was a movement held together by the strength of his personality, courage, and commitment. There was purpose to the impromptu visits, the long dinners, the costume, the theatrical behavior. That is what mobilized the troops to fight the fascists in the streets. His followers believed in him.

Not every Italian anarchist was a follower of Tresca, however. Not by any means. Many first- and second-generation Italian Americans, including anarchists, found his old-fashioned dress, manners, and speech an embarrassment. He personified the very things they wanted to escape. Then there were anarchists with whom he feuded for personal, essentially egotistical reasons—rivals such as Armando Borghi, whom Mussolini forced into exile, a leader of the Italian syndicalists and second only to the great Malatesta in prestige. Others, such as Valerio Isca—a thoughtful, sensitive, and intelligent person, whom I knew and visited my entire life up until his death at age ninety-four—took a balanced position. Valerio was put off by Tresca's bombast, bad treatment of women, and political machinations: especially his willingness to work with the communists until the 1930s, although most anarchists got off the boat after the Kronstadt Revolt of 1921. However, he gave Carlo great credit for his days as an IWW organizer and for battling the fascists in the streets. It comes down to taste in the end: Valerio respected modest men. He thought neither Borghi nor Tresca the equal of Rudolf Rocker in character or depth of thought.

Sam knew all these men well. He considered their criticism of Tresca part of the normal give and take of a public life. The man himself made no claim that he held a monopoly on virtue or judgement; for example, he mentioned privately to Sam that he got burned by the Stalinist betrayal of the anarchists in Spain—their sickle in the back of the Spanish Revolution. They were blood enemies and he should have known. But nothing—nothing in Sam's opinion—justified the out-and-out viciousness of the attacks on Tresca by the Galleanisti, the most influential—and largest—group of Italian anarchists in America. Luigi Galleani was a man of formidable intellect and courage who advocated an austere brand of individualistic anarchism—or at least, Sam said, that is how his many followers interpreted his teachings.

"Galleani rejected all forms of organization—trade unions as well as political parties—as harbingers of authoritarianism," Pernicone notes, pointing to the man's view that "the anarchist movement and the labor movement travel along parallel lines…that do not meet and never coincide.'" Even the IWW was too tame, too compromising for Galleani, who preferred direct forms of revolutionary violence. As Avrich explains, "Such activities…were replies to the monstrous violence of the state. The greatest bombthrowers and murderers were not the isolated rebels driven to desperation, but the military resources of every government—the army, militia, police, firing squad, hangman." The Galleanisti practiced what Galleani preached. As part of a plot to retaliate for the persecution of radicals during the Red Scare of 1917–1922, they bombed the home of Attorney General Palmer of Palmer Raid notoriety. There were many other similar acts.

Sam never bought into the doctrine of violence—The Propaganda of the Deed—as a useful form of protest. He rejected the tactic, except in the most extreme cases—assassinating Hitler would not be a bad idea. And he rejected the doctrine on moral grounds. "You want to use guns? Plant bombs?" he admonished romantic hot-heads in the 1960s. "Remember, they have a hell of a lot more of that stuff than you. In any case, who gives you the right to mete out punishment? We want to change the *system*. Self-defense. Strikes. Protest. That is another matter." Nevertheless, he said many times the Galleanisti were merely following in the nineteenth- and early-twentieth-century tradition.

The Galleanisti distrust, nay hatred, of Tresca stemmed all the way back to the great Lawrence, Massachusetts textile strike of 1912. It branched onward and upward for thirty years into an entangled complex of valid criticism, half truths, lies, character assassination, attacks on his sex life, his finances, his personal appearance, his bowel movements, you name it. Carlo sold out the Lawrence strikers, Carlo was looking for glory during the Sacco-Vanzetti trials, Carlo shook the hand of Coolidge, Carlo was a stool pigeon for the FBI, Carlo was a gigolo, supported by rich women, Carlo was a coward (can you imagine?), Carlo, Carlo! Sam judged that some of their hatred of Tresca was principled, but old-fashioned jealousy, rationalized, was behind most of it. They envied his prominence.

Their abuse of Carlo cut deep. The Galleanisti—formally known as the L'Adunata dei refrattari group—were his countrymen, his natural allies, his spiritual home, and they cast him out. Were not their goals the same? True they differed on tactics, but no one had ever accused Carlo of being a follower of Gandhi, after all. It was remarkable the way these fervent proselytizers of the primacy of the individual could conform like a disciplined army. Sam remembered getting into a subway car with a group of them, only to have them desert the car en masse and on cue to the neighboring car. Left behind in humiliation was Armando Borghi. He was being punished, he explained vehemently, for his affair with a comrade's wife. Never mind she chose to leave voluntarily, that the husband mistreated her, he said. He had violated the code: thou shalt not fuck a comrade's wife. Borghi's pain was palpable.

The part Sam found difficult to explain was that one-on-one the L'Adunata comrades were fine men: loyal, ethical, generous, and it may surprise you, gentle. Sacco and Vanzetti, universally described in glowing terms by those who knew them personally, including Carlo, were Galleanisti. Twenty-five years after Carlo's death, in the midst of the Vietnam War, Sam tried to arrange a meeting of the surviving L'Adunata comrades and a fresh crop of anarchists: protesting students for the most part. What I'd give to have been there! Can you imagine these long-haired, Up Against the Wall Motherfucker kids reaching out across a lifetime of experience and an ocean of culture to the elderly, conservatively dressed, conservatively living Italians?

First I'll give you the idealized version: There was communion despite the differences as the young anarchists explained the world as they saw it. And when the young folk passed the collection hat around it came back green.

Now I'll give you what really happened. The Motherfuckers—the name came from the way the police spoke to them when commanding them to line up—proclaimed, "The cities are the new front line of the war. We defy law and order with our bricks and bottles, our shit, our long hair, our drugs, our rifles and fires. We are the forces of chaos and anarchy! We lie, we swindle, we hide, and we kill!" Despite their uncompromising stance the Motherfuckers needed money for bail and lawyers to navigate them through a sea of legal troubles, so they came to Sam to see if they could arrange a meeting with the Italians to help finance them. Sam was reluctant but felt obligated to help them; they were young people and could be facing serious jail time. So he introduced them to the L'Adunata secretary in Brooklyn. The meeting did not go well!

What do you mean Motherfuckers? We respect and revere motherhood. What kind of anarchist uses language like that? Ok, you hate the police, but what of the firemen who come to put out the fires you start? You want to kill them too? On and on like this. The secretary, an educated man and no fool, said that the Motherfuckers had no moral right to ask the Italians for help since they had committed themselves to a course of action in violation of their principles without the courtesy of consulting them. (For the record, Sam recalled that the Motherfuckers "were actually very gentle people absolutely incapable of putting their threats into effect.")

Carlo took his ostracism hard, though he never let on in public that it fazed him. Rather than withdraw from the mainstream as the Galleanisti had, Carlo engaged the political and cultural world around him. He had even authored a well-received play in 1925, a satire on Mussolini and fascism, directed by Salvatore Pernicone, Nunzio's father. "The town anarchist," as Nunzio called him, became the darling of the liberal and social democratic left. They held a Tresca Jubilee in his honor in 1939, to which Tresca consented, not out of ego but to raise funds for the perennially bankrupt *Il Martello*. Everyone from Ernest Hemingway to Margaret Sanger to Edmund Wilson to John Dewey to Leon Trotsky sent greetings. Sam said Carlo would trade all that for the friendship and understanding of his Italian comrades. Still, Carlo had contacts; access to powerful people. Quietly, on the side, many of his L'Adunata haters would approach *the evil compromiser* for a favor. "Carlo, I got something to ask of you heh, heh. My son, he just got out from the can. Can you get him a city job?" Stuff like that. According to Sam, "Carlo never turned them down. And never said a thing about it."

Carlo was murdered Monday, January 11, 1943, at 8:40 pm. Sam found out about it upon returning from work late in the afternoon the next day. There was pain and grief but not quite surprise. Carlo had told Sam often that he did not expect to live long and probably not his natural span. He was profoundly fatalistic. He was in poor health; a lifetime of overeating, smoking, and not taking care of himself had caught up to him. His two brothers, Ettore and Mario, had died of cancer within months of each other, in 1942. And the threats, the constant threats to his life. How long before one of them made good? More than once Sam said Carlo may have welcomed it in a certain sense.

When Sam got the news something like rage came over him. Without thinking, as if driven by compulsion, he boarded the F train three stops to the Cobble Hill section of Brooklyn and the silent L'Adunata hall. A number of comrades sat alone, staring vacantly. They felt terrible, Sam said. No one wanted this to happen to Carlo. But Sam could not, would not, control himself. "Well, the great impediment to the revolution is gone. The traitor holding you back all these years is gone. So, what's stopping you, go make the revolution!" Sam had worked himself into a fury, his sarcasm a lash.

The old men sitting in the silent hall let him go on. Finally, one of them answered, softly, "Sammy, you don't understand. You're not Italian."

You may notice that I have said nothing about who murdered Carlo. Well, there is no suspense to it. Everyone who has investigated the case concludes it was a professional hit man: a Mafioso named Carmine Galante. As to who ordered the hit, there is much disagreement. Carlo had all the right enemies; he was on all the lists. It is interesting that Sam refused to speculate. "What difference does it make?" he said. "The man is dead." Carlo had his dark side, Sam would say sometimes.

I for one agree with Dorothy Gallagher and Nunzio Pernicone that it was a straightforward Mafia hit. About three months before his murder Carlo attacked his nemesis, the publisher Generoso Pope at a public meeting he had not expected him to attend (otherwise Carlo would not have.) "Not only is the fascist Pope, but even his gangster is here." Tresca said in a loud voice. The gangster he referred to was Frank Garafolo, right hand man of Mafia chieftain Joseph Bonanno and a close associate of Pope. "Within a week I'll show Carlo Tresca who I am," Garafolo told those at his table. That's not the half of it. Garafolo flew into a rage soon after and beat his mistress when she disclosed to him that she had appealed to Tresca not to run an embarrassing story about her in *Il Martello* and he complied. *A favor from Tresca regarding his woman?*

The murder took a few months longer.

Dorothy Gallagher mentions in a footnote an incident reported in *Time* magazine that I had read earlier. Turns out that after many years Carmine Galante rose to become boss of the Bonanno crime family. Well, he "got his," classic Mafia style, in a Brooklyn restaurant in 1979, thirty-six years after Carlo. Naturally a crowd formed outside the restaurant as Galante's blood-splattered corpse, wrapped in a blanket, was wheeled on a gurney to the waiting ambulance. From somewhere in the crowd an elderly man emerges; he spits conspicuously on Galante. The reporter smells a story. He approaches the man. "Why?" he asks.

His answer resonates with me. "When I was young I went with Carlo Tresca to break up the fascist meetings in the streets." The old man then stared at the Galante corpse in complete contempt. "He killed a hero and then he sold drugs to school children. So I spit on him."

I do not want to leave Carlo like this. So I save for last a happier time: the day he brought Freddie Miller home. It was Mother's fondest memory of Carlo; she glowed when she spoke of it. I include a photo of Freddie in this book. He is wearing a suit and overcoat and is cradling the infant me in his arms as we stare out across an expanse of Manhattan harbor into the distance. A nice photo, sent to me by Olga Baer, a few years ago. She had been a good friend of my parents and she wanted me to have it, now that she was in her ninetieth year.

Freddie looks healthy, even a tad prosperous, but that is not how he appeared the day Carlo brought him home. A Wobbly from a Pennsylvania mining town, who spoke with a distinctive small town accent, Freddie was an ex-marine, and he knew how to handle a rifle. He had taken that knowledge to Spain where he fought on the side of the anarchists in the Durruti Column, until he was captured and spent a year or so—I do not know precisely how long—in a Franco prison camp. Not a health spa. He was starved, lost his teeth, was beaten with chains. He was among the last prisoners exchanged (Mother said the last) between Franco and the United States following the fall of Spain. He had fought bravely and survived.

Mother remembered Freddie entering through the door of our home: frighteningly thin, looking half dead, with that large head and shining eyes starved people get. Carlo's arm is wrapped around him as he enters, as if he is guarding something precious. Carlo, Freddie, and the half-dozen happy Wobblies that came with them find places around the dining table. Mother sets out the food. She would never forget the expression on Carlo's face, the joy. He sat next to Freddie, one arm loosely around his shoulder. Carlo's other arm was beneath the table and he kept talking so as not to embarrass Freddie as he slipped him a wad of bills thick enough to bulge his pocket.

# 21
## VANGUARD, ETC

Some time back, I took a course in music appreciation at the Julliard School. I remember few of the details but remain impressed by the way the instructor was able to "open up" a complicated piece and reveal its structural elements. Well, it occurs to me that something of that sort may serve as a way to describe Sam's radical activism in the 1920s through the early 1940s. The Wobblies supplied the rhythmic undertone; he never strayed far from their beat. You can say that the Russian, Finnish, Spanish, Latin American, and Italian comrades—whom Paul Avrich might call the "ethnics" because they conducted their meetings in their native languages—supplied the rich orchestration and coloring of his life; his standing was high with all of them. The melody or theme—the scaffolding upon which these other elements rested—consisted of a series of English language groups with a strong Jewish flavor, thoroughly seasoned, to mix metaphors, with discarded anarchists the world over who had washed onto the American shore:

*Road to Freedom* (1920s): Cheeky Sam, having been given his start by Walter Starret Van Valkenburgh, the editor, promptly started his own sheet, *Friends of Freedom*, which lasted a few issues. True to form, Van encouraged him in the endeavor.

The Free Society Group (Chicago, late 20s–late 30s). A polygot group of Jewish, Italian, Spanish, and Russian comrades that held weekly lectures and forums. Free Society was the most active Anarchist organization in the United States and exerted influence beyond its numbers. Sam soapboxed for Free Society in Bughouse Square, and it was at Free Society where he came under the influence of the Russian anarchists, especially Maximoff, as I have described. In 1937, Free Society paid his expenses from New York back to Chicago where he spoke in commemoration of the fiftieth anniversary of the state murder of the Haymarket Martyrs. Less triumphantly, Sam also addressed the Midwest Anarchist Convention, sponsored by Free Society, where he read his anarcho-syndicalist manifesto to a nearly empty hall. A lot more can be said about Free Society, an interesting group in many respects, but I will leave that to the historians.

*Looking Forward* (1932–1934) was basically a mimeo-sheet that Sam, Esther, and a few other comrades put out in protest at the way the Ferrer School and the Stelton Colony were run.

The Vanguard Group and its publication *Vanguard* (1932–1939): In its heyday, the early to late-30s, this was the group and publication Sam was most proud of. He was instrumental in founding it, together with Mark Schmidt, Louis Slater, Abe Bluestein, Sidney Solomon, and Clara Freedman (later Solomon). Sidney had been a high school classmate of Sam's younger brother, my uncle Tommy, who also signed up for a short time. All of them with the exception of Lou Slater who had "issues" with Sam, were household staples of mine growing up.

According to Sam, the group propagated "the ideas of Bakunin and Kropotkin. It disagreed sharply with the Stirnerites, individualists, and bohemians. Under the influence of the Depression, it believed…that…a realistic program of action was needed to win support from the workers and intellectuals, to organize an anarchist-communist (i.e. communalist) federation throughout the United States as a prelude to the social revolution."

Heady stuff coming from a handful of first- and second-generation Jewish kids! The anarchist-Wobbly Franz Fleigler, a few years older, was his usual phlegmatic self. "Who the hell are these snot noses to call themselves a Vanguard? It's pretentious. Change the name!" But he was an active member. And so were they all. They started with a typed mimeographed sheet of a few pages and from that built a well-written, well-edited publication with a peak circulation of several thousand.

Sam was proud of the intellectual content of *Vanguard*. Emma Goldman communicated regularly with the group. Gregorii Maximoff, Rudolf Rocker, Armando Borghi, Augustin Souchy (who was to become a close friend of Sam in later years), Alexander Shapiro, and many others—they all wrote for *Vanguard*. According to Sam, it "was highly regarded as one of the best English-language publications [of its kind] in the world."

Sam specialized in writing about the American labor movement in his regular feature "On the Class War Front." It was the time of the New Deal and the reforms of the Wagner Act, of a new partnership forged between the AFL/CIO and the Roosevelt Administration. Liberals, social democrats, and even some conservative Wobblies and anarchists were ecstatic. Sam for his part saw the government's embrace of the unions as the herding of cattle into the chute.

A privilege granted by the State can as easily be withdrawn, he warned. It was a prescient remark in view of the sorry state of today's mainstream unions—eunuchs standing with a tin cup outside the door of the Democratic Party. The lenient laws of the '30s and '40s that enabled unions to swell their membership have given way to a host of straitjacket regulations. Union membership has shrunk back to where it was a century ago. But to Sam the domestication of the labor movement had implications beyond union issues. You need a militant left, and the IWW was the only organization conceivably up to the task. Many anarchists were purists and disdained the Wobblies for their Marxist tendencies and for what they perceived as their anti-intellectualism.

In 1935 Sam wrote: "Both the CIO and AFL are...intimately connected with the Roosevelt administration and are helping the government to regiment the labor movement into the pattern of emerging state capitalism. The attitude of many anarchists toward the IWW must be changed. The IWW represents most closely in America the type of revolutionary unionism we are talking about."

The collaboration of the AFL/CIO with the Roosevelt Administration was on sickening display two years later during the Spanish Civil War. Three representatives of the largest union of Spain, the CNT—1,500,000—strong, came to the United States to seek the support of the American labor movement. They received none, beyond that of a few fringe groups.

From my perspective, the best quality of the predominantly Jewish group was their tolerance and openness. You must remember the time! Glenn Carrington, a black homosexual wrote regularly for them and was welcomed without the condescension afforded blacks by the communists. And my parents and Abe Bluestein spoke fondly of two Chinese comrades: "Yat Tone and Eddie Wong, who had come from the Equality Group (P'ing-she) in San Francisco." They were dedicated men. Bella Friedman, from Poland, fell in love with Eddie and became Bella Wong.

"My husband was born Wong Chay-tin near Canton in 1900," Bella relates. Rebellious from the start, he cut off his queue (pigtails) as a boy to signify his liberation. "He later took the name Edward from the English Socialist Edward Carpenter." But his father "married him off at seventeen and Eddie hated him for that. He and his wife had a son but separated soon after." Eddie came to San Francisco around 1920. "He lived in humble, unbelievable poverty.... He worked fourteen to sixteen hours a day in the fields, picking peas. When his knees began to bleed he stopped. Then he worked as a busboy in a restaurant for five or six years. During this time he attended night school and engaged in radical agitation, speaking in Chinese on street corners as a soap boxer."

Eddie came to NY in the early '30s: worked as a waiter; joined the Vanguard group; married Bella. The couple moved into an apartment near Ida and Valerio Isca, two very active Vanguard members. Eddie and a few other waiters pooled their money, opened a restaurant, the Jade Mountain, on Second Avenue and 12th street. Naturally, he donated some of the profits regularly to *Vanguard*. Bella recalled that Eddie's "best friend at the time was Yat Tone, a devoted anarchist. Yat held back his own food money and gave it to the movement." He was of medium height, wore glasses, and spoke little English. And Sam recalled sadly that "Yat Tone traveled to Spain in 1933 to be among the anarchists. He then returned to China to set up a Modern School but was arrested and executed."

Mark Schmidt served as *Vanguard*'s internal explosive device. I have described Schmidt warmly, because I remember him that way at our apartment in his later years: a kindly man, good to our family, until Sam finally choked on his Stalinism and they had their falling out. He had been a key founder of *Vanguard* fifteen years or so earlier, wrote under the pen name Senex, and was at first highly respected. Those days he worked as a laborer on the docks, which contrasted with the well-dressed, professorial air he projected in our living room. A brilliant guy, really, and self-educated. Also, pathologically conspiratorial. He set up little spy systems within the group, having Faction A report to him about Faction B: a Stasi bureau of one, especially as he began his drift from anarchism to Stalinism. The atmosphere grew rancid.

No one respected Schmidt more highly than Lou Slater. Lou's best friend from high school—the long defunct Townsend Harris, for "gifted" kids—was Uncle Tommy. He was also close to Sid and Clara Solomon. Lou and Sid looked up to Sam, the Wobbly adventurer, who introduced them to a lifetime of anarchism. But Schmidt became Lou's mentor, confidant, older brother, father figure. So it was natural in those Depression years that Schmidt moved into the apartment of Lou and his companion, Elsie Milstein, also a member of the Vanguard group and a young woman. Do I need tell you what happened next? Elsie switched to Schmidt.

Lou took it as a stab in the back. Engorged with rage, grief, and righteous indignation, he brought the matter before the group, insisted Schmidt be expelled or otherwise censured for unethical behavior. The Vanguard group exploded, the shrapnel flying in all directions. Abe Bluestein said it was a private matter, not the business of the group, and quit in disgust to publish *Challenge*. Others took sides. And here is where Sam lost a friend. Lou described to Sam how the older, more sophisticated man wedged his way between the couple, subtly undermined him, and for one reason: he wanted Elsie. That is why he had moved in. It took him months. Sam told me years later he believed every word Lou said. But there was an important principle at stake: Elsie was not property. She had the right to live with whom she pleased. Lou misinterpreted Sam's stance to mean he was siding with Schmidt. He never spoke to Sam again.

This incident may appear a trivial, long-ago scandal to some, not worth mentioning. I disagree. It raises interesting questions about what is public and what is private in a tightly knit group. It most certainly was not taken as trivial by Vanguard.

I have my own subjective opinion on the matter. A straight right delivered by Lou to Schmidt's highly intellectual nose would have done each of them a world of good. Not that Schmidt's time with Elsie lasted long. They soon split up and the rumor circulated sub rosa through the group that Schmidt was impotent. I might add that Lou Slater was no shrinking violet. In later years, he owned a Brooklyn printing shop. When, in 1973, a gunman burst in and ordered Lou and his partner to put their hands up and face the wall, the crusty old anarchist said, "Why don't you work for a living?" Upon which the gunman opened fire and murdered him.

Mother, circa 1908, standing in front of her parents, Grandmother Ida and Grandfather Abraham, who is holding infant Aunt Sarah in his lap.

Mini me, Stelton Colony, NJ, 1939 or so.

Esther and Sam Dolgoff, March 29th, 1959.

Sam, Mother (holding infant Abe), and Stelton colonists having fun, 1933. Notice Sam's raffish pipe and lean physique.

Sam speaking at Waldheim Cemetery, Chicago, in commemoration of the fiftieth anniversary of the execution of the Haymarket anarchists; November 11, 1937.

Fred Miller, a Wobbly seamen who fought in Spain and survived a Franco prison camp, holding me in his lap as we faced NY Harbor. (Photo, Olga Baer, a talented photographer and wife of Sam's close friend Dave Baer)

The New Society Group, Chicago (1931?). Sam is last fellow on the far left, top row; Maximoff is fourth from right, same row. Rudolf Rocker is the prominent person, third row, third from left. (Photo courtesy of the Kate Sharpley Library)

South Street, early 1940s on the way to the 510 Hall at 134 Broad Street. (Charles Cushman Collection: Indiana University Archives, P02305)

Jews without money. A few buildings up from where our family lived on Clinton Street in the 1940s. (Charles Cushman Collection: Indiana University Archives, P02521)

The great Russian anarchist Gregorii Maximoff, who was Sam's mentor and father figure.

Russell Blackwell, 1950s.

Carlo Tresca, 1910 or so.

Diego Camacho (aka Abel Paz), Liberto Sarrau, and
Federico Arcos on the streets of Barcelona.

Detective examining Carlo Tresca's body January 11, 1943. Photo by Weegee.
(Used by permission from Corbis)

The great Wobbly Ben Fletcher holds Benjamin Harrison Fletcher Homer, Andrew Homer's son.

At an anarchist picnic in the Bronx (June 1956). I am second from left, age nineteen. Russell Blackwell is at my right. The anarchist Sasha Zagar is to my left. Russell's middle son, Arthur Henry, is next to Sasha. The Hispanic boy couched in front of me decided to get into the picture.

*Vanguard*, December 1936 with article by Sam Weiner.

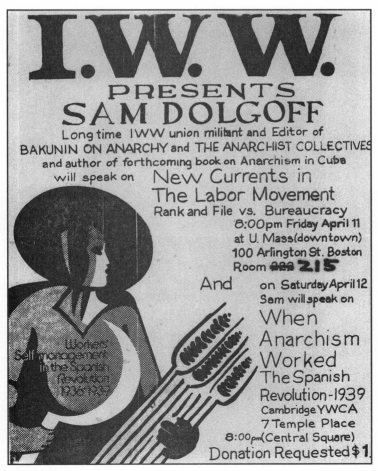

Sam in the 1970s. Still at it. Boston.

Murray Bookchin at an anarchist teach-in, Hunter College, NYC, 1976. (Photo by Mimi Rivera)

Sam and Paul Avrich, far left, at same teach-in as above. Notice Sam's careful attire. Since it was a public meeting, and not at home, he is wearing shoes. (Photo by Mimi Rivera)

Mother and Sam, early 1980s.

**Left to right:** Pura Arcos (who was nearly blind), Federico Arcos, Sam and Mother, at my parent's apartment, NYC, mid-1980s.

Dieter Gebauer, Paul Avrich, and me. Near Columbia University, 2000

Sam. May 11, 1990 in Windsor, Ontario.

Me. July 17, 2015 in Berkeley, California.

# 22
## SERIOUS MATTERS

The Schmidt/Slater incident did the Vanguard group no good. But it was world events that tore it apart. I refer of course to Hitler and the run-up to World War II. So many academic histories; so many grainy images; so many films and memoirs and realistic novels: What is left to say about his rise and the rise of his militaristic, fascist state? Well, I have a few things to say.

Mother spoke often of the guttural, ranting maniac who came to us over the radio. That voice! And of the newsreel footage of obedient throngs shouting "Heil Hitler!" and the goose-stepping soldiers on parade saluting him. The entire spectacle left her in fear and shock—shock, because she considered German culture—its science, its music, its literature—to be the envy of the world: this, despite World War I. And the persecution of the Jews? Unthinkable in such a modern, civilized nation.

Naïve and wrongheaded as Mother's admiration may appear today, it was a view shared by many Jews of her time. Brother Abe's father-in-law, Frank Kagan, was orphaned during World War I and left to wander on the Russian front. A pint-sized boy, big nosed, who spoke mainly Yiddish, it was the German soldiers who kept him alive, adopted him as a mascot. He never forgot the moment one of them handed him an orange. He had never seen such a wonderful thing and the taste, so sweet! Frank was grateful to the German soldiers, remembered them fondly. He simply could not, would not believe that which was unfolding before his very eyes. Until, of course, he did.

To join in the war effort or oppose it? There was no avoiding the issue.

To many Jewish anarchists Franco's conquest of Spain was an open wound. And they were witness to the Japanese murder and enslavement of the Chinese and other Asian peoples. It was their view that the rise of world-wide, aggressive, militaristic fascism should not, could not be seen through the lens of classical anarcho-pacifist theory. But, of course, their argument was based on things deeper than the intellectual, as well it should have. Some Jewish anarchists enlisted. Others joined the merchant marine. Still others took to wearing yarmulkes (traditional skull caps), not out of religion, but in solidarity with their persecuted people.

There were also a sizable number of anarchists, some of them Jewish, who, while appalled at events in Europe and Asia, refused on principle to align themselves with American militarism and the Allied Powers.

Some were committed pacifists who would not kill under *any* circumstance.

Others saw all states as oppressive institutions, and war between them as no business of anarchists. They employed a World War I model to what was happening in Europe and Asia: a fight between imperial powers. The Galleanisti and many of the Spanish anarchists, for example, took a fervent antiwar stand. This, despite the conquest of Italy and Spain by the fascists and their marriage to Hitler.

These arguments raged with concentrated intensity within Vanguard. The contradictions proved too strong. Comrades no longer felt they could work constructively together; indeed they were at cross purposes. The little group, admirable in many ways, collapsed; *Vanguard* ceased publication in 1939 and Vanguard itself faded out of existence by 1941.

My parents did not give up easily and, in 1943, together with the remnants of Vanguard, and other recruits, formed Why?—a name changed shortly thereafter to Resistance (as with Vanguard, both groups brought out publications under the same names). The enterprise was not successful from Mother's, Sam's, and many of the older members' point of view, and they ended it in 1946 or so. For my part, I find the Why?/Resistance groups interesting from today's perspective, although that does not mean my parents and friends were wrong in their opinions.

While I do not agree with the antiwar stance some members of Why?/Resistance took, I do admire their backbone. Dave Koven registered as a Conscientious Objector (CO) when called late in the war, but was fortunate not to be imprisoned. Dave Wieck refused outright to serve and did three years in a Danbury, Connecticut,

Federal Penitentiary. (In a similar vein, Vernon Richards of the London-based Freedom group was imprisoned by British authorities for his antiwar stance.)

The conflict between the "war" and "antiwar" camps within the Why? group grew increasingly bitter and personal, in part, I think, because each side, deep down, could see the other's point of view and thus was not entirely comfortable with its own. I also think that, aside from the war, Why? was torn by generational, cultural, and lifestyle issues. These same issues, played out on a much larger scale, served as well to tear apart the radical movement in the 1960s. One incident in particular crystallized the conflict. You need some background information to appreciate it, so bear with me.

Rudolf Rocker is hardly a household name today even in anarchist circles. Not so during his lifetime. Albert Einstein called his *Nationalism and Culture* (1937) "an extraordinarily original and illuminating work." To Bertrand Russell, Rocker's book was "an important contribution to political philosophy, both on account of its penetrating and widely informative analysis of famous writers, and on account of the brilliant criticism of state-worship, the prevailing and most noxious superstition of our time."

The man's life is worthy of a PhD thesis.

According to Avrich, "Rocker, although a gentile, became the apostle of the [immigrant] Jewish workers of London in the years before the First World War. The story of how he came to Whitechapel and became a Yiddish writer and editor is one of the most fascinating of that period. A German by birth [1873] and upbringing [childhood in a Catholic orphanage] he had not so much as met a Jew until he was eighteen. Yet he settled among the Jews, took one of their daughters as his wife, learned how to speak, read, and write their language and shared in their poverty and suffering." He also led thousands of Jewish textile and garment workers in a series of strikes that tied up factories and shops throughout London and elsewhere.

Rocker and his wife, Milly Witkop, were imprisoned as enemy aliens by British authorities for their opposition to World War I, despite the fact they were equally opposed to the German military machine. Upon release, the couple moved to Berlin, where he became principle founder of the International Working Men's

Association, the so-called Anarcho-Syndicalist International, established in 1922.

In the course of his eventful life—and believe me, I have barely given you a whiff of it—Rocker formed close friendships with the leading, and to my mind legendary, anarchists of the time. People like Peter Kropotkin, Errico Malatesta, Louise Michel, Élisée Reclus, Max Netlau, Fransisco Ferrer, Gustav Landauer, Nestor Makhno, Buenaventura Durruti (in fact, Rocker's son, Fermin, an artist, knew Durruti when he was on the lam from virtually every police department in Europe—and forged the passport that enabled him to remain in Berlin).

When Hitler took power in 1933, Rocker and his wife fled for their lives to Switzerland on the last train out of Berlin. They took with them the clothes on their backs and the manuscript of *Nationalism and Culture*. They were admitted to the United States under the same law that allowed entry to distinguished refugees such as Einstein.

The incident I referred to earlier concerns a speech Rocker gave in Brooklyn before members of the Why? group and other anarchists toward the end of World War II. Rocker made no secret of his views on what the anarchist stance should be: "The present war cannot be measured by the standards of military conflicts of the past." Rather, "the struggle against totalitarian slavery and its bestial achievements is the first duty of our time."

With this stance, Sam readily agreed: there was no other choice. Hitler and his Japanese partners had to be defeated. Period. Their victory meant the end of civilization.

Now I have a question to ask of you. Agree with Rocker or not, do you think a man of his caliber has earned the right to courteous treatment before an anarchist audience? Well, such treatment was not forthcoming. They heckled him. They interrupted him. Instructed with pointed finger where he was "wrong." By "they" I refer to the younger "lifestyle" members of the group. Sam, Mother, Franz Fleigler, and the older, more Wobbly-oriented members, were appalled. The incident stuck in their throats. I heard about it for years. And there, in my view, you have the nub of the generational/lifestyle conflict: the hecklers were interested most of all in ego and self-expression. They did not give a damn about Rocker's reputation—fuck the established norms. On the other hand, my parents, and others, did not think one's ego and self-expression were all important, especially if it came to acting out cruel impulses. They were at heart deeply conservative people; their militancy, paradoxically, grew from their conservative roots.

My parents found the behavior of many "lifestyle" anarchists infuriating and I can see their point. For example, what was one to make of the guy who entered the main lobby of the Metropolitan Museum of Art, dropped his trousers in full view, and proceeded to take a shit, shouting, "This is what I think of your fucking system," as he pulled up his pants? Had "propaganda of the deed" come to this?

Granted this idiot, whose name I do not know, was an outlier. But there was far too much "self-expression" going on for my parents and their friends to feel comfortable. Many of the self-expression types became followers of Dr. Wilhelm Reich. Not the earlier Wilhelm Reich, brilliant colleague of Sigmund Freud, militant, and author of the seminal *The Mass Psychology of Fascism* (in which he drew parallels between Stalinism and Fascism). Rather, they were enamored of the later and—naturally enough—crazy Wilhelm Reich, inventor of the orgone box, within which you sat naked while it focused the cosmic energy of the universe on your orgasm. You see, this cosmic energy was colored blue, which explained the color of the northern lights, the Aurora Borealis. Paul Goodman became a Reichian therapist.

To be fair, Reich and the power of the orgone box were all the rage in the artistic, intellectual, and even some scientific circles of the time. And there is no doubt the U.S. Government's imprisonment and persecution of Reich on fraud charges in the late 1950s was a cruel travesty. But Reich was crazy and my parents could not see what a goddamn box you sat in naked had to do with anarchism, revolution, or social justice. The whole bunch of lifestyle recruits, most of them derived from middle-class, bohemian circles began to repel my parents.

"I am sick and tired of these half-assed artists and poets who reject organization and want only to play with their belly buttons," Sam said to Paul Avrich.

But that was not Sam's full opinion. He was on good terms with many of them and he was especially fond of Paul Goodman. He thought Paul and his brother Percival's *Communitas* a pioneering work as he did Paul's much later book, *Growing Up Absurd*—his deeply felt depiction of the problems facing the young in a regimented society. But Sam could not resist the title. "Your autobiography?" he would ask Paul mischievously, and Paul would answer with an affectionate smile.

Franz Fleigler expressed a harsher judgement of the "lifestyle" anarchists. "There was a certain selfishness or self-centeredness about them, a lack of true compassion and broad humanity. In their crackpot group, a new deity emerged—Wilhelm Reich and his orgone box!... They were seeking adventure, I think. Maybe I had my adventure pounding the seas and they had it in other ways."

Other ways indeed. In 1935, when the chief concern of the State Department was not to antagonize Hitler so that he pay back the First World War debt, and distinguished citizens such as Charles Lindbergh were on good terms with him, Franz and a few comrades boarded the German ocean liner, the *Bremen*, in New York Harbor, and tore down the swastika flag.

To join the merchant marine seemed a suitable compromise for many radicals who did not want to serve in the military. Woody Guthrie is posthumously famous for having "shipped out." But shipping out was no haven; it was easily as dangerous as being in the official navy. The merchant ships that made the North Atlantic crossings of WWII were loaded with the supplies that kept nations alive and armies fighting. They were also ducks in a pond for the free ranging German U-Boat submarines, especially in the early years of the war. Life for the seaman working one of these defenseless ships was an exercise in sustained fear—a prolonged game of Russian roulette played with exploding torpedoes. It was pure chance. Many a ship went down in sight of the East Coast, and many a merchant seaman's body washed ashore, Wobblies among them. The North Route, whereby supply convoys reached the Soviet port of Murmansk via the Arctic, was especially hellish. Murmansk was open for only a few months of the year before freezing over and the merchant ships had to run the gauntlet of the German Navy to get there. Franz served as helmsman on the lead ship of the first convoy going in.

And in the aftermath of the war, thousands of Jews—men, women, children—were left to rot in the camps. No nation wanted them, least of all the British who blockaded entry to Palestine. This is of course well known, and the cause of the Jews to enter Palestine and kick out the British was supported by radicals at the time, including the IRA! What is not well known is the role of the Wobblies in defying that blockade. I knew a half-dozen who did precisely that—most fondly, three short, barrel-chested seamen, so close in friendship that nature was cruel in not making them brothers: Franz Fleigler, Ed Mitchell, and Dave Baer. They were a constant presence in my childhood and later years. Hardly a day passed without seeing at least one of them around our kitchen table or in our tiny living room, or, on an odd Sunday, at the Five-Ten Hall. That is, when they were not at sea. (More about Ed and Dave later.)

Franz? I concentrate—and the damnedest image pops into my head. Totally symbolic, it is piece of grilled steak. Not the tender portion, but the bone and gristle. The hard to chew stuff that wedges between your teeth. There you have Franz, not the ingratiating type, whose every word seemed to have escaped the side of his mouth. He was the kind of fellow you liked in spite of himself! Nothing of the venal, brutal side of human nature surprised him. But he served as Captain of that leaky bucket, the *Josiah Wedgwood*, and smuggled its suffering cargo past the British war ships to Haifa—which made him the quarry of a British manhunt. That was 1946, one year before the voyage of the more famous *Exodus*. It is said Leon Uris modeled one of the characters in his novel of the same name after Franz.

Franz's gentle wife Gussie bounced me on her lap when I was an infant and cared for me as if I were her own son. She died suddenly of leukemia around 1971. There is no describing the depth of Franz's grief. He survived her three decades but never remarried and would not be consoled. The tough Wobbly-anarchist with the soft heart.

# SAM'S VIEWS ON THE WAR

It should be clear at this stage that I am no historian—a teller of tales (true as far as I know) is more like it. But I think few would disagree that WWII was the most shattering event in history measured in terms of geographic scope, its destructive scale, the number of deaths—military and civilian—and in terms of its utter sadism, racism, and savagery. Who could imagine that it would reduce World War I, which ended a mere twenty years earlier, to the status of a dress rehearsal or warm-up act? One would have to go back to the bubonic plagues of the Middle Ages to find a human catastrophe to rival it. No surprise then that in the War's wake and in the reconstruction that followed, thoughtful people would draw differing conclusions concerning the War's meaning, and the course of action anarchists should follow.

Put yourself in the place of Rudolf Rocker, Diego Abad de Santillan, Augustin Souchy—European men who had been dedicated anarchists through two wars, two revolutions, the rise and fall of fascism and, in their time, the all-powerful Communist State. They had seen enough suffering and suffered enough personally. By comparison the Western Democracies, instrumental in defeating Germany and Japan, seemed a plausible compromise. That is, they came to reject revolution as a means of social change. In the advanced nations of the United States and Europe, they contended, there exists a tradition of civil liberties and freedom of expression that allows one to work peacefully within the system toward the realization of anarchist ideals. "Evolution rather than revolution."

Sam drew different conclusions in the wake of the War. It was fortunate in his view that the political and military imperatives of the Allies happened to coincide with the defeat of fascism: that humanity persevered over barbarism. But there was nothing inevitable about that alignment. Freedom and morality and humanitarian values are not inherent qualities of the Western Democracies and certainly not the motivating factors of foreign policy. A different set of military and political circumstances could have easily mandated a different set of alignments. Well into the 1930s, you can find any number of admiring comments concerning Mussolini's Italy and Hitler's Germany from representatives of these self-same democracies. On the eve of World War II, Chamberlain signed a pact with Hitler. Was it a maneuver, with the tacit approval of the U.S. and France, to direct Hitler's fury to the East? Chamberlain, Roosevelt, and the "socialist" Leon Blum, to their shame, also made the conscious decision to let Republican Spain die.

As for officially sanctioned atrocities, the allies committed their share: The Dresden destruction; the induced famines of India due to the diversion of grain shipments to English troops; the fire-bombings of Hamburg, Tokyo; and, of course, Hiroshima and Nagasaki. I cannot convey to you Sam's revulsion after the A-bombs were dropped. Forty years later nothing changed him on that score. I remember mentioning the pressures on Truman that led to his decision (though Sam added racism and vengeance to my list). I mentioned the American troops waiting to land, the immense American casualties certain to occur, the terrified young soldiers on the ships who exploded in cheers at the news the bombs were dropped. What choice did Truman have, I asked?

I remember my father pausing for a moment and then twisting his torso as if freeing himself from a physical constraint. And he spat out the words as he spoke: "I am not Harry Truman. I don't care about his choices. The man dropped an A-bomb. That's all that matters!"

Sam saw WWII as a form of realignment. He predicted that from its ashes would emerge the Cold War, Mao's China, and an American Empire, oligarchic at home and militaristic abroad. So he respectfully disagreed with the "live and let live" attitude of his old comrades.

Better than trying to describe precisely what the National Confederation of Labor—known by all as the CNT—meant to Sam, I can tell you Sam's favorite story regarding that great union. It is several years before the Spanish Revolution and the government has decided to build a new prison. Which it does. However, the last phase involves installing the iron bars. But, you see the iron workers are members of the CNT; they do not believe in prisons. So, you wound up with a brand-new prison devoid of bars! Which rendered it useless, of course. I can still see that mischievous light in Sam's eyes. As with the IWW, the spirit of independence pulsed through the arteries of the CNT. The CNT was an anarchist union. Nobody gave these men orders.

Am I being tedious if I mention again that such was my parents' devotion to the cause of the Spanish Revolution that they saddled me with the middle name Durruti? Well, their devotion went deeper than a name. I was conceived on or about the official birth date of the Revolution, July 19, 1936. No accident, there: a new son, dedicated to their faith in the new society forged in anarchist Spain. With Mother and father long gone now, my dear brother Abe reminds me gently of this fact.

I remember Federico Arcos up on the platform at Sam's memorial service in 1990 as he struggled to convey to a modern New York audience what it was like to live through a genuine and complete social revolution. Federico is a short, solidly built, gray-haired man, wears glasses. He speaks softly, his cadence more Spanish than English, and you can sense his frustration getting the right words across. Finally, he faces us square on, leans forward with clenched fist, his voice rising in exaltation, "You have no idea what truly free feels like. No authority above you, no one below you. To walk down the street and meet each man's eye."

Federico was speaking of the streets of Barcelona, his boyhood home. Many people have described what that special freedom feels like, of course. This famous passage from Orwell's *Homage to Catalonia* brings it home to me:

> Barcelona was something startling and overwhelming. It was the first time that I had ever been in a town where the working class was in the saddle. Practically every building of any size had been seized by the workers and was draped with red flags and with the red and black flag of the anarchists; every wall was scrawled with...the initials of the revolutionary parties.... Churches here and there were being systematically demolished by gangs of workmen. Every shop and cafe had an inscription saying that it had been collectivized; even the bootblacks had been collectivized and their boxes painted red and black. Waiters and shop-walkers looked you in the face and treated you as an equal. Servile and even ceremonial forms of speech had temporarily disappeared. Nobody said "Señor" or "Don" or even "Usted"; everyone called everyone else "Comrade" or "Thou," and said "Salud!" instead of "Buenos días"... almost my first experience was receiving a lecture from a hotel manager for trying to tip a lift-boy. There were no private motor-cars, they had all been commandeered, and the trams and taxis and much of the other transport were painted red and black. The revolutionary posters were everywhere, flaming from the walls in clean reds and blues that made the few remaining advertisements look like daubs of mud. Down the Ramblas, the wide central artery of the town...crowds of people streamed constantly to and fro.... Except for a small number of women and foreigners there were no "well-dressed" people at all. Practically everyone wore rough working-class clothes, or blue overalls or some variant of militia uniform. All this was queer and moving. There was much in this that I did not understand, in some ways I did not even like it, but I recognized it immediately as a state of affairs worth fighting for...so far as one could judge the people were contented and hopeful. There was no unemployment, and the price of living was still extremely low; you saw very few conspicuously destitute people, and no beggars.... Above all, there was a belief in the revolution and the future, a feeling of having suddenly emerged into an era of equality and freedom. Human

beings were trying to behave as human beings and not as cogs in the capitalist machine.

Some pages later, Orwell adds: "As far as my purely personal preferences went, I would have liked to join the anarchists."

Orwell is describing his impressions of Barcelona. The revolution went deeper and was more transformative. This passage from the historian Gaston Leval, a close observer and participant, gives a sense of its scope:

> In Spain during almost three years, despite a civil war that took a million lives, despite the opposition of the political parties (republicans, left and right Catalan separatists, socialists, Communists, Basque and Valencian regionalists, petty bourgeoisie, etc.), this idea of libertarian communism was put into effect. Very quickly more than 60% of the land was collectively cultivated by the peasants themselves, without landlords, without bosses, and without instituting capitalist competition to spur production. In almost all the industries, factories, mills, workshops, transportation services, public services, and utilities, the rank and file workers, their revolutionary committees, and their syndicates reorganized and administered production, distribution, and public services without capitalists, high salaried managers, or the authority of the state.
>
> Even more: the various agrarian and industrial collectives immediately instituted economic equality in accordance with the essential principle of communism, "From each according to his ability and to each according to his needs." They coordinated their efforts through free association in whole regions, created new wealth, increased production (especially in agriculture), built more schools, and bettered public services. They instituted not bourgeois formal democracy but genuine grassroots functional libertarian democracy, where each individual participated directly in the revolutionary reorganization of social life. They replaced the war between men, "survival of the fittest," by the universal practice of mutual aid, and replaced rivalry by the principle of solidarity....

This experience, in which about eight million people directly or indirectly participated, opened a new way of life to those who sought an alternative to anti-social capitalism on the one hand, and totalitarian state bogus socialism on the other.

War between men replaced by the universal practice of mutual aid, rivalry replaced by the principle of solidarity: These are the things that gave meaning to Sam's life, and to Mother's as well. And so the events of 1936 forced my parents to face a wrenching dilemma. Sam felt compelled to join the revolution in Spain. Mother understood this. But she was pregnant (with me) and Abe was barely three years old. We had nothing, even by Depression standards. One might comment in retrospect that there were ways to express joy at the dawning of the New Age other than getting Mother knocked-up, but human beings are not usually logical, are they? The guilt Sam felt was overwhelming, but he nevertheless made the decision to go. Despite the pain, mother supported him in this. How she and Abe were to live I do not know. Sam literally packed his bags—or I should say bag, because there was not a hell of a lot to take. He was *that* close to leaving for Spain, but then comrades intervened.

I mentioned earlier that Carlo Tresca felt protective toward Sam and he showed that side of himself again. "Sammy, they don't need blind house painters. They got plenty of men. You do more good here!"

His advice was not strong enough. What convinced Sam were discussions with his old friend from the Free Society Group in Chicago, Maximiliano Olay, a Spanish anarchist born in Asturias who came to the U.S. before World War I and spread anarchist propaganda among the cigar workers, at the waterfront, and any place the Wobblies and the Latin American anarchists needed him. In later years, he operated a translation bureau in Chicago, but when the revolution broke out he became the representative of the CNT in New York. Olay advised Sam against going. So did Marcelino García, editor of *Cultura Proletaria*, the leading Spanish anarchist publication in North America. You could not find men more informed about the situation on the ground in Spain. The anarchists did not lack for men, they told Sam. The anarchists lacked arms and money and support. Sam could put himself to far better use if he were to publicize their cause in the U.S. Not the Republican cause. The Anarchist Cause. Do not go to Spain, they told Sam. Stay here!

So Sam stayed and was a key participant in what is in my opinion one of the finest things the American anarchist movement did in the twentieth century: With Spain in revolution, the anarchists tossed aside their differences in language, culture, lifestyle, political philosophy, and other petty bullshit and combined to form the United Libertarian Organizations (ULO), which operated out of Wobbly/Anarchist headquarters at 94 Fifth Avenue. Russell Blackwell, who fought in Spain and was an astute observer of the time, has this to say about the ULO:

> The United Libertarian Organizations embraced the Jewish Anarchist Federation (publishers of *Freie Arbeiter Stimme*), the Russian Federation (Dielo Truda), the Vanguard group, several branches of the Industrial Workers of the World (IWW), a federation of Spanish-language groups publishing *Cultura Proletaria*, Carlo Tresca's group publishing the Italian newspaper *Il Martello*, several Canadian anarchist groups, some Italian groups in New England, and a scattering of others. Although not actually affiliated, the Gillespie, Illinois branch of the Progressive Mine Workers of America contributed substantially through a regular monthly assessment on its membership. [Sam's old friend from his Wobbly coal mining days, John Bautello, was secretary.] Mass meetings were held in many cities and thousands of dollars were collected.

Sam wrote that, "According to the U.S. State Department, which ruled that all organizations collecting funds for antifascist Spain must report how much was actually sent to Spain and how much was retained for expenses, the Communist Party-dominated Committee to Aid Spanish Democracy transmitted only ten cents of every dollar collected to Spain and ninety cents of every dollar went to 'expenses.' The ULO, on the contrary, sent every cent collected to Spain with no deductions for expenses." The Communist Party swindle is no surprise to those who have followed them through the years. They pulled the same crap when they exploited the Sacco-Vanzetti case to their advantage and never accounted for the funds. But financial dishonesty was of course the least of their betrayals.

I bring up finances because Sam collected most of the money that went to the ULO. That is, he hit the road again, as he had years earlier for the IWW—up and down the east coast and as far west as St. Louis. Street corners, union halls, private settings, wherever a crowd, or not so much of a crowd, would hear him. He flopped in comrades' homes, and when not available, flea-bag hotels. No money for expenses, as I have stated, all out of the pocket of a Depression-era house-painter. I've asked Abe how we lived and for the life of him to this day he doesn't know. Seems Sam took jobs on short notice he could finish quickly. He'd work a few days, slip Mother the money and he was off.

But fundraising was not Sam's only concern. He served on the editorial board of *Spanish Revolution*, which is considered today perhaps the finest running account in English of that revolution—in other words of the reconstruction of society according to anarchist principles. *Spanish Revolution* was a monthly that ran from 1936 to 1938 until the revolution was deemed lost and funds dried up. It was concerned not with battles, covered in the everyday press, but with the issues for which the battles were fought, which the press ignored: the constructive and economic achievements of the revolution. The format and articles of the paper seem blunt and harsh viewed by today's standards but not through the eyes of those engaged in a life and death struggle: Peasants Build a New Economy; Statistics on Industrial Socialization in Catalonia; Organizing the Textile Industry; Industrial Democracy; Running a Department Store; Telephone System Run by Workers; the Peasant Communes in Aragon; etc. Taken together, they stand as a refutation to a major, and crippling, charge against anarchism and anarchists: That they were—and are—impractical dreamers and anarchism can never work.

Fenner Brockway was Secretary of the Independent Labor Party (the ILP) in England. He traveled to Spain after the May events in Catalonia (1937) and he had this to say: "There are still some Britishers and Americans who regard the anarchists of Spain as impossible, undisciplined, and uncontrollable. This is poles away from the truth. The anarchists of Spain, through the C.N.T., are doing one of the biggest constructive jobs ever done by the working class. At the front they are fighting Fascism. Behind the front they are actually constructing the new Workers' Society. They see that the war against Fascism and the carrying through of the Social Revolution are inseparable."

Sam recalls that, "When Barcelona fell, according to Rocker, who was with him at the time, Maximiliano Olay burst into tears."

He was not alone. One can well understand the tears, and the sense of betrayal that arose among the surviving comrades in the face of bitter defeat. I have heard and read innumerable discussions of Spain and the Revolution down through the years. Save for Sam's *The Anarchist Collectives*, published in 1974, few were devoted to the constructive work that went on. Instead they turn on this question: In the face of Franco's invasion, was the anarchist leadership correct in joining the Republican Government, as they did, or should they have stayed out and fought the fascists independently? It is a sulfurous argument. Many comrades I respect—Federico Arcos, Russell Blackwell, Abel Paz, for example—were in Spain at the time and state categorically that the anarchists should never have joined the government and carried out their dictates; it was the death knell of the Revolution. That is also the undying opinion of *Freedom's* Vernon Richards and Sam's sometime friend and crusty antagonist, Murray Bookchin.

I see their point. However, and while I am no expert, I ask myself whether the choice was that simple. A well-armed fascist army, supported by Hitler and Mussolini, was driving across Spain. With what were the anarchists to fight? Their pitchforks, their shoes? Excepting courage, they lacked for everything. There were no guns, tanks, petrol. Another point, often overlooked by critics: though powerful, the anarchists were no means the majority of the Spanish population. Were they, in this desperate situation, to ignore that fact and go their own way? And what of the CNT? To restructure the economy—and society—the membership may well have agreed with, but how long would they have agreed with a policy that remained aloof from the rest of the antifascist population while Franco slaughtered his way to Madrid and Barcelona? So, in the hope of fielding a well-armed united front, the leadership joined forces reluctantly to what they thought was a coalition government capable of attracting the support of England, France, and the United States. Agree with this decision or not, is it reasonable to call it a "betrayal"?

Sam thought not. On this he ran afoul of Murray and Vernon Richards, and even his dear friend Federico. The record showed, he said many times, that most of the anarchists in the Republican Government were sincere comrades and those executed by Franco died bravely. It was not true that most became corrupt and bureaucratic and lost sympathy with the Revolution. Sam did not like the idea of scapegoating and slandering people, many of whom were not in the position to answer. Was it wrong to join the government? Probably. Was it wrong not to join the government? Probably. Sam's overarching view from the perspective of many years after the event was deeply pessimistic: the Revolution was doomed from the start. The Western democracies were not going to intervene to save the Republic. And suppose, by some miracle, the Revolution survived. Does anyone seriously believe England, France, and the United States would tolerate an anarchist society in their midst? They'd rather have the fascists!

# 25

# THE COMMIES

The true betrayal of Spain came from Stalin and his followers. Or is "worshipers" the better word? The record is absolutely clear. I quote here passages taken from two essays. They were written by a man you can trust, as I will explain later.

> Russian state policy at that time was based on the formation of Peoples Fronts in all countries. This meant alliances with such diverse elements as Chiang Kai Shek, Franklin D. Roosevelt, Fulgencio Batista and Leon Blum, and a denial of revolution everywhere including Spain. The Stalinists claimed that in Spain there was purely and simply a civil war between democracy and fascism, and that to work for a social revolution was "counter-revolutionary...."
>
> They entrenched themselves by appealing to the capitalist and petty-bourgeois elements, recruiting thousands of the latter into their party, and into "unions" and auxiliary front groups to serve their purposes. From a small minority party they became a powerful movement....
>
> Eventually they were able to crush the revolution, largely through political and military blackmail. Stalin's Russia sent in a limited amount of supplies, always paid for in gold in advance, and on condition that Stalinist policy be followed. Their personnel flooded Spain. Starting with technicians and advisors, they shortly introduced the GPU [the Soviet secret police] and its methods of terror against the revolutionary movement. The libertarians were no match for the Bolsheviks in political intrigue. For the sake of a false unity against fascism, the libertarians yielded one revolutionary position after the other until the revolution was lost. And with the revolutionary fervor gone, the military fight against Franco (an unequal one at best) was also lost.

[The ULO's *Spanish Revolution*, however, was no rubber stamp.]

...The editors of the paper [Sam being an influential one] found it impossible not to criticize their Spanish comrades. In the issue of January 8, 1937, Emma Goldman attacked the softness of the anarchists in yielding to the Stalinist pressure and political blackmail. Other material in the same vein is to be found in succeeding issues, and there is a rising tone of criticism.

*Spanish Revolution* reported step-by-step the unfolding of events, the developing political crises, and the barricade struggle of the May Days, 1937, in Barcelona. The latter marked the last point at which the Stalinists could have been crushed and the revolution possibly saved.

After the May Days, the Largo Caballero government was overthrown by the Stalinists and replaced by the Government of Juan Negrin. This regime, heralded as the "Government of Victory" by the Communists and by itself, proceeded to lose the war piecemeal, due largely to the demoralizing effect of its anti-revolutionary policies on the morale of a revolutionary people.

Upon taking power, Negrin crushed the POUM [the anti-Stalinist Workers Party of Marxist Unification, a relatively small but influential group] and brought its leaders to trial as fascist agents, just as many of the Old Bolsheviks in the Soviet Union had been framed and liquidated by Stalin, accused of being Hitler's agents. The Russian GPU operated actively and almost openly in Spain. Andrés Nin of the POUM and many anarchists as well as a number of foreigners of anti-Stalinist Marxist groups, were murdered by its agents.

The CNT now went into open opposition where it was joined by the Left Socialists around Largo Caballero. [But it was too late. One of Sam's recurring regrets was that the CNT "didn't turn around and give those Commie bastards a dose."] The repression reached mammoth proportions. The press censorship was crippling and the anarchists and socialists issued illegal papers in order not to lose their identities altogether. The Stalinist International Brigades were taken into Aragon to smash the peasant collectives by force of arms.

# 26

# RUSSELL (PART ONE)

The above passages are from *The Spanish Revolution Revisited* by Russell Blackwell, as well as from his introduction to a collection of the ULO's bulletins on the Revolution. Both were published in 1968, the year before he died. He and Edna were close friends of my parents. I shared the same bed on occasion with their eldest, Steve, at an age when we were barely toilet trained, and Russell remained a fixture in my life into my twenties. It is tempting at this point for me to go on about Russell. His life could comfortably fill three novels: his youth in the 1920s as an organizer for the Communist Party in Mexico, Guatemala, and Honduras; his middle period when he stowed away on the French luxury liner the *Normandy* to get to Spain, hooked up with the POUM, switched to the anarchists, was wounded on the barricades of Barcelona, and barely escaped execution by the GPU at the intervention of the U.S. Secretary of State; and his later period, when he and my parents founded the Libertarian League; and a hell of a lot more. Yes, it is tempting to go on about Russell. I will remain relatively disciplined, however.

Russell is not alone in calling the Barcelona events of early May 1937, the turning point of the Revolution. You can read the accounts of Augustin Souchy and George Orwell, for example. From 1936 and up to May, the Stalinists had been gathering strength; their military and assassination squads were functioning well, and they were starting to dominate the government. They had been chipping away at the anarchist system of workers control throughout Spain. The anarchists put up with these provocations so as not to destabilize the United Front. But matters came to a head in May when the communists assaulted the Telephone Exchange in Barcelona, which was under control of the CNT, and attempted to expel the workers. The entire city rose in spontaneous revolt. Barricades went up. There followed a period of fierce street fighting, the POUM and CNT on one side, the well-armed Stalinists and police, far smaller in number, on the other. And, the anarchist leadership, those who had joined the government, blinked. They negotiated, agreed to a shitty compromise, which was not a compromise because it affirmed the authority of the government—and therefore the Stalinists, over the CNT.

Russell was there from start to finish. That is where he saw the whole sorry business unfold. Outside the Telephone Exchange. In the streets. That is where he was wounded. That is where he became an anarcho-syndicalist and cast his lot with the Friends of Durruti, a no-compromise band of rebels within the CNT opposed to joining the government. Among them, though Russell did not know them at the time, were the teenagers Federico Arcos and Abel Paz. Russell proclaimed many times it was the last chance the anarchists had to crush the communists or at least beat them back. If not a sell-out by the anarchists of the United Front, it was a gross miscalculation of what the May Days meant.

Russell was hunted for months following the May Days. In time, he was arrested and confined to a prison in Madrid. The American Council in Valencia secured his release on the understanding he be placed on an English ship bound for Marseilles. But the GPU boarded the ship in port and brought Russell to a dungeon for two months where he was beaten and tortured, before being put on trial for treason. This was tantamount to a death sentence. However, Edna raised heaven and hell in the States and managed to enlist the support of important people on the liberal and noncommunist left. Their appeals reached the U.S. Secretary of State who intervened on Russell's behalf. The Stalinists did not want to antagonize the U.S. and the GPU was ordered to ease-up; there were plenty of others to murder. And so they found Russell not guilty at trial, and he was returned to the States in early 1939.

I feel a swell of emotion when I see Russell's picture on the Internet. It is all there: the patrician WASP manner; tall, slightly stooped posture; the threadbare gray suit and vest he seemed always to wear; the large nose and large hat from the 1940s that seem of one piece; the kindly face, the charm of the man. You have probably gathered by this time that Russell was not easily silenced. He spoke out against the role of the communists in Spain immediately upon returning to the States. The domestic communists did not like what he had to say. And, please, these were not the gentle Jewish "misguided" communists of a "red diaper baby" memoir—the kind of people Vivian Gornick and Carl Bernstein describe. These were a different breed. So this is how they replied to the man. They attacked from behind while he was out walking one day. They punched and kicked him until he lay on the pavement semi-conscious. But one should not conclude from this that they lacked compassion, because Steve was left unharmed in the baby-carriage Russell was pushing at the time.

# 27
## LINCOLN BRIGADES - MEDIA

This is not an "objective" memoir. I have warned you of that from the beginning. So, bear with me while I ventilate on a subject dear to my spleen: The Abraham Lincoln Brigade. I have seen its veterans over the years taking credit as the brave antifascists, lone defenders of the Spanish Republic. I have seen them hijack public meetings, basking in the applause of an ignorant audience. I have seen the documentaries, the panels, the symposiums. Their exploits have passed into myth. And please do not misread my intentions. Many of these men were indeed brave and idealistic. Why, after all, would one go? Nor do I object to an old-timer, so few of them left, getting his moment in the sun. At some place, at some time, however, reality must enter the picture. The Lincoln Brigade was part of the International Brigades, an organization founded, controlled, and dominated by the Soviet Union. This passage, taken from "The Spanish Revolution: A brief introduction" by Charlatan Stew, describes matters well.

> The daily experiences of the Lincoln Brigade participants generally differed significantly from both those of Spanish and non-Spanish fighters in the popular militias. Jason Gurney, in *Crusade in Spain*...notes that the International Brigades claimed to be a "people's army." Nevertheless, it more closely resembled a professional military because of its openly hierarchical, authoritarian military officer structure. Gurney gives many examples of participants' reports of officers demanding absolute obedience and openly resenting questions from the ranks. Gurney also notes that the officers at company and platoon level were chosen for their political views and connections. Only Communist Party members were trusted to hold senior positions.
>
> Cecil Eby in *Between the Bullet and the Lie: American Volunteers in the Spanish Civil War*...found that some volunteers

had been affiliated with non-Communist socialist or anarchist organizations, such as the Wobblies, and others were not affiliated with any group. However, they generally reported that the Lincoln Brigade, as part of the International Brigades, was always under the management of the Communists.

Those in the Lincoln Brigades who did not submit to discipline were severely punished. And punished is a kind word. Many were hunted down and assassinated; the GPU was relentless. The victim need not have been a Wobbly or a Socialist. Some were simply men of goodwill who came to Spain to fight fascists. My colleague, Harold Lipson, was one of these. "It was a reign of terror," he said, and he fled from the Brigade—alone, knowing little Spanish, and broke. He believed to the day of his death years later in New York, that he owed his life to a brave Spanish lady, who, understanding his desperation hid him out until he could escape. So spare me the Lincoln Brigades! As for their parent outfit, the International Brigades, I mention again Russell Blackwell's account that "The Stalinist International Brigades were taken into Aragon to smash the peasant collectives by force of arms." A Brigade capable of that is capable of anything.

I find galling the praise afforded the communists by "liberals," "objective scholars," and various media types.

They, the communists, are presented as the true antifascists who fought for democracy! We should be grateful! It is a form of collective brain-lock of the same type that continues to venerate Mao and that bogus folk hero Che. And while I am in the combative mood, I will say a few words about the esteem afforded Ernest Hemingway, champion of the Spanish Republic! Spain was the ideal stage for him to prove that the hair on his chest was indeed real and not pasted, as Max Eastman suggested. Hemingway was held in universal low regard by those anarchists and Wobblies who knew him in Spain. Holed up in the best Madrid hotels, in tight with Stalinist operatives, commandeering the best wines, his favorite maneuver was to befriend some poor devil removed from the front, ply him with wine and maybe a hot meal, and file his story as a dispatch. Although Sam respected the Hemingway of the Nick Adams stories, and *The Sun*

*Also Rises*, he called his Spain opus, *For Whom the Bell Tolls*, "senti-mental drivel." Federico Arcos for his part regarded the book with a detached contempt. "Can you imagine the Spanish anarchists (!) need a guy come all the way from Montana to teach us how to use explosives!" he spat out in rapid spanglish. Taken that way the plot does seem a touch implausible—and patronizing.

The Spanish anarchists who draw occasional mention from the liberal media and "objective" scholars are too often depicted as impractical church burners: Violent dreamers. If only they had listened to the dictates of Stalin and obliterated their revolution to his specifications. This was the opinion of Sir Raymond Carr, historian and practical guy, who seems oblivious, for all his wisdom, that Stalin signed his pact with Hitler three months after the defeat of the Republic.

# 28

# SPANISH EPILOGUE

The official end of the Spanish Civil War was 1939. The War in Europe ended in 1945. The former is often referred to as a warm up or unofficial start of the latter, and most historians and journalists let it go at that. The two wars are treated as separate, distinct events. However, that is not how the anarchists and militant defenders of the Spanish Republic saw things. Some quarter of a million refugees (a conservative estimate) fled across the Pyrenees to southern France in the wake of Franco's triumph. They were confined to camps no better than prisons. Democratic France fell soon after and was replaced by the puppet Vichy regime; by 1942 the German Army occupied Vichy territory. To the Spanish anarchists fascism was fascism! They formed the backbone of the "French" resistance and were responsible for the liberation of countless French towns including Toulouse and of course Paris. They were the first ones in.

Indeed, the first units to enter Paris and reach the Hôtel de Ville were anarchists who comprised the Ninth Tank Company of the French Second Armored Division. You can see in the old photographs the names of the Spanish battlefields painted on their tanks—"Guadalajara," "Teruel," "Madrid," and "Ebro." Some 3,200 served, many of them veterans of the Durruti Column. They went on to help liberate Strasbourg and, irony of irony, ended their campaign by calling at the "Eagles Nest"—that is Hitler's idyllic retreat at Berchtesgaden. Too bad he was not home.

> Captain Raymond Dronne, commander of the 9th Company, remembers that the Spanish anarchists were "both difficult and easy to command." In accordance with their libertarian principles, "it was necessary that they accept for themselves the authority of their officers.... They wished to understand the reason for that which was asked of them." However, "...when they granted their confidence it was total and complete." "They were almost all anti-militarists, but they were magnificent

soldiers, valiant and experienced. If they had embraced our cause spontaneously and voluntarily it was [because] it was the cause of liberty. Truly they were fighters for liberty."

In all, 25,000 Spaniards (conservatively) died fighting the Nazis or in concentration camps such as Dachau and Mauthausen.

With the German surrender in 1945 many of the Spaniards again turned their attention to Spain and to the unfinished business of overthrowing Franco. The anarchist tank brigades turned from Paris and Germany back to the Pyrenees. It was a plausible objective. Without the support of Hitler and Mussolini, Franco was vulnerable. But they needed the help of the allies and that did not happen.

I have a photograph of three sixteen-year-old boys, strutting proudly together down a street in Barcelona. It is 1936. Federico Arcos gave it to me. One of them is Federico. The other is Diego Camacho, who in later years would go on to become the great historian of the Revolution, writing under the pen name Abel Paz. The third is Liberto Sarrau; notice the name, *Liberto*. You can see their pride, their affection for one another. Confined to a French refugee camp with the fall of the Republic, they slipped back into Spain in 1942 and joined the underground. Franco's police closed in. Diego was captured eventually and did eleven years in a Franco prison, as did Liberto, who was captured some years later. Federico managed to escape. He kept battling until his recent death at age ninety-four.

# 29

# FAMILY STUFF - OSCAR - RED

My maternal grandparents died before I was born, as did my father's mother, Anna. Grandfather Max I knew only slightly and that when he was old, unhappy, and sick. Abe and I had a fair share of uncles and aunts. We saw them from time to time, but were not close. Geographical separation and the separation of politics isolated us. My parents, and therefore Abe and I, were radioactive to my uncles on both sides of the family, because they held sensitive Government jobs during the time of Senator Joseph McCarthy and the red hunters.

I remember Uncle Sid, a government scientist, hunched around our kitchen table, speaking to Mother in plaintive yet defiant tones: "The day I can't visit my own sister, that's enough!" But they mostly stayed away. There were other reasons as well. Mother could be hell on wheels to the inherently unworthy women who had the temerity to entrap her innocent, godlike brothers in marriage (never mind they seemed happy; they were deluded). And, as I have said, Mother's siblings, respectable first-generation strivers, were scandalized that she had run off with a Wobbly, a filthy hobo house painter!

Mother regarded Rose and Elaine, Sam's sisters, from a lofty height. It was not Mother at her best. As for me, I liked them both. They were unpretentious and native-smart in a way mother was not. They were of a generation, and culture, that regarded marriage as a woman's first imperative, though both worked hard. To discuss their lives takes us too far afield even for this rambling memoir. I confine myself to a single anecdote.

Rose and her husband owned a neighborhood hardware and knick-knack store in Hoboken, New Jersey. Hoboken is a narrow strip of a town sandwiched between the Palisades Cliffs and the Hudson River that faces the lower Manhattan skyline. In those days, the early 1930s, it was a gritty, grainy Italian community: overcrowded, working class, tightly knit. Rose became friendly with

Dolly Sinatra, a woman her age who dropped by the store from time to time. Dolly was a nurse of some kind, active in local Democratic Party politics, and leaned quite far to the left. Her only child showed talent with pad and pencil, and her ambition was to make him an architect or at least a good draftsman. But her plans for him were not working out.

"I don't know what to do about my Frankie," Dolly would lament to Rose, "All he wants to do is sing songs and hang out with bums!"

Rose told that story with relish. Then she would add that Dolly was the community fixer. She would arrange abortions for the women. It was an open secret she was proud of.

"Do you know what it was like in those days if an Italian girl got pregnant? Not married? My God!" Rose said. "They'd throw her out on the street! And the family! The disgrace! Even the married women went to Dolly. So many kids, so poor! The women couldn't stand it!"

The Wobblies were my true extended family. No doubt they set a bad example, none worse than Oscar Sokol: elderly, short, bald, brusque of manner, with a German accent that I cannot attempt to put down on paper. Oscar was head superintendent of a sprawling apartment building on Eighty-First or Eighty-Second Street and Broadway, I forget which. It was a responsible job with a large staff under him. He was the kind of fellow who arranged for the parole of men imprisoned for strike-related crimes; he provided jobs for them and gave them a place to stay in the basement of the building.

One day Oscar gets a phone call: "This is Agent X of the FBI. We are giving you the opportunity to serve your country! There is a person of interest in your building, a Mr. So and So, apartment #__. We need a better idea of his opinions and what he is up to. You are in position to earn the applause of a grateful nation should you collect the literature and letters he disposes of."

It is a flattering request and no doubt a matter of overwhelming national security.

Oscar's response, with the accent thick as a thicket? "Do you know who pokes through people's garbage? A rat! You are paid to be a rat. You could not pay me enough to be one!" And he slams down the receiver.

Sam loved that story. Oscar was not a reasonable man. Nor was his son, whom I did not know personally or was too young to remember. What reasonable man, going for his PhD at Harvard, would refuse to register for the Draft because he was a pacifist? My childhood was filled with "unreasonable" people of that sort.

I'd like to depict some of these "unreasonable" people: Wobblies, anarchists, hangers on, drunks, violent types, fringe people, artists, poets, on and on. They mostly knew one another and constituted a complex affinity group distinct from the Vanguard–Freie Arbeiter Stimme–Rudolf Rocker–Jewish anarchist comrades Sam also associated with, although there was overlap. I have said many times Sam's soul lay with the Wobblies and other bums: the untamable bad-boy that coexisted with the "sober" article-writing activist.

The IWW Five-Ten Hall at 134 Broad Street is a good place to begin. Sam loved the place, as I have described. He'd go there to pal around with his buddies and forget for a few hours that he was a hardworking house painter chained for life to a life-companion and two children. Typical of these pal-around buddies was a scapegrace seaman by the name of Red Shannon. Abe remembers from childhood that he was heavy set, with, of course, flaming red hair, and a red beard, and that he had a fascinating, intricately veined bulbous nose. Abe liked him. Together they would forage the streets for fire wood to heat our cold-water flat on Avenue D; Red, like so many others, flopped on our couch for days on end.

Red was irresponsible, though, as far as Abe and I can tell, not toward our family. His chief claim to fame—or at least the story Sam told many times—concerns the time Red was arrested for vagrancy or some such crime and found himself a "guest of the county" in a small town jail. Seems there was something wrong with the plumbing and all the toilets were backed up flooding the place. The floors were wet and the place stank and the police did not like stepping in the stuff.

"I can fix that," Red says. "I'm a plumber!"

"You are? If you can fix that, we'll let you go right away. And what's more, here, you can have some of our steak and not the crap we feed you!"

Give me the wrench, Red says and he goes down to the basement. Now you should understand that Red is not a plumber. Does not know the first thing about plumbing. But he sees where the sewage lines are and he simply disconnects them. The police are delighted as everything seems to work, unaware as they are that they are shitting in their basement. By the time they discovered this uncomforting fact, as they certainly did, Red was far away on an overland freight.

That was Sam's buddy, Red Shannon. At least he was not dangerous in the manner of John S. (Sneak Punch) Morgan—an affable fellow when sober, but watch out when he was drunk. Morgan would all of a sudden cold-cock you with a right hook and lay you out in front of the bar for utterly no rational reason. You had to watch the guy, but he was fine sober.

I'll leave Red Shannon to history soon, but not until I share the tale of Sam and Red's encounter with a group of beauty parlor workers: hairstylists, facial specialists, and the like. The way Sam told the story the women called the Five-Ten Hall to inquire about affiliating with the IWW: Serious business and an opportunity for the Wobblies, whose fortunes were in decline, to make a comeback and branch into new territory. Unfortunately or fortunately, the only Wobblies in a position to meet with them at the time were Sam Dolgoff and Red Shannon. A most inappropriate looking pair: Red with the pot belly, unkempt beard, bulbous nose, and construction-worker clothes; Sam with the thick glasses, bad teeth, and painter's fingernails. They met the women delegates in a mid-town shop and things did not develop as you might expect.

The women did not give a damn the way Red and Sam looked. They were all business: tell us about the IWW, what you stand for, what would joining your union do for us. Sam took the lead and things went swimmingly well. He suggested calling a strike. The women seemed to agree. But then matters came to a crashing halt when they discovered Sam's idea of a strike meant they would have to carry picket signs in front of their shops. No way! That was beneath their dignity! They were professionals. What would their customers—excuse me, clients—think? They were *ladies*.

Sam spoke from the heart. To walk the picket line and carry a sign in the assertion of your rights is the highest form of dignity. It is a noble thing to do. You are letting the world know you are not a slave, that you have a voice: that you are standing up for your self and in solidarity with your fellow workers. You are part of a grand tradition. And so on.

The women were having none of it. They affiliated with the AFL, who promptly hired Bowery derelicts at a dollar or two a day to do their picketing. A more dignified arrangement.

Sam and Red's effort ended in failure. They obviously did not understand the psychology of the women and their work environment. But there is another way to view the encounter. Perhaps these women lacked the courage to be worthy of the IWW! If you are in the anarchist tradition I am sure you know of Louise Michel, Emma Goldman, Lucy Parsons, Voltairine de Cleyre. And probably the great IWW orator who later became an important official of the American Communist Party, Elizabeth Gurley Flynn. In the strictly feminist tradition we have of course the nineteenth-century pioneers, followed by Margaret Sanger and, much later, Betty Friedan and Gloria Steinem.

I'll bet not many people have heard of Jane Street. The late historian Franklin Rosemont devotes a wonderful chapter to her and to Wobbly feminism in his *Joe Hill: The IWW and the Making of a Revolutionary Working Class Counterculture*. He notes that: "One of the IWW's most innovative and successful organizing campaigns of all time was Jane Street's unionization of the housemaids in Denver, 1916—a movement which soon spread to Salt Lake City, Duluth, Chicago, Cleveland and Seattle." They were a brutally exploited lot, whose labor, Street said, bore "the deepest taint of chattel slavery handed down from the time when it was a disgrace for a member of the master class to lace his own boots." Together, though, they would build a union of women who "don't believe in mistresses or servants. They would do away with caste altogether. They believe in removing the degradation from domestic service by teaching their employers to look upon the hands that feed them and wash for them, and scrub for them with respect or fear and humility." Out of their struggle came the IWW song "The Maids' Defiance":

We've answered all your doorbells and we've washed your dirty kids,
For lo, these many weary years we've done as we were bid,
But we're going to fight for freedom and for our rights we'll stand.
And we're going to stick together in one big Union band.
We've washed your dirty linen and we've cooked your daily foods;
We've eaten in your kitchens, and we've stood your ugly moods,
But now we've joined the Union and organized to stay
The cooks and maids and chauffeurs, in one grand array

A reporter asked Elizabeth Gurley Flynn the reason women were so prominent in Wobbly strikes and demonstrations. "The men don't hold us back, and we choose to go to the front," she said.

The wives of the miners of Colorado, Arizona, and Montana regularly joined the IWW. They and their husbands, together, were considered an economic unit. No decision to strike was taken without their participation. At the founding convention of the IWW Lucy Parsons spoke poignantly to her male audience of the desperation of poor women in American society. She advocated organizing prostitutes. They were workers, she said, and, rather than objects of contempt, should be treated as the victims of exploitation—(they are) "my sisters whom I can see in the night."

Wobbly women were every bit as tough as Wobbly men. Big Bill Haywood recalled that, during the epic Lawrence Massachusetts Textile Strike of 1912, "One cold morning, after the strikers had been drenched on the bridge with the firehose of the mills, the women caught a policeman in the middle of the bridge and stripped off his uniform, pants and all. They were about to throw him in the ice river, when other policeman rushed in and saved him."

Perhaps Sam and Red were not naïve to expect more of the Beauty Parlor workers.

I am five or six years of age at the Five-Ten Hall. While a small clutch of men, including my father, speak animatedly about things that buzz above me, my eyes are locked on one man in that group. I follow him wherever he steps, at a certain distance, too shy to approach. I am engrossed in the light that reflects purple and dark blue off his forehead and cheeks and by the contrast of his totally black skin and the whites of his eyes. No doubt such interest is not new to him. When our eyes meet he smiles at me in a kindly way. The name of this blackest of men was Benjamin Harrison Fletcher. He was among the greatest of IWW organizers and one of the pioneer civil rights leaders of the twentieth century: unsung and forgotten today.

Ben Fletcher was my first conscious knowledge of the black race. He appeared an old man whose health was shot when I knew him: a bit heavy with a paunch and with thick working man's shoulders that sloped oddly—the result of a stroke, my father told me years later. All in all, he did not cut the heroic figure of a black man white people of the 1940s found acceptable. He looked nothing like the relatively light skinned heavyweight champion Joe "a credit to his race" Louis, or, a generation later, like Sidney Portier: handsome with ramrod straight posture, who wore his dignity as a suit of armor. Instead he projected good humor and decency—you wanted to be in his company—but there was something sad that seeped through. Matilda Robbins was a Wobbly organizer who knew Ben in the full bloom of his youth and power, at a time when he was responsible for the organization and welfare of ten thousand men. She remembered Ben as "soft spoken" and that "his eyes seemed to reflect the tragedy of his race."

Sam called Ben Fletcher "undoubtedly the most eloquent, humorous speaker I have ever heard (which is saying quite a lot). His ringing voice needed no microphone." He was fond of retelling the incident Ben had recounted to him of the time his black skin saved his life.

It is 1912 or thereabout, and Ben is on the soapbox addressing a crowd of longshoremen on the Norfolk Virginia docks. Remember this is one-hundred years ago. Ten men, all white and all business join the audience. They are interested in nothing Ben has to say, save the answer to this single question that pierces the air: "Nigger! What do you think of miscegenation?" The crowd tightens around Ben like a noose; it is a classic lynching set up. For a full tense minute Ben's eyes size-up each and every member of the crowd. "Well," Ben says at last, "I see a whole lot of folks here whiter than I am. And you damn well know how that happened!" It takes a moment to sink in. The tension is broken. The moment has passed. It is hard to work up whatever it takes to murder a man when you have just laughed at his joke.

I cannot imagine the courage of a man such as Ben Fletcher to stand exposed in front of a hostile crowd in the jaws of the Jim Crow South of 1912. Espousing revolutionary unionism and racial integration, no less, at a time when a black man in the South had to step out of the way of an approaching white man. When a black man faced prison or worse for the crime of pissing in the same pot as a white man. When a black man imprisoned for the most trivial offense—or no offense at all—could find himself in chains and on a plantation work gang. It was a time when an entire nation was whipped into a state of hysteria because a black heavyweight, Jack Johnson, defeated every last one of his white opponents. It was a time when a film extolling the virtues of the Ku Klux Klan, *The Birth of a Nation*, was a huge sensation. It was a time when a rabbi's son, Al Jolson, who as a boy roamed the same streets as my father, could make a fortune prancing on stage with black grease-paint smeared on his face.

I add that it was a time when the Great Statesmen—you know, Woodrow Wilson—in one of the first acts of his first term, sought fit to protect the racial purity of the Civil Service by segregating the facilities of Federal employees: installing separate bathrooms and partitioned lunch rooms and the like. This, after our paragon of integrity had appealed to black voters for support in the campaign of 1912.

In the face of that gale of racial hatred, Fletcher and his fellow Wobblies, white and black, organized and led thousands of

Philadelphia dock workers in what was surely the largest interracial union of its time. That union was known as Local 8, a branch of the Marine Transport Workers, IU 510, of the IWW. According to Peter Cole's superb *Wobblies on the Waterfront*,

> Local 8 was a black-led, black majority organization that included in its ranks African Americans, West Indian immigrants, Irish Americans, other European Americans, as well as Polish, Lithuanian, and other European immigrants. These men included Catholics, Protestants, Jews and freethinkers. They worked in a variety of waterfront trades, although the deep-sea longshoremen (those who loaded and unloaded cargo vessels in international trade) always were the core of the union. Anyone interested in inclusivity in a diverse society need go no further than Local 8, a union of unskilled workers who managed to do what most American institutions still have not achieved: equality and integration within its own ranks. And for many people, Local 8 was synonymous with Ben Fletcher.

Cole describes one of Local 8's business meetings:

> No finer spirit of brotherhood can be found anywhere than exists in this organization. Upon entering the hall, during meetings, one is met with the fact of a Negro chairman and a white secretary sitting side by side and conducting the meeting.
>
> From the floor, white and colored workers rise, make themselves heard, make motions, argue pro and con, have their differences and settle them, despite the Imperial Wizard William Joseph Simmons' and Marcus Garvey's "Race first" bogey. At picnics, the workers mingle, fraternize, dance, eat and play together. Nor do Negro workers, dance, eat and play only among themselves; but both white and black men, white and black women, and white and black children eat, play and dance together just as they work and hold their meetings together.

There are numerous similar examples in *Wobblies on the Waterfront*—and all of this, the tangible expression of Martin Luther

King's Dream, Ben Fletcher and his fellow Wobblies, white and black, accomplished before King was born. They were in the tradition of the abolitionists, of John Brown and Frederick Douglass, of those who dedicated their lives to the proposition that no man should be another man's slave. Compare the vision and humanity of these forgotten men to their conservative rival, Samuel Gompers, president of the American Federation of Labor (AFL). Asked the goal of his organization, his answer was a simple "More." More, that is, for white workers having skilled trades, the so-called "aristocrats of labor." Black workers need not apply, as noted by Booker T. Washington, who criticized the AFL for its racism.

When the IWW declared they were for the solidarity of all labor they practiced what they preached; they would not tolerate racism. Big Bill Haywood was for many years the public face of the IWW and respectable society's favorite villain. This is what "The Menace to the Republic" said to white timber workers in 1912 in apartheid Louisiana, where it was illegal for blacks and whites to conduct meetings in the same room: "You work in the same mills together. Sometimes a black man and a white man chop down the same tree together. You are meeting in a convention now to discuss the conditions under which you labor. This can't be done intelligently by passing resolutions here and then sending them to another room for the black man to act upon. Why not be sensible about this and call the Negroes into this convention? If it is against the law, this is one time the law should be broken."

That is what Brotherhood of Timber Workers did. They broke the law and affiliated with the IWW as a fully integrated union. The IWW would have it no other way. It was the only organization to confront the most powerful interests of the white South. And let's be clear the Wobblies were seeking to emancipate the timber workers from a system of slave labor every bit as vicious as existed before the Civil War. They were men of rare courage. Philip Foner describes their struggle well in "The IWW and the Black Worker."

Let me tell you of an encounter I had over breakfast a short time ago. In Berkeley California, where else? A lady and her husband at the next table happen to look over my shoulder. They see my copy of Peter Cole's *Ben Fletcher: The Life and Times of a Black Wobbly* on the table.

"Wobblies? You know about the old-time Wobblies?" the lady asks.

Her husband—in his late sixties I guess—then mentions that his grandfather helped to organize Asian and Portuguese plantation laborers, the semi-slaves of long ago Hawaii. The Wobblies were there, too, he said. At that time, fifty years before Hawaii became a State, agriculture and not time-shares was the chief industry. The Wobblies? His grandfather spoke of them often and fondly. "The Wobblies were in California, too, among the Japanese and Chinese farm laborers."

In Arizona, too, I might add, where they organized a series of strikes in the copper mines strung out along the Mexican border. The Wobblies demanded among other things that the Mexican miners be paid the same wages and have the same rights as their "white" counterparts. It was vicious, bloody combat. In the most notorious incident, the Bisbee Deportation, thirteen-hundred striking miners were forced onto cattle cars by rifle-carrying "deputies"; transported under supervision of the Gatling gun sixteen hours into the desert, and abandoned without water or food.

Back to Ben. No greater brute labor was required of a man in the early 1900s than the loading and unloading of cargo from the bowels of deep sea vessels and similar waterfront work. It was hard, dangerous, unsteady, and low paying. But it was work. Thousands of desperately poor southern blacks migrated to coastal cities, north and south. So too did thousands of impoverished white immigrants from Europe: Polacks, Honkies, Mics. The ship owners and stevedoring firms loved this arrangement since they held the power to hire and fire at will. Their strategy was blunt and effective. Keep the blacks in segregated work gangs. Play black off against white. Keep black and white dependent on them for their children's bread.

Desegregation of the work gangs was the first demand the Wobblies made of the ship owners. The second was elimination of the humiliating "shape-up" during which the men stood in front of the hiring boss each morning like cattle, to be chosen or passed over by him for his own reasons. You are mistaken if you think the men

joined the IWW purely for more money. The union was the instrument these men used to assert their self-respect; they were not to be
treated as animals, even if their employers and respectable society
viewed them as such. Matilda Robbins recalled Ben Fletcher's role
in organizing these men.

> On one of my organizing assignments which took me from the
> textile towns of the South to those of the North I stopped in
> Philadelphia where Ben was organizing longshoremen. I met
> him for the first time when I heard him speak one night at the
> IWW hall. I remember how strongly he held the attention of
> the grim-faced, work-marked men. How their faces brightened
> with understanding of...the need for solidarity and resistance
> against the shipping companies who kept them divided. Ben
> won the confidence of both Negro and white workers by his
> exposition of how they were being used against one another....
>
> Day after day and night after night he covered the water-
> front, twenty miles of it, repeatedly at the risk of his life. He
> took me to the slums in the City of Brotherly Love where
> longshoremen and their families lived. He agonized over their
> degrading poverty. He was of them. He was with them.

Born in 1890, Ben was about twenty-three years old at the time.
His early life and background are obscure to us, though we suspect
his family traveled north to Philadelphia—as did thousands of other
Southern black families—in the late-nineteenth century. By 1910,
he was registered as a laborer on the docks. Mother reiterated on
many occasions that Ben told her he was influenced by the Quakers
growing up, and that "he could have had an easy life as a member of
the black bourgeoisie, working in the printing trades, and gave it all
up." But she was vague about the facts. In any event, he wrote and
spoke in the language of an educated man.

I add, in view of the current sickening state of most American unions, that Ben was never a "union boss." The Philadelphia
longshoremen were responsible for their own union. The black
and white chairmen and secretaries that conducted the Local 8
meetings were rotated on a regular basis with strict adherence to

the rule that all ethnic and racial groups get an equal chance. The Wobblies trained their fellow workers, many of whom were illiterate, to administer union affairs. Union dues were collected by the union, and not deducted from the men's wages by an employer-run check-off system. Bargaining with the ship owners was conducted by elected committees. There were no contracts. Agreements were enforced by the solidarity of the men.

Ben was not worshipped as some kind of mystical savior; black candidates caucused and ran against him. Nor was he a "token black" or front man. He was instead respected for his character, his dedication, his powerful speaking ability, and above all for his strategic and tactical sense. He and the other Wobbly organizers received nothing material for their efforts. They worked on the docks alongside the men, or held side jobs to keep alive. They generally "hopped a freight" to get from one city or port or mining town or lumber camp to another. There was no such thing as drawing obscene salaries or passing the union on to your son as if it were your family business.

Class warfare on the Philadelphia docks left no place for the faint of heart. I am in a position to affix a footnote concerning the tactics of the Wobblies; my parents were friends not only of Ben Fletcher, but of several of Ben's comrades—among them Manuel Rey, and especially the Irish-American organizer John "Jack" Walsh. Jack had devoted fifteen years of his life to Local 8 and to the ideals it embodied. He was a taciturn, solitary man and so Mother considered it a coup when he agreed to address the IWW "forum" my parents conducted alternate Sunday afternoons at the Labor Temple on Second Avenue and Fourteenth Street. The Temple, a labyrinthine structure of many rooms and passages, was not a temple at all but the Presbyterian Institute of Industrial Relations; it has long since been converted into a residential condo.

We got the tiny room via the good offices of the superintendent, Pete Peterson, a Stockholm Wobbly and one of Sam's drinking buddies, who ran a guerilla war against the conservative management until they gave in. I realize now this was not an easy decision on their part. It was 1952, the time of Senator Joseph McCarthy and of the Korean war, an ugly period in American politics. The IWW was on the U.S. Attorney General's list of Subversive Organizations, those that advocated overthrow of the government by "unconstitutional means"—a term of convenience designed to help Government lawyers circumvent the Constitution. My parents' purpose in running the forum in these tough times was "to keep our ideas alive."

I remember Jack Walsh vividly: a thin man, sharp featured, white hair impeccably combed. He wore neatly pressed jeans and a tweed jacket over an open blue work shirt. Today this is the standard uniform of the university professor, but in those times jeans and a jacket were an anachronism—a statement of eccentricity or in Jack's case, poverty. He came across as a man of intelligence, with the pointed, biting turn of phrase typical of many Wobblies. And he proceeded to give a lecture on the history of the Philadelphia waterfront worthy of the best university professor. The usual eleven people were present, three of whom were certifiable, and one in from the cold. The rest of us witnessed a bygone age come to life.

Jack described in detail in that sparse, tiny room the full spectrum of power the ship owners and stevedoring firms employed to crush the revolutionary union: goons to intimidate the men; police and courts to beat and jail organizers and strikers; "scab labor" to break strikes and usurp jobs; the press to lie about the men and impugn the motivations of the Wobblies; and, to this list, add the special services of the Mafia. The Wobblies answered back, and though I remember no specifics from sixty-odd years ago, this I do recall: The Mafia, at the behest of the ship owners carried out a systematic campaign of terror against Wobbly organizers and the longshoremen they tried to reach on the docks. They would break up the crowds around Wobbly soapboxers by clubbing listeners, and were especially vicious toward those who took Wobbly leaflets. Some of the speakers they beat until near death. But—to use a contemporary phrase alien to the Jack Walsh vocabulary—this time the Mafia fucked with the wrong bunch.

As Jack described it, the Wobblies were cool and measured in their response. They observed carefully the Mafia chain of command: who the errand boys were, to whom they reported, and so on up. It took a while. Then, when they were ready, they pounced, grabbed a Mafia boss—not a low-level guy—and dragged him to the Wobbly hall where they proceeded in silence to beat him to a pulp. The moment before tossing him out onto the gutter, they gave him an instruction: "Tell this to your friends: 'For every one of us, two of you!'"

Jack called it the work of the "Education Committee."

The Mafia lay off. They were nothing if not businessmen.

It is a colorful story, but I hesitate telling it, because it seems to reinforce the stereotype that union people, and the Wobblies in particular, were a violent bunch—an impression that is to me laughable in view of the violence, state-sponsored and otherwise, that they were up against. The Wobblies were determined men who lived in a hard world. But the record is clear that their "violence" amounted to self-defense in response to deliberate provocation. Even the fights that erupted around the introduction of scab labor are exaggerated. The Wobblies realized the desperate conditions that caused men to "cross the line" and sought to convince them to join their union instead. A large portion of Ben's time was spent traveling to ports up and down the East Coast doing precisely that.

The sit-in. The sit down strike. The freedom ride. The "freedom march." The jails filled with men and women willing to pay that price. The songs that bond and inspire. The mass meeting as a show of strength. The Wobblies anticipated the nonviolent tactics that the modern civil rights movement employed to catch the conscience of the nation, although I doubt many civil rights demonstrators had heard of the Wobblies. Martin Luther King, who I am sure had heard of the Wobblies, called these techniques "passive resistance." The Wobblies called them "direct action." Can there be a more Gandhian protest than a man clinging to a lamppost and reciting the Declaration of Independence while clubbed by the police? This the Wobblies did too, in the San Diego "free speech fight."

Direct Action on the job? When, in 1923, the dock bosses refused the Wobblies' demand for an eight-hour day, the men of Local 8 simply walked off the job at eight hours, and that was that!

# 31
## BEN ON TRIAL

In 1918, Ben Fletcher was sentenced to prison for ten years in a sensational Chicago trial that dragged on for months. The offence was violation of the Espionage Act passed a year earlier in the run-up to World War I. He was found guilty along with a hundred other prominent Wobblies, including many who worked closely with him on the Philadelphia waterfront: Jack Walsh, Walter Nef, E. F. Doree, and Manuel Rey (later Sam's Stelton buddy). There were similar mass trials in Kansas and California. Eugene V. Debs was convicted under the same Act in a separate trial.

The years 1917–1922, roughly, bracket the Red Scare: the paranoid fear that the nation was being subverted by radicals, socialists, foreign elements. It is a chronic disease, latent in the national bloodstream, that erupts from time to time with sudden ferocity—a political malaria akin to the bouts of hysterical anti-Semitism of other cultures. The hysteria is whipped up and orchestrated by interested parties: the Federal Government, business interests, demagogic politicians, and so on. The Red Scare meant open season on the IWW, on the Socialist Party, on all political nonconformists—or alternately on those people the dominant culture simply did not like, such as the devout Mennonites, the homeless, and the undeserving poor.

The IWW marked a dividing line in American society, Helen Keller wrote. You hated them or loved them and that was that. She came to the defense of the IWW in a remarkable document written on the eve of the 1918 Chicago trial and in the midst of the Great War To End All Wars.

The Wobblies were regarded as no better than vermin by the powerful and "respectable" elements of society. I am not speaking metaphorically. It is a literal truth that reflects the foul odor of the times.

A Tulsa, Oklahoma newspaper wrote: "The first step in the whipping of Germany is to strangle the IWWs. Kill them, just as you would kill any other kind of a snake. It is no time to waste money on trials.... All that is necessary is evidence and a firing squad." Another paper referred to the IWW simply as "America's cancer sore." On the other hand, we have the impeccable standard of journalism of the *Los Angeles Times*: "A vast number of I.W.W.'s are non-producers. I.W.W. stands for I Won't Work, and I Want Whisky. The average Wobbly, it must be remembered, is a sort of half-wild animal. He lives on the road, cooks his food in rusty tin cans...and sleeps in 'jungles,' barns, outhouses, freight cars.... They are all in all a lot of homeless men wandering about the country without fixed destination or purpose, other than destruction."

The myth of the Rootless Wobbly Wild Man! Yes, many of them were indeed rootless—a byproduct of their poverty. But not all of them by any means. I suspect most of those who were not migrant workers—and many of those as well—were family men. It was true of Ben and E. F. Doree and Walter Nef and Herbert Mahler and Ralph Chaplin and Big Jim Thompson and Bill Haywood.

In 1923, five years after the war ended, Kennesaw Mountain Landis referred to the Wobblies in Ben's trial as "scum," "filth," and "slimy rats." The comment is noteworthy because Landis was the judge who had presided over that Chicago trial. In his viciousness and vindictiveness, he was furious at Calvin Coolidge for commuting the sentences of the Wobblies still in jail.

John Reed attended the trial and had another impression of the Wobbly defendants. "These Hundred and One are outdoor men, hard-rock blasters, tree-fellers, wheat binders, longshoremen, the boys who do the strong work of the world. They are scarred all over with the wounds of industry—and the wounds of society's hatred.... They aren't afraid of anything."

You see the rugged faces and ill-fitting suits in the old photographs of the Wobblies, and you understand what Reed meant. They were working men radicalized by the harsh condition of their lives and of those around them. They were not smooth; they had rough edges. Judge Landis in a show of humanity saw to it that spittoons for tobacco juice be placed where they sat.

Big Bill Haywood certainly had his rough edges. He lost an eye when he was nine, the year he began working in a Utah mine.

That kind of thing stays with you. But he never wore a patch or a glass eye. What you saw was what he was. Whether he should have defected to Moscow instead of serving his twenty-year sentence is debatable: he left the Wobblies in a terrible fix trying to make good on his bail. On the other hand he was in poor health and he probably would not have outlived prison. Can you imagine the guards licking their chops at the thought of getting their hands on him? Upon his death half his remains were interred in the Kremlin Wall, the other half at Waldheim Cemetery in the company of the Haymarket Martyrs.

Reed's description of Judge Landis is classic: "Small on the huge bench sits a wasted man with untidy white hair, an emaciated face in which two burning eyes are set like jewels, parchment-like skin split by a crack for a mouth; the face of Andrew Jackson three years dead."

Ben, who rarely spoke of the trial, despised Landis. He saw the plantation owner, the man with the whip. "A cracker!" he spat out years later to Mother, which for him was strong language. Many of Ben's fellow Wobblies, naturally enough, sought to offer documents and testimony in their defense, hoping to get off or at least draw a lesser sentence. Not Ben. One glance at Landis and he knew the effort was hopeless.

Instead, he put energy into lightening the burden of his fellow prisoners. The only black man in the court room, he'd crack that he was glad to add a bit of color to the proceedings. When it was his turn to speak during the punishment phase of the trial, he commented to Judge Landis that his grammar was poor. "Your Honor, your sentences are too long." Landis chuckled and down went the gavel: ten years. Mother insisted Ben said this directly to Landis rather than to his fellow Wobblies, as Haywood recalled in his biography. I add that Mother said Jack Walsh probably did his cause no good on the witness stand by referring to the Prosecutor as "fellow worker" in a tone dripping Irish acid.

Peter Cole recounts that, "While waiting in the infamous Cook County jail—the same prison where the Haymarket martyrs were hung thirty years before—to be loaded on a train for Leavenworth, Fletcher again sought to make light of the situation while simultaneously calling into question the authority of the entire proceedings. Years later in Moscow, Haywood recalled Fletcher holding a mock court. Imitating Judge Landis, 'looking solemn and spitting tobacco juice,' Fletcher 'swore the prisoners as a jury; calling the guards and detectives up to him he sentenced them without further ado to be hanged and shot and imprisoned for life.'"

A little-known facet of the Chicago trial—to anyone but students of IWW history—was that the leadership was split on the stance the organization should take toward World War I. Yes, the overwhelming majority privately opposed it, but there was the question of tactics. Bill Haywood and Herbert Mahler, for example, feared militant opposition invited a massive crackdown that would crush the organization. And for what? The IWW did not have the power to influence U.S. entry into the war. Better to hunker down and keep organizing, building the strength of the union. Frank Little, for his part, thought the IWW should oppose the war with every fiber of its being, as he did personally. "They're going to come after us anyway," he said. "So we might as well go down swinging!" Ralph Chaplin took a stance somewhere in the middle. As a compromise, the organization issued a general statement against the war, but left participation up to conscience of the individual members and locals.

Ben and the other leaders of Local 8 took an extreme position: they supported the war effort. I know it does not sit well with later admirers of the Wobblies but it is the truth. Many have cited realpolitik reasons. Philadelphia was the main shipping port for supplies sent to Europe; business was booming and the men never had it so good. Opposing the war would split this altogether admirable union the Wobblies worked so hard to build.

I think there were deeper reasons as well. Ben knew the character of his black membership better than anyone. They were militant, believed in solidarity, could buy into a socialistic message. But they were at heart profoundly patriotic men despite a government and a society that treated them so shabbily. They would never go along with refusing to aid the war effort, refusing to load ships, refusing to support the troops, refusing to register for the draft. And Ben at heart may have felt that way, too. Patriotism tapped into emotions that sometimes transcended the class war.

Support of the war effort had no effect on the fate of Ben and his Philadelphia comrades. They were, after all, Wobblies. Justice had nothing to do with it. Walter Nef drew a twenty-year sentence despite a letter from a Federal Agent that he was among the finest men he had ever met and that he was instrumental in keeping the waterfront humming and strike free. Of course, there were other reasons for the harsh sentence: Nef, perhaps the greatest of Wobbly organizers, had been the driving force behind the AWO, the IWW union of migrant harvest workers—35,000 strong. More to the point, a Haywood memo in the confiscated IWW files suggested that Nef take over as General Secretary in the event he was jailed.

So Ben was sent to Leavenworth, the only black man among his one-hundred fellow Wobblies. However, he was not an isolated black man. Ben's standing among the black longshoreman of Philadelphia and up and down the east coast waterfronts was huge. He had the respect of the black leaders of his time, as I have mentioned: among them W.E.B. Du Bois and A. Philip Randolph, editor of the *Messenger*, and President of the Brotherhood of Sleeping Car Porters. Forty years later, Randolph would play leadership roles in the March on Washington and passage of the Civil Rights Act. He worked tirelessly for his friend's release.

# 32
## INSIDE GOLGOTHA

The title of this section is taken from Part 11 of Stephen Martin Kohn's essential *American Political Prisoners: Prosecutions Under the Espionage and Sedition Acts*. For the nonreligious, Golgotha is the hill near Jerusalem where Jesus was crucified. The broader meaning refers to a place of suffering or sacrifice, a place of burial. All senses of the word apply to the convicted Wobblies. A number of them did indeed die in prison, from abuse and disease. Those who did not die suffered egregiously. Some were driven mad. It was hard labor and hard time under strict regulation. Ralph Chaplin witnessed practices in Leavenworth Federal Penitentiary, 1918, right up there with the Spanish Inquisition: "A dozen [Mennonite objectors] refused to work because their beards were cut off and were not permitted to remove buttons from their clothes, as their religious beliefs required. They were handcuffed to the bars of cell block B (arms over head) for more than two weeks. They had to stand on their toes to keep the cuffs from cutting into the flesh of the wrists. When they grew too tired to do this, 'their fingers would swell, turn blue and crack open and blood would trickle down the upraised arms.'"

Other torture practices were less creative, such as throwing into "the Hole" those Wobblies who protested inhumane working conditions on the coal pile. There, prison guards—some with machine guns trained on the men, and others wearing baseball masks for protection—"proceeded to club them senseless."

We have Kohn's account that "Fletcher was punished for a variety of offenses, such as 'loafing,' 'disobeying orders,' 'creating a disturbance,' and 'talking.'" But I have no idea what exactly he was subjected to. Being a jet-black man did not help, of that I am sure. Ben spoke to Mother of many things; her innate compassion had that way of drawing stoic men out. However, he never spoke to her of his prison experiences. He was a gentleman of his time and such things were not for a lady to hear.

The Wobblies refused to grovel. Warren Harding in response to protests and appeals and the waning Red Scare offered them the opportunity to apply as individuals for pardons. Most refused. Fifty-two signed a petition saying that since they were unjustly convicted as a group, they should be pardoned as a group. Calvin Coolidge finally pardoned them in 1923. The War was over. The men had been imprisoned five years. The government's point had been made. The Wobblies' wings had been clipped, or so he thought. It was time for a new chapter.

Ben returned to the Philadelphia docks where he encountered markedly changed circumstances, not for the better. Despite Local 8's decline and demise, I am impressed that the Wobblies were able to hang on for as many years as they did, considering the forces pitted against them: the imprisoned leadership; the changed composition of the work force; the reactionary, racist International Longshoremen's Association (ILA) in partnership with the stevedoring and shipping firms; the rule-or-ruin, newly emergent Communist Party; the pervasive racism and hostility of the culture. You can add to these things the disastrous effects of an ill-timed strike called by those who led Local 8 while Ben and his comrades were in jail.

So Local 8 went down. Ben remained a Wobbly lifer, doing what he could. He traveled all over, mainly to the East Coast ports where the Wobblies still had influence. By all accounts he retained that power as an orator who could bring men to their feet. He never wavered in his belief that the best way to promote racial integration was to unite men in common cause against economic tyranny; that in struggle both white and black workers would learn love and brotherhood. To his last day he believed these things.

# 33

# BEN AS WE KNEW HIM

How should a black man whose health was shot after twenty-five years on the docks and in prison earn a living?

Ben found work hand-rolling cigars in Philadelphia and New York. Cigar making was a traditional Cuban trade, and long a focus of anarcho-syndicalist activism. I suspect Spanish Wobblies—perhaps Manuel Rey or Frank González or Marcellino García—helped him out. But hand-rolling cigars is not easy work either.

Ben moved to Brooklyn in the 1930s within walking distance of his old Philadelphia comrades: E. F. Doree's widow and Walter Nef, who was married to her sister. They constituted a support group. Ellen Doree Rosen writes fondly of Ben in her moving family memoir, *A Wobbly Life*. She writes that Ben had married a much younger woman, Clara, who made him pretend in public he was her uncle or some sort because she was ashamed of the age difference between them. Granted I was a child, but I do not remember Clara that way and my parents who knew them well never mentioned it. I remember Clara as pretty, extremely polite with exquisite manners. Classy, you might say. And she was definitely the boss.

Clara was a nurse. Ben found work as a janitor. Later they lived in a brownstone, at 813 Hancock St in the Bedford Stuyvesant section of Brooklyn, long a black neighborhood. I do not know if they owned the building, but they had some kind of arrangement where they rented out rooms. By the time I knew Ben he was not able to work much; he took care of things, kept the place clean when Clara was on the job.

Ben's life was not at all solemn. He had a great sense of fun, especially when "hanging out" with his Wobbly buddies. Probably his best friend was a colorful character on the fringes of the Wobblies named Andrew Homer—who happened also to be a close friend of our family. So we saw a great deal of Ben. Andy was white and from rural Mobile, Alabama, the product of an old and large southern family. "Homers all over the place," as he put it.

Andy was a character out of the pre-modern south of Ben's generation. Erskine Caldwell captured his flavor in *Tobacco Road* and *God's Little Acre*; the *Beverly Hillbillies* TV series of years ago is the more up-to-date, white-bread version. Andy was a refrigeration mechanic. He wore blue coveralls with shoulder straps over his pot belly all the time and beady glasses over his veined blob of a nose. The backyard of his North Bergen, New Jersey home was his shop: rusty machinery scattered all over the place; a broken down wreck of a car shorn of tires; a big vat of chemicals in the center of the yard with a tripod pulley system over it to dunk his customer's malfunctioning condensers. All in all a nice complement to the well-trimmed, flowered lawns of his neighbors—and you can be sure they fully approved of it.

More than a first-rate mechanic, Andy was a first-rate businessman. He specialized in air conditioner house calls and he made sure those he sent out bearing the Homer name were men of the highest integrity, and if you believe this I have a Brooklyn Bridge to sell you cheap! He specialized in cheating the region's housewives—sending out slime-bucket assistants while their husbands were at work. I remember Andy's description of a particular favorite: "Got this here Coobahno! Heh, heh! The little son-of-a-bitch has laar-sen-y in his heart!"

Above all, though, Andy was a world-class Vulgarian and a sex researcher of practical bent ("Quarter-inch of tongue is worth a yard of the other stuff!"). I well remember Andy lounging on his cushiony seat in the corner of the living room of his ramshackle home, his feet up on the foot stool. Facing him was his enormous cabinet radio, later a TV set. Close to his left leg was the spittoon. Taped to the wall behind it was a liner of clear plastic. And Andy would lie back and spit tobacco juice. Half the time he'd missed the spit bucket. That was what the liner was for.

Andy was given to folk cures for his hangovers. After a prodigious night of bourbon, you'd find him next morning in his cushiony living room seat wrapped in blankets, sweating profusely, feet soaked in a pot of hot water, steam rising from his bald round head. "Poopy, Ahm dyin. Ahm dyin. More hot water!" he'd shout to wife, Anne. How much can a woman take?

Andy had his good points, however. He was loyal. I remember him over at our apartment the time Grandfather Max left his bed in the middle of the night, went to our roof, and walked off. Was it an accident? Did he jump? Sam was crushed, weeping uncontrollably, and it was Homer who showed up, "You all have got to get out of here," he said and drove us to New Jersey. His home was my second home for many years growing up. I slept in the same bed as Larry, his oldest son. There was also a room for Mother and Sam and for Abe, as well. Whenever we wanted it.

And he had a deep, soft heart. He was beaten as a child. Escaped from a reformatory—and I can only imagine what reformatories were like in the Alabama of 1910 or so. But Moms was long dead and there was his father, Pops, white haired, suspenders over long underwear, silent, a fixture in the house, destitute, and Andy took him in and cared for him. The two grown men had an interesting way of displaying affection. Andy would follow Pops wherever he stepped, lower his head and nudge him gently between the shoulder blades.

"Old man, yuse a goat," he'd grunt and then he'd make a goat sound. "Goat! Goat!"

Pops would put up with it, ignore Andy stoically for as long as he could. Finally, when he had enough nudging and grunting he'd respond in a low baritone: "Son, you aint got no more sense than a hound dawg!" More grunt-grunt and nudge-nudge. I kid you not.

Somehow Andy became an air force pilot, 1918 or so. I have no idea how. Andy chuckled when he mentioned to us that his mother sent him a worried letter imploring him not to fly too high. Apparently he did and crashed his plane in Panama. I have no idea why or what he was doing there. In any case he was injured badly enough to receive a veteran's pension, and of more importance was laid up next to a Wobbly with a broken back named Lawrence "Dutch" Ecker. No one knows if he was really Dutch but that is what he was called. While there, over a period of months, in the tropical heat, Dutch in his strange accent proceeded to educate Andy. Gave him pamphlets on Marx, anarchism, the IWW. Andy became a life-long Wobbly.

He made it a practice of naming his children after his Wobbly buddies. The first, Larry, was named for Lawrence Ecker; the second, Herbert, for Herbert Mahler, whom I have mentioned and will return to again. The third was named Benjamin Harrison Fletcher Homer! As you may guess, Andy had a way of wearing out wives. So Sam had to wait for the new wife and her first child, for his namesake: Sammy Weiner Homer.

Ben and Clara were delighted with little Ben. He was the grandchild they would never have. They doted on him. I have a photo of big Ben, his beautiful face filled with pride, holding little Ben close to him.

So here was Andy, crude white man from the deepest South, who had not a racist bone in his body. I can tell you it was not simply a matter of naming his child after Ben. Andy loved Ben. Each week he made the inconvenient trek to central Brooklyn by car to collect Ben and Clara and return them in the evening. He had a school boy's respect for "teacher" Clara. He talked dirty, scatological to Ben's glee when she was out of earshot. But when she was near, Andy was all attention, good manners, and charm! He'd clean the tobacco juice from the walls before she came, was on his best behavior, because he knew Clara would not put up with his "stuff." Toward Mother, Andy behaved differently. She would make faces and turn away from Andy's vulgarity in pain; that amused him and he laid it on thick for her benefit.

I'll not forget my last image of Ben. Sam took me to see him one Saturday afternoon, 1948 or so. He would die less than a year later, in 1949. He was not well at all and looking back I am sure it was the reason for our visit. Clara and Ben lived in the basement of their brownstone; the windows were high at street level and the rooms were dark. Sam and Ben had a good time laughing and gossiping about the old days. Clara went off to work. Ben flipped on the TV set, one of those anti-diluvium Dumonts with the round, ten-inch screen. We had no TV so I stared in awe at this marvel of technological progress.

Ben had on the ball game. It was the Brooklyn Dodgers. Ben watched the tiny black and white action intently. Suddenly the tension was broken. With the poor camera work of the day you could barely see the flickering image of a player no larger than an ant scooting around the bases. Ben thumped his hands up and down in joy. He turned to me, his eyes bright in the dark room as Sam and I prepared to leave.

"He got a hit! He got a hit! You see that? He got a hit!"

It was Jackie Robinson.

Ten years after Ben's death, in 1959, I met Martin Luther King. He had just finished an address to the faculty of Miami University (Ohio); a graduate teaching assistant, I was technically faculty and allowed in. The leader of the Montgomery Alabama bus boycott and the awakening Civil Rights movement of the Deep South, he was a figure of interest, nationally known, but not yet of transcendent importance. Selma, The March On Washington, I Have a Dream, the Memphis Balcony, all lay before him. The meeting was well attended; fifty or so liberal professors, all white. I felt he was speaking cautiously to his audience: a little stiff, not in his element, alert not to offend. He was seeking support, funds. On a speaking tour, some behind him, more to go, maybe a bit tired. None of this subtracted from the feeling that you were in the presence of an impressive man. He had that ability to resonate emotionally with an audience, chest to chest, to make each individual feel he was uniting to a cause larger than oneself. Like Sam and some of the old-time Wobbly and socialist speakers I've heard.

He came to the center of the room after his speech where an informal queue waited to shake his hand. And that is how we met. Ten seconds at best. There was nothing special to note about the encounter and I would have forgotten it except that the hand I shook that day was the hand of Martin Luther King.

What I gave a damn about was not shaking his hand but the opportunity, however brief, to stand in front of him and look him in the eye. His coloring was dark brown and not jet black like Ben's. I was surprised he was not taller than he was; he had a kind of barrel chest, strong looking, the build of a middle-weight wrestler. His nose was long and delicate; the plains of his face flat, and without the fleshy appearance his cheeks took on as he aged. It was a youthful face, in my recollection markedly different than the one evident in the last photographs. When our eyes met I saw a young man; he was after all only eight years my senior.

"Dr. King, I enjoyed your speech," was all I could think of to say under pressure of those waiting behind me. If each of us knew then about events to come, I could have said more; that my parents and I knew a good friend of his, Bayard Rustin, who was instrumental in helping him formulate his philosophy of nonviolence and who was a key figure in the March on Washington.

That night I called Sam. I told him I heard King speak and shook his hand. What do you think of him, Sam asked?

He's an impressive fellow, I answered. Sam paused. Then I heard him harrumph in that way he had when not comfortable with the conversation.

"Let's see if he measures up to half the man of Ben Fletcher," he growled.

# 34

# HERBERT MAHLER, COCKROACH BUSINESSMAN

We were poor—not starvation poor, but poor nonetheless. My parents took no part in the relative prosperity of the post WWII 1940s and early 1950s. Almost my entire world consisted of the Lower East Side. We were the residue of a vast Jewish population, a million strong, that fled its American ghetto of a few square blocks, and spread out to join the wider America—leaving behind abandoned synagogues and socialism and the Yiddish language. The escapees were second, third, fourth generation Jews who looked down on those that remained behind for their ethnic coarseness and working-class status. I was of this left behind world.

On the other hand I had the riches of my imagination. I was of a generation of Lower East Side boys, who like Martin Scorcese of neighboring Little Italy—and so many others—circumvented a restrictive life by escaping into the dark of the movies: To the Loews (we pronounced it "Low-ease"), Delancey, the Canal, the Palestine (a different connotation then), the Windsor. Third-run houses. The "big sky" westerns were my favorites, the ones featuring open space, jagged cliffs, cactuses, towering trees. My favorite heroes of the west, though, were not to be found in these movies. They were called Wobblies.

We will take another long walk now, not to the Five-Ten Hall this time, but to Herb Mahler's place. It is a suffocating August night, 1948 or so, the kind of night that pastes your shirt to your back. Air conditioning? Science fiction. We pass through lower Manhattan streets not to be gentrified for fifty years. Streets teeming with Puerto Ricans gesticulating in Spanglish over board games and dominoes. And working-class Italian housewives in slippers and house dresses that had grown too tight for them, gossiping on the "stoops" fronting their ancient tenements, gulping homemade iced tea from glass milk bottles. And kids of diverse sizes, shapes, and colors running underfoot and between parked cars and around traffic, and hitching rides from the backs of slow buses. And naked children, in a state of delirium, splashing in the wake of open fire hydrants: two to a block, gushing water full blast. The atmosphere is saturated with smoke from sausages, and the ingratiating, oily scent of chuchifritos. It is a lost New York.

The hike up from the bottom of Manhattan where we live to Mahler's place on Seventh Avenue and Fifteenth Street is bracing. But you will hear no complaint from me. You see, Mahler and his wife Bessie own a hole-in-the-wall candy store. The sight of all that free stuff intoxicates me, although in practice I am allowed two things. I settle for ice cream and a coke, which is an eating and drinking experience different from the same junk today. Ever have a Melo-Roll? It was a vanilla cylinder of frozen cholesterol, naked on top and bottom, encircled in rough paper. You stabbed it in the center with a thin wooden stick, unwrapped the paper, and sucked, bit, and licked away—while the melting white paste stuck to your fingers and dripped down your chin to your neck. You needed the coke to wash the guck down your gullet. You drank the coke from its iconic glass bottle. There was no plastic.

We all sat toward the back of the one room shop, on folding chairs and cartons, next to the waist high ice cream freezer, away from the heat, while Herb tended to the passing street traffic that formed his livelihood: "Lucky Strikes and matches? There you are! Butterfingers and Jujy Fruits? There you go."

After a busy spurt, as things quieted down, Herb would wander back to us wearing a sheepish expression. Then he'd untie the white apron from around his waist, which he did unconsciously, for he would only have to retie it.

"Herbert Mahler, cockroach businessman!" he'd exclaim, while exchanging a glance of deepest irony with my father. It was an irony earned: this man of action and purpose and high drama washed by the tides of history onto a candy store at Seventh Avenue and Fifteenth Street.

It was in that tiny candy store, near the freezer in the sticky evening heat—with his beloved Bessie at his side—that Herbert Mahler, self-proclaimed "cockroach businessman," proceeded to bring the old West to life before my eyes; the Wobbly West, that is. Mahler's life was with the Wobblies of the West. When he spoke of that life, in an inflection that was definitely not New York, it came across as a saga of an America long gone. There was an epic quality to it that reminded me of the "big sky Westerns" I absorbed in dark movie theaters after school. The American West. The Wobblies. The America of Myth. It all fused together in my romantic, sub-teenage soul.

Mahler pronounced his name "Mailer" rather than with the broad sound used for the great composer Gustav Mahler. I find that worth noting, although I cannot say exactly why. He was a man of dignity: tall, handsome, blue eyed, white haired, though when I knew him he panted from heart trouble and was a bit thick about the waist. He had the bearing of a distinguished lawyer, which in effect he had been for many years. He was born in 1890, just over the border in Chatham, Ontario, the last stop on the Underground Railroad, and he spoke fondly of his far-away youth among the children and grandchildren of the escaped slaves that had settled there. As a young man, I do not know exactly when, he tried his hand at boxing, and developed into a good light heavyweight. For a time, he palled around and trained with a heavyweight by the name of Victor McLaglen. Mahler said the man could take a hell of a punch. However, acting was the easier way to make a living. Film buffs may recall that McLaglen won an Oscar in the early 1930s for his portrayal of Gypo Nolan, an Irish revolutionist turned rat, in John Ford's *The Informer*, and he had a long career as John Wayne's perennial sidekick and foil in all those Ford westerns. He was the one with the gnarled head and the face like a side of beef; like many of the old Wobblies I remember.

In 1910, Mahler headed to the Canadian Northwest in search of work, and found it as a riverboat pilot, and then as an itinerant tall-tree logger in the lumber camps of the Canadian forests. It was there, in the camps, that he met up with the Wobblies, and became one himself. The man was a born organizer. Nor did it hurt his cause that on several occasions he was able to square off and flatten a company goon in full view of the loggers gathered round in a circle. Just like in the movies! And just like in the movies, to my impressionable mind there were the good guys—the Wobblies—on one side, and the bad guys—the greedy Capitalist Lumber Trust or Mine Owners or Ranchers or whatever the incarnation—on the other. You knew for whom to root once the shooting started and the bodies fell.

I loved to listen to the man! "You could tell the work a man did in the West by his deformities," Mahler would say to us there in his Fifteenth Street candy store, and the images he left me are indelible. A one eyed stiff? Dead giveaway of the hard rock miner—from blasting and the rock bursts that sent chips whizzing past his head at the speed of light. All long-time miners spit, and wheezed from lung disease. A severe gimp? Mark of the timber beast; they'd most all of them broke a leg in time that had not been set properly, maybe not at all! And don't forget the bronchitis phlegm or the "white cheese" from the touch of TB. Missing fingers, sometimes an entire hand up to the wrist? Signature of the shingle weaver. The man had to stand between two huge saws, blades like shark's teeth, each rotating two hundred times a minute, and shape and slice log segments that came to him from a conveyer belt he was powerless to turn off! Ten hours a day, six days a week. Inhaling cedar dust for years and years of his life. Sooner or later the blades were bound to find him. Usually happened late in the shift, as exhaustion set in. "The Weaver did not hold a job; he was trapped in a nightmare."

Mahler said the Wobblies called the loggers "Timber Beasts," because in fact they were treated as such. According to one Wobbly organizer:

> Now the logger, he walks out in the woods and he looks around at a wilderness of trees. He works hard in there. And what does he get? He gets wages that are below the dead line, I say dead line in wages means below the line necessary to keep him alive.... They are being murdered on the installment plan....
>
> They breathe bad air in the camps. That ruins their lungs. They eat bad food. That ruins their stomachs. The foul conditions shorten their lives and make their short lives miserable. It rains a great deal and they work in the rain...When they come in from the camps, they are wet.... They go into a dark barn, not as good as where the horses are, and the only place to dry

their clothes is around the hot stove.... Those in the top bunk suffer from heat; those far away, from the cold.... Business is business. And so the logger, he finds that he is nothing but a living machine.

The man was testifying before a federal commission of the time. The cadence, the poetry could as easily been Mahler's. All this for less than $2.50 a day—and yeah, yeah, I have not adjusted for inflation.

If anything, the testimony downplays the squalid, fetid conditions that existed in the camps. There is no mention of the lack of water for a man to wash; of the garbage piled high; of the lice and bed bugs; of the revolting smell of the sweat-stained clothes drying over the fires; of the bad-to-nonexistent first aid in a job that was surely dangerous. It says nothing of the human lice that preyed upon the men in the camps: the "sharks" seeking phony employment fees, the swindlers, the pimps, the "hijackers" who robbed them at gunpoint.

The aim of the Wobblies was to help "the timber beast" become a "lumber worker." Mahler played a large behind-the-scenes role in the success of that effort.

When young I was most impressed by Mahler's recounting of the free speech fights and pitched gun battles the Wobblies fought in the Northwest. They were impressive, more exciting than the Hollywood westerns that mostly covered the wrong battles. But the Wobblies were not all about blood and guts. Mahler labored to weave them into the fabric of Seattle life, to dispel the hostility against them—this notion of them as "the other," the foreign menace, rather than working-class Americans opposed to the wage-system. So the Wobblies had their baseball team. Each weekend they played against their supposed enemies: teams fielded by churches, banks, local civic groups.

Mahler's strict orders: you wear the uniform of the IWW! You are not the troublemakers! Under no circumstances are you to argue with the umpire no matter how outrageous his decision. Under no circumstances are you to show up drunk or spit tobacco juice and adjust your crotch in front of the ladies in the stands!

The same kind of behavior, though looser, was expected at the amateur boxing matches. No arguing with the referee! No hitting below the belt! No rabbit punches! Mahler trained the men with particular attention to the volunteer organizers.

And no heavy drinking at picnics, where everyone was invited.

Mahler was thinking ahead to the reception Wobblies could expect at open-air meetings and in courtroom jury selections. Mahler was always thinking ahead. His specialty became getting innocent men off murder raps.

Sam became fast friends with Herb Mahler during his Chicago days of the late 1920s and early 1930s. He served as Mahler's confidant and sounding board during his heartfelt courtship of Bessie, though I doubt Sam was the first person one would turn to seeking romantic advice; Bessie, in her youth a great beauty with flowing dark red hair, was much sought after. By the time they met, Mahler's most active and bloody days were behind him: the Everett massacre, the founding of the General Defense Committee of the IWW, his stint in Leavenworth Penitentiary. The man had been a confidant of Big Bill Haywood, Frank Little, James Rowan, Ralph Chaplin. He'd learned practical lawyering at the side of the attorneys that represented the IWW in their murder trials and free speech fights.

Membership had shrunk to ten- or fifteen thousand when Mahler became General Secretary-Treasurer of the IWW in 1931, and the bickering, the backbiting had increased in proportion to the decline. I suspect it is the fate of many a declining movement. Nevertheless, the organization was still active and not the nonfactor many historians and detractors seem intent on describing. They had a small presence in Harlan County, Kentucky when the coal mines erupted in the first of what was to be a series of epic strikes. The strike at its core pitted desperate locked-out miners, many of them homeless and destitute, in a life and death struggle against coal company agents and local authorities. Mahler had the approval of the IWW General Executive Board (GEB) to step in and lend support to the strikers. What he saw there—the brutality of the police and the mine owners, the literal starvation of the miners and their children—reached the core of the man. This is why he had become a Wobbly.

On May 5, 1931 a large group of armed miners attacked a convoy of deputies; a heavy exchange of fire, lasting thirty minutes, left three deputies and one miner dead. Local union officials W. B. Jones and William Hightower and more than forty miners were arrested in connection with the killing of the deputies. Mahler committed himself and the IWW to their legal defense. At this point events grow murky. The upshot is that the GEB, probably for good tactical reasons, ordered Mahler to pull the IWW out of Harlan County. Mahler refused; he had given his word to these men. They had put their faith in the IWW and he would not abandon them. So, after a nasty internal fight, Mahler was forced to resign as General Secretary-Treasurer and was expelled from the IWW.

Sam said to me many years later, recounting the incident, "Do you know what that meant to a man like Mahler, who gave his life to the organization?"

But Mahler did not, would not, leave the Harlan Kentucky miners. After several trials, Jones, Hightower, and six others were convicted of conspiracy to commit murder. By that time, the powerful United Mine Workers under John L. Lewis; the communists; the liberals; and the editorial writers had faded away. But Mahler remained, fighting to have their sentence reversed. As Sam put it:

> Herbert Mahler has been dead many years now. Let it be known that he had been given far less than the recognition he so richly merits for the part he played in exposing the Harlan County, Kentucky gunman paid by the mine owners to break the strike and destroy the mine workers' union. Mahler succeeded in organizing the defense and achieved the release of innocent workers framed and sentenced in 1931 to life imprisonment. Mahler devoted ten years of his life from 1931 to 1941 to unremitting efforts to secure the release of William Hightower, Elzie Philips (in May 1935) and William Hudson (December 1935)....
>
> People tended to forget the plight of the four other imprisoned miners.... But Mahler did not in the least relax his efforts to secure their freedom. Seven years later, in 1941, at the risk of his life, he came to Pineville and other Harlan County

locations to gather the incontrovertible evidence that brought their release. The approved parole papers were delivered to the Kentucky Reformatory by Herbert Mahler of the Kentucky Miners Defense.

What must Mahler have felt? Sam recounts the celebration at the Five-Ten Hall when Mahler brought Hightower there. Eighty years of age, the old boy had plenty of juice left. He had recently married his thirty-year-old sweetheart!

Mahler died in 1961. Sam called me with the news. I felt a sadness that went beyond the death of a man I knew many years ago, who was older than my father. I remembered our long walks to his candy store. Cockroach businessman indeed! Now, as I write this, I am reminded that Herbert Mahler and Ben Fletcher were deep friends. Both men were born in 1890, served time together in the same prison, gave their lives in the same just cause of others. I am also reminded that Mahler wrote a poem in eulogy to Ben at his funeral twelve years earlier. The words apply equally to him:

> Rest, rest old fighter, rest
> Scars of battle on your breast
> Prove that you have done your best,
> Rest, rest old fighter, rest.

# 35

# THE DRINKING LIFE

I have put off discussing Sam's ugly side. It is painful. However, I have committed myself to telling the truth about his life and times; biased, but the truth nonetheless. My father was a drunk. I prefer not to use the word alcoholic. His mid-thirties and forties bore the brunt of it, and, although he had relapses, he tapered off to the point where he hardly drank at all his last forty years. Nevertheless, that hard drinking mid-period had a near devastating impact. What started him off? Why did he continue for as long as he did?

Marten Pine was a Sam protégé who is as close to me as a brother. He offers the occupational hypothesis: that Sam was a typical old-time house painter who drank and smoked to mask the disgusting taste of the paint fumes in his mouth. A longtime home builder and contractor, he knows the trade.

Mother offered the evil friends hypothesis: That many of his supposed friends were jealous of his abilities and sought to get him drunk by taking advantage of his trusting nature. She insisted, and I believe her, that Sam was not a heavy drinker when she met him.

These explanations may have some truth to them but do not quite make it. For example, Sam's longtime friend and comrade, the anarchist Jack Frager—veteran of the Russian Revolution—was also a house painter and never touched a drop. And many of Sam's drinking buddies—such as Andy Homer—were manifestly Sam's true friends and found no pleasure in belittling him. Each of these hypotheses runs the fault of letting Sam off the hook. They do not explain the fact that when Sam finally decided not to drink any more, or at least not to get drunk, he quit.

I do not know precisely what caused Sam to drink so hard for so long: I suspect there is no "precisely."

He enjoyed it. He might have picked up the habit in a hobo jungle or on that ship to Shanghai he took after he ran away from home. Ben Reitman wrote him prescriptions for booze in prohibition Chicago. The Wobbly seamen of the Five-Ten Hall and of the

Newark, New Jersey branch, whom he hung with quite a bit, were, with notable exceptions, a drinking crowd. Getting drunk to many of them was simply life. There was no disgrace to it and if they acted amused by Sam's antics that does not mean he was victim of a plot. Sam liked to drink, probably in the same way that young people today enjoy getting high. It was a release from being harnessed to the responsibility of providing for a wife and small children. It was a release from hard work. If he could not be free he could at least have the illusion of freedom for a few short hours. I doubt if he thought of the reasons for his drinking. He was not given to introspection of that sort.

Sam's drinking had somehow fused with his egalitarian, communal philosophy. It was an obligation willingly assumed by my parents that no "fellow worker," no "comrade," no one of the "movement" be denied a "flop," a meal, a warm welcome—no matter how poor we were or how cramped our apartment. This insured Wobblies were all over my life as a boy, not always to wholesome effect. Hardly a day or week passed without waking up to a Wobbly snoring on our sagging couch or stretched out on our living room floor in underwear and stinking socks. Often Abe and I would come home from school to find complete strangers around our dinner table acting as if they owned it. Then there were the late nights Abe and I were awakened to Wobblies escorting Sam home drunk, bellowing revolutionary songs.

What is worse for a boy to see: His father reduced to a fool or his mother's anguish?

Sam's drunkenness carried over to public places. He had a genius for making a spectacle of himself at the large, dignified gatherings of the Finns, Hungarians, and other "ethnic" Wobblies. It may surprise you, for example, that the Finns owned their own building in the 1930s and could draw crowds of over five hundred at annual events for class war prisoners and the like. When I knew them in the late '40s the crowds were down to 150 or so. Sam spoke at these events and was well received. But he invariably got plastered afterward. "Friends" egged him on and he'd start singing and rumbling about like a dancing bear to their amusement in full view of the same audience that had applauded him earlier in the evening.

Again, I cannot begin to describe Mother's humiliation before the other women present who stared pityingly at her. And how were we to get him home? Taxis were expensive. Often an understanding comrade would drop us off.

Sam's drunkenness at public events and at committee meetings was *prima facie* evidence that he lacked self-control, a trait not desired in a revolutionist. So his reputation suffered. The Wobblies may have been tolerant of his drinking, but that does not mean they respected him for it. Public drunkenness is especially frowned upon in old-fashioned Jewish culture; the drunkard is an object of contempt, and that rubbed off on Sam. You could see some of his *Vanguard* and *Freie Arbeiter Stimme* comrades snigger when he was barely out of range. He had earned the reputation as a drinker; only his energy and sincerity, and occasional brilliance served to balance things out somewhat. The irony of it all is that Sam's critics probably consumed more alcohol than he did. My father's problem was that although he liked to drink, he could not hold his liquor.

Now I should clarify things. Sam was not always drunk at public meetings, mostly not. He never drank at home; rather he would return home drunk, which was bad enough. He was never violent toward Mother or Abe and I. He did not drink continuously or most of the time, and in the time he was not drinking, a boy could not ask for a better father. These mitigating factors had the perverse effect of making matters worse when he was drinking, for the contrast was stark and the adjustment more difficult.

Sam's drinking nearly destroyed us. The intervening years—all the events of a life between then and now—have no effect on the clarity of my misery. I remember lying in bed in the little room Abe and I shared, listening in the dark for him to stumble home, while Mother waited for him at the kitchen table in a state of wretchedness and fury. Her shouts, her screams, her sarcasm echoed down the halls of our apartment house and out the windows onto the street, while Sam played the bass part to her tortured melody, mumbling semi-apologies. Finally, he would calm her down to muffled whimpers and sobs. Probably they had sex, although I did not know of such things then, for they usually woke the next morning in a more cheerful mood.

Those evenings are probably the origin of Abe's anger toward Sam—an anger that lingers though Sam is long dead and Abe is in his eighty-third year. Yes, he appreciates Sam's good points, even acknowledges he was touched by brilliance, but always with a wry smile and a comment pointing to how impractical he was, how self-ish in his drinking, how he could have afforded Mother a better life.

I began to have nightmares. What set me off was a scene in *The Lost Weekend*, long considered the classic Hollywood film about an alcoholic. The year was 1945. You may think it strange that Mother would bring us to such a movie, but she did. She took comfort in the company of her sons. I forget now the intricacies of plot, although I remember vividly Ray Milland's desperation while hiking the entire length of Third Avenue in the shadow of the elevated train tracks, all in search of a drink. And THE SCENE: Milland, far gone in his drinking, contracts the "DTs," that is the Delirium Tremens. He sees a rat crawling out of a crack in the wall, then a bat flapping above, and the bat devouring the rat. It was terrifying! I was afraid the same thing would happen to Sam; that Sam would get the DTs, that he would go mad. I started to shriek. Mother and Sam rushed to my bedside. Sam held me close, his arm around my shoulder.

None of it is real, he explained as I clung to him. It is a movie; they are actors. They go home after work, eat dinner! But his words could not stop me from shivering.

"Do you see what you are doing to your child," Mother pleaded.

Sam was crushed, though he did not stop drinking. But I think, finally, that Mother had gotten through to him and he knew he would have to stop.

I have often tried to pin down the deeper reason the DTs scene in *The Lost Weekend* terrified me so. And I have come to the conclusion that it depicted the consequences of a man lost, completely unable to control events, and that is how I saw my father. A father who has lost control. A mother driven to hysteria. Who then is to protect a small boy against the world?

There were practical consequences of his drinking. To put the matter bluntly, Sam often drank up his pay, which placed Mother in a state of panic, because we had no money in the bank, and therefore no way to meet the monthly rent or to feed us. Things got so bad that Sam was forced to work out an arrangement with John, the owner of the corner grocery store and butcher shop. John also owned several slum buildings in the neighborhood and the deal was Sam would work off in the spring the debt he had incurred in the winter. I'll let you guess who got the better of *that* arrangement.

Sam was usually paid each Friday afternoon when working for a contractor. Mother's campaign began the next Saturday morning. Where are you working? When do you finish? How long does it take you to get home? What subway do you take? Unbeknownst to Sam she enlisted his friend Chris Hansen to go the job site and cut him off at the pass before he drank his pay. I was taken along for effect. We were successful once or twice until Sam stopped supplying the information. He was not pleased to see us on the job, to be treated as a child not to be trusted, and he became surly on the way home.

Foiled at cutting Sam off at the pass, Mother was forced to employ a "blanket strategy." That is, we searched as many crummy bars as we could between Fourteenth Street and South Street east of Third Avenue. He had a preference for Polish, Russian, and Ukrainian dumps that smelled of pickles and rancid meat, the perpetually dark ones thick in sawdust as from a sand storm, where he'd bellow folk songs in bad, generalized Slovak. Never mind he was Jew. Sam was always welcome, since he never counted his change. Abe did this more than me, as he was four years older. Fortunately, Sam's favorite was a dive on the corner of Jefferson and Henry streets, about four blocks from home. He seldom protested when Abe came for him.

"This is my oldest son," he'd announce proudly as twelve-year-old Abe entered. Then Abe helped him stagger back to our fourth-floor refuge at 250 Clinton Street. His repertoire changed on the way to such revolutionary standards as "The Red Flag." The neighborhood children heard the words so often that one peaceful Sunday they gathered beneath our window to serenade us to "The worker's flag is deepest red/ It shrouded oft our martyred dead." They sung it in key, better than Sam, though clearly their purpose was not benign. Sam gave Mother a sheepish grin. Mother nodded to him significantly. Understatement was best.

# 36

## CHRIS TAKES ME TO THE FIGHTS

Others came and went, but there was always Chris—Chris Hansen—a family fixture, over for dinner virtually seven days a week. Chris Hansen was Mother's ally in her lonely battle to get Sam to stop drinking. He was the grandfather I'd never known. Chris had been a drinker himself and was an early follower of Alcoholics Anonymous (AA).

"Admit to a higher power? What the hell kind of Wobbly are you? Why, they're part of the Catholic Church!" Sam would growl at him, taking advantage of an easy way to avoid the stop-drinking issue.

But Chris persisted nevertheless. He and Sam went way back. A ship's carpenter, a product of the Norwegian stronghold of Bay Ridge, Brooklyn, he had joined the IWW early on, and had been a friend of Jack Walsh, Walter Nef, and Ben Fletcher on the Philadelphia docks. He had also been a stage hand in a burlesque theater in his youth, and served as a chiropractor and masseur to a troupe of traveling chorus girls, circa 1910, supplying a "twist in the legs" when needed—and did that get a snort from his fellow Wobblies, no matter how sincere his tone. Chris had been a man of many aspects and spent years as a trainer of boxers. He did have his prejudices, however. No, he was not a racist; he was an ageist. Old was automatically better. There had not been a good fighter since Jack Dempsey! "The man was born old!" Sam said crankily. I loved Chris for that. He taught me things. I took to walking like Chris: leaning backward slightly and stepping slowly forward with legs widespread in that gait some old people get.

Visiting Chris was my first destination when I became old enough to navigate the streets of the Lower East Side. If there was no school, I was out the door in the early morning, down the four flights onto the street, turn right and hike straight up Clinton, past Delancey, past Houston, trudge past Tompkins Square Park into the tough Russian neighborhood, where you had to watch your ass, and, finally, Eleventh Street, where I turn right two blocks to one building short of Avenue D. Five flights up the rickety stairs and thump on Chris's door. A pause, some rustling about, and Chris opens the door wide, wearing pants with suspenders over his long underwear.

"Hey, Hey!" Chris smiles, as I pass him.

The place has a strong doggy smell from Spot and Pork Chop, wire-haired terriers, father and son. Spot is so old he can barely wag his stump of a tail and Pork Chop is not far behind. I hug them, frazzle their tight hair.

"Want some breakfast?" Sure.

Chris gets an ancient glass into which he pours orange juice, splits open an egg and lets the yoke drop, adds a tablespoon or two of honey, mixes thoroughly. "It's good for you! Better than cake. Better than candy. Don't eat that stuff!"

I gulp the mixture, standing in the tiny kitchen. Actually, it tastes good. I must stand because there is no place to sit. Chris is a hoarder. Except for his bed, lost somewhere in the back, the entire place is covered floor to ceiling with every object imaginable. What I especially remember are two hollow columns—stage prop ruins of ancient Rome—truncated, about four-feet high.

"Chris, what do you need them for?" I say.

"They're good. Hard to find them!" Inspecting the stuff other people threw away was his favorite activity.

Following "breakfast," and with Spot and Pork Chop in harness, we begin our long meandering walk—during which Chris sniffs each garbage can and his two roommates piss on each hydrant. Destination? Back to our place, in time for Abe's practice session. Abe will never experience a more fervent audience. That is, Spot and Pork Chop howl like hell the instant he starts on the clarinet.

Chris took me on a memorable trip when I was twelve or so. For some time before that I had been listening to his stories of the old-time fighters he knew or knew of. I became enamored of the heroic battles they fought in the ring, epic struggles involving Jack Johnson, Jack Dempsey, Stanley Ketchel, Harry Greb, Harry Wills, Benny Leonard, and the like. Many of them were Wobblies, according to Chris! And that connected me to the stories Herbert Mahler told of himself and the Wobblies of the west. It all fused together in my feverish imagination. I'd thrash my arms about in fantasy struggles behind the closed door of our bedroom when Abe was away, knocking out fantasy opponents while Don Dunphy, the "Friday Night Fights" radio announcer, gave the blow by blow inside my head. One day after an orgy of fury I opened the door and announced that I was becoming a boxer. Mother was mortified.

"Chris, Chris, he wants to a boxer! He'll ruin his face! His face!" Mother implored him in whispers so I would not hear.

"Don't worry, Esther, I'll take care of it!" Chris promised.

Chris took me on my memorable trip to assuage Mother's fear. He took me to Fort Hamilton Arena. In those days boxing had a far larger following than today and television had not yet smothered local spontaneity. Each neighborhood fielded its baseball team and staged its "club" fights at the local stadium that sat perhaps five hundred or so. Fort Hamilton Arena, in far away Brooklyn was among the largest of them. They featured fighters who would never make it, part timers who doubled as garage mechanics, long-faded headliners, and the occasional prospect.

My first brush with the reality of boxing occurred outside the Arena. "Hi, Chris!" the old-timer selling programs greeted us. His dark brown face was a mask of disfigurement; Punch Drunk Morse of the Five-Ten Hall looked handsome by contrast. The old man limped. He looked unsteady.

"This is my friend, Dootsie [a bastardization of Durruti]," Chris answered, and then to me: "Tommy here had 150 fights!" Tommy smiled proudly, showing no teeth as we walked away. Chris said nothing more until we were seated in the open-air twilight as the lights lit up the square ring.

The bell rang, the fighters engaged, and started swinging. There are few sounds as nauseating as a fist landing full force against unprotected flesh. I held back the urge to vomit. The romance of boxing fled from me in an instant. I wanted to go home, but did not want to appear soft. So I stayed and watched. The crowd roared and whistled as the sounds intensified and one of the fighters crumpled. They hooted and booed during the next match as two black fighters seemed to waltz around the ring. But Chris took a keen interest. "The crowd only wants blood. These fellows are professionals. You see how they slip the punches? Look at their feet! See, see, always in balance." Chris was the only one clapping at the end.

I wanted to go home. My stomach was upset. But Chris insisted I go with him to a rickety wooden structure behind the stands. It was the fighters' dressing rooms. We entered to a blast of sweat and gore. There, in a side room, we saw a boxer being attended to by what I hope was a doctor who was sewing up a bloody cut around his eye.

Chris saw my revulsion. "He's the winner!" he informed me in a quiet, meaningful tone. He had promised Mother he would handle things.

Chris was uniformly loyal and decent. Mother felt alone and isolated in dealing with Sam, and Chris was someone she could rely on. Looking back, I think he was sweet on her—but in a platonic way. He respected Sam despite his drinking and he was a *very* upright and old-fashioned man. He was Chris, of our family.

## 37
## I START TO GROW UP

I'll never know precisely how old I was, nor is it important. But I remember vividly the day the morning sun flooded my bedroom, spread across my naked body, and exposed a soft mat of pubic hair: not nearly a full grown bush, but unmistakable nevertheless. I was shocked. Surely I could have seen the growth earlier and maybe I had, and yet this was my first conscious discovery of it. I searched out the fuzz in my armpits, chest, and cheeks. No doubt about it: I was growing up.

My world was expanding along with my body. I was required to walk a greater distance to school, to navigate unfamiliar streets and neighborhoods on my own. I learned not everyone in the world was Jewish. We lived close to the waterfront and in those days working men tended to live close to where they worked. So I ran with the children of longshoremen—mostly Italian and Irish longshoremen: Tommy May, Spud Gerry, Jim Cody, Eddie Falco, Frank (Chico) Carbone. We got along fine except when we did not and I had to learn to take care of myself in those times, too: whom to fight and whom to avoid, when to be a lion and when a fox. I learned that most fights were not fair and that most bullies, contrary to moralistic folklore, were not cowards.

Richie Carlson was an early nemesis. Two years older, four inches taller, and twenty pounds heavier, he knew my schedule and lay in waiting for me to show up at school where he emptied my pockets and confiscated my sandwich. He pulled this on the other smaller kids as well; a shakedown artist in miniature. It got so I was afraid to show up. Finally, desperate, I did what I promised myself I would not do: I whined to Sam about it.

Sam gave me a bit of advice, no doubt learned the hard way. "Hurt him! Think of nothing but that. It doesn't matter how." So the next day, shivering fear, I would not let him put his hands in my pocket. He punched me in the face, my nose bled, but I locked on to a single thing. I bent back the pinky finger of his left hand full force gripping it in both my hands. I would not let go. I attached myself to him, followed him wherever he squirmed, until he howled in pain and begged me to stop. He said I was a little prick, that I fought like a girl. He ridiculed me in front of his friends or, I should say, those he intimidated into acting as if they were. All of that. But he kept his hands out of my pockets and I ate my own sandwich.

Beyond fights, of which there were plenty, I learned of the social cruelty of children. Whether this cruelty is culturally or genetically inherited I do not know, but it led me to doubt early on the inherent goodness of The Child, a hypothesis of many sincere anarchists. I'm thinking of the treatment the neighborhood kids afforded my dear brother Abraham. The concrete rectangle of a park across the street from our house crawled with boys his age: laughing, scrapping, playing in all kinds of ways. But it was obvious Abe could not see well since he wore eyeglasses thick as a glass Coke bottle, and he bent forward, and he couldn't react rapidly enough to things that whizzed by him. So he was ignored. He did not exist, which is perhaps the greatest humiliation of all, and I watched silently, ashamed I chose not do more, as Abe—a lonely boy—returned upstairs to his music.

I learned the games of the city streets, many of which I am told date back to the Middle Ages: ring-o-leeve-eo, Johnny on the Pony, skelly. When I was a bit older there were ball games: stickball, a variation of baseball played with a pink rubber ball, a broom handle of a bat. In those days of lesser civilization, traffic was maybe one-tenth of what it is today and children could still play stickball in the streets, the hydrants and manhole coverings serving as bases. We played in packs. We ran in packs. Our life at home, at dinner with our families, running chores, our time at school, were apart from our real life. Our real life was the pack, on the streets. The pack had its own rules, enforced mostly by a few dominant individuals, not necessarily the strongest but the most charismatic. They were boys like us but with that indefinable quality that made you crave their approval.

I can well understand the gang cultures of Latino and black Los Angeles, of Chicago, of Detroit, and other cities. They are commonly explained in racial terms, but as an early graduate of a gang culture, I am convinced race is not the fundamental factor. Territory, the physical control of space, an area in which you feel free and have, above all, a defined status: that is the controlling factor. Your turf! And woe to the poor fish who wandered in without permission. We'd fight boys from three, five, or six blocks away from working-class families like our own, for hardly any reason at all: a perceived slight, a move onto our park to play games, a flirtation with someone's sister. Our fights were of the primitive variety reflective of the times. Ordinary firearms were hard to come by. Instead we had the zip-gun, made from rubber tubing strapped to a block of wood, and a stiff rubber band to activate the firing pin. Trouble is the bullet could go backwards as easily as forwards or the whole thing could explode in your hand. But zip-guns were exotic. Typically we fought with weapons that, like our games, went back to the Middle Ages: a chain with a heavy weight on the end, stickball bats with nails attached, knives and the like. I participated in a couple of these nasty jousts. Terrifying! Ten kids on each side swinging those things, ducking behind park cars, chasing one another down alleyways. The best protection you had was mutual fear of getting maimed, so you and your opponent ended up swinging at relatively safe distances.

We were boys, not snarling wolves or killers, and our bad behavior ran more to the nasty prank than the criminal. Summer Saturday nights were especially fruitful. The heat emptied the apartments of their inhabitants and life moved to the streets—to the men and women on the stoops fronting their buildings and the children playing in the wake of the open hydrants. The entire block served as an informal reviewing stand for the young men on the way to pick up their Saturday night dates, a formal procedure in those days. Most of them were from middle-class families, the type the girls hoped to snare, and each wore a suit and a tie and carried a bouquet. And their young ladies—the older sisters and cousins and neighbors of the pack—waited in their best dresses and fresh hairdos. Our job was to make sure things did not turn out as planned. We'd drag the poor, unsuspecting fellow under the hydrant and not release him until soaking wet and dripping—to the hilarity, if mock disapproval, of our block-long audience. The nice thing about it is that most of the victims, resigned to the situation, laughed with us. What choice did they have?

Though I feel I can understand today's gang cultures, I am not implying equivalence. We had our share of vicious characters, many of whom graduated to the Mob. Some became known killers, not all of them Italian by any means. Murder Incorporated, whose prosecution sparked the career of Thomas Dewey, Republican presidential candidate, was a Jewish outfit. Closer to home, a few blocks from us, we were treated to the sterling example of Abraham Telvi, whose most notable achievement was throwing acid in the face of labor journalist Victor Riesel—this at the behest of Telvi's racketeer employer. But for most of us the natural progression of events, the centrifugal forces of the world, worked against the gangs. The expanding economy and geographic mobility of the post World War II years trickled down to the Lower East Side. Jimmy So and So may have dropped out of high school but his uncle got him an apprentice spot in the electrician's union. Frankie H. passed the post-office exam the third time around. Spud G. had a child, got married, and drifted away. Harry L's parents made a little money and moved the family to the suburbs. If all else failed there was that old stand-by: The U.S. Army.

The situation is not the same for the young of today's ghettos, trapped in a destructive synergism of poverty, racism, drugs, non-education, and a level of violence we never came near experiencing. Gangs are the de facto government and their reach extends into the prisons and the better neighborhoods.

Looking back, I am struck by the compartmentalized life that I led. At home there were my parents, Abe, Chris Hansen, history, literature, music, the Wobblies, the anarchists, a kaleidoscope of colorful characters—and I was one kind of Anatole. Away from home, on the street, or acting up at school, I was another kind of Anatole. I was vaguely aware that the two Anatoles were fundamentally incompatible, but as in a bad marriage, I found a way to make it work. I kept my parent's radicalism, that part of my life, separate from my friends. I remembered the shock that reverberated through the auditorium when Mother refused to stand and salute the flag at school assembly. I had heard the sneering response of my friends to Sam's singing Wobbly songs drunk in the streets. I sensed the hooded contempt of the neighbors as I walked alongside my parents. I internalized that stuff. I treated our radicalism as a shameful secret. Not that he was aware, but my best friend was Montgomery Clift who starred opposite Elizabeth Taylor in *A Place in the Sun*—a great film of the time. Clift plays a poor boy who arrives in a factory town after having been brought up in an obscure religious cult that holds street corner meetings, sings hymns, and harangues passersby. The cult is run by his puritanical, moralistic mother. Could I relate to all that! Cliff wants only to succeed, to fit in, to conform. I was convinced Monty and I would understand one another if only I could meet him.

I return now to the peach fuzz on my groin, growing darker and more insistent by the day: that is, to my awakening sex drive. I am not self-serving, merely truthful, when I say I differed from my street companions—whose behavior resembled wild dogs in heat. They hunted in packs, sought out the vulnerable girls, and pounced. I was constitutionally unable to do such a thing. I was shy, self-conscious to a fault, and nursed my erections in private. Believe me when I tell you I did not know exactly what to do with them. My introduction to sex came when I was twelve or thirteen years old and had a result opposite to what one might expect. I do not think it was planned, certainly not on my part.

You see, Mother insisted we have all kinds of pets in our apartment: turtles, goldfish, a cat, and a grey-haired sheepdog named Shnuffitz. Her theory was Abe and I would learn to care for people by taking responsibility for the animals. My job was to walk Shnuffitz, get him to move his bowels in the street. However four flights to the street is a long way early in the morning. Easier to take him up two flights to the tar roof, take off his leash, and let him run free. So that is what I did one morning.

Up on roof was Alice hanging her sheets and laundry to dry. I remember her as a delicate thin woman, almost boyish, with short, clipped hair and hardly any breasts at all. She had no child that I recall and she lived on the fifth floor directly above me. You could hear her and husband George, a Greek truck diver, argue a lot, but who paid attention? You heard all sorts of stuff in the halls.

"You like sneakers?" she asked. "George has an extra pair I think maybe can fit you."

She led me into their bedroom and sure enough there were the sneakers. I tried them on sitting on the edge of the bed. She sat next to me, stared at me with a strange expression. Ever so gently she pushed me back onto the bed.

"Here," she said. "Let me help you. Has anyone ever did this?" And she proceeded to open my fly and take me in her mouth. I was too confused to say or do anything. It was wonderful, it was terrible. "This is our secret," she said afterward. "Only this one time."

We'd pass each other in the hall and on the street as if nothing had happened.

I kept that secret well into adulthood. To be initiated by an older woman is many a man's fantasy. I should have been raring to go from then on. However, it had the reverse effect. I felt used, not right. The experience added to my shyness and I retreated from sex for several years after that.

In sum, the early 1950s was an important time of life. I gained a degree of emotional independence from my parents, which is by and large a good thing. I discovered I was a sexual being, not that I acted much upon that knowledge. True, I ran for a time with nasty kids and have some chipped teeth and a broken nose to prove it—but in retrospect there was little chance I'd end up like them: not with the parents I had and the values anchored in my soul. I left the gangs as I grew older and found my confused way through high school, and almost by accident entered Hunter College, a branch of the City University of New York. I was a mediocre student who did enough to get by.

# 38
## THE DEATH OF THE MTW

I mentioned that Sam's drinking began to level off in his late forties and early fifties—gradually at first. Like a listing ship that rights itself, he seemed to have rediscovered his equilibrium. I do not know why, exactly, if there was an "exactly why." However, I remember his fiftieth birthday. He had a job painting one of the local synagogues and I visited him there. He seemed subdued, thoughtful; the back and forth rhythm of the brush always helped him to think. He spoke to me of the recent loss of three people who were dear to him.

Grandpa Max in 1948. Too old and sick to care for himself, he refused the care of his wealthy daughters. "I want to go to my son," the old man said. Our living room became his bedroom, until, his memory shot, and suffering depression, he went up to our roof in the middle of the night.

Ben Fletcher in 1949.

Gregorii Petrovich Maximoff, his life-model, in 1950. The death of these men weighed on him.

"I'm going to devote the time I have left to the propagation of our ideas. To the anarchist movement," he said simply. And that he did. Whether this decision was the cause or effect of his tilt away from the drinking life I do not know.

Since Sam was born in 1902 his mid-century coincided with the H-bomb, the State of Israel, the Cold War, the zenith of the Soviet Empire, Mao's China, the Korean War, Red hunting, anti-labor laws, and the general suppression of the radical movement. He took the collapse of the IWW, the IWW of his youth, especially hard, and he writes movingly about the fall of the Five-Ten Hall, the hall of my childhood, in *Fragments*: "The disintegration of the MTW was primarily due to unfavorable circumstances beyond its control. It had neither the financial resources nor the backing of the immensely powerful AFL-CIO.... The new generation of maritime workers who were enjoying all the benefits which the MTW and other militants had forced the ship owners to grant...had no desire to join 'subversive' unions like the IWW. A lot of good rebels were lost at sea during World War II. Many of our best fighters were beset by the infirmities of old age and many retired and passed away."

The Five-Ten Hall closed for good in 1964. Long gone were the days when the MTW controlled the Philadelphia waterfront and were a potent force up and down the East Coast, and the Great Lakes. Long gone were the days when the MTW seamen and long-shoremen, in tandem with the Wobbly lumber workers, tied up the entire Pacific Coast from San Pedro to Seattle in a series of epic strikes. The MTW accomplished these things in the early to mid-1920s, despite the passage of Criminal Syndicalism laws that jailed hundreds of Wobblies—and, I add, in contradiction to the commonly held view that the government crackdown of 1917–1918 finished the IWW.

Sam had a thirty-year association with the MTW. He remem-bered the Depression years of the 1930s when the Five-Ten Hall "was from early morning until late at night in constant turmoil," serving as homebase for a small band of militants who "distributed thousands of bulletins and leaflets all over the waterfront; con-ducted outdoor street meetings throughout the city ([he] addressed several); staged protest demonstrations in city welfare centers and charitable agencies demanding more help for the desperate unem-ployed that crowded the waterfront"; opened and operated a soup kitchen for hungry seamen and longshoremen.

"The MTW fought the early threat of government control of unions, particularly the Copland Continuous Discharge Book—bet-ter known as the 'Fink Book.'" The Fink Book listed all the places a seaman had worked, rated his willingness to obey orders and submit to discipline, his patriotism, and his record as a subversive.

The death of the MTW affected Sam as would the death of a dear friend. He mourned the passing of a self-regulated, working-class culture, its raffish, improvisational style. "Mari-time workers not only worked together, but lived together as they constantly shifted and intermingled from one ship to another and again intermingled between voyages in Atlantic, Gulf, Pacific and foreign ports. The international character of the marine industry and the cosmopolitan lifestyle of the marine workers stimulated international solidarity, 'the brotherhood of the sea.'"

The Wobbly seamen were an absurdly egalitarian bunch. I remember a half-dozen of them over at our apartment one Sunday. As usual, they simply burst in. They had all chipped in for a great meal featuring porterhouse steak. Philip Mellman—who had served time with J. B. Chiles for Criminal Syndicalism in the 1920s—did the cooking. Things went immediately wrong as Mellman, a feisty guy, got into an argument and forgot to tend to the steaks, which burned. Smoke rose from the stove, making the kitchen nearly uninhabitable for fifteen minutes or so. But what seriously pissed off the Wobblies around the table was the way Mellman apportioned the steak. Though all got the same amount, two or three Wobblies accused Mellman of reserving the tenderest, most succulent cut for himself, while consigning the bone, gristle, and fat to others.

It is difficult to convey the fury Mellman's alleged action precipitated (he denied the charge). Our tiny kitchen erupted. Mother pleaded for peace. Blows were avoided. But a happy visit turned sour. Years later I reminded Sam of the incident. I attributed the anger to the background of poverty of these men. Why else such anger over a scrap of meat. Sam disagreed. Mellman had broken a serious moral code in the eyes of his Wobbly comrades. No privileges, no matter how slight, at the expense of the group.

I find it instructive—and amusing—the way the MTW handled its internal affairs. There was no set term for a branch secretary or an "official," as the men drifted from port to port. His salary did not exist. A seamen who volunteered to serve as branch secretary paid for his own food and lodging. When his money ran out he slept in the back of the hall and ate in the hall's soup kitchen. Flush Wobbly seamen, just off a ship, would slip money in his pocket to "help him out." Next month or next year or whenever, their roles may well have reversed. Decisions that involved the MTW as a whole were made at regional or national conferences, subject to ratification by the membership.

Sam mourned other things as well. His voice would thicken whenever I brought up the old Five-Ten Hall and the subject would shift to the men who trod there:

To T-Bone Slim, who wrote a column for the *Industrial Worker* beneath a T-bone steak logo. Even non-Wobblies would line up for it, for he was a brilliant essayist: playful, superficially upbeat and deeply sarcastic. Listen to, or, better, sing his classic lament "The Popular Wobbly" and you will see what I mean. Sam remembered T-Bone by his real Finnish name, Matti Valentine Huhta, and he remembered how T-Bone and Ben Fletcher loved "to chew the fat" at the old Hall on Coenties Slip, and he remembered the late 1930s night T-Bone slipped overboard while working a tug in the harbor and drowned.

To Nick the Greek, to Sammy Weinstein, to Punch Drunk Morse, to Bob Willock, to Red Shirt Anderson, to J. B. Chiles, to Phil Mellman, to 350-pound Claude Marty, to the aptly named Cockeyed Cunningham, and so many others.

You could hear the ancient floor timbers creak.

Now, Sam said, it had all come to this: "The MTW as an organization was dead. Bob Willock...could not be called 'Branch Secretary' of a non-existent MTW. He was actually the caretaker of the defunct New York Hall—soon to disappear. It was no longer even a social center....The hall was practically deserted—a ghostly reminder of its former vivacious self. Bob could not even get together an ad-hoc committee of fellow workers to liquidate the hall, dispose of its excellent library, furniture and office equipment, the records, the artistic paintings and ships models and other artifacts accumulated through the years. Bob was forced to dispose of everything. In desperation he gave everything away indiscriminately, free of charge, to anyone willing to take what they liked.... Bob, in poor health and low spirits, disappeared."

I've often wondered what happened to the ship's steering wheel with the bold IWW logo in the center that had covered an entire wall and had so impressed me as a child.

The rickety old building at 134 Broad Street, home to the MTW Hall, was demolished and replaced by an enormous, monolithic office tower covering an entire city block.

# 39

## BILL ROTH, MONARCH OF THE LIVING ROOM

It is possible that I am reaching now, but I think the gradual collapse of the IWW in New York (and nearby Newark, New Jersey) affected the surviving Wobblies in strange, sad ways. Our tiny Clinton Street apartment, already as private as a bus station waiting room, became way-station to disparate jetsam and flotsam that normally washed up onto the Five-Ten Hall: all sorts of cranky codgers—some lovably obnoxious, others simply obnoxious. Somewhere between these two extremes one would have to place a short, wide-bodied Wobbly and anarchist named Bill Roth. The man would come each Sunday morning of the early 1950s to sit on his throne—that is our sagging armchair—and preside over his kingdom, which consisted of our open living room-kitchen-dining area. And he would sit and sit and sit. Well after dark he would take the subway back to his solitary room in the Bronx, leaving Mother to pick up after him. She never seemed to mind that part of it and it was plain my parents respected him. Sam knew Bill, who was in his eighties, from his Chicago days on the loose in the 1920s: the two naughty boys exchanged a knowing wink when they recalled those times.

What did I care if Bill had been a close friend of Emma Goldman, close enough to observe Emma "pick the tar out Ben Reitman's asshole"—as he lay stark naked and face down on a hotel room bed in the aftermath of being brutalized during the San Diego free speech fight of 1912? (And yes, that's a direct quote.)

What did I care if Bill had been Joe Hill's roommate? I did not like him so much.

He was a stern old man, and not a hell of a lot taller than me, or so it seemed when he leaned forward. His outsized, gnarled head, rope-textured gray hair, and above all, his rough gravel of a voice, intimidated me. Seems he had been a chiropodist or podiatrist or some similar thing, and so Mother, a worrywart when it came to her children's health, brought me to his living room throne for his professional opinion of my flat feet. His thick hands felt gentle as he inspected them. Then he had me stand up straight and twirled me in a circle before he delivered the devastating diagnosis. One of the worst cases he had ever seen! Corrective shoes with severe arch supports, rigorous exercises, and long-term posture lessons were essential to avoid crutches by adulthood! There could be no doubt of it!

Who knows, but one of these days I may take his advice. In any case, this session, and similar encounters in the same spirit, set us off on the wrong foot.

On the positive side, Bill arrived each Sunday morning with shopping bags of food suspended, Willy-Loman-style, from each arm. Like many a working-class man come of age in the late-nineteenth century, Bill was a jack of all trades, and had earned his living in his youth as a chef on merchant ships and in the lumber camps of the Pacific Northwest. He was determined to cook for his adopted family whether we liked it or not. Massive pork roasts, pans of roast potatoes, turnips, sweet potatoes, tossed salads, not one but two, three thick-crusted apple pies, juicy. Mother's tiny oven groaned from the labor. The man's repertoire was geared to "timber beasts"—hordes of them, and he would comment dryly that if they were ever fed this well there would have been no Wobbly strikes. "Cholesterol" was a thing he knew not of. The smells that spread from our kitchen are still with me. As are the tales of Bill and the old revolutionaries who broke bread with us.

Bill had a romantic nature or so Mother insisted. His early life was for her ears alone, as she pulled a kitchen chair close to him, the better to catch his low growl, punctuated now and then by his short, bitter laugh. Bill recalled to her his tyrannical, rabbinical father; the man's abuse, his belittling scorn. He recalled his coming of age, a hard-working, obedient young man, and then—the pivot point of his youth—falling deeply, intensely in love with a respectable young lady above his station. She jilted him without warning to marry a more promising man. Her idea? Her parents'? The shock, the pain numbed his brain and he passed into a kind of trance, from which he suddenly awoke, a full thirty days later, at the edge of a pier, the ocean beneath his feet. No, he did not want to die. From that moment he would no longer live for the approval of others. He would find his own way.

His way led to the sea, to the rails, to Chicago's skid row, to the lumber camps of the Pacific Northwest. To the anarchists and the IWW.

It took quite a few of his visits, and largely in retrospect, for me to appreciate that Bill used gruffness and irritability as a shield to protect his sentimental core. There were times, however, that core stood naked, as when he recalled his friend and fellow Wobbly, a tall, thin Swede named Joel Hägglund. The two roomed, and "were on the bum" together, in San Pedro or Portland, I forget which, around 1912—I really do not know and have no way to check. More than a century ago as I write this! In that time the man, Joel Hägglund—the impoverished immigrant who survived by cleaning spittoons in Bowery saloons when he landed in NY, and who went to wherever there was work, including the docks of far away Hilo, Hawaii—that man has long faded into the common soil of the past. In his stead we have the legend known by the name he anglicized and shortened, Joe Hill.

At this late date I will not go into the Joe Hill case. I am sure you are familiar with it. He was convicted of shooting to death a Salt Lake City, Utah retired policeman and grocer, John Morrison, and executed for the crime two years later, in 1915. No use recounting the details of the murder and trial here. I refuse to be objective. However, my prejudices are beside the point in this instance, as every "objective" legal scholar, journalist, and historian who has reviewed the case agrees there is no evidence linking Hill to the shooting. Even those unsympathetic to Hill admit that the reasonable doubt in the courtroom testimony was wide enough for a truck. I suggest William Nagle's *The Man Who Never Died*, which is probably the definitive account of the life and times of Joe Hill. In it, Nagle establishes Hill's innocence beyond any reasonable doubt and makes a strong circumstantial case against the likely murderer, known to the police at the time. The Hill case is one of the great frame-ups of the early-twentieth century.

Do not expect me to reveal unknown or surprising things about Joe Hill. Bill did not mention any. In 1947, the august Wallace Stegner—man of letters and lofty reputation, chronicler of the American West—published a poisonous article, "Joe Hill, the Wobblies'

Troubadour." In the *New Republic*, where else? He followed that up with *The Preacher and the Slave*, a mean-spirited novel, in which he portrayed Hill as a solitary, vicious gunman who consciously sought martyrdom. The heroes and injured party in his account? Why, the Utah authorities! Mother was outraged, as were many New York comrades, not all of them Wobblies. She and Herb Mahler organized a lively picket line in front of the *New Republic* office that got some publicity. Way out in the northwest, the *Seattle Times* carried a front page spread, "The Ghost Walks Again." Eventually, the *New Republic* agreed to print a rebuttal, which is all Mother and Mahler wanted.

Bill shared Mother's outrage, but his response was softer, inward. He said simply, "I don't remember Joe this way," and you could sense his sadness. Then he'd tell of penniless Joe Hill foraging for food that he cooked for his friends, and of his love of the violin, and of his appreciation of a pretty woman.

Bill took a dim view of Joe Hill the mythical figure, as opposed to the man. He was scornful of "I Dreamed I Saw Joe Hill Last Night," which may seem surprising because it is a beautiful song, especially as sung by Paul Robeson (and later by Joan Baez at Woodstock). That beauty was precisely the problem for Bill. Look at or listen to the lyrics. Hill comes to you as a saintly figure in a dream and who can disagree? This is Joe Hill safely defanged, which is why the song is popular around the fires of liberal summer camps, and with slightly drunk leftists at parties. Bill Roth remembered Joe Hill, the rifleman who fought alongside Flores Magón in the Mexican Revolution. Joe Hill was not a flower child.

But Joe Hill certainly was a poet. I repeat his last will, written in pencil on a bit of paper the night before he died.

> My Will is easy to decide
> For there is nothing to divide.
> My kin don't need to fuss and moan,
> "Moss does not cling to a rolling stone."
> My body, ah, if I could choose,
> I would to ashes it reduce,
> And let the merry breezes blow

My dust to where some flowers grow.
Perhaps a fading flower then
Will come to life and bloom again.
This is my last and final will,
Good luck to all of you,
Joe Hill

He added that the Wobblies could spread his ashes wherever they wished, except Utah. He didn't to be found dead in Utah.

A few years ago I was surprised to see on the front page of the *New York Times* that the archives of the American Communist Party contained the original copy of that very Will! No doubt it was put there by Elizabeth Gurley Flynn, who had been a great Wobbly organizer before she became a Communist, and who had befriended Hill in prison. There it was, the original copy from so many years ago, reprinted in the *New York Times*, which treated its find with a certain bemusement, as an archaeological curiosity.

Bill made it to the late 1950s or so. I accompanied Mother to his last home, a hospice bed in the Bronx run by the Working Men's Circle. He was grateful to see her, near weeping. He was all alone. I confess I behaved badly, refusing to engage him humanly, pacing back and forth, and forcing Mother to shorten her stay. I was too young to grasp fully the situation and felt oppressed by the pervasive presence of death.

# 40

# "IT AIN'T THE WORK, IT'S THE LABOR INVOLVED"

Sam was fond of saying things like that.

He loved Dickensonian puns. (Mr. M'Choakumchild, the spirit-strangling teacher in *Hard Times* was a favorite.)

He loved obvious jokes ("Every time I finish eating I lose my appetite"). He'd tell them over and over until you found yourself laughing—not from the jokes, but from the delight he took in seeing you laugh.

He loved sentimental songs like "Danny Boy" sung by the Irish tenor John McCormack, got bleary eyed from the pathos of it all.

He loved old-time vaudeville, the old-time pratfall clowns, considered it authentic American folk theater.

He loved the Yiddish theater on Second Avenue: Hams like Maurice Schwartz that did Shakespeare in Yiddish, comic actors like Menasha Skolnick, ingénues like Molly Pecan.

He loved recounting the time he worked for a dry cleaning establishment and delivered a costume to the dressing room of Enrico Caruso. "I can tip you with money or a ticket, which is it?" the great man asked fourteen-year-old Sam. "A ticket, of course." Standing room, way up in the top-most tier, Caruso tiny in the distance, his voice filling the space between them, what a thrill!

Sam loved that kind of stuff. He was not all about politics and social upheaval. He professed to hate baseball and all organized sport where one group rooted against the other. "Tribalism! Patriotism in miniature! Perverted civic pride! Why the players don't even live in the cities they play for, they're hired guns," he would sneer. Then one day I come to visit. He is in his eighties and he is in front of the TV watching baseball! He did not know a damn thing about the game, or who was winning or losing. He simply liked to watch the players.

"Look at them. Like dancers. So graceful." He especially liked the way infielders settled under pop-ups.

I mention this side of Sam to dispel the impression he was a solemn guy. And he had this way of speaking, as if from a hip time-capsule—"half New York, half Joe Hill," Paul Berman put it—that was humorous and serious and irreverent at the same time.

"What the hell did he contribute to literature? Short sentences? Read Sherwood Anderson!" he'd proclaim of his favorite punching-bag, Ernest Hemingway. You knew he knew better, which was part of the fun.

Sam hit it off well with all kinds of people you would not expect to be his type: counterculture icons like Tuli Kupferberg of The Fugs; Judith Malina and Julian Beck of The Living Theatre; Dorothy Day of the Catholic Worker; ultra-orthodox rabbis, cynical shipping executives. They were drawn to this rough gargoyle of a man. Everything about him was genuine. When Robert (Bob) Calese, a librarian and scholar, first saw Sam speaking at a Libertarian League forum, he thought "Sam looked like he combed his hair with an eggbeater. His eyeglasses were covered with paint. His teeth were rotten. He mispronounced every other word. But he made the other speakers look like junior high school students." Bob was a notably unsentimental man, a combat veteran who fought his way across Europe under George Patton. But he wept openly on the platform at Sam's memorial service.

These "unexpected" friendships are not to be tossed off as novelties. Tuli and Sam were quite close for a time in the years before he hit full stride in the 1960s. I am not sure his fans of later years realize how deeply intellectual a man Tuli was, or how firmly rooted was his anarcho-pacifism in the tradition of Kropotkin and Tolstoy. Sam and Tuli (though a much younger man) meshed well. Both of them were Lower East Side Jewish boys of immigrant families: irreverent, unconventional, though in different ways. Tuli, a cum-laude graduate of Brooklyn College, and a talented writer, saw the potential of Sam's catch phrase "It Aint the Work, It's the Labor Involved" and ran with it. That is, he wrote an essay on the nature of work under the capitalist system, concentrating on the coercive aspect, and the harm that does to the personality of the individual. It was written playfully and poetically and is not at all solemn. Sam thought it was terrific. I've since tried to run it down, whether in the *Industrial Worker* or some other place, but cannot seem to find it. My point is that there was serious intent behind Tuli's later *1001 Ways to Live Without Working* and similar satiric books.

In those days, he and "Shush" (from the Hebrew Sho Shona, meaning Rose or Flower) were still together. I visited them several times in their first-floor flat on Columbia Street a few blocks from us. I remember the remains of a meal left to rot on his kitchen table and roaches crawling over it. I hadn't realized I was fastidious, but I found myself admonishing him, "Tuli, the roaches are all over the food." To which he replied, deadpan, "Its ok, they don't eat much."

In the late '40s or early '50s, I witnessed an incident that I hadn't planned to mention in this book. Then I read something on the Internet that I hadn't known about Tuli and that I doubt Sam knew: that Tuli, in a state of despair, had jumped off the Manhattan Bridge in 1944 and was rescued by a passing tugboat. He suffered serious injuries and was not proud of the incident. He regretted that his friend Allen Ginsberg refers to it in altered form in his famous *Howl*. But the incident I had planned to leave out? Tuli and Shush had a son named Joseph, an energetic little boy with a mop of black hair like Tuli's. They—or at least Tuli and Joseph—visited us one stifling summer afternoon at our fourth-floor apartment on 250 Clinton Street. The place was crowded; it was some kind of party or gathering. We had no air conditioning. My parents, mindful there were children present, kept the bottom windows closed but slid down the top windows full to let air in; otherwise our apartment would have been insufferable. If you counted the space below the windowsill, and the closed bottom window, there was fully a six-foot barrier a child would have to climb.

What child would do that? Joseph! Tuli rushed into my parent's bedroom a split second before Joseph's torso, bent over the open top window, disappeared. Desperately Tuli lunged at Joseph's ankles, the only part of him that remained within the room. He pulled Joseph back in, hugging him in tears, and then collapsed on the bed, holding Joseph to his breast.

Tuli and Sam drifted apart from the mid-50s onward. Though friends, they went different ways. Sam was a traditional radical: committees, programs, organization, demonstrations. Tuli believed in the propaganda of the deed, though not in the nineteenth-century, bomb-throwing sense. His life, his very being was the deed, designed to dramatize one individual's response to a brutal, unjust society.

"Tuli was a true American maverick original in the best, Whitmanesque sense of the word," says guitarist Gary Lucas. "He contained multitudes. A genius poet/Zen songwriter/deadpan Jewish anarchist/comedian/insurrectionist of a million minds, his songs with the Fugs stormed my teenage consciousness and greatly affected the warp and woof of late-'60s counterculture in general—a Golden Age."

As years went by, I watched Tuli perform as part of The Fugs at rallies in Central Park and other places, wearing trousers with a different color for each leg and weird costumes. I'd pass him on the street in the East Village. He did not recognize me and I was too shy to introduce myself: what the hell, I thought. It was nice he came to Sam's memorial and sat quietly in the back. He sang along with "Solidarity Forever" at the end and found time to have a heartfelt conversation with brother Abe.

# 41

# THE FOOTLOOSE BOHEMIAN GIRL

The most vivid image I have of Dorothy Day dates back to 1956 or so. It is of this severely handsome woman in her late fifties, her gray hair swept up in a bun the way Mother sometimes wore hers: no lipstick or makeup whatsoever to alter or conceal the wrinkles of her neck and face; her only coloring the natural flush of her cheeks. She is impeccable in a long simple dress and completely unadorned. She is addressing the young Catholic women of the Newman Club at Hunter College, my school. She sits up front on a stool unprotected from the audience by table or desk. It is just she and the room full of conventionally religious young women sprinkled with a few young men. I decided to attend the moment I read the Newman Club notice on the bulletin board. I had not seen her since my boyhood and was curious.

The Cold War was at its nastiest and most threatening; H-bombs were being tested. She could have spoken against militarism. Civil Rights agitation was beginning in the deep south; she could have spoken on what should be the proper Catholic response to racism. She could have spoken of how young Catholic women should dedicate their lives to the poor and tie that in with her feelings about wealth and poverty and the class struggle. She could have spoken of the virtues of a life of intense spiritual devotion. She could have spoken of any number of things and had the audience on her side. That is why they crowded into the large classroom; to see and listen to this woman they heard so much about, this woman of substance who had founded a radical form of Catholicism, the Catholic Worker Movement.

Instead, she chose for her subject the virtues of sexual chastity. She castigated the young women for their make up, for their suggestive dress, for their flirtatious body language. Sex was for procreation only, and only after marriage in the Catholic Church, and birth control a sin contrary to God's will. This the young women had not expected from her. Worse than the message was the tone of disdain, which suggested that students having a natural hormonal curiosity were tramps. You felt the hostility well up in the room, the veiled hisses. Some women turned their backs to her insolently and left the room, an unheard of insult of the time. Dorothy seemed not to give a damn. She sat through the hour, unbending and as unreachable as a marble statue. This great woman—an adjective I use in the sincerest sense—was going to say what she had come to say. She had faced tougher audiences than this.

That night I told Sam about the meeting. "I knew Dorothy when she was a footloose bohemian girl," he said, his voice a mixture of irony and humor, and his smile suggestive of bygone times.

Sam was referring to her free-living, anarcho-syndicalist youth when she worked as a radical journalist and committed all the sins—and more—for which she admonished the young Catholic women of the Newman Club. Her spiritual journey from this supposedly degenerate state of affairs to her embrace of the Church to her nomination for sainthood ten years after her death is well documented, although her chief advocate for sainthood, Cardinal Dolan of New York, seemed more enamored of the sinner-to-piety narrative—the Mary Magdalene bit—than with the anarchism she never abandoned. The conservative hierarchy aside, however, her admirers universally depict Dorothy Day as an authentic Revolutionary, a rebel within the Church.

Sam begged to differ. "The best Dorothy was the old Dorothy," he said often. By which he meant the young Dorothy—Dorothy the atheist. To Sam, the new Dorothy was not an anarchist at all, despite her rhetoric and her respect for Kropotkin and the Wobblies and all that. As Dwight MacDonald once wrote in the *New Yorker*: "She has always insisted she is a Catholic first and a radical second. 'The hierarchy permits a priest to say Mass in our chapel,' she told me in 1952. 'They have given us the most precious thing of all—the Blessed Sacrament. If the Chancery ordered me to stop publishing the *Catholic Worker* tomorrow, I would.'"

"What the hell kind of an anarchist takes orders from Cardinal Spellman?" Sam railed. "You know what the *Catholic Worker* is? A safety valve to let youngsters who might leave the Church blow off steam!"

Sam respected Dorothy despite his fulminations. My parents visited the Catholic Worker House of Hospitality on Christie Street around the corner from the Bowery on occasion. They were fond of the volunteers dedicated to practicing true Christianity—who prepared meals for the down and out, without pay, and who slept and ate among them. Sam liked especially that they served the drunks and other specimens of the undeserving poor. Nobody preached at them and they could stay as long as they wanted.

Sam took me along to Christie Street when Dorothy invited him to speak at Catholic Worker forums. As I think back, I am struck by the nonverbal communication between them. Sam enters the large room on the second floor, nods to Dorothy. Dorothy calls the meeting to order with a brief prayer. Sam keeps his head down as a courtesy, but he and Dorothy know no praying is going on. Then Sam delivers his speech dealing with the IWW and labor issues to the small audience of Worker folk. Questions from the audience follow and so on. Then, when it is time to leave, he and Dorothy lock eyes in a significant nod—for old-time's sake. Not a word spoken between them.

I wish I could leave Sam and Dorothy at peace like that. But truth is they had it out one night at the Libertarian League Forum, as I will describe later.

# 42
## TOUGH TIMES IN THE FIFTIES

Even leaving aside Senator Joseph McCarthy and the Red Hunters, the 1950s were a tough time to be a radical. Some comrades dropped out of the movement. Others became liberal Democrats—a few using it as waystation to becoming conservative Republicans, can you imagine. Still others hunkered down like turtles in a shell, waiting for better times. My parents pushed on as best they could. We held forums of the IWW at the Labor Temple, as I mentioned earlier in connection with Jack Walsh and Ben Fletcher. Chris Hansen made the biweekly sign to be posted in the Temple lobby, our sole publicity. He blocked out the letters in a clear blunt style, circa 1910 (at the time my father still went by Sam Weiner):

IWW Forum
The Importance of a Revolutionary Labor Movement
Sam Weiner
Sunday May 19, 2pm
All Welcome, Refreshments

My job was to see Chris got the sign posted by Wednesday to give the expected throng time. This was not an easy task because Chris tended to get lazy and I had to keep after him. But he generally got it done.

Though the radical movement had fallen on hard times, especially so in the early 1950s, it was far from dead. Sam has the date wrong in *Fragments*, but in late 1951 or 1952 he and Russell got wind through the Spanish comrades that at least eleven members of the CNT faced death sentences for underground activities against the Regime. Here was an issue around which the various groups could coalesce to form a surprisingly effective united front: Opposition to Franco. Sam, Russell, and Mother contacted Herbert Mahler's friend Roland Watts, secretary of the Workers Defense League, an attorney who spent his life exposing exploited workers trapped in the legal system. He was one of Mother's favorite people. She remembers him attempting to go before the U.N. to report examples of slave labor in the United States; J. Edgar Hoover had him investigated instead of the charges. Watts took the matter to Norman Thomas, head of the Socialist Party: "For only his close connections," Sam thought, "could rally the liberal, socialist, religious, labor and progressive political parties to exert maximum effective pressure, locally and nationally (and internationally) to save the workers threatened with death. Thomas agreed, and the Committee to Defend Franco's Labor Victims was formed."

Abe remembers the picket lines in front of the Spanish Consulate and Tourist Office in Rockefeller Center and the mass meetings he attended at Freedom House across from the New York Public Library. Many distinguished speakers. Similar protests were held in cities around the country. The cause of the condemned Spanish anarchists spread to England and France. According to Sam, "Thomas took an active part. A full-scale publicity campaign was launched; the mass media, which paid no attention to us before, carried reports. Telegrams, cablegrams, protest demonstrations on a vast scale (many of them addressed by Thomas himself), petitions to the State department, Congress and the president himself... finally prompted the State Department, through its Ambassador to Spain to ask for an explanation."

Then an unexpected turn of events: Sam recalled that, "Without a word of explanation, the Committee to Defend Franco's Labor Victims suddenly ceased to exist. When we came to attend a scheduled meeting of the committee, the door was locked." Only later did they learn that Thomas had withdrawn because it was a "hot potato."

There are several versions of what happened, all pointing to more or less the same conclusion. Abe recalls that Russell told him that Secretary of State Dean Acheson sent for Thomas. Present at the meeting was the Spanish Ambassador. The Ambassador proceeded to defend Franco's actions. These men were not workers but dirty anarchists: common criminals, terrorists plotting to assassinate the Head of State, Franco. Does not every government have the right and duty to defend itself against people of that sort?

Apparently Thomas bought into the theory that a tyrant who conquered his democratic country with the help of Hitler and

Mussolini, who was an ally of Hitler during World War II, who was responsible for the deaths of easily a million people, had by some mysterious alchemy become "legitimate" five years later—and those looking to overthrow him were terrorists. The real issue was something else entirely. The Cold War was firing up. The U.S. Air Force needed Spain as a base for its A-bomb-toting Strategic Air Command, and Franco made a bid for respectability, seeking diplomatic recognition and economic aid to shore up his regime. To be fair, Acheson and Truman personally despised Franco, thought him odious, but they held their noses and yielded to the generals.

Thomas was either told or got the hint he should lay off. Abe was present when he said before a large audience that I know you are not going to like this, but the U.S. should extend diplomatic recognition to Franco.

Russell and Sam refused to give up. In 1956 the reconstituted Committee to Defend Franco's Labor Victims—about fifty comrades consisting of the Libertarian League, the Young Socialist League, the IWW, and the Catholic Worker—picketed a reception in honor of the Spanish Ambassador held at Gracie Mansion, Mayor Wagner's residence. Photographers were taking pictures everywhere, though none of it reached the press. No doubt a bonanza for the Red Squad! And I received a lesson about power in this land of free speech and free assembly. We were given a narrow strip to pace back and forth with our handmade signs. It was a block away and around the corner from the reception so as not to offend the distinguished guest. The police were everywhere, a sea of blue, far more of them than us, so that we were immediately branded as troublemakers and crackpots by passersby. We tried to shout over the cops and were warned about disturbing the peace. Passing priests called us church-burners.

The result of our efforts? Hard to say. Russell was sure, through various sources, that over the time of its existence the Libertarian League saved the lives of at least five Spanish prisoners. It was a sensitive time for Franco.

Abe reminds me that the most dynamic speaker by far at the protest meetings for the Spanish prisoners was a thin, balding Basque nationalist named Jesús de Galíndez. More about him later.

We tried our best. We teamed up with Norman Thomas again on other ventures. Mother became one of his stalwarts on Civil Rights picket lines, protesting hiring practices at Woolworth's and so forth. But it was not an easy time to be a radical.

Most discouraging of all was the attitude of the working class, that object of so many illusions. Fully thirty percent of all jobs were unionized; the power of the AFL/CIO was at its zenith. And contrary to revolutionary theory, this served only to make the workers less militant. You could not call them working class! It was a badge of shame. Rather, everyone was middle class, in the manner of Garrison Keillor's fictional Lake Woebegone, where all the children are above average. Better yet, America was a classless society! The nation and its workers seemed to feast on the post-war boom. People wanted things. All the cheap cars—the Plymouths and Chevies—sported tail fins like the top of the line Caddies. Refrigerators, TVs, hi-fis, stereos, a house in the suburbs. A plastic watchband to match your plastic belt. That is what the 1950s seemed to be about.

Many a Wobbly reacted with a deep cynicism to hide his disappointment.

"The fires of revolution quenched in a bowl of soup!"

"The boss throws them a bone and they gnaw on it!"

"Is this what our men got beat on the head for, went to the can for, died for?!"

Dave Baer carried his bitterness to the extreme. He was a short man of sallow complexion, married to the talented photographer Olga Zagar. For a time during the late 1930s and after WWII, when all of us lived on the Lower East Side, they were part of a closely knit affinity group of Wobblies and anarchists that included Franz and Gussie Fleigler, Ed and Sarah Mitchell, and Fred and Wanda Miller. My parents were at the hub and, as far as I can tell, we all got along well.

Franz, Dave, and Ed were especially tight: three stocky merchant seamen who braved Nazi torpedoes during the war, and in
the aftermath of that war, smuggled the Jews that survived the
death camps past the British blockade of Palestine. To my limited
worldview, Ed Mitchell was the most exotic of the three. The only
gentile, he was from Memphis, Tennessee and he and his brother,
Harry Leland Mitchell, were instrumental in founding the groundbreaking, fully integrated Southern Tenant Farmers Union of the
1930s. Ed claimed that race was not a factor; black and white saw
plainly their common interest. What I liked best about Ed were the
stories he told. He opened worlds to me: of life in the rural south; of
Baptist revival meetings in the hills so intense that the parishioners
babbled "in tongues"; of his own youth during which he stuttered
so badly he could hardly get out a word, and of how he somehow
forced himself to speak in public and testify before Congress on
behalf of the tenant farmers.

Dave was the most outwardly emotional of the three. By the
time I got to know him a bit, in the mid 1950s, we had moved
from Clinton Street in lower Manhattan to the Bushwick/Bed-
ford-Stuyvesant section of Brooklyn, and Dave had graduated to
executive status. He was vice president of Maritime Overseas, a
shipping corporation. He'd come over on a Saturday or Sunday and
rail away for several hours at the "woiking class." He was a good
mimic, especially of Yiddish accents, and he cut deep in the manner
of comedians like George Carlin. Towards the end he would set his
sights on Sam and abuse him personally. "Look at how you live! For
what! The 'woikers?' Do they give a shit about you? When will you
give up? Still slinging a brush in your fifties! You look like shit!"

Sam took it all, each visit. Finally, after one particularly lacerat-
ing session, I asked, "Why do you let him speak to you like that?"
Sam answered simply, "He keeps coming around, though."

Sam saw into Dave's heart. I'll skip ahead four or five years to
1958. I'm accepted to graduate school in Ohio. Scholarship money
has not yet come through. I need cash. And for that Sam broke
a cardinal rule. Up until this point I had never heard him ask a
personal favor of anyone. Never! The act was foreign to his nature.
But he broke down for my sake and asked Dave to get me seamen's

papers and help me to ship out. It was more money than I could possibly make otherwise—short of armed robbery.

"I'm not promising, but give me a week or two. I'll see what I can do!"

Ten days later I'm in Dave's dingy office on lower Broadway near the Battery. Dave, looking small and not well, flips me an envelope from behind his desk: my papers. "Hold on to this. Not easy to get!"

Then he dials the phone and proves he's an equal opportunity abuser. He calls Paul Hall, president of the Seafarers International Union (SIU), a labor leader of the Jimmy Hoffa school.

"Paul, this is Dave, Dave Baer! Listen I got a kid… No, no Paul, he's not a Congressman's son, he's not a businessman's son… Paul, Paul, listen: HE CAN'T DO ANYTHING FOR YOU! Guess what, he's a woikin' man's son. You're the head of a fuckin' union? How 'bout givin' a woikin' man's son a break!"

I could hear laughter on the other end. Send him over! Dave rises from behind his desk and does a shocking thing: he hugs me. "Take care of yourself."

I checked in at the SIU Hall on Fourth Avenue near the Brooklyn waterfront. Ed Mitchell, who apparently was waiting, ushered me in through a side entrance to the back room. Facing me was Paul Hall, a physically powerful man and a fearsome guy. Five goons encircled him. He barely acknowledged me. I was not to see such an arrangement again until thirty-two years later when, walking on Mulberry Street in Little Italy, I saw Mafioso John Gotti exit Benito's Restaurant, goons first. I remember the incident vividly because Gotti's fleshy face leered at my wife. It amazes me that Dave—or anyone—would have the balls to speak to Hall directly the way he did.

Dave died a few years later. Sam knew he had heart trouble for many years.

# 44
## THE SIA HALL

In the opening pages of this memoir I remarked that "Climbing the rickety stairs of ancient lofts would turn out to be a staple of my childhood." The stairs I climbed that day were at 134 Broad Street and they led up to the old Five-Ten Hall. But I had another set of stairs in mind as I wrote that line: those at 813 Broadway that I climbed to get to the SIA Hall. Although the old SIA Hall has long been converted into a residential flat, the nineteenth-century structure stands. The building is just south of 12th Street in a funky/chic neighborhood of antique shops and expensive facials. The famous Strand Bookstore is diagonally across the street, and a block or two down you will find the landmark, high WASP Grace Church. The neighborhood was grungier in the 1950s: mostly union halls, cut-rate haberdasheries, hole in the wall offices, dark beaneries.

SIA is the acronym for Solidaridad Internacional Antifascista. It was an organization dedicated to aiding imprisoned and exiled anarchists and other victims of Franco. Lucía Sánchez Saornil served as the chief officer of SIA from 1938, which is interesting because she was also the founder of Mujeres Libres. The Free Women of Spain were dedicated both to the social revolution as fought by the CNT and to the absolute equality of women in Spanish society— not "come the revolution" but NOW, as the Revolution was being fought. In 1936, at the outbreak of the Civil War, Mujeres Libres had over thirty-thousand members. Among them were Pura Arcos, wife of Sam's dear friend Federico, and also the Free Women of the SIA Hall at 813 Broadway.

These women fascinated me. Exotic creatures, their cheeks heavily rouged, their lips lacquered vivid red, their hair a wild nest of henna. No American woman wore make up or dyed her hair that way, and their clothes were brightly colored. The women were undoubtedly aware of the latest American styles; they did not give a damn. Their appearance was off-putting at first, but they were sweet natured and generous when you got to know them. One lady, a survivor of the French refugee camps following the fall of the Republic, made it a point to arrive early, before the scheduled activities, and teach Abe Spanish. I was taken to task gently because of my reaction to the outsized anthropological display that hung on the long wall opposite the tables. The display purported to classify all the races of the world and their habitats, as keyed to a large map in the center. The races were in native attire and arranged around the map in boxes—each race confined to a box. They stared out at you mournfully in sepia tone as if from cages. The entire display had a centuries-old, antediluvian quality to it. Depressing but engrossing to me. "No, no, it is not depressing," a free woman comrade protested. "It shows all the races of mankind. It shows we are all one!" So, there!

The Free Women prepared the monthly Friday night dinners at the SIA Hall. The event had been going on for years and they were totally organized by the time I attended. Each individual's movements were so patterned that, viewed from afar, the group appeared choreographed, to be performing a sort of ballet. There was no need for any of them to speak. The menu was undeviating: arroz con pollo, salad, crusty Spanish bread, a carafe of red wine. The men helped by arranging and setting the tables along the length of the hall and by cleaning up. On a good night, maybe thirty or forty people attended: veterans of the Spanish Revolution and Civil War; exiles; comrades who had come to the U.S. long before the War and who were active in the IWW; increasing numbers of Cuban comrades—refugees from the Batista, and, later, the Fidel Castro regimes. They were working men: elevator operators, janitors, factory machinists, food preparers, cigar makers, longshoremen. Few spoke English well. They were Sam's kind of people.

The SIA Hall was an essential place to be if you really wanted to know what was going on in Spain and Latin America. Sometimes you got the information in a formal way: there were after-dinner speeches, almost always in Spanish, although Sam spoke in English. Russell Blackwell made a strong impression. His Spanish was impeccable, his appearance—in black suit, vest, and hat—striking. And the SIA group knew he had put himself on the line with the Friends of Durruti in the streets of Barcelona. Often, however, you got the information informally: after the speeches and the voluntary contributions on the pass-around plate—when comrades were free to wander around the hall, have espresso, and chat.

Here's a case in point. In early 1957, the *New York Times* had just carried the first of Herbert Matthews's articles on Fidel Castro, front page. Matthews had interviewed Fidel at his camp in the Sierra Maestro, and a more fawning, uncritical piece of writing about a human being you will not find short of a press agent. The articles had a huge impact, far better than paid propaganda. Che Guevara said later that the article was worth more than winning battles; in 1997 Fidel had a plaque commemorating the interview installed where it took place.

But some of us knew better. A year before Matthews idolized Castro in print, I remember sitting with Russell and Sam at the far end of the SIA Hall around the edge of one of the long tables. Next to us is an elderly Cuban gentleman, whose name, though I have racked my brain and inquired about it, I cannot remember. He speaks no English. "What about this Fidel?" Russell asks him. The old man shakes his head slowly while waving two fingers in a gesture that means no good. "*El Caudillo*" was all he would say: The chief, the charismatic leader, the man on the white horse, the plague of Latin America. Sam and Russell exchanged significant glances. That is all they had to know.

Later Russell told me the old man's son had fought with Fidel and Che in the Sierra Maestro. "Fought" in both senses of the word. He found them too dominating and left. Several years later, after the collapse of the Batista regime, Fidel and his men came down from the mountains and made their way methodically across Cuba to Havana, stopping in every town. The purpose was to eliminate potential opposition. In each town, Fidel had to approve a list of those to be executed. The old man's son was on one of the lists. But in a display of princely compassion, Fidel crossed his name off. Before being sent into permanent exile he was made to sign a statement that he would never publicly criticize the Castro Government.

# 45

# THE LIBERTARIAN LEAGUE

The SIA Hall became the first home of the Libertarian League. Rent free, of course, but equally important: it was welcomed there. I do not recall a compelling reason Sam, Mother, and Russell decided to found the League; no international or political crises beyond the awful ordinary: it was July 1954. They simply felt it was time for a fresh try at an American organization advocating anarcho-syndicalism, though they were not doctrinaire about the label you wore. I was present when Sam sat down at the dining room table and composed the first draft of the League's opening statement, "What We Stand For." Russell sat next to him and the two men and Mother tinkered with the wording, back and forth. The idea was to keep it short and plain:

### LIBERTARIAN LEAGUE: "WHAT WE STAND FOR"
(1963)

The "free" world is not free; the "communist" world is not communist. We reject both: one is becoming totalitarian; the other is already so.

Their current power structure leads inexorably to atomic war and the probable destruction of the human race.

We charge that both systems engender servitude. Pseudo-freedom based on economic slavery is no better than pseudo-freedom based on political slavery.

The monopoly of power which is the state must be eliminated. Government itself, as well as its underlying institutions, perpetuates war, oppression, corruption, exploitation, and misery.

We advocate a world-wide society of communities and councils based on cooperation and free agreement from the bottom (federalism) instead of coercion and domination from the top (centralism). Regimentation of people must be replaced by regulation of things.

Freedom without socialism is chaotic, but socialism without freedom is despotic. Libertarianism is free socialism.

These ideas are expanded upon in the provisional statement of the principles of the Libertarian League and in other literature that will be supplied free on request.

---

LIBERTARIAN LEAGUE
P.O. Box 261, Cooper Station
New York 3, N.Y.

= = =

For those interested in a scholarly history of the League and its related activities I recommend Andrew Cornell's fine dissertation, *For A World Without Oppressors*, which is available online. There are other sources as well. My intentions are modest: to describe some of the League members and those in its orbit. Strictly my impressions! I also want to describe Sam's central role in the concerns and activities of the League. It was a remarkable organization through most of its ten year existence.

First, a word about the meaning of "Libertarian." Sam and Russell meant it in the sense of "libertarian socialism," which they considered the same as anarchism, but without the negative connotations. Sam had always preferred it as a means of emphasizing the constructive aspects of his philosophy. Libertarian Socialism had been used as a stand in for anarchism for over a century. However, "Libertarian" has acquired a far different meaning since the late-twentieth century. True, these modern Libertarians want to severely limit government (especially when it helps the poor)—or do away with it altogether. Some have even adopted *Nationalism and Culture* as a seminal text in their analysis of the state; I am sure Rudolf Rocker has turned over in his grave. But the modern Libertarians consider private property sacrosanct—and I am not referring to the shirt on your back, your apartment, or your toothbrush. I mean mines, lumber, farms, factories, all the fish in the sea, the intellectual efforts of others. They believe in the sanctity of Capitalism. They have usurped the name. Instead of a Sam Dolgoff or a Murray Bookchin you have David Koch.

Second, a word about membership. I doubt the league had more than twenty members at any one time, not more than half of them currently active. It was never able to break through to a wider audience. There were many reasons for this, which I will not go into here, but I believe, above all others, it was the climate of the times: few people were interested. Nevertheless, the League exerted influence beyond its numbers through its publication, *Views and Comments* (most of it written by Sam), its forums and discussion groups, and other activities.

The League was not perfect. It was composed of fallible human beings who tried their best. Earlier I quoted Robert Calese to the effect that "Sam looked like he combed his hair with an eggbeater." Now, Bob was a good guy. I do not want to come down hard on a man who loved my father. His remark was essentially complimentary. But it did not seem to occur to him that Sam's disheveled appearance and the paint and all that came from a hard day's labor, after which he ran to the SIA Hall to deliver a lecture. The rotten teeth were product of a lifetime of poverty. Teeth were expendable when there were children to feed. He was an old-fashioned man in many respects.

Let's look at some League people as I remember them.

# 46

# RUSSELL BLACKWELL (REVISITED)

Russell's friendship with my parents began well before the start of the League, all the way back to his return from Spain in the late 1930s. Our families were intertwined for a time. Mother was close to Edna, Russell's wife, and she regarded their three children—Steve, Arthur Henry (A. H. ), and Claudia—as an extension of her family. The League was but a prolonged episode in a thirty-year relationship. So forgive me if I seem to wander in my description of this man who, I repeat, deserves the efforts of a talented novelist.

The quality I remember most vividly was the irresistible charm of the man: his antic humor, his quirky sense of the world. How many fathers do you know take their children hitch-hiking for vacation? ("You meet the most interesting people that way!") His conversation was playful, never malicious; scatological, never vulgar. "Is *this* what the common people call farking?" he'd exclaim in an overbearing English accent, breathing heavily. "Too good for them! Far too good for them!"

Simply walking with Russell could turn into an adventure. On second thought, there was no such thing as a simple walk with Russell. He kept a "studio" on Fifty-Third Street near Lexington Avenue. In reality it was an old-fashioned bathtub-in-the-kitchen-toilet-in-hall dump in a walk-up tenement long-since demolished. It was a great place for assignations. Russell let me use it when I was older. This day, circa 1954, we are walking up Madison Avenue to his studio in the bright sunshine. Not that the season mattered to Russell who wore his signature black hat, gray suit, black tie and vest, with bulging Adam's apple. Sounds like respectable clothing for a Madison Avenue workday. But not on Russell; there was always something off about it, hard to explain. Anyway, who should we run into in the opposite direction on the backside of Saint Patrick Cathedral? His buddy and fellow cartographer, Ricky Harris.

Russell regards him with mock suspicion. He flaps his elbows in and out. He leans forward in a strange posture, his hat and head perched precariously. He starts to circle Ricky in a crouching, hop-ping motion, his elbows flapping wildly. He emits a series of star-tling cackles: "Auk, Auk!" Russell has turned himself into a rooster!

Ricky, a respectable, well-dressed fellow with a cultivated mus-tache—the kind you might expect on Madison Avenue—he takes the cue. The two roosters, grown men, hop around each other flapping their elbows, crowding out the sidewalk. "Auk, Auk! Auk, Auk!" It goes on like that. People avoid them, think they are stark raving mad. Finally, finally, "How are you, Ricky?!" "Fine." And they go on their way.

Russell was not a clown. He was a serious man with a playful sense of fun. Perhaps I am the only one who cares at this late date, but Russell was a first-rate cartographer; this before the digital age when maps were by hand. He did beautiful work on Abe's PhD thesis at Rice University; his colleagues marveled, where did you get this guy? He worked for all the big map and atlas makers: Rand McNally and the UN, where he was ultimately fired for his anar-chist beliefs. A mismatch when you think about it. The man knew the latitude, longitude, altitude, temperature range, rainfall pattern, vegetation, population, racial-ethnic composition, culture, sexual mores, diet, and primary products of virtually every point of human habitation on this Earth. I exaggerate slightly.

I could talk to Russell for hours.

Behind the façade, he was a man of vast experience, who had encountered life as few people have. I do not know how he ended up as the chief Communist Party youth organizer in Mexico, Guate-mala, and Honduras through the 1920s and early 30s (he went under the name Rosalio Negrete). I suspect his childhood was profoundly unhappy, as the only relative he mentioned affectionately was his uncle Henry, after whom he named his second child. I remember vaguely his running away often and setting out on his own early.

Russell could tell you what it was like to be an itinerant organizer moving from village to village in those days. He could tell you what the Mexican Communist Party was like. He could tell you of his friendship of a sort with Vittori Vidali—Communist hatchet man most infamous for his role in the murder of Leon Trotsky—who in the course of his life also came to be known as Erea Sormenti,

Jacobo Hurwitz Zender, Carlos Contreras ("Commandante Carlos"), I may have missed a few. The last name on the list is decidedly Spanish; that is because he served as chief murderer for the GPU in Spain; the man's hands were immersed in an ocean of POUMist and anarchist blood. Since Vidali was sent to Mexico to enforce party discipline and Russell had become a Trotskyite or something close to it in the late 1920s, the "friendship" was a dicey affair—although Russell said characteristically that Vidali was a pleasant fellow.

He was on a firmer footing with Diego Rivera. They were expelled from the Party at about the same time, although for different reasons. Of course, they took Diego back in later: He was after all *Diego Rivera*. But the two men were genuine friends. And here is an image I will not forget: Russell keeping Diego Rivera company as he constructs his famous murals that depict the history of Mexico on the walls lining the steps of the National (President's) Palace in Mexico City. It was brutally hard work. It was hot. Diego, a large man, sweat profusely. Russell brought him cold drinks and they often lunched together, eating their sandwiches in the shade of the Palace steps, the masterpiece surrounding them.

I've written earlier about Russell's activities in Spain, so I'll say no more about them. For a time, following his return, he left the movement and put his energies into raising his family. Edna's brother died while serving in the merchant marine during World War II, and they used the insurance money to buy or rent a nice house in Sunnyside, Queens. I stayed there fairly often, sleeping in the same bed or room with Steve. Sunnyside seemed like a vacation in the country to me, though it is about a mile from Manhattan. And I liked Edna, too.

Russell comes back into my focus during the 1950s and 60s when he and my parents founded the League. He was involved in all of its activities, but two incidents demonstrate the loyalty and courage of the man. Perhaps you have heard of the Galíndez Case? It caused a sensation some sixty years ago. On the evening of March 12, 1956, Jesús Galíndez taught a class at Columbia University. A student gave him a lift downtown to Columbus Circle, where he was to hop the subway a few stops to his apartment near West Fourteenth Street and Eighth Avenue—in those days a neighborhood of many Spanish émigrés. He never made it home. He simply vanished.

Born in Spain in 1915, Galíndez was a political activist, a committed antifascist and perhaps above all, a militant Basque nationalist. None of this endeared him to Franco, and with the fall of the Republic, he was forced to flee for his life. By 1939, he was allowed to enter to the Dominican Republic—where, as a trained lawyer and scholar, he grew useful to the tyrant Trujillo—doing various intellectual work and, I believe, tutoring his children. But Galíndez found that fascism and corruption polluted the Dominican Republic as well; on the bad side of Trujillo, he was forced to run again and, in 1946, emigrated to New York City.

In New York, while "working on his PhD in political science from Columbia University, Galíndez found the time to teach college classes, write a newspaper column which was syndicated throughout Latin America, and represent the Basque government-in-exile. He was a busy man." He also spoke at rallies in support of the Committee to Defend Franco's Labor Victims and attended SIA Hall dinners. He was not an anarchist, but was on friendly terms with my parents and Russell and many other comrades; the Basque nationalists and anarchists had made common cause during the Civil War. Abe spoke with him several times, but has told me recently that he was put off by the way Galíndez could speak ringingly in support of the men facing the death penalty and then mutter under his breath something about "dirty" anarchists.

Galíndez's PhD thesis was a thorough documentation of the corruption, crimes, and horrors of the Trujillo regime. He knew the man and his family intimately and considered him a monster. Trujillo was not inclined to forgive or forget, and he had a long reach. He had murdered one of Galíndez's friends in Manhattan in 1952. Yet Galíndez courageously refused to back down on his thesis, and he went so far as to state in a letter, that in the event of his disappearance and/or death, Trujillo had ordered it.

The abduction and apparent murder caused a huge sensation; *Life* magazine investigated and charged that Galíndez had been kidnapped, drugged, flown by private plane to Ciudad Trujillo, where he was shot to death in the presence of the sadist.

Russell took the whole thing hard. You can see his picture in *Life* taken during a demonstration in front of the Dominican

Embassy sponsored by the League and others. You can bet Trujillo saw Russell's picture as well. Mother was near tears over Galíndez's death. She knew him to be a kind man of courtly manners, a man of principle.

Galíndez was also a complicated man. Apparently, he angered Trujillo in the Dominican Republic when the great man asked him to mediate a labor dispute involving sugarcane workers and he ruled in favor of the strikers. Not a smart career move. On the other hand, I wonder what Russell, Sam, and Mother would have thought of Galíndez if they had known he was an FBI/CIA informant. Still, he wrote his thesis even when his handlers urged him not to because they would not be able to protect him. Trujillo being more important to U.S. interests than Galíndez.

The second incident that comes to mind when I think of Russell's courage was the trip he took up to Harlem during the riot of 1964. The riot was in response to a police shooting of a black teenager. The streets erupted. It was a bloody, violent affair, blacks battling cops and in some instances each other. All kinds of factions entered the fray. "When Bayard Rustin, who had organized the March on Washington in 1963, pleaded for peace," said the *New York Times*, "he was called an Uncle Tom and showered with boos from an angry crowd that chanted instead for Malcolm X." To which Rustin reportedly replied, "I'm prepared to be a Tom if it's the only way I can save women and children from being shot down in the street, and if you're not willing to do the same, you're fools."

Although Rustin's plea did not accomplish much, he was able to rescue Russell. Rustin happened to be passing by as a street mob got hold of Russell. They were in no mood for white visitors. Who was this guy? A cop? What did he want? Desperately, Rustin prevailed upon them. He explained who Russell was, begged them to release him. And Russell barely got by, white skin intact. Rustin escorted his friend and comrade to the subway station and made sure he boarded the train. A rational person might have thought Harlem was a good place to avoid that first night. Not Russell. He had advocated that blacks revolt for years. He thought it the harbinger of the revolution to come. He may have remembered his Barcelona days.

Sam loved Russell so dearly that he hesitated to write of his declining years. His health failed. He had a painful gall-bladder and kidney-stone operation. He convalesced a long time at our apartment under Mother's care. His marriage to Edna, never an easy one, had gone bad, to disastrous affect on A. H. and Claudia. Edna's mental health deteriorated and she was placed in a state asylum much like a prison. Exactly how or why I am not sure. But then Russell did something as uncharacteristic as it was unforgivable in Sam's eyes. The authorities were willing to release Edna if Russell would take her. She begged him, but he refused. "When you were in Spain, and your life hung on a thread, I was there for you. I raised heaven and hell to get you out. And now I ask you for this and you say no."

Fortunately, his better angels prevailed, and he signed her out, but it was awful. The process repeated itself several times. Years later, in preparation for this memoir, I spoke to Russell's son, my old friend Steve, about Russell's attitude, and he took a more tolerant stance toward his father than had Sam. Edna was extremely bipolar, refused medications, and was altogether impossible for Russell, a sick man, to deal with. Steve insists he did the best he could.

Russell dropped away from the League in the early 1960s, though he wrote several excellent articles on the history of the Spanish Civil War and Revolution. Sam and I visited him on occasion in his run down flat on Sixth Street and Avenue C in the middle of what New Yorkers called Alphabet City: a Puerto Rican/Dominican slum at the time. The door was always open and neighborhood kids ran in and out and all over him, taking what they wanted. He had no sense of private property or privacy; he gave them everything. Friends looked after him, as did Steve. He had heart trouble and died of a heart attack in 1969. He was sixty-five years old.

I attended his memorial service at the liberal Community Church on Thirty-Fifth Street. Sam gave the eulogy. Herb Miller, to whom I dedicate this memoir, sat next to me in the audience. He was a professor of Speech and Rhetoric at the City University. He said he had never heard a more moving, finer address.

Russell was loved by many people. Murray Bookchin attempted to hang the black anarchist flag, the flag of the CNT, outside the church: the only flag under which Russell fought. An idiot church official tried to prevent Murray, and Murray near came to blows with him until he relented. "Who are these people?" the respectable churchman asked.

47

# DICK ELLINGTON

Forgive me, but the most vivid memory I have of Dick Ellington's physical appearance was his infirmity. The man was in his
mid-twenties and already arthritis was bending him and deforming
his arms and wrists. The condition would grow worse as he suffered
stoically through a lifetime of pain. I found him a terrific person to
be around; in my opinion perhaps the best of the many people Sam
influenced in a positive way. He was a full-grown adult individual,
an Army veteran when he showed up at the SIA Hall soon after the
birth of the League. I am not sure how he heard about us. What I
do remember is he was from Seattle, Washington and had decided
to come to New York after his stint in the Army; he was the product
of a working-class, Irish-Catholic family.

Dick was a science-fiction "nut," but you knew better than to
say that to his face if you valued your smile. He took the genre
seriously, and it was through his association with like-minded people that he came in contact with the League. I do not know the
exact connection, because no one I can recall at the League was a
science-fiction enthusiast.

Dick's anarchist instincts were in place before he came to the
League. What they lacked were a sense of context and intellectual
rigor. Years later, living in Oakland California, Dick would describe
what it was like to meet people who "had the same fucking ideas
I did politically, but they had a fucking political theory about it...
and a history!" As David Jacobs put it in a remembrance he wrote
of Ellington, "Dick met up with History itself, in the sense that he
came into direct contact with Spanish anarchists, with Americans
who had fought in Spain on the anarchist side, with people who had
known Kropotkin and Nestor Makhno, with the friends of Carlo
Tresca and Emma Goldman. His and Pat's interest in the ideas
behind this history would lead them into contact with the English
anarchists around Freedom Press; history would also give them the
name they chose for their daughter, Marie Louise, named for the

anarchist Marie-Louise Berneri (wife and comrade of *Freedom*'s Vernon Richards)."

Sam, Russell, Boris Yelensky, the comrades of the SIA Hall, and many others, did more than educate Dick; they provided him an emotional home.

Dick repaid in kind. Before computers, before self-publication, before all the marvels of the digital revolution, getting your message out was a major problem—especially so if you were a tiny group of working-class radicals. No grants or trust funds anywhere in sight! A skilled printer and typesetter—actually a skilled mechanic in all things—Dick made *Views and Comments* legible. The first few issues were mimeographed but the group soon chipped in and bought an old multilith that Dick ran. Pat and Dick made a huge difference. They were the nuts and bolts of the League. New York's loss became Oakland's gain.

However, I do not want to leave the impression Dick was valued for his Jimmy Higgins skills alone. He had fine judgment. He had a great sense of fun. He was creative. He and David Van Ronk teamed up to write and publish a parody on the Wobblies' famous *Little Red Song Book*: *The Boss's Songbook*. It contains a pitch-perfect take-off on "This Land is Your Land," which is a bit unfair because the intent of Woody Guthrie's classic was revolutionary; not his fault the patriots hijacked his song.

# 48

# DAVID VAN RONK

Finally, I can write about someone my age! A New York City kid at that, an attendee—I'm not sure he graduated—of Richmond Hill High in Queens. The school is proud of him, as well they should be. He is listed in their Hall of Fame; you can look it up. Another working-class, Irish-Catholic kid, despite the Dutch name, a street kid. Someone I can relate to. Also, a brilliant kid. I close my eyes and can still hear him speak authoritatively on so many topics at League forums. At nineteen years old! Had he really read all that stuff or was he "improvising?" Maybe a bit of both. I've seen a thousand photographs of him over the years. Nearly all of them show this huge, fleshy overweight person with hair all over the place, sometimes a beard. That was David the legend, the seminal figure in the Greenwich Village folk scene of the 1960s. I remember him as tall, thinnish, somewhat round shouldered. His reddish hair was cropped short exposing a fine pair of jug-ears. An appealing, likeable face.

David and I were on good terms, although not close. Looking back, he had broader experience, was more sophisticated and street smart than me, and I was Sam's son, which, because of my parents' presence and status, probably inhibited him. But we mingled for a time. We were close enough that he stole my girlfriend. Well, okay, she was not my girlfriend—we had never even discussed the matter—and David did not actually "steal" her. It simply felt that way at the time. I was a square kid despite all the radicalism at home and Heather was my first adult sexual relationship. I really did not know what to do in bed, although I was willing to learn.

Heather was a bohemian girl, a bit older and more experienced than me—an NYU student who had rented a loft on the Bowery. A daring thing for a young woman in those days. You might say she was a pre-hippie. I remember she had to step over a derelict or two sleeping in the hallway before she could climb the stairs to her loft. Anyway, I took it hard for a time but got over it. If I were Heather I probably would have chosen David, too, although I'm not sure how long that lasted, either.

David was an active participant in the League from the mid- to late 1950s, spilling over maybe into the very early 1960s. He regarded Sam as a mentor and surrogate father figure for a time— perhaps more so than he did Russell and some of the older members, although David seemed to like them all. He dug Sam's erudition, the way he carried it off in an earthy style, and he loved to get Sam going on tales of the old-time Wobblies and legendary anarchists like Carlo Tresca. But they seemed to wear on each other after a while, which was sad. David, I believe, wanted action, more militancy from the League. Sam and Russell did not object to the idea—but in what direction, to what purpose? Certainly not for its own sake. David expressed affinity for the Trotskyites at this time, wanted to make common cause with them. Sam and Russell distrusted Trotskyites. But David committed or attempted to commit the League to an alliance without the approval of the group. It was a long time ago and I do not find the specifics important.

David gives his version of the break up in *Mayor of MacDougal Street*, published after his death. He keeps referring to Sam's being drunk and hounding him until David felt driven to punch Sam out: a good thing he did not, because Sam was middle-aged, nearly blind without his glasses, and never could fight his way out of a paper bag. I have a different recollection. David taunted him, was sarcastic, and Sam was not prepared for that from him. Looking back on their fallout, from the height of my of old age, there is no question in my mind that Sam shared the greater blame. He was a mature man with two sons close to David in age. He should have kept a sense of perspective.

Sam knew this. He felt sheepish about it after he cooled down. He invited David and his girlfriend (or was it his wife? I do not remember) over to our apartment. I was away at graduate school at the time. David writes generously that it was a nice visit, that Sam went out of his way, even presenting David and friend with a hand-drawn print of anarchists fighting in the Civil war and a fedora worn by Carlo Tresca. But he also says it was not the same for him, which may mean that David had outgrown the need for a mentor. Mentor or not, I find it revealing that David considered himself an anarcho-syndicalist throughout his life and never let his membership in the IWW lapse.

Though definitely not gay, at least as I remember him, I find it gratifying that David "was among the thirteen people arrested at the Stonewall Inn June 28, 1969—the night that the Stonewall Riots, which many cite as the night the gay rights movement, began."

Last year I saw the Coen Brother's *Inside Llewyn Davis*. The film, as most people probably know, was not about David as such, but was inspired by incidents in David's life as recounted in *Mayor*. However I ask myself: If one is going to make a film of the Greenwich Village folk scene of the time and base it on incidents from David's book, then why not make it about David? Why not attempt to capture David's rough, noncomforting voice, his intricate guitar work, his originality? Why not try to convey his generosity of spirit? For he was definitely not the selfish, depressive creep pictured in the film.

I lost track of David in the 1960s. We went different ways. But I can add one more footnote. I've read—or heard—that David was hurt and a bit rueful that Dylan had copied David's version of "House of the Rising Sun" for his first album. Now, let's be clear that the song is a standard. Dylan had every right to sing it, but to use David's version? I'd heard him sing it many times at the SIA Hall.

# 49
## THE LIBERTARIAN LEAGUE FORUMS

The League sponsored "Forums" every Friday night. Invited speakers or in-house League members would address the audience, followed up with questions and back-and-forth debate. On a good night maybe twenty people would attend; on a poor night eight or ten. As often as not, I found the Forums tedious: a group of tired people—some dedicated and some with nowhere else to go—going through the motions. So why write about them? Because just as often they were remarkable. I marvel at the quality of many of the speakers and of those who showed up to listen. They came out of respect for Sam and Russell and the Spanish anarchists. They came because they could say what was on their mind without the need to pull punches. They came to try out new ideas, new theories. The place to be for a time in the 1950s and early 1960s was at the Forums of the Libertarian League.

There were nights that historical figures—men who made history—told you things only they witnessed. Case in point: The night I. N. Steinberg, Peoples Commissar of Justice in the Soviet government from December 1917 to March 1918 and a central figure in the drafting of the Soviet Constitution, came to tell us of his private, face-to-face meeting with Lenin in that sparsely furnished Kremlin room where he forged the Communist State. Steinberg had been there to protest the vicious crackdown of the Cheka on all dissent and suspected dissenters. Vanishing people, torture, murder—all without trial or even a hearing—and that he, as People's Commissar of Justice, was being ignored.

It was late in the afternoon. Lenin stared up at him from behind his simple desk and greeted him warmly. He appeared tired. He denied none of Steinberg's charges. He shook his head sadly: "Yes, yes comrade, but these are special times. We have many enemies. Steps must be taken." Steinberg was not having it. He mentioned victims of the Cheka who were loyal revolutionists. "Why call me Commissar of Social Justice? Why not Commissar of Social

Extermination?" Steinberg asked, exasperated. Lenin peered forward, smiled ambiguously: "That's it!" he said, waving his arms, "but we can't say it!" And he kept his eyes on Steinberg. Was it his ironic humor? Steinberg felt a chill; he knew he was on the list, or would be sooner or later, and went into exile.

Where do you learn things like that? Steinberg went on to say Lenin and his Bolshevik comrades were not monsters in the conventional sense. They were not sadists and took no satisfaction in the imprisonment and murder of others. Nor were they corrupt; they sacrificed hugely for their ideals and truly felt they were the vanguard of a new era for humanity. But, you see, they were history's instrument. Their decisions were governed by the unbending logic of a Marxist dialectic that led to the inevitability of the Communist State. Certain acts were an historical necessity—a necessity that transcended mere morality or personal loyalty.

Mother expressed the matter metaphorically. "Nice men! They'll serve you tea and sponge cake while they explain to you the historical necessity of keeping their old friend chained in the basement."

Several years later and by total coincidence, my wife Jessica took an Art History course at Hunter College. She mentioned over dinner with my parents that the otherwise excellent instructor made her uncomfortable with constant demeaning references to his father. What an idiot he was, what a clown, etc. He would invite the class to laugh, which they did uneasily. Then she happened to mention that the instructor was Leo Steinberg. She had no idea who I. N. Steinberg was. When Sam informed her, he asked, "Does that man seem like a fool to you?" Sam found it sad. Leo Steinberg would go on to a distinguished career as an art critic and scholar. His obituary was carried as front page news in the *New York Times*.

No one bothered to keep a list of League speakers—or high-powered audience members. I'll list a few names to suggest the flavor:

- Michael Harrington of the Catholic Worker and the Socialist Party, later the author of *The Other America*.
- Bogdan Denitch: in his youth a Trotskyite of some kind, later a great scholar of the history and politics of the Balkans, and

Chairman of the Department of Sociology at the Graduate
Center of the City University of New York.

- Bayard Rustin on several occasions. I remember him as lean
and handsome with a hawk-like nose and reddish brown
complexion. He resembled a stereotypical American Indian,
with his shock of black hair pitched forward high on his
head. He spoke in a high tenor: more of his pacifist antiwar
activism than Civil Rights. His focus was to change soon, as
we know.

- Ammon Hennesy: Catholic Worker, pacifist, anarchist,
Wobbly. Cell mate of Alexander Berkman during Berkman's second imprisonment, this time in Atlanta Penitentiary for opposing World War I. What he loved to speak
most about was his time with the Hopi Indians of the west;
their mores and anarchistic lifestyle and so on. Forgive me,
for he was a terrific story teller and had a lot of interesting
things to say, but what I remember most vividly was that he
was all gums, with one green tooth that stood as a sentinel.
Like the discovery of someone's toupee, I could not take
my eyes off it.

- Conrad Lynn, the great black Civil Rights lawyer: defender
of conscientious objectors, various radicals, framed and
unjustly imprisoned citizens, participant in the first Freedom Ride through the South in 1947, and on and on. He
spoke incisively on the criminality of colonialism in Africa—
especially on Portuguese rule, which he found vicious. He
had an eloquent and poetic mode of expression. "I admire
the Wobblies. They were a movement that had the courage
to sing."

- Jim Peck, a white man, pacifist, conscientious objector,
close friend of Russell and Rustin, and the only participant
in both the first Freedom Ride of 1947 and the next one in
1961. In Birmingham he was beaten to the point of nearly
bleeding to death and received fifty-three stitches. All this
while the FBI on the scene turned away. The son of a rich
man, graduate of exclusive Choate, he entered Harvard
with his future laid out for him. Only it was a future he did

not want; he left in his freshman year for a lifetime of radical activism. He spoke to us sometime in the late 1950s. He was among Mother's favorite people.

- Dorothy Day. She spoke admiringly of the devotion of the Mexican peasants to the Catholic Church. This angered Sam, which led him to dress down the future Saint. I'll let him describe the incident:

> At one of our meetings, Dorothy Day described her pilgrimage to the shrine of Mexico's patron Saint, the Cathedral of the Virgin of Guadalupe in Mexico City. In glowing tribute to the devotion of the Mexican people who crawled on their knees to the holy shrine, the symbol of their eternal faith in their savior and his eternal Church, Dorothy exclaimed: "She (the Church), as strong as ever, continues to live in the hearts, the minds, in the very soul of her faithful children, the Mexican people." During the discussion period I took the floor and rebuked her in the following terms: "The oppressed Mexican people, peasants and workers, and with them the anarchist militants, the Magón brothers, Práxedis Guerrero, Librado Rivera, Camilo Arriago, Juan Sarabo, and so many others in the glorious Mexican Revolution of 1910, fought, bled and died to break the power of the Church over the life of the people and achieve freedom and social justice. That you, a professed anarchist… should now glorify the Church and ignore their valiant struggles is an intolerable insult to their memory."
>
> When, several months later, she complained to some comrades that I mistreated her, they told her that, "If he did, he probably had a very good reason for doing so."

It turns out that I happened to have been to that shrine. I have seen the devotion Dorothy Day described. Facing the church is an enormous open expanse of concrete with embedded pebbles that gives the ground an incredibly rough texture. The faithful Dorothy Day so admires crawl over this concrete, their knees bleeding, mumbling entreaties to Jesus to help them, for many are deformed and sick and all of them in poverty.

In 1956 I discovered something about Sam I had not consciously realized. You see, Sam lectured at the Forum more than anyone else; not because of ego, but to fill gaps in the schedule. It was difficult to come up with a speaker each Friday. To fill these gaps and also the gaps in the education of some League members, he decided to deliver a series of lectures: The classical anarchists, starting with William Godwin and continuing on up through Max Stirner, Benjamin Tucker, Pierre-Joseph Proudhon, Michael Bakunin, Peter Kropotkin, Élisée Reclus, Rudolf Rocker, Errico Malatesta, and Luigi Galleani. Each week a different anarchist—his life and times, his historical context, his principal contributions, his faults. To Bakunin, he devoted several weeks, because he required an analysis of his relation to Karl Marx, the First International, and the dark figure of Sergei Nechaev. The scope of these lectures was vast. Taken together they painted a panorama of nineteenth- and early-twentieth-century history. On other occasions there were other subjects: The Medieval Guild System; Adam Smith and the Origins of Capitalism; the Knights of Labor; the Roots of Spanish anarchism; Corruption in the AFL/CIO; Mistakes of the IWW. By this time I had listened to a hundred lectures at college delivered by dozens of professors, men and women with PhDs and all the 1950s pomposity that went with it. Not one of them came close to my father; not one in depth of understanding, in conviction, and yes, in scholarship. All this knowledge he gained by himself after hard labor and hernias and his drinking and his activism and the demands of a wife and children. And this is the thing I discovered about my father that I had not consciously realized: that he was a brilliant man.

Speaking of a brilliant man, I'll skip five years ahead, circa 1961, and recount to you an incident my parents told me about.

A dreary evening at the League Forum, half dozen in attendance. Clump. Clump. Feet struggle up the wooden stairs to the SIA Hall. In walks a smallish, elderly Chinese man—well-dressed in suit and tie. At his side is a hulking young American man, sloppily dressed, in need of a haircut. They sit down politely and wait for the meeting to dribble to an end.

The elderly Chinese man holds a copy of *Views and Comments*. "Can you tell me who wrote this, please?" It is an article on Mao's

China, specifically about the regimentation of Chinese society, and the disastrous affects of Mao's Great Leap Forward. It lays the blame squarely on Mao and the Communist Party, and it eviscerates sympathetic press agents like Herbert Read who travel the length of China and are blind to what is happening.

"It is the best article I have read in English on the situation in China," the elderly man says. "Can you tell me who wrote it?" (*Views* articles were unsigned.)

"I wrote it," Sam says, pleased.

"And with what university are you affiliated?"

"None."

"And how do you earn your living?"

"I'm a house painter."

The old man is visibly stunned. So is his young companion. He is a professor at the University of Delaware or some such place, and he is accompanied by his graduate student who is also looking after him. They traveled all the way to New York by bus to meet the author. The visit turns into a love-fest and it goes on into the night. They wait while Sam and Mother close the Hall.

"Have you eaten?" Mother asks.

No.

"Do you have a place to stay?"

They haven't thought about it.

"Well, come home with us." And so the four of them take the subway back to our apartment at 481 Van Buren St. buried in the Bushwick/Bed-Stuy section of Brooklyn. Mother goes to sleep. Sam and the old man and the bleary-eyed grad student talk the night away. The old man tells Sam some amazing stories. Seems he has known Mao since childhood. They were classmates! He is not the least bit in awe of him. Rather he holds Mao in contempt. He remembers that when the teacher left the room and the children acted up, maybe did some mischief, Mao stood up and denounced them when the teacher returned.

"Mao, the class snitch!" Sam exclaims, delighted.

"Yes indeed." The old man says.

The old man's analysis of Mao went far deeper than that. He was a serious scholar of anarchistic bent.

What was his name, I asked Mother and Sam. Where exactly did he live? Work? Do you have his phone number? Nothing? Maddening! My parents were often that way.

# 50

# VIEWS AND COMMENTS

*Views and Comments* (*VC*) in the main consisted of views and comments on the events and concerns of its day: Civil Rights and black liberation; the rise of new states from the polluted soil of traditional colonialism; the crimes of Mao's China, Castro's Cuba, Franco's Spain, Peron's Argentina, Stalinist Bulgaria; the Cold War; militarism; etc. To this stew add a sprinkling of radical history, for example, a brief account the Haymarket Affair, or a book review. And do not forget that old standby, the corrupt, collaborationist labor movement. Don't panic. I have no intention of recounting all of this stuff. However, I will say that many of *VC*'s insights were prescient and seem surprisingly fresh after fifty years.

Sam wrote and edited most of the articles, although it is hard to pin down authorship because, in the custom of the time, the articles were usually unsigned. You have to read them for style or, in my opinion, the lack of it in Sam's case, for he paid almost no attention to "style." He was concerned only with getting his meaning across as directly as possible, which on second thought is a kind of style. Whatever eloquence or grace he may have achieved came straight from conviction. Sam had been writing articles for years, all the way back to the days of Walter Starrett Van Valkenburgh and the *Road to Freedom* group of the early 1920s. They are scattered throughout the anarchist and Wobbly publications since then. He wrote under the name Sam Weiner, but again, because most were unsigned, his output is difficult to trace. He continued to write articles, probably a score of them after the League folded. His work at *VC* should be judged as one episode in a lifetime of activism.

He had a nose for the buried fact, the relevant detail, for the thing unsaid. He poured over obscure foreign-language publications few people paid attention to: material sent to him or that otherwise reached him:

From the Jewish anarchist federation of Argentina, which told him a great deal about anti-Semitism and the Peron regime not covered in the mainstream press.

From the Cuban underground during Batista and after Castro, and later the Cuban anarchists in exile. (He was on excellent terms with the Cubans, as I will discuss later.)

From the Bulgarian anarchists—some forced into exile in Paris—others persecuted and murdered by the Stalinists.

From the Spanish Cultura Proletaria and the SIA Hall group, of course.

From the anarchists of Tel Aviv, who sent him *Problemen*, one of the few surviving anarchist publications in the Yiddish language.

From the comrades of Mexico, Nicaragua, Costa Rica.

From the Korean anarchists, who Sam claimed were part of a surprisingly active movement.

From China, and on and on.

If Sam could not read the language pecking through it with a dictionary, he called on others to translate for him.

These sources alerted him to events not covered by the "mainstream" media. One source described the eruption of slave revolts in Vorkuta and throughout the Soviet gulag that began in the late 1940s. Sam published the news before the *New York Times* broke the story. "I scooped the bastards," he cried, shaking his fists. Too bad so few people read his scoop.

Sam could print nasty stuff. For example, this item from a Mexican paper (*Esto*):

> One of the most vociferous of the anti-falangist agitators during the student strike in Madrid was none other than the youngest son of Don Alberto Martín Arrajo, foreign minister and a power in the Franco government.
>
> Rumor has it that the young man was sent away to continue his studies in England, where he would not be exposed to the seditious influence of the young people of his own country. Once in England, he promptly went over to the Protestant faith and proceeded to publish denunciations of the Franco regime and his own father.

The Spanish Gestapo, the D.F.G., sent a little group of plainclothesmen to shadow him. They followed him until he made a trip to Paris, and there they pounced. The young Arrajo was bundled into a car and spirited over the Spanish frontier. In Spain he was declared hopelessly insane and committed to a luxurious asylum where he has been locked up ever since.

Foreign Minister Arrajo was the gentlemen whose appearance at Gracie Mansion we had been picketing.

He could be acid when it came to union tyrants. Of David Dubinsky, long-time boss of the International Ladies Garment Workers Union (ILGWU), he had this to say: "The members who built the union and whose dues paid his salary and the salaries of the hordes of lesser officials, are (in Dubinsky's opinion) incapable of running their own union.... 'The increasing complexity of union affairs make it necessary to rely on men trained as lawyers, accountants and technicians for much of the union's future direction.' It is natural that this state within a state, which is called a union, needs an army of bureaucrats and politicians to regulate the organization and its members."

# 51
## SAM ON CIVIL RIGHTS

On December 1st, 1955 Rosa Parks was arrested for the crime of refusing to surrender her seat to a white man on a Montgomery, Alabama bus. You cannot overestimate the impact of that revolutionary event.

"A Negro woman! She refused to accept her inferior status. Do you understand what that means?" Mother exalted, turning to Sam.

Sam well understood. He had been monitoring the stirrings that preceded the Montgomery Bus Boycott and he was convinced the issue cut deeper than civil rights in the American South.

"All over the world the submerged peoples are rebelling against the imperialist exploitation which is based in large part on the false doctrines of racial superiority. The struggle of the Southern Negroes is part of that movement," he wrote in the February 1956 *Views and Comments*, in an article entitled "The South's Negroes are in Motion."

Sam approached the Civil Rights struggle from a consistent anarcho-syndicalist point of view. This usually served him well, but it also led him to take rigid and unrealistic positions at the onset, which in time, I am pleased to say, evolved for the better.

In 1957, Governor Orville Faubus used the Arkansas National Guard to block entry of nine black students to Little Rock High School. This was counter to the 1954 U.S. Supreme Court Brown v. Board of Education decision that ruled segregation in public schools unconstitutional. The Faubus action caused an uproar. President Eisenhower, after some dithering, called in Federal troops to enforce the enrollment on the grounds that, whether or not he agreed with the decision, the authority of the Federal Government is paramount and must be upheld.

Sam's stance? Obviously he supported the rights of the black children. But he pointed out that Eisenhower had done nothing for these children. He was upholding the power of the state. If the situation were reversed and the Supreme Court had ruled to allow segregation, he would have called in troops to block their entry to the school. The better path was to win the grassroots support of the white working class, the unions in particular. I say good luck with that! How long would it take? Perhaps until the nine students were eligible for Social Security benefits?

To my thinking Sam contorted events to fit his convictions. The state was evil and must be opposed even if in this instance a centuries-old wrong was liquidated. He completely missed the human dimension. The blacks wanted justice within the system; they did not want to overthrow the system. As for his idea of seeking grassroots alliances with white workers, it was wildly impractical, given the polarized state of race relations in the South of that time. However, it made sense to Sam if you consider the Wobbly tradition of racial inclusiveness: a tradition that included an integrated union among the timber workers of Texas and Louisiana—the deepest South. There was also the example of the integrated Southern Tenant Farmers Union, forged by the Mitchell brothers of the 1930s. So the possibility of a working-class coalition of blacks and whites was not a fantasy to Sam. Nevertheless, he well knew these unions were a long time ago. He had let his distrust of the state get the better of him.

But he evolved. He absolutely supported the Freedom Riders' penetration of Alabama and Mississippi. "You must go to the center of the infection." He reveled in the development of a mass movement that practiced civil disobedience: shades of the old-time Wobblies, though more widespread. By the early 60s Sam had made an unconscious 180-degree turn: The largely white union movement needed an infusion of black militancy more than the blacks needed white union support. He respected Martin Luther King for trying to broaden the Civil Rights movement to include *all* poverty stricken people and he appreciated his moral courage in taking a stand against the war in Vietnam, a stance that could not have helped his alliance with President Johnson. I visited Mother and Sam the evening of King's assassination. They were deeply saddened. Sam noted that he met death after he came to Memphis in support of striking sanitation workers. Sam took that to be the essential part of the man.

As for me, having locked eyes with him ever so briefly, I cannot forget his youthful face.

However, Sam distrusted many aspects of the Civil Rights movement. He attacked the NAACP as an authoritarian organization. He disliked the anti-white turn of the Student Nonviolent Coordinating Committee (SNCC), thought the Black Panthers proto-fascist and not so proto at that. The Black Muslim's were anathema, as was Malcolm X: not for his militancy but for his racism, his not so veiled anti-Semitism, his support of reactionary Muslim states (though, Sam knew he was "evolving"). The respectable Protestant Church, bedrock of the movement, was not his cup of tea either. They spawned opportunist politicians and businessmen who used the movement as a springboard to power. In sum, Sam was an anarchist and the Civil Rights movement was basically reformist. The blacks wanted in, not out, which is why the movement was in large measure successful. The establishment was under no threat in letting them have a place at the trough.

# MARTIN LUTHER KING AND THE PRINCESS

The Princess was, of course, Princess Alexandra Kropotkin (1887–1966), the only daughter of Prince Peter Kropotkin (1842–1921), and the direct descendant of the first Russian Czar, predating the Romanovs. Peter Kropotkin considered it an insult to call him "Prince." He gave all that up and was disinherited by his father. He turned his back on privilege, and spent years in prison and, following that, years of exile in London, where Alexandra was born. He was perhaps the greatest anarchist theorist—also a first-rate scientist, and pioneer in fields as widespread as geology, biological evolution, history, sociology, economics, and philosophy. But most of all he was an anarchist, and he believed in a stateless society, organized through voluntary, free association and direct, though nonviolent, activism. Princess Alexandra did not give a damn about her title, either. She used it to make a living in NY where she came to live after leaving Russia in 1921 following the death of her parents. She wrote articles on etiquette for the old *Liberty* magazine, a rival to the *Saturday Evening Post*, and the Princess title served her well.

Princess Alexandra was a complicated person. Not only did she toss anarchism aside, sort of, but she voted for Barry Goldwater in 1964 and "felt sick" that he lost. Many anarchists despised her for desecrating the name of her beloved father. My parents knew her well and liked her very much. They found her a charming person and not the arch reactionary that she proclaimed to be in public. Sam said, with characteristic irony, that the daughter of Peter Kropotkin was a closet anarchist. Nobody, least of all the worshippers of her father had to remind Alexandra who her father was. She adored him and honored his memory, and was especially close to Rudolf Rocker, whom she knew from her childhood days in London.

Alexandra took a liking to Mother and enjoyed regaling her with tales of her childhood and young adult years in London. Here is one for you. The Kropotkins were socially prominent among the intellectual elite of 1890s and early-twentieth-century London.

They ran an open-house salon on Sundays where Madame Kropotkin prepared a buffet of the best available Russian delicacies. All
welcome. However, there was a guest she came to loath: a young
law student with a thick Indian accent and peculiar voice who lectured the other guests on their dietary habits. They should turn
away from the meat and the vodka Madame served and become
vegetarians. The young fellow was aware of Madame's dislike of
him. Somehow he learned her habits—maybe Peter told him. He'd
lurk around the corner from their house and scoot up the back way
when he saw the old lady go out the front to shop. Then he'd get
into long, complicated discussions with Peter.

That young Cambridge law student was Mohandas Gandhi.
Yes, the great Gandhi would scoot up the back way so as to avoid
the old lady. What an image! Of course, Gandhi did not know at the
time he was to become *Mahatma Gandhi*.

You can trace the lineage. Gandhi was heavily influenced by
Kropotkin and, later, Tolstoy. Bayard Rustin was in turn heavily
influenced by Gandhi. Rustin brought Gandhi's humanistic philosophy of opposition to state power through nonviolence, derived
from Kropotkin and Tolstoy, to Martin Luther King. A nonviolent mass movement committed to passive resistance was probably
the only effective strategy open to the Civil Rights movement, and
in keeping with its Christian tradition. Sam thought it depressing
but not surprising that the establishment has expropriated Martin
Luther King's life and image to serve its purposes. King's rough
edged, socialistic, nay anarchistic, qualities have been smoothed
over and polished to near oblivion. Substituted for the real King is
the inoffensive one, espousing a platitudinous tolerance acceptable
to white people—a modern day Founding Father, perversely, in
Sam's opinion, undercutting black militancy.

Aside from the usual suspects, Sam found himself at intellectual war with a new adversary: the statist mindset displayed by many of his comrades on the Left. Indeed, some were members of the Libertarian League. This mindset took a variety of forms:

- support of the new states emerging from the collapse of European colonialism;
- support of the new states emerging from national liberation struggles, "socialist" Cuba being a prime example;
- support of the new state of Israel emerging in the aftermath of the Holocaust, or alternately support of a Palestinian state, emerging in the aftermath of Israel.

Sam supported none of these on principle, though the intensity of his opposition varied in particular instances for practical and emotional reasons.

Here he is, early 1958, on the creation of a new state (Ghana) in the aftermath of colonial rule:

> Behold! A new state is being built! The power of foreign colonial rulers is now wielded by the new government. The new government makes and enforces the law of the land. It creates the machinery of domination. It organizes the army, police, jails, judges, courts, schools, radio stations. It appoints swarms of officials who poke their long noses into everybody's business, regulate everything, and exact tribute (taxes) which supports the parasitic state apparatus.
>
> To the native governing class, independence meant the right to abolish the natural, social, cultural and communal institutions that were developed by the people, and impose from above, by force, an artificial scheme of life, which nullifies or distorts their natural development and paralyzes their creative

capacities. The new rulers secretly admired the colonial gover-
nors and administrators. They envied the easy, luxurious life of
their masters, their power, their prestige....They soaked up the
teachings of their masters like a sponge absorbs water.

And let us not forget, Sam said, these new states are artificial
entities. Their boundaries were carved out by the European powers
without regard for the cultures and allegiances of the people within
them. The stage was set for internal conflicts and regional wars.

What I guess most infuriated Sam's critics was that he refused
to grant that the people of these new states were by definition, or
through some moral calculus, better off for having governments
run by native rulers. After Idi Amin of Uganda and Mugabe of Zim-
babwe (formerly Rhodesia) and the genocide in Rwanda, who is to
say Sam did not have a point? But it was a point no one wanted to
hear. As in his criticism of Cuba and Israel he was branded a reactionary, out-of-touch crank.

"That don't bother me one little bit!" he'd snort.

As a Jew at one with the historical suffering of his people, including the Holocaust, and as a committed lifetime anarchist at war with the concept of the state, Sam was torn apart by the creation of Israel, the Jewish State. He would have preferred, he said many times, that there be no State of Israel or any kind at all; rather a loose confederation of peoples where all religious and cultural rights are guaranteed. The wolf will dwell with the lamb, the Torah tells us, but we know this makes no ecological sense. In other words, as Sam noted ruefully, "My solution is no solution because none of the participants would agree to such a fantastic thing, and the outside powers would never allow it to happen if they did."

Mother grew soft and tearful on the subject of the old-time Zionists; a branch of her family on my grandmother's side had settled there under the Turks and helped form a kibbutz. She insisted the Jews and Muslims got along well: worked in the field together, dined in each other's homes. They were farmers. She may well have been right about that, but she could not face up to the way the Jews took over Arab land during fighting leading to the formation of Israel in 1947–1948. She insisted sentimentally that the Arabs were bought out or left voluntarily at the insistence of their leaders who said it would be a short war and they would return in a few weeks after the Jews were killed. Some of that may have happened but the evidence is overwhelming that many if not most of the Palestinians were driven from their homes by force of arms and in fear of their lives.

Sam had no trouble admitting to this reality. All nations are formed in blood if you go back in history far enough, he insisted. Well-meaning liberal supporters of Israel—I include Mother—emphasize the fuzzy, social democratic, kibbutznik origin of Israel. Sam did not dismiss this, but pointed out that the Stern Gang and the Irgun, the underground fists of the nascent Israel, were the direct descendants of Zionist fascists—admirers of Mussolini—who regarded the Arab Palestinians an inferior race and culture. From the statements of Ze'ev Jabotinsky in the 1920s, through the Israel at the time of Sam's death in 1990, through to the present day, there is remarkable consistency in Israeli policy toward the Palestinian Arabs. Jabotinsky spoke of an iron wall, which to him was probably a metaphor, but we know today is a reality. Jabotinsky also wrote that the Palestinians would never accede to this state of affairs, nor would he if he were they. Therefore, he predicted total conflict until, by repression, the Palestinians gave up all hope. Then bargaining could begin.

Sam parted company with the anti-Israel brigade, however, when it came to their support of the Palestinian resistance: not the mass of the Palestinian people, who are victims, but their fascistic, corrupt leadership. How could any person calling himself a socialist break spiritual bread with Yassar Arafat and the thugs surrounding him, he asked? Should Israel fold its tent before people like that? How would that further the cause of socialism? And what of the Muslim rulers supporting the Palestinians—the Jew-hating rulers of Egypt, Iraq, Saudi Arabia, Iran? The scum of the earth! The truth of the matter is these people would not be happy until every Jew was either dead, expelled, or both.

That is what Sam felt. Not every problem has a solution, he often said. But he continued to view what he considered to be the moral deterioration of the Israeli state with increasing sorrow. I remember his spontaneous elation at Israel's lightning victory in the 1966 Six-Day War. But soon it became clear Israel had no intention of surrendering the West Bank.

"So now the Jews are in the imperialism business," he said, shaking his head sadly.

Sam did not live to see current developments. I am convinced I know his heart and mind well enough to speak for him. He would have mourned the decline of the kibbutz movement into farms that exploited immigrant labor for profit. He would have been appalled at the social and economic segregation of the Israeli Arabs. He would have found the Wall a spiritual atrocity, especially so coming from the descendants of millions who died in concentration camps. He would have thought Israel finding common ground with racist Christian reactionaries in the U.S. repulsive.

The murder of children in Gaza? The ultimate moral degeneration of the Israeli people.

He would not accept Israel's pseudo-logical reasons for why this was regrettable but unavoidable: the Hamas rockets and tunnels, the use of women and children as shields. He would have answered, "I am not God. I am not Netanyahu. You do not murder children. Period!" He would have agreed that his was a sentimental and unrealistic stance. Nevertheless, as a Jew of the old-school humanistic tradition he held Israel to a higher standard than its enemies.

# 55
## CUBA

Sam considered it a form of blindness that some of our allegedly leftist comrades are incapable of distinguishing true revolution from the capture of state power. Especially so if those seizing state power spout the correct—that is Marxist—rhetoric. Sam considered this blindness to be the "triumph" of the Bolshevik interpretation of Marxism in the twentieth century. The brutality of the victorious "revolutionary" regime is denied or explained away as necessary to protect the supposed revolution—which is in fact a counterrevolution. The civil libertarian critics, including the anarchists, are derided as impractical—and I guess they are if your aim is to multiply state power. An unconscious lust for power or the urge to be close to power does not improve the eyesight of these alleged comrades, especially those of intellectual bent useful to the regime.

Sam saw the pattern repeat upon the overthrow of Batista's Cuba. The tyranny was installed. There was the cult of the God-like leader, Castro this time rather than Stalin. The anarchists and other's concerned with liberty were knifed in the back. Sam had information from the underground in Cuba and from exiles at the SIA Hall. He had his eyes and ears and his own instincts. His "blood was up." He was not going to sit by while the anarchists were persecuted once again. He was going to challenge the regime's intellectual mythmakers and apologists. His challenge turned into a fifteen-year war against the pro-Castro Left. His enemies were influential. Substitute Cuba for Russia and Castro for Stalin and it was the 1930s all over again in miniature. It was a lonely time in some ways for Sam and the few comrades at his side, but it did not bother him one little bit. He relished the isolation.

Cuban anarchism had a long and honorable tradition that existed well before Batista and Castro. The historian Frank Fernandez recounts that tradition in his excellent *Cuban Anarchism, The History of a Movement*. He devotes an interesting chapter to the MLCE (Cuban Libertarian Movement in Exile). Those anarchists not imprisoned, or worse, were deported. They set up shop in Miami and as their name indicates proceeded to do their best to oppose the Castro regime as they had in Cuba. However, because most people on the Left were ignorant of Cuban anarchism and Cuba in general they bought into the slander spread by Castro and his ass-kissers that the MLCE was a CIA front; it was an easy thing to believe in the wake of the Bay of Pigs debacle. Sam and Russell knew this to be a lie. No activity in Sam's seventy-year commitment to the radical movement brought him more satisfaction than his campaign on behalf of the exiled Cuban anarchists, coupled with his exposure of Castro from the Left. Frank Fernandez writes that "without doubt, the primary source of solidarity and cooperation for the newly arrived Cubans was the New York-based anarchist Libertarian League, led by Sam Dolgoff and Russell Blackwell.... Without the collaboration of the members of the Libertarian League, the task of the Cuban anarchist exiles would have been much harder."

I've mentioned many times that for Sam history was not an academic exercise. He took what he perceived to be matters of historical betrayal and intellectual dishonesty personally. And two living, breathing individuals with whom he had worked and knew quite well in the past came to personify that betrayal and dishonesty. They were David Dellinger and, to a lesser extent, David Thoreau Wieck.

Now, to be fair, they were men of personal courage and high reputation: longtime anarcho-pacifists and conscientious objectors who had served time in federal prison during World War II. Sam and Wieck went way back to at least 1945 when they worked together on *Why?* (later named *Resistance*). Wieck went on to earn a PhD in philosophy from Columbia University and for many years taught at Rensselaer Polytechnic Institute in upstate NY. Dellinger's radical pacifist resume would fill several pages. While in prison, he led a demonstration to integrate the dining hall. He drove an ambulance in the Spanish Civil War. He was for a time active in the IWW. He founded major pacifist organizations. He was a founder and editor of the important anarcho-pacifist *Liberation*, along with Wieck and Roy Finch of Sarah Lawrence College. He was one of the famous Chicago Seven on trial for disrupting the 1968 Democratic Party convention in opposition to the war in Vietnam. He traveled in a huge circle of important friends and contacts.

That these were men of substance infuriated Sam the more. They should know better. They had to know better. They were either willfully blind to Castro or hypocrites, which amounted to the same thing. In 1964, Dellinger returned "from Cuba after the May Day celebrations in Havana (the trip being paid for by the Castro regime)—with, of course, the obligatory military parades, Soviet slogans, and 'The International' as background music," and proceeded to write "a pro-Castro piece which was published in...*Liberation*."

Sam described the article and its aftermath in a *VC* piece titled "Cuba: Dellinger Returns from Animal Farm": "The first lengthy installment of his [Dellinger's] report reminds us of the glowing, equally 'objective' accounts of many international travelers of the 1930s whose chronic euphoria prevented them from seeing Stalin's most glaring atrocities. All is well in Paradise. They saw and heard no evil. As to Cuba, Castro himself had been far more critical of the defects of his 'revolution' than Dellinger. Dellinger pretends to be an anarchist but he has become an apologist for the Castro dictatorship."

The article goes on to quote from a leaflet of the MLCE:

An old tyranny has been replaced by a new one. Castro's government has denied the right to strike and the right of a free press. It has made state agencies of labor unions. In place of the heralded agricultural cooperatives, the Castro-communist government has set up a [regimented] system of State working conditions dictated by State employees. The so-called voluntary militias—(have) been superseded by a policy of military conscription, the conscripts being used as forced labor. The autonomy of the University has been suppressed for the first time in Cuban history. Private capitalism and exploitation has been supplanted by state control. People are encouraged to spy on their neighbors, for the secret political police, through local "Committees for the Defense of the Revolution."

...Sixty thousand [resisting] Cuban WORKERS now languish in prison. Other thousands, including Castro's closest early collaborators have escaped into exile.... [We] are against both capitalist imperialism and communist imperialism, both of which would exploit the country as a semi-feudal sugar plantation. The Cuban workers need not choose between Castro and the CIA, both of which represent counterrevolution.

Sam and comrades attempted to distribute that leaflet at a public meeting sponsored by *Liberation* where Dellinger spoke on Cuba. Dellinger, surprised, was visibly shaken by the picket line. Sam writes, "He was even more embarrassed when I, and a few other comrades, denounced him as a liar and a turncoat. I challenged him to debate the issue anywhere, anytime and at our expense. My challenge was greeted with catcalls and demands that we be forcefully removed from the meeting."

Paul Berman described the reaction of the audience this way: "Middle-class radicals looked at the old house painter and called him—him!—a reactionary."

I was not present at the event. I can well imagine that the anger some people felt toward Sam and the League was a natural reaction to having their meeting hijacked. It was a meeting they had taken the trouble to attend, that featured a man they respected, and now this man was under attack. True enough, probably, but I bet many of the throw-the-bums-out crowd were indeed intolerant snobs. I am referring to Sam's working-class appearance and to the more substantive matter of his anti-Castro stance.

The vast majority of the "New Left" of the time, which constituted Dellinger's audience, enthusiastically shared his pro-Castro euphoria. They listened avidly to their "house organ," WBAI radio. It was an extremely popular station that catered to the left and left liberals of the day, amplifying their sanctimony and hypocrisy. Am I abusive? You be the judge. WBAI invited Roy Finch, Russell Blackwell, and Sam to present their disagreements with the Castro government, uncensored (Finch had resigned from *Liberation* in protest of its support of Castro and other third-world regimes). Sam and Russell then made the audio tape that the radio station had requested, pulling no punches; Finch acted as moderator. But WBAI refused to air the tape on the grounds it was too controversial and would disturb their listeners.

David Wieck did not turn the other cheek to Sam's criticism: "My old friend Sam is now sucking the CIA tit," he wrote to him insolently. The Cuban anarchists were "counter-revolutionists" he said, and had to flee to Florida. Sam and Castro's critics had no right to call him a communist. Unfortunately for Wieck, as Sam writes in *Fragments*, "Castro himself confessed, the very next morning [after Wieck's letter] that he was, and would remain a communist to his dying breath."

Back and forth the argument went. I take a more charitable view than Sam did of Dellinger and Wieck. Clearly they were mistaken. But their mistakes were motivated by enthusiasm for what they thought was a genuine revolution of the poor and downtrodden. They fell in love and love can be blind. Sam himself had often said, "Show me the man who has not made a fool of himself on occasion."

Sam's book on the Cuban Revolution was published in 1976. I find the proofreading terrible, the mechanical editing poor, and the layout confusing. All this makes for a difficult read in places. In spite of these shortcomings it is a groundbreaking work, in my opinion a classic. Frank Fernandez noted in *Cuban Anarchism* that "It wasn't until 1976 that the atmosphere of suspicion and distrust of the MLCE began to dissipate, with the publication of *The Cuban Revolution: A Critical Perspective*, by Sam Dolgoff. This book…had a demolishing impact among the left in general and anarchists in particular. It was the most cutting critique Castroism had received in these years…and was the decisive factor in the change in attitude toward the MLCE within world anarchism."

I can still see Sam sitting in his vakokta shorts at his self-made desk in his bedroom on East Broadway as he hunted and pecked the keys of his ancient typewriter: articles in Spanish all over the place, cut-out strips of paper all over the place, writing his heart out.

"Enough of this talk about me! Let's talk about you. What do you think of me?"

I get Oscar Wilde's point. This book has been about me even if the narrative has been mostly focused on Sam. Now it is time for me to step directly into my own memoir: The years I have been describing these past several sections, roughly from the early 1950s through the mid-1960s, were the years I grew up. Around 1953 or so, the city authorities pried us loose from our pre-Civil War apartment on Clinton St. in order to put up a public housing project, and we decamped to 481 Van Buren St. in the Bushwick/Bedford-Stuyvesant section of Brooklyn. It was in many ways an improvement.

250 Clinton Street had run downhill steadily. The Bank owned it when we moved in near the end of World War II. Rent was $24 a month. For that we got mopped hallway floors, steam heat in the winter and electricity that worked. Then a Jewish family took it over and the radiators went cold. Mother, her teeth chattering, the windows icing over, could not take it any longer. She sent me to Mr. Cohen.

"Tell Mr. Cohen we're freezing. He's got to send heat!"

And at this point I learned a life lesson. The Cohens lived on Grand St. My eyes blurred with tears from the warmth of their steamy hallway as I entered their building.

"Tell your mother the boiler's broken," Mrs. Cohen said as she slammed the door.

Things got worse when the Cohens sold the building to a middle-aged Chinese fellow. You saw him once a month when he knocked on your door to collect the rent personally. To save money he installed a burly black guy to live in the basement and act as our Super. He was an intimidating fellow, very shrewd at extorting the tenants. He'd knock at the door with one excuse or another while the men were at work. The women would give him a few dollars for a "favor," the favor being to keep him the hell out of their apartment. He ran a whore house out of his basement, one dollar a shot. The broken, disheveled women, blouses open, tits hanging, lounged in slippers in front of the building. Sleepy summer afternoons our Super provided entertainment. He and his buddy would stage mock knife fights on the corner sidewalk across from my window. Drunk, shirts off, sweating, they'd slash playfully at each other's torso, maybe inflict a cut or two, and then stagger together arm and arm in brotherly harmony down the block. This went on for eighteen months until the tenants rose in revolt. The Chinese guy had bought the building low, thinking that it would be torn down by the city and he'd reap a profit, which he did.

The Van Buren Street apartment, as I've said, was an improvement. We lived on the second floor facing leafy backyards. Abe and I each had our own bedroom for the first time in our lives. The four story building was kept spotless. The neighborhood was in transition from white to black. The candy store around the corner from us on Patchen Avenue was owned by a Jewish family. They were proud that a young black fellow who used to shop there by the name of Floyd Patterson grew up to become Heavyweight Champion. The neighborhood was in fact in better shape than any place I had lived in before. We played together, black and white, but now the game was basketball in the open school yard a few blocks away on Ralph Ave. I wasn't bad for a short-sighted white guy who couldn't jump. I had a good sense of positioning under the boards, using my arse as an antenna, and had a soft one-hand jumper. Of course, this was half-court basketball. My good friend was Jay, who went on to Columbia University on an academic scholarship, unusual for a black kid at the time.

I was still in high school, finishing up. I remember the lurching stops on the elevated Broadway-Brooklyn line that I took each morning to get to Seward Park High in my former neighborhood: Kosciusko, Myrtle, Flushing, Lorimer, Hewes, Marcy, over the Williamsburg Bridge, into the tunnel, and finally, Delancey Street where I got off and walked two blocks. I was a bit of a wise guy, too clever, and that nearly cost me my graduation. Dr. Schliefer was an old-fashioned math teacher, a nervous, elderly fellow. We sat in rows and each row lined up to bring their homework and other assignments to his desk where he sat and graded you, one after another. His florid cheeks shook as he flashed his red pencil across the problems on your paper. I was the last kid in the last row and the last one he graded. By this time he was tired and pissed off and ready to blow. Schliefer grades my homework, checking that the answers lay out in the boxes the way he designed it. Check, check, cross, his exasperation multiplying. Finally, he looks up at me and smiles. I knew I was in for it.

"Dolgoff," he says, oozing concern, "what are you going to do when you graduate?"

I shrug.

"Going to college? Get a job?" He stands up suddenly. "I'll tell what you're gonna do. You're gonna write Chinese laundry tickets!" With that he crumples my home work violently, rises to full height, and flings it to the floor. "Get the hell out! Come back when you can write so a person can read it," he shouts, pointing to the door. And with that he banished me for the day.

I counter-attacked next time in class on a beautiful late-spring afternoon. It is ten minutes to the end of the very last period. Dr. Schliefer knows this. He can breathe humanly at last. Fire-engine sirens wail in the far distance on Delancey Street, the sound wafting up through the huge fifth floor windows of our classroom. Dr. Schliefer turns his head absently, smiles benignly toward the sound. A fire somewhere, out there in the city. The sound blares louder, more insistent. The devil grabs hold of me, an inner compulsion. I stand up, stare out the window.

"Looks like #132, doc," I cry out, alarmed.

Now Dr. Schliefer was neither a doctor of mathematics or education. He was a doctor of dentistry and his office was #132 Delancey Street. Everyone knew this. He runs to the windows in a panic, tears one open, and thrusts his body out to the point the class feared he was about to jump. But of course I had no idea where the fire engines were headed and as the sirens faded it was clear it was not #132. The entire class roared. I was for a brief moment elevated to heroic status.

Dr. Schliefer regained his composure. His eyes leveled with mine, his voice a threatening stick: "Dolgoff, you fool around too much!"

That's all he said. He kept me out of class. Each day I'd show up and he told me to fuck off, not quite in those words. This lasted a month until the last day of class. I was unprepared for the state-wide Math final that I needed to pass in order to graduate. I almost did not make it. I managed to squeak through with a 65, the minimum. Those days you never complained to the authorities. My parents knew nothing of it.

Contrast my wayward behavior, dating back at least to junior high school and the days Mother rescued me from the clutches of Mrs. Halinan, with Abe's exemplary approach. He was attending City College, the "slum kids Harvard," in the words of an anonymous *Time* magazine wit. He got A in everything. Was Phi Beta Kappa. Played first clarinet in the orchestra. Received the History medal, although he did not major in history. I've mentioned his IQ is extraordinary, but a great deal of his success came from the fact that he had extraordinary will power.

Case in point: Friday evening after dinner and Abe is at the table working integral calculus and differential equations. I leave for the movies. Saturday morning I am up for breakfast. Abe has finished breakfast and is still sitting there working the same problem. On through the afternoon, I'm out of the house to play basketball. Abe is still there over the same problem. On like this to Sunday night. At last, Abe closes his note book with a smile of satisfaction.

"Why do you work like that over one stinking problem?" I ask.

"Do you think I'll forget how to do it?" he answers, and I guess he never has. The thing about the problem, though, was that it was not assigned to him. Abe would polish off the assigned problems and then proceed to work every problem at the end of each chapter of the calculus text. Why? He was not a Math major and it is the rare major who would attempt that.

Abe's answer: "Those problems are listed for students taking this course. I am taking this course. I should be able to do each problem." And that is how Abe approaches things. He went on to a National Science Foundation (NSF) Fellowship and, as I've mentioned, earned his PhD at Rice University.

I began gradually to drift away from the IWW, from the SIA Hall, from the Libertarian League, from the world of my parents. It was a drawn out process and not a conscious break on my part. The easy explanation is that I was getting older. I had graduated from high school June 1955 and entered Hunter College in the Fall; lots of work, new friends and all that. The truth, however, is more complicated and involves a complex of emotions I am still trying to sort out. I mentioned earlier that I was two Anatole's growing up. One inhabited the world of my parents, the other the world of the streets, and that I somehow kept their dual demands within my conflicted self. I had kept the lid on by treating the radical side as a shameful secret. Like a closeted gay man of the period.

This inner conflict intensified in my later high school years and upon entering college. My street friends would question me: where do you disappear every Friday night with your parents? My evasive answers did not satisfy them. If you attended college in the 60s or thereafter, you may remember that many students considered extreme radicalism chic and imagine that I would find a niche there. Perhaps, but my time was the mid-50s and a different universe. And, as I look back I had led a remarkably compressed and sheltered life for a young man whose parents were worldly and sophisticated in so many ways. But in the ways of normal middle-class life they were willfully ignorant. Mother had consciously run from it. Sam had no use for it. Neither of them aspired to it.

Hunter College was hardly a rich person's school. It was, and still is, a part of the City University of New York system. The student body was drawn from the city public schools. There were no dormitories. You needed good grades, not money, to get in; admission was free. The college even went so far as to distribute worn out textbooks which you could either buy at a discount or return. Hunter had that year switched from all girls to coed and they needed boys. So they scraped the bottom of the academic barrel to fill the male quota. That is how I got in with my 78 average. There was a catch, however. Hunter in those days was a two-campus college. Midtown Manhattan was still girls only. We boys had to travel way out to Bedford Park Boulevard, the last stop on the D line in the farthermost reaches of the Bronx. And then walk about half a mile. It was a two hour trip each way for me, buried as I was in central Brooklyn.

Hunter drew students from the upper Bronx: the Grand Concourse, Bronx Park East, Riverdale, Van Cortland Park. This meant the basic population was Jewish and middle class. The girls looked like jewels to me; heavily made up, lacquered hair, the latest skirts, sweaters, and blouses reinforced by tight bras and similar arrangements. Some drove cars, can you imagine! I was too intimidated to speak to them. Just as well, because the zeitgeist of the day was that you married young. Their ambition, their social scheming had but a single objective: to land a Jewish Prince, that is, a Columbia University med student. The dating pecking order descended from there. Goes without saying guys like me were at the bottom of it. Most of the students knew each other from high school and they formed social cliques. The huge dining hall was filled with tables reserved for them. Boys and girls, laughing, having a good time, helping each other cheat on their assignments—a big advantage. Nobodies like me found a stray table in the corner to nibble on the paper bag sandwiches our mothers packed.

I am ashamed to say I wanted nothing more than to be a citizen of that shitty little world. The ultimate status symbol to me, the mark of ultimate acceptance, was to have the right-looking girlfriend and hold hands with her as we walked across campus from one building to the next. Just like the prestige guys who drove their father's Oldsmobile. My erotic fantasies seldom got past that point. I felt an overwhelming pressure to conform. What room was there in this Anatole for Buenaventura Durruti?

I met Jessica Reiner at Hunter College my senior year. Very pretty, the kind you wanted to hold hands with walking the campus path. She did not want a Jewish Prince although she could have had one. She wanted me. We remained married twenty-five years, had two children, and remain good friends. Therefore, please do not misinterpret the reason I discuss Pauline, her mother. I do this not to rehash old stuff no one cares about; rather to illustrate my mania to conform, the depths of my feeling of inferiority.

Pauline was boss; she was the family earner, a bookkeeper and accountant of a sweat-shop factory in the garment district. The shameful secret Jessica made me swear not breathe was that several years earlier, Will, Pauline's husband, worked as a waiter at

Grossingers, the great resort in the Catskills frequented by rich Jews. He took the job in order to support Pauline, Jessica, and her sister Gloria when times were tough. Never mind that. Pauline wanted a husband who could take her to Grossingers, not a husband who waited tables there. That Will's father, a poor immigrant, died when he was ten; that Will was forced to support his destitute mother and two younger siblings working nights carting vegetables in the Washington Markets—all that was long forgotten, as was the ulcer operation that turned him into a semi-invalid for years. He was incapable of earning a living. That is what mattered. He was not a full man in Pauline's eyes. She ordered him around like the domestic servant he had become. The girls never forgave her. They wanted a father they could respect and she had taken that from them.

I thought Will was the nicest person in the family, but Pauline was the one you were obligated to please. To please her I was willing to humiliate my parents and myself. I'll not forget her appalled expression the moment she and Will stepped into our Van Buren street apartment on her one and only get-acquainted visit. Nor will I forget her disappointment at the sight of Mother and Sam, which she hid instantaneously. They—we—were everything she did not want for her daughter: Shabbily dressed people in a shabby apartment in a black neighborhood in Brooklyn. Crazy communists! Kept talking about strikes and politics. And Mother and Sam bent out of shape in the effort to please this unbending woman. All to please me.

The worst of it was to come. We were to be married in a Grand Concourse synagogue. Proper dress required, of course. White wedding dress for Jessica, dark formal suit for me. But I did not own a suit and Pauline insisted she pick one out for me. She took me to Moe's Clothes on Twenty-Third Street, walked with me through the racks, fiddling with one jacket sleeve after another. Exasperated, she called for the salesman and pointing at me up and down in total contempt, snapped "Look at him! Take him! Do something!" I stood for this passively. So suppressed was my ego that I did not as much as ask myself if I should be offended.

The question of Mother's appearance was of utmost importance to me. I insisted she get her hair done, probably for the first time in her life. Then she went shopping and came up with something hideous between a dress and a gown in pink. The shopping experience was foreign to her and so were fashions. Sam looked equally awkward in suit and tie. And I paraded them down the aisle. They were happy because I was happy, but there was no joy in it for them. I would apologize to them if I could.

In time I learned Pauline was a better person than I have described to you. Her bosses treated the poor black and undocumented Hispanic women who worked the machines as their harem. They'd walk the aisles, reach for their breasts in full view of the floor, and turn the vulnerable and desperate ones into mistresses. Pauline stood up to them, attempted to shame them out of it, threatened to tell their respectable Jewish wives. The women on the floor looked upon her as their champion. Courageous and advanced for her time and situation. She did after all need the job.

I could go on, but my life on its own account is not worthy of a memoir. There was graduate school, then two children, one of them mentally handicapped, which was very painful. I became a professor at a branch of CUNY, teaching mostly poor students from central Brooklyn and working-class immigrants from every nation, kids scratching for a toe-hold—the kind who drive cabs at night and work unseen in high-end supermarkets. There was a divorce, and a remarriage ten years later. Another divorce, quickly this time. In time, I shed my youthful desire to slavishly conform and the Anatole I grew up with made a gradual comeback. I had never lost contact with my parents and Sam always filled me in on their activities in a general way.

Abe had moved to Houston and then Chicago 1960 or so and never returned except to visit. I remained behind and became the son Sam confided in most—and deeply so as the years went on. We saw each other or called several times a week. Although Sam's activism continued unabated it had shifted in emphasis, in part because his life was changing. His body was shot, his torso thickening, his voice a rasp from smoking two packs a day for fifty years. The day before his third and last hernia operation the doctor showed him an x-ray of his lungs. "You have emphysema," he told him. "You will die from it. The question is when. If you quit smoking now and quit abusing yourself you have some good years left. If not I give you two or three."

The night before the operation Sam grew restless and began pacing the ward before he settled back in bed. Presently the night nurse admonished him: "Mr. Dolgoff, the women are upset you walked through their section."

It had been an innocent mistake; his mind had been on other things. "I'm a sixty-eight-year-old man with a hernia. Tell 'em they don't have a thing to worry about," he growled, which brought a smile from the nurse.

Sam retired from house painting immediately after his operation and he quit smoking cold turkey. He nearly went crazy: gobbled peanuts, candy, raisins, compulsively—gained weight, but never again took a puff. Retirement served him well. Mother and he lived on a small union pension, social security, and from time to time—more so later in life—Abe and I helped out. He experienced sustained rest for the first time in many years. And he had the time and energy for long-term projects.

# 57
## THE STUDENT SIXTIES

I dropped out of the Libertarian League well before it folded in 1964. They had moved a few years earlier from the old SIA Hall at 813 Broadway to a smaller space on Lafayette Street, as I remember. Russell paid for the move out of the small inheritance his Aunt had left him. Sadly, the remaining Spanish comrades were to likewise abandon the old Hall as their children deserted the cause and the old folks died off. Although I am not familiar with specific details, I could sense the League's premature move was accelerated by a certain tension building between the Spanish anarchists and the new people the League attracted. Sam found it hard to admit this was so. You could call it petty, but for me looking backward, the attitude of these people presaged much that I did not like about the 60s.

The new crowd glommed on to the monthly dinners staged by the Spanish comrades. Hordes of young *pishakas* in hippie costume descended on the old hall. A free meal! That it was served by old-time Spanish people, groovy. Where do you find that in the suburbs? They cared not a wit for the history the Spaniards represented, nor for their labor in preparing the dinner, nor for the purpose of the collection taken at the end of the dinner. You can give what you want; so nothing or throw in a dollar for appearance sake. It's enough! More than once I'd seen a young man attempt to add a few insufficient dollars to the collection plate only to have his arm blocked by his girlfriend. The new crowd was not poor. They would spend more on pot later in the evening. They simply did not give a damn. There was selfishness about them, a willful lack of knowledge. They personified everything the communal Spaniards abhorred.

Sam was conflicted about the young 60s radicals: the whole counterculture, hippie thing. He certainly appreciated their courage in opposition to the draft and to the War, which they were instrumental in stopping; if the young had not risen in revolt, who knows, we might still be fighting there! And he stood with them in their revolt against an authoritarian, conformist culture. Still, Sam was in many ways an old-fashioned man with an ingrained sense of what constitutes ethical behavior. That was the reason he was an anarchist. He was also a crusty S.O.B. and he did not buy into that guilt inducing "don't trust anyone over thirty" crap, as he put it: the concept, prevalent at the time that the young were somehow possessed of greater wisdom or moral purity than the old. He observed Paul Goodman and later Murray Bookchin become gurus based on what he called their "youth worship."

"I don't kiss anyone's ass," he said. He found youth worship patronizing of the young and he discouraged the reverse—the guru stuff—in the young radicals who found their way to him.

Sam considered the behavior of many young radicals inexcusable. Especially so their rhetoric: a kid who never lifted an object heavier than a cereal box, who never did a day's hard labor in his life, calling a middle-aged construction worker "pig" and "honkie." How are you going to build a coalition with people you have insulted? Or maybe you have no intention of doing so, but need to vent your alleged superiority like a spoiled brat? I have mentioned that the "Up Against the Wall Motherfuckers" asked Sam to contact the Italian anarchists in order to raise funds for their legal defense. Sam had been reluctant because he knew the reaction in advance.

Sam's objection to most of the young radicals went deeper than language and lifestyle. He distrusted their politics. He blamed "ambitious, power-hungry, young Lenins who...were reenacting the same [Stalinist/Trotskyist] scenario that I witnessed thirty years before" and precipitating the collapse of the Students for A Democratic Society (SDS). He reached this conclusion after a heated meeting at Hamilton Hall of Columbia University.

Now Sam was eighty-three years old when he wrote of that meeting. His memory may have failed him a bit or maybe he did not regard the circumstances of his visit to Hamilton Hall as important. But he recounted to me at the time that several students came for him—I suppose he knew at least one—and said "you will have to trust us." They drove Sam around for a while and then blindfolded him; they led him by the hand and did not remove the blindfold until he found himself facing an eager group inside Hamilton Hall. The students were occupying the Hall. It was during the great

Columbia University student revolt of 1968. There was bedlam outside. They had heard of Sam the anarchist-Wobbly and sat back waiting to bask in his praise.

They were disappointed. He did praise them highly for their struggle to ban the military and secret government work from campus. He also praised them for their sincerity and courage. However, he said there is a huge difference between a revolution and a coup. They were a attempting to seize power and bend the huge college community to their will—a community that included faculty and administrators as well as students, of which they were a minority. That to him was a coup. When he asked the students their program for running Columbia University in a capitalist economy—in other words their constructive plans—he was greeted with hisses and cat-calls. Get the old bastard out of here!

Sam chuckled as he told the story. "I kiss no one's ass," he repeated.

Frankly, I found Sam's remark uncharacteristically smug and I called him on it. How does not being an ass-kisser justify being tone deaf, I asked him? You say the students have engineered a coup when in fact they have spearheaded a revolt against the very things you praise them for opposing. They are not living in Russia 1917 or Spain 1936. They are living in NYC in 1968. What exactly are these miniature Lenins going to take over? Columbia University? The student body? Have they a secret police—perhaps the janitors— at their disposal? Then you chastise a group of twenty-year-olds for not having at their finger tips a detailed proposal for running Columbia University. No wonder they booed you! As Sam listened to me beat up on him his weathered face took on the expression of a small boy being scolded by his teacher for wetting his pants.

Of course my parents were in sympathy with the students and antiwar activists. My parents carried signs in parades, spoke at meetings on campuses, followed events closely. The sight of the police attacking demonstrators in the streets during the Democratic Convention later that year sent Sam into a rage. Then he grew saddened at the sight of the bloodied young people who had come to Chicago with a noble aim in mind. Brother Abe, who lived in Chicago, happened to be visiting us in New York at the time. He sat in Mother and Sam's living room and watched the same TV images that we all did: only he came to a different conclusion.

Now I must fill you in on Abe and Sam as background to the confrontation that was to take place. They had "issues." Abe, four years older than me, recalled Sam's drinking years more sharply than I. He remembered Mother's anguish and he never forgave Sam for it—even if Mother had. He resented that Sam seemed always to have time for "the movement" and his half-crazy comrades despite his hard work, but not for his family—not for Abe. Sam tacitly agreed and felt guilty about it. Invariably he assumed a defensive posture when it came to Abe.

Hence, the confrontation.

Sam: "Look what the cops are doing to these young people!"

Abe erupts in a fury. "You don't understand! You will never understand! These people are having the time of their lives. They will never forget this. They'll tell it to their grandchildren. They are middle class! They have credit cards! They fly! Their parents pay the bills! Do you think they have felt the lash like you, forced into slavery at the age of eight?" His rage subsided. "Exempt them from the draft, you watch!"

It was then that I realized how deep was Abe's understanding and love for his father—feelings he never verbalized or admitted to. Sam stood by humbly and said nothing.

Abe's cynicism regarding the motivations behind the student antiwar movement turned out to be well founded. President Nixon ended the draft and the antiwar movement collapsed like a deflating balloon. The rich kids went on to school or wherever, and the poor kids, those with no options? Let them go! This of course was the difference between them and people of true conscience. The Wobblies and Emma Goldman and Eugene V. Debs and Sam and Russell and Jim Peck and David Wieck and David Dellinger and Bayard Rustin and Martin Luther King and so many others would not let the poor kids go.

I'll skip ahead three or four years to the early 70s. I'm on the ground floor of my school outside the lunch room.

"Professor Dolgoff!" I turn to the voice and find a light-skinned black kid with glasses. He's huge, three-hundred pounds. His face is familiar but I cannot place him. "You don't remember me. Greene!" he says, giving his last name. "I was in your four o'clock lab."

I remember now. It was maybe five years ago. Greene was a skinny kid. Now he is bloated. "What the hell happened to you? You got fat!" I had that direct way of speaking, inherited from Sam.

"Yeah, I got shot up," he says, and he lifts his trouser to show me his plastic leg.

"Jesus, I'm sorry," I say.

"That's ok. I'm back. Remember Moore and Rafael? The three musketeers? In the back row? We liked to break your balls?" he adds, joking.

I remember. Their young faces return to me, piercingly.

"We all enlisted!"

"What the hell did you do that for?"

Greene shrugs, as if my question is of no consequence at this late date. "I ran out of money. We had to drop out. Well, Moore, he bought it. I don't know what happened to Rafael."

Three poor kids from Brooklyn. But Nixon abolished the draft.

Nevertheless, self-interest is not a crime. The student revolts at Berkeley and Columbia sparked a series of campus riots that hastened the end of the Vietnam War. Student uprisings in Paris led to the demise of the De Gaulle Government. You have to go back many decades to find a mass movement to match what the students accomplished.

# 58

# YOUNG FRIENDS – A NASTY FIGHT

Sam's crusty attitude toward the student movement notwithstanding, a floating nucleus of young people flocked to my parents. It was a trend that began with the Libertarian League and continued to the last days of their lives. All kinds of young people: academics, students, actors (the entire Living Theatre group joined the IWW, of course including Judith Malina and Julian Beck), young anarchist writers such as Paul Berman, factory workers: I did not know and can't remember them all. They did not agree with my parents on every issue and some differed with them sharply on major points. That did not seem to matter. My parents had introduced them to a world few knew existed. They regarded my parents as living history. They respected Sam's intellect. Ultimately, they were drawn to my parents for reasons that transcended ideology: their integrity, their humanity.

Wobbly and anarchist Jeff Stein met my parents in the 1970s. I am going to let him describe his feelings toward them. He presents a unique portrait of Sam the Wobbly activist and recounts vividly his role in a bitter internal battle within the IWW few people know about. The discussion is a bit complex but worth the effort. Jeff writes:

> Although he does not mention us by name in…*Fragments*, Sam refers to us when he wrote about a group of young members of the IWW that supported his ideas in the mid-1970s. If you can look up this passage in *Fragments*, he is talking about Mike Hargis, Jon Bekken, and myself. This is the core group of younger (at the time) activists who later began publishing *Libertarian Labor Review*, to which Sam was a frequent contributor.
>
> I first met Sam on a trip that Mimi Rivera (my long-time companion, wife, and co-revolutionist) took to New York to visit her parents. We had reprinted Sam's "The Relevance of Anarchism to Modern Society" in our anarchist newspaper, *The Walrus* in Champaign, Illinois in 1972. I remember being

impressed at the time by Sam's writing and clarity of vision. When we were in New York in 1974, I looked up Sam Dolgoff in the phone book, and called him to see if he would meet. I was amazed to meet a man in his 60s since to me his writing always emphasized what was happening at the moment instead of events long past (not to mention the only anarchists I knew at the time were young people like myself).

Sam told me he was working on a discussion paper for the IWW, which later became "Notes for a Discussion on the Regeneration of the American Labor Movement." The gist of this paper was that in the 1970s young workers were starting to buck the union establishment of the time. Sam thought the IWW and anarchists in general needed to reach out to these young workers and help them organize and build a new, more revolutionary labor movement. He suggested I get ahold of Mike Hargis, since he was also discussing these ideas with Mike. As it turned out both Mike and I had recently joined the Chicago branch of the IWW, so I already knew Mike. (We did not meet Jon until a few years later, since Jon was living in California at the time, a member of the San Diego IWW branch.)

Mimi and I also met your mother, Esther. I remember her as a firebrand in her own right. She shared Sam's ideas but also wanted to preserve the history of the Jewish anarchist movement. She was working on a translation of the movement in Philadelphia written in Yiddish. Both she and Sam had many stories to tell, like how Ben Fletcher had once visited their home and bounced you (or perhaps it was Abe) on his knee.

Mike Hargis and I tried to get the IWW to adopt Sam's program. Unfortunately we ran into a lot of resistance. I did not know at the time that hard feelings remained over the Cleveland branch of the IWW and how they had split from the union in the 1950s over the Taft-Hartley law. The Taft-Hartley law required union officers to take loyalty oaths and swear that they were not members of the Communist Party or any other group wanting to overthrow the U.S. government. The Cleveland branch thought this was a mere technicality, since the IWW was always opposed to the Communist Party and that they could sidestep the issue of wanting to "overthrow the government" with semantics. Sam and Esther had been in the opposition. They felt that to sign Taft-Hartley was a move toward business unionism and relying upon the government to help organize workers into docile unions loyal to capitalism. Rather than wait to convince the rest of the union to their position, however, the Cleveland branch left the IWW and joined another union. The IWW never recovered from the split, and many still had hard feelings toward Sam over his vocal opposition to the Cleveland IWW. Instead the IWW moderates proposed a program of pooling all the financial resources of the IWW and to concentrate on organizing the way it had been done in Cleveland. These IWW members formed the "Industrial Organizing Committee," which tried first to organize metal-working shops in Chicago (similar to Cleveland in the 1930s) but this drive collapsed after the failure of an organizing effort in Virden, Illinois. No lessons were learned from that failure and the "IOC" lingered on mainly as a faction within the IWW, intervening in other organizing campaigns, until they were disbanded about ten years later.

Having been rebuffed from the IWW, we looked for other opportunities to promote Sam's ideas outside the IWW. This culminated in the organization of the "Anarchist Communist Federation." Sam and Esther were very supportive of this effort, attending many of the meetings that led up to it. The "Libertarian League" that Sam and Esther had organized in the 1950s was something of a model. However, although we were friendly to the IWW, unlike the Libertarian League, members of ACF were not required to join the IWW as well. [Jeff is mistaken here. LL members were not required to join IWW.] This was probably what led to the breakup of ACF. Some of the members who joined ACF were hostile to the IWW and wanted to "bore from within" the AFL-CIO. Since the labor movement was a big focus of the new organization, this created political strife within the new organization. I remember Sam became very frustrated at the New York area members of ACF, who were the most hostile to the IWW, perhaps because they had once tried to get the New York IWW branch to adopt the "bore from within" program and, having failed to win converts, now wanted to hasten the IWW's demise. The ACF collapsed within a couple years after it was organized.

It was not long after this we met Jon Bekken. Jon had come to Michigan from California to go to school and became a member of the IWW Ann Arbor branch. The Ann Arbor IWW branch had been formed by members of ACF wanting to organize in workplaces. Although they received help from the IOC, Frank Cedervall (Sam's old Cleveland rival) in particular, they were as much a product of ACF, as they were of the IOC.

With Jon and a number of like-minded IWW members, we formed a group called the "Rank-and-file Organizing Committee" (ROC) dedicated to promoting Sam's ideas within the IWW. One of the things we accomplished within the IWW was to organize an international conference of revolutionary unions in Chicago in 1986 to coincide with the hundredth anniversary of the 8 hour day strike. We invited the CNT (Spain), and SAC (Sweden), the two largest syndicalist unions, as well as smaller groups from around the world. Sam came and gave a talk at the conference on high technology and its implications for the labor movement.

The last time I saw Sam was in 1990 not long before his death. He was visiting Abe and Hadassah in Des Plaines. Esther had passed away and he was making one last trip to see family and friends. He invited several of us to meet with him. I am not sure but I think Mike was there that evening. He was still optimistic about the future of the anarchist and labor movements, and wanted to give us all some encouraging words. He knew that this would be our last visit.

My impression of Sam is that in his own way he was sort of an anarchist "rabbi," a teacher and mentor in the best sense of that term. He always was willing to share his time with younger people because he knew that it would be up to us to carry on his work. Esther was his partner in all his efforts. I know he shared his ideas with her before trying them out on others and that she helped him hone his ideas by pointing out facts he got wrong, or faulty reasoning. He would not have accomplished as much as he did without her. We miss both of them very much.

Was Sam right in opposing the Cleveland branch's willingness to take the Taft-Hartley loyalty oath? I find it a most interesting dilemma. Sam's faction stuck to its principles and the IWW lost the last local that actually had job control: that is the power to bargain with the factory owners over working conditions, pay, and the hiring and firing of the workers. As a practical matter, union dues sent to Chicago from Cleveland had kept the rest of the organization afloat.

I can well understand the Cleveland local's attitude. To hell with Taft-Hartley. Why let that define you? Sign the damn thing and live to fight another day. On the other hand I can well understand Sam's objection. Sign the damn thing and you are no longer a revolutionary organization. Sounds good, but Sam's attitude consigned the IWW to the same fate as the Shakers, who were at one time very well-known residents of Cleveland, Ohio. Ever hear of them? They were a religious sect with many admirable qualities. However, they practiced celibacy and survived by adopting children. Well, eventually they ran out of children and they remained pure to the last Shaker.

In my view, the dispute was a moot point. The Cleveland branch wanted out. That is why they did not attempt to debate the issue.

# 59
## BAKUNIN

I've come to a subject I am not comfortable writing about. I am not a Bakunin scholar and the man meant so much to my father. More than any nineteenth-century anarchist—and Sam held Kropotkin, Reclus, and Proudhon in high regard—he admired Bakunin. He was at one with the man's insights into the nature of power, his encompassing humanity, his vitality, his vision, his moral and physical courage, his warm yet difficult personality. Sam loved to go on about Bakunin. He could talk about him for hours, especially in the heat of toiling over his groundbreaking *Bakunin on Anarchy*. In fact, so absorbed was he by Bakunin the theorist, Bakunin the anarcho-syndicalist, Bakunin the rival of Marx, that he was unprepared for a simple question I put to him one day.

"Forget all the other stuff. If you had known the man would you have liked him?"

Sam recoiled, startled. "I'm not sure," he stumbled. Then he thought a bit and added, "Probably not."

His answer surprised me. "Why not?"

"I don't know. It's a feeling I have. He was a towering figure."

So there you have it: an example of one of the many kinds of love. Sam loved the towering figure, not necessarily the man, though he was in sympathy with his life.

Sam wrote *Bakunin on Anarchy* as an expression of love, you might say homage, for yet another man: Gregorii Petrovich Maximoff, the great Russian anarchist had who befriended Sam as a footloose young Wobbly. Maximoff admired Bakunin. More than any other figure it was Bakunin's writing that had brought him to anarchism. Maximoff considered his *The Political Philosophy of Bakunin: Scientific Anarchism* a payment of his debt to Bakunin, so to speak. It was published in English translation in 1953, shortly after his death. Sadly, Sam found the book to be only a partial success and somewhat of a disappointment. Yes, it contained prestigious introductions by Max Nettlau, whom Sam regarded among the foremost historians of anarchism, and by Rudolf Rocker. And yes, the body of work consisted of a vast number of passages from Bakunin's writing. The fault in Sam's view lay in the organization of the book, which reflected a fundamental error in judgment. The book is divided into a series of preconceived categories—"boxes" if you will—that are logically arranged so as to provide the entire spectrum of Bakunin's thought on the topics Maximoff considered essential.

What, you may ask is wrong with that? Everything, Sam felt. Bakunin wrote voluminously—probably millions of words in many languages. Few of his works were ever finished and he'd go off on tangents. His writing was at times brilliant, at times turgid, and often reflective of the pressures he was under at the moment. Maximoff would snatch a paragraph from one work and a page from another written at a different time and place. All of them he stuffed into his boxes, as if each paragraph, each page were not taken from disparate works but instead were intended by Bakunin to fit into the boxes. Lost is a sense of context and history, the flavor of the man's prose, the salt of his personality. Maximoff had inadvertently put Bakunin in a straitjacket. "There is no such thing as 'scientific anarchism,'" Sam wrote. The term is uncomfortably close to the "scientific socialism" of Marx, which Bakunin abhorred. Sam's *Bakunin* lets Bakunin breathe freely.

Sam lets Bakunin breathe by allowing him to speak for himself. He does not string together excerpts from separate works. This sounds simple but in reality it becomes a formidable task, for "Bakunin's literary output is a bewildering mass of fragments, articles, letters, speeches, essays, pamphlets, highly repetitive and full of detours and dead ends, yet flashing with insights throughout." Sam tackled Bakunin head on: "Most of the selections in the present volume," he wrote, "have either never appeared in English at all or appeared only in disconnected excerpts. All of them have been freshly translated to convey not only the sense but also the spirit in which they were written (all translations by the editor, Sam Dolgoff, except as indicated below). Each selection is accompanied by a brief editorial note; editorial amplifications within Bakunin's texts are bracketed." And, of course the volume is heavily footnoted. In short, Sam produced "the first comprehensive collection in English from the works of the founder of anarchism—culled and newly translated from Bakunin's writings, published and unpublished—including manuscripts unfinished or unrevised at the time of his death almost [now over] a century ago."

*Bakunin on Anarchy* was designed as an introduction to Bakunin's anarchism for literate readers. It is nearly fifty years old now. Some scholars have found what they claim are mistakes. Others question his selections or editorial decisions concerning the manuscripts. That is understandable because a typical Bakunin essay may be compared to a magnificent tree that must nevertheless be pruned—that is, choices are unavoidable if we are to publish a single volume people are willing to read. And, yes, being no Bakunin expert, it seems natural to me that more recent works may have surpassed Sam's book in certain areas. All of that is in the nature of scholarship.

But I make no apology for the pride I take in the accomplishment of this man who began hard manual labor at the age of eight, whose formal education ended with grade school, and who slung a brush his entire life until his body gave out.

Sam had slaved over the book; Mother as well, all day, every day and on into the night. No computers, word processors, Internet, or email then. Old-fashioned, seat-of-the-pants scholarship around the ancient hunt-and-peck typewriter on top of the bedroom desk. At times the task seemed to bury them amid a mountain of detail, the physical manifestation of which was mounds of paper and books piled on the desk and nearby floor over which they were forced to step leaving the room. They took a break late Sunday afternoons when Jessica, the children, and I came for dinner.

Sam was in the tradition of a nearly dead breed: the working-class intellectual. However, one stronghold still existed: the comrades of the Libertarian Book Club. There is debate over its origin. Paul Avrich states it began after World War II in 1945. Sam attributes the idea to Maximoff in 1950, who died before the organization took shape. He goes on to say that as a practical matter it was founded by he, Mother, and a number of *Vanguard* and *Freie Arbeiter Stimme* comrades in the early 1950s. For many years, homebase was space in the Working Men's Circle Hall in the Penn

Station South Housing Cooperative on the west side of Manhattan. Roger Baldwin, Paul Goodman, Paul Avrich, Alexandra Kropotkin, Herbert Read, Dwight Macdonald, James T. Farrell, Murray Bookchin, Daniel Guérin, Sam Dolgoff—they all spoke at the Book Club, at either their monthly lectures or annual luncheons. Like the Libertarian League, with which it was *not* affiliated, it was a major alternative intellectual center frequented by writers and university professors as well as working-class intellectuals.

The main purpose of the Club was to publish anarchist literature in English. Its output was low over the years because the Club lacked manpower and resources, but what it published proved meaningful. I find symbolic that the Club chose as its first project *The Unknown Revolution*, Volin's classic history of the role of anarchists in the Russian Revolution and their death struggle against the new Bolshevik tyranny. Volin, whose real name was V.M. Eikhenbaum, was, like Maximoff, confined to Taganka Prison, where, following their hunger strike, he was eventually sent into exile. It was very hard to come by books written by men like that in the 1950s.

I mention the Book Club here, though, because along with the Five-Ten Hall and the SIA Hall, it was home for Sam, and he received help in working on Bakunin—especially from my parents' old friends Ida Pilot, a professional translator, and her life-companion Valerio Isca.

Sam did not regard Bakunin as an historical relic. He found many of his insights prescient, especially those concerning the nature of hierarchal authority, and they were the bedrock of Sam's classical anarchism. You can see the influence of Bakunin in Sam's analysis of parliamentary—or "representative"—democracy in this passage from "The Labor Party Illusion":

A capitalist democracy is a competitive society where predatory pressure groups struggle for wealth and prestige and jockey for power. Because such a society lacks inner cohesion, it cannot discipline itself. It needs an organism which will appease the pressure groups by satisfying some of their demands and prevent the conflicts among them from upsetting the stability of the system. The Government plays this role and in the process enacts more and more laws. The bureaucratic governing group thus becomes a class in itself with interests of its own, and becomes more firmly entrenched as it extends its influence....

At this stage in its drift towards totalitarianism, the governing group cannot rule alone. It needs the financial and moral support, at any given time, of most of the influential power groups: the financiers, the labor movement, the farmers, the press, the churches, as well as the military and civilian bureaucracies. Despite their differences, all these institutions and groups are inter-dependent and no one of them can stand without leaning on the others. Parliamentary democracy is, at this stage, the political system which safeguards the unjust economic and social order.

The actual rulers in a parliamentary democracy are the class of professional politicians. In theory, they are supposed to represent the people, but in fact they rule over them. They do not represent. They decide.... The political parties, or more accurately, the inner clique that controls them, select the candidates for whom the people vote. The candidates express the will of the party and not that of the people. The platforms of the contending parties are adjusted to trick the voters into balloting for their candidates. Then the immense machinery of mass hypnotism goes into high gear. The press, the radio, television and the pulpit brainwash the public. The stupefied voter casts his ballot for candidates that he never nominated and never knew, whose names he forgets, and whose platforms he has perhaps never read. The electoral swindle is over. The voters go back to work (or to look for work) and the politicians are free to decide the destiny of the millions as they see fit. The democratic system is actually a dictatorship periodically renewed at election time.

Sam wrote these words in 1961. You can trace the consistent line of attack back to Bakunin.

Paul Avrich dispels a misconception of mine that Bakunin, concerned as he was with the overthrow of European monarchies, had little knowledge of, or interest in, the United States and representative democracy in general. If you share my ignorance I suggest you read Paul's "Bakunin and the United States." In fact, Bakunin observed America closely during his short stay in the States following his spectacular escape from Siberian exile. He spoke passable English and seems to have had a grand time meeting some of the leading citizens of New York, Boston, and San Francisco, who held him in high esteem: abolitionist senators, the poet Henry Wadsworth Longfellow, old comrades from Germany now well connected to the newly formed Republican Party; even an official of the Confederacy. He held a letter of introduction to General George McClellan, commander of the Union forces. This was a man a few months relieved from twelve years of prison and exile. The freedom and openness of American society appealed to him. He went so far as to fill out the preliminary citizenship forms, and he imagined how different and happier his life may have been had he been born in the States and settled in the forests of the west.

But he held few illusions. The year was 1861 and he had interesting things to say, both positive and negative, about the Civil War, American society, and the limitations of "democratic" government. I for one am struck by how fresh he sounds from a distance greater than 150 years. Does the incessant commercialism and the trumpeting of "American exceptionalism" get to you? Well, it got to Bakunin—who spoke of the "banality of soulless material prosperity" and the "infantile national vanity" that he observed in American society. But these traits did not obscure the potential he saw in America. The Civil War—a war against slavery—might restore America's "lost soul." He predicted that America would become a great power after the war: "more individualized, so to speak and better poised in her social life, and that her great trial could bring out great men, indeed greater than she had ever known." Comments made, I repeat, in 1861.

However, Bakunin was not blinded by the "promise" of the United States, for he observed the wretched slums of New York, Philadelphia, and Boston, where "masses of proletarian workers" were in a condition "analogous to that in the great manufacturing centers of Europe."

Before long, Bakunin predicted, the American laborer would be no better off than his European counterpart, the victim of rapacious capitalism and centralized political power. No state, he insisted, no matter how democratic, could get along without "the forced labor of the masses.... On this point, not even the United States of North America can as yet form an exception."

"What do we really see in all states, past and present, even those endowed with the most democratic institutions, such as the United States of North America and Switzerland?" he asked in 1867. "The self-government of the masses, despite the pretense that the people hold all the power, remains a fiction most of the time." The masses are "sovereign in law, not in fact." For "ambitious minorities," the "seekers of political power," attain predominance "by wooing the people, by pandering to their fickle passions, which at times can be quite evil, and, in most cases, by deceiving them." While preferring a republic, therefore, "we must nevertheless recognize and proclaim that whatever the form of government may be, so long as human society continues to be divided into different classes as a result of hereditary inequality of occupation, wealth, education and rights, there will always be a class-restricted government and the exploitation of the majority by the minority."

Parliamentary regimes elected by universal suffrage quickly degenerate into "a sort of political aristocracy or oligarchy," he wrote in 1871. "Witness the United States of America and Switzerland." And again in *Statehood and Anarchy*, published in 1873, he writes that, in the United States, "a special, thoroughly bourgeois class of so-called politicians or political dealers manages all affairs, while the masses of workers live under conditions just as cramped and wretched as in monarchic states."

Back in the '50s my sociology and political science professors never tired of referring to the genius of Alexis de Tocqueville. They considered his *Democracy in America* the penultimate account of nineteenth-century American society. While it is true Bakunin wrote no book that focused on America, I wonder if any of my professors had read him on the subject—or on any subject at all.

# 60

# MY PROBLEM WITH BAKUNIN

As I said, I am not comfortable writing about Bakunin. There are also deeper reasons. To put the matter bluntly, Bakunin was an anti-Semite. His anti-Semitic rants would please Hitler, even if his anti-German invective would give Hitler pause. Indeed, an Internet search will reveal that modern anti-Semites praise Bakunin as a nineteenth-century visionary. Now, I in no way hold Bakunin responsible for Hitler. I take Sam's word that Bakunin wrote in a style of overblown invective not simply reserved for his comments about Jews. Most of his anti-Jewish rhetoric was in knee-jerk response to slanders coming from Marx and his followers. It was the nineteenth-century style of revolutionary discourse and no, never would he have approved of Hitler's Final Solution or in any way would he have approved of persecution of Jews as a social policy. As Mark Leier points out in his biography of the man, in calmer moments, "Bakunin asserted that he was 'neither the enemy nor the detractor of the Jews' and that he did not support such a barbaric position."

Sam cites Bakunin's broad humanism. On the other hand Bakunin was close to Proudhon, whose hatred of Jews does indeed approach the Hitlerian. He wanted them expelled from Europe, their property confiscated, their civil rights revoked.

It does me no good knowing that anti-Semitism was rampant in nineteenth-century Europe or that Proudhon expressed his views in his private diary and not for publication or that nineteenth-century intellectuals thought in terms of classifications: attributing character traits to an individual based on his nationality and so on. Nor does it give me comfort knowing Marx was probably as much a bigot as Bakunin—judging his rival Ferdinand LaSalle a "Jewish nigger" for his "nigger hair" and supposed conniving nature. The great scientific socialist believed in phrenology and racial types. My question to Sam was, why did he not mention Bakunin's anti-Semitism in his book? And then, the broader question: how is it that so many Jews—Emma Goldman, Alexander Berkman, Sam

Dolgoff, and so many others—were drawn to a movement whose founders hated them?

Sam answered that he was not trying to excuse Bakunin's anti-Semitism. It is reprehensible. Nor was he trying to hide what was all too well known. But his book was about the constructive aspects of Bakunin's thought. In this, he has support. Bakunin's anti-Semitic "remarks make up a deplorable but minuscule part of his thought, never becoming a consistent theme in his writing." However, scholarship is one thing; emotions are another. Sam said Bakunin's anti-Semitism was a major reason he probably would not like him personally. As to why so many Jews, including Sam, gave their lives to the anarchist movement in light of the anti-Semitism of its founders, Sam shrugged. "You had to have a thick skin." Frankly, I am not satisfied with Sam's answer. You have to look for psychological factors.

# 61

# MURRAY BOOKCHIN

Sam had help in finding a publisher. He lacked academic credentials and *Bakunin on Anarchy* was a scholarly work. The manuscript bounced from here to there, almost accepted but not quite for one reason or another. Certain professors, seeing the basic quality, sought to piggy-back on the project, offering their prestige in return for being listed as co-author. Eventually Sam found a publisher through the generous efforts of Murray Bookchin and Paul Avrich. At this stage of my story you may have realized that Sam had a strange way of revealing certain facts while keeping others hidden. So, it was through Mother that I learned the publisher, Alfred A. Knopf, sent Sam's manuscript to ten academics of high reputation for their appraisal. Nine out of ten approved it for publication—a difficult percentage to achieve, as I know, being an academic myself.

About Paul and Murray: these men played a major part in the later stages of Sam's life, of which the Bakunin book was but a single episode. Sam's connection to Paul remained warm and loving. The connection to Murray was complicated, sad in certain ways. I say sad because they started as close friends and ended, I am sure in Murray's eyes, as something less than that. I see no need to defend or condemn either of them, and in any case I doubt they would need my help. Verbal pacifists they were not. And they are both long dead.

My best memory of Murray was from the 1960s when Sam and I took a long walk with him through Lower Manhattan: I, a fly on the wall, as the two not-so-old codgers remained locked in discussion over the state of Murray's marriage, Bakunin, Kropotkin, Marx, the labor movement, the Spanish Revolution, and, most importantly, how best to adapt anarchist ideas to modern life. How I wish I had a tape recorder! They relished each other's company.

I hardly knew Murray personally. I had faded away from the day-to-day activities of the Libertarian League in the early 1960s and was lost in my own pursuits: marriage, children, job, things like that. Murray lived with his wife on La Guardia Place and Houston Street just south of NYU in a nice co-op apartment. He had recently written *Our Synthetic Environment* (under the pen name Lewis Herber), and it was an advanced book for its time, earlier though not as famous as Rachel Carson's *The Silent Spring*. His career as an anarchist scholar and theoretician lay before him.

Sam spoke of Murray virtually every time we met. They were at heart two Russian Jewish boys of the Lower East Side—born poor, working class, and brilliant—that found their way to the anarchist path. Murray this, Murray that: one way or another his name always came up. I remember that time well. Sam was genuinely fond of Murray. He respected him and was grateful for his help.

But now for the break-up, starting with Murray in "A Meditation on Anarchist Ethics" from 1994:

> I helped him prepare his book on Bakunin after he despaired that he would never be able to publish it, and I personally presented it with a strong recommendation to my editor, Angus Cameron, of Alfred A. Knopf, which did publish it. I should add that it was I who suggested that Dolgoff edit a book on the Spanish collectives (he initially wanted to write an account of Bakunin's relationship with Nechayev), and I wrote the preface for it, which he then censored because I expressed my disagreement with the CNT's entry into the Madrid government.

Murray's account is accurate as well as I can remember. Sam agonized over his decision to cut a passage from Murray's introduction to the *The Anarchist Collectives: Workers' Self-Management in the Spanish Revolution, 1936–1939*, although it was not Murray's criticism of the CNT that he objected to, but the one-sided and unfair way in which he thought Murray presented his case. Sam felt that, as written, Murray had undercut his book before the reader had a chance to read what he had to say. He agreed that Murray had a right to write as he pleased, but let him choose his own book to do so. On the other hand, an Introduction is analogous to a letter of recommendation. Do you ask a friend to write such a letter and then edit it?

I am in no position to pass judgment on the incident. I have not read the passage or the context in which it was placed. I do not know the manner in which Murray was informed or consulted on the matter—or if Murray was amenable to compromise. I seem to remember it was a last-minute decision and it tore at Sam's heart because he knew he was hurting a friend. In this he was surely correct; I am convinced this incident had a great deal to do with the estrangement between them. *The Anarchist Collectives* was published in 1974; Murray marks 1965–1976 as the time he knew Sam well.

Murray wrote "A Meditation on Anarchist Ethics" in response to Ulrike Heider's *Anarchism: Left, Right, and Green* that surveys the state of anarchism in America by interviewing Sam, Murray, Noam Chomsky, and others. Murray despised the book and its author, whom he accuses of a pervasive dishonesty as well incompetence:

> After three or four days of probing and note-taking, expressing a minimal number of her own opinions, she returned to her home in New York City and proceeded to write a book in her native German, *Die Narren der Freiheit* (*The Fools of Freedom*)—possibly one of the most malicious, fatuous, and basically immoral books I have encountered on the left in decades. I say this quite soberly…seldom have I encountered such blatant character assassination and such deliberate distortions of ideas.…This book, alas, has now been translated—with suitable modifications, additions, and deletions—into English under the title *Anarchism: Left, Right, and Green*.

Ulrike describes Mother accurately and compassionately—even lovingly—in her book, and I quote her later in that context. And she treats Sam admiringly. Nevertheless I can understand Murray's anger, though I think the origin of what he considers Ulrike's sins lies in language difficulties, a misreading of American culture, and the fact she was in over her head. She distorts Sam as well as Murray, as Murray notes. I am most interested in the last page or so of "A Meditation," where Murray pivots away from Ulrike toward his reminiscence of Sam:

One may reasonably wonder which tried, fast, and unswerving anarchists Heider actually does admire. After all, she disposes of Malatesta as a "utopian" (p. 90); of Fourier as a quack, "often comically naive" (p. 91); and of Kropotkin as a queasy "vacillator." Let it not be said, however, that Heider is without heroes. The looming figure in Heider's book is really Sam Dolgoff, a man I knew well from 1965 to 1976.... Many of Dolgoff's more ungracious attitudes resurface in her treatment of the Spanish anarchists, as well as Malatesta, and Vernon Richards (whom Dolgoff detested for his criticism of the Bakunin book and of the CNT-FAI's entry into the Madrid and Catalan governments in 1936).

With these words Murray opens up an ungracious attack on Sam, whom he notes was not alive to defend himself. Sam was not perfect, nor did he profess to be. However, in his seventy years in the radical movement, no one—and I repeat no one—has ever accused him of being small minded and petty. No one that is, except Murray. Sam did not detest Vernon Richards. He admired him for his courage in opposition to World War II, for which he was tried and sent to prison. He read his publication *Freedom* regularly. He simply disagreed with Richards's intolerant attitude toward those of the CNT-FAI who joined the government at the start of the Spanish Civil War. Probably the decision to join the government was wrong as events played out, he conceded, although hindsight is always easier than foresight. But the intention of these men was to defeat Franco, not to sell out the Revolution. It was time to put an end to character assassination, Sam pleaded, to show some degree of compassion for those who tried to cope with an impossible situation. In any event, the fate of Spain was out of the hands of Spain. Can we end the bitterness and hatred after all these years, Sam asked?

Murray goes on to accuse Sam of "political pragmatism," a dirty word in his dictionary. If only it were true, Mother would have led a far more comfortable life and Abe and I would have been better off as well! I have no doubt the uncompromising Murray, on the faculty of several colleges, led a softer existence than the hernia-ridden, compromising Sam. Forgive me for being facetious. In the eyes of the circumcised Murray Bookchin you were not a principled anarchist for supporting the Allies over Hitler in World War II. His punchline is that this made Sam no better than the social democrats—as if agreement on the necessity of fighting Hitler made him automatically wrong. Spanish anarchists, fighting under the command of the Free French, liberated Paris in 1944. Were they mistaken to do so?

I think Murray was tone-deaf when it came to Sam. They were emotionally incompatible, which is, finally, the reason for their divorce. Consider this last quote from Murray: "Thus it was not because of our political disagreements that Dolgoff and I 'parted company,' as I believe he says in his Memoirs [*Fragments*]. Quite to the contrary, we retained a very close relationship well into the 1970s. His account of our relationship in his memoirs is simply false."

It does not occur to Murray that Sam did not want to expose private matters in public; that in citing "political differences," and not personal ones, he was making a plea for Murray's friendship. Sam continued to speak well of Murray until his final day.

# 62
## PAUL

The quintessential Paul Avrich: Late afternoon of a raw November day, darkness closing in. The French anarchist Ronald Creagh, Paul, and I have just left a warm Thai restaurant where Paul insisted, as always, on paying the bill. We are at the corner of 112th Street and Broadway. A frail, tiny old lady shivers forlornly at the curb. She faces the north wind defeated and alone as taxis whiz by her. Paul goes into action immediately. You need a cab? He steps out into the path of the oncoming Broadway traffic, waving his arms. He gets in front of a speeding cab, forcing it to stop. He opens the back door and cradles the old lady into her seat. I'm sure he was ready to pay her fare, except the taxi accelerates. Paul returns to us triumphant. He was a kind man.

Paul Avrich was the author of ten books on anarchists and anarchism, four of them short-listed for a Pulitzer Prize. He wrote more than a hundred scholarly articles. He held the title Distinguished Professor of History at the City University of New York. One day he told me the story of how he discovered the major theme of his scholarly life.

In 1959, in the midst of the Cold War, Nikita Khrushchev attended the General Assembly of the United Nations in New York, where he electrified the world by pounding his shoe on the table in mock indignation. He also found time to visit Columbia University in upper Manhattan. We are an open society, he proclaimed. To prove it, he was willing to conduct a scholarly exchange. Ten American scholars were welcome to go to the USSR where they would be allowed full access to the archives of the Kremlin; anything they wanted. In exchange, ten Soviet scholars would be sent to the United States. As it turned out, naïve Columbia sent real scholars. Khrushchev sent KGB. Paul Avrich was one of the scholars; he jumped at the chance, having learned to speak and read Russian fluently at Cornell University. While in Moscow, he discovered the anarchists through a sociological survey taken soon after the Revolution, and buried in the basement archives. The survey, quite well done, recorded the attitude of various segments of Soviet society toward the new Bolshevik regime. The most cogent, and humane, comments came from the anarchists. Paul was hooked.

Paul's PhD advisor at Columbia University cautioned him against specializing in anarchism. With his knowledge of Russian, and with the Cold War in the deepest freeze, there were myriad fruitful opportunities out there for him to pluck. (For example, Paul could have become a Soviet specialist like his colleague Condoleezza Rice, whom he liked very much, and who in those early days was a liberal.)

"It's a dead end. No one gives a damn about anarchism," his advisor warned Paul. He did not understand that Paul's commitment to anarchism transcended detached scholarship. "In America, such individuals and groups…were pioneers of social justice," he explained in a 1972 *New York Times* interview. "Many of the anarchists in this country and in the world have either been neglected or scorned, and I would like to play a role in resurrecting them."

"He considered himself a scholar, teacher, and chronicler of the movement and had great sympathy and affection for them," his wife, Ina Avrich, said many years later after Paul's death, "and he took issue with the prevalent image of the anarchist as violent and amoral."

He certainly had great affection for my parents and if "resurrect" is not the proper word for Sam, he certainly did much to introduce him to a wide audience. He wrote the preface to Sam's *Bakunin on Anarchy*, which lent heft to the project and reassured Alfred Knopf. The affection was mutual, although a sociologist may have found the ethnic character of Sam and Paul's interchange amusing. I certainly did. I remember on several occasions entering my parent's apartment to find Mother sitting by her lonely self in the living room. From the bedroom behind her came heated argument and raucous laughter, interspersed with muffled tones of serious discussion. Joyous sounds.

"Paul is in the bedroom with your father," she'd say, with her usual obliviousness to innuendo. "I'm letting the men have a good time."

Talk, talk, talk—I find that to be a Jewish thing. It is a verbal culture. Heated discussions, antagonistic argument—the very things that alarm, say, the Danes—are the tools of affection, the means of affirming intimacy. And Paul and Sam had so much to talk about. Sam was the living embodiment of Paul's research—not that he was the only such person. But he spanned fifty years of the anarchist and Wobbly movement at the time they met, and he knew—or knew of—perhaps the majority of the individuals Paul had studied. Beyond that Paul recognized Sam as a scholar of anarchist history. The two men communicated at a high level—anarchist theory and key events and all that—and also at a low level: salacious anecdotes, and the like. Name your topic, Paul and Sam could discuss it on equal terms. They learned from one another and they relished their disagreements. Sam took a more tolerant view of Bakunin's relationship with the psychopath Nechayev than did Paul; he considered it overblown and exploited by his enemies and he felt Paul recycled some of the destructive myths about Bakunin. None of that mattered between them.

Mother had an easier way of expressing affection for Paul and his family. She simply *kvelled* at the site of Paul's young daughters. I guess the best translation of this untranslatable Yiddish term is "to coo with delight." "Look at them! Angels! What beautiful children, darling girls!" she'd say to Ina and repeat it later to me.

I could go on about Sam and Paul but do not want to bore you. No conflicts, no scandals, no deep personal secrets to report. Affection and respect throughout the years is boring to write about. I will add, however, that Paul regarded Sam as more than an interesting historical figure, rigid and unbending, a living fossil of nineteenth-century ideology. He appreciated the fact that Sam remained contemporary. Read Sam's *Third World Nationalism and the State*, for example, and *The Relevance of Anarchism to Modern Society*, written in 1970 and revised in the late 1980s. He showed these and other works to Paul regularly.

Paul officiated at the memorial service for Sam in 1990, as he had for so many comrades over the years. He took Sam's death hard.

Paul and I remained friends and we became close the last five years or so of his life. I attended several Stelton Colony–Ferrer

School reunions with him, which he chaired. It was one of his favorite activities, though not mine. But I so enjoyed the ride down to New Jersey with him that I never entertained the possibility of refusing his invitation. You felt revived having spent the day in his company. Another of Paul's favorite activities was inviting Federico Arcos to stay at his home; he never failed to pick him up at the airport upon his flight to NY from Detroit. Like Sam, Paul adored Federico; they were buddies. I especially enjoyed the lunches the three of us had in the Columbia University neighborhood where Paul lived. You learned more about the Spanish Revolution and anarchism after ten minutes in their company than from a graduate seminar, believe me.

When we lunched alone Paul mentioned things about his life that I do not flatter myself were confidential, but are probably not too well known. I had not known that Paul attended Cornell University as a candidate for Officers Training School; he learned Russian that way, and he graduated as an Air Force Lieutenant. They stationed him at the huge U.S. base in Germany where his job was to monitor the in-flight conversations of the Russian pilots. By piecing together the many fragments, Paul was able to locate a key military installation: I am not sure which one, but I believe Paul said it was a nuclear arsenal. His superiors were delighted; it was a major coup. He and his coworker were promoted on the spot! A parade was sponsored in their honor. Upon debriefing, he was asked about his plans after re-enlistment. He was the fair-haired boy, Paul said, and could have written his own ticket up the ranks.

Paul informed them he was not re-enlisting. They were shocked. Why? "Because I want to be a college professor," Paul answered.

His superiors were incredulous. "A fucking college professor! You want to be a professor!" Why, it was as bad as confessing you were a homosexual, Paul chuckled.

I saw Paul every three months or so in his later years and his decline was sadly evident to me. At his last Ferrer School meeting he lacked force and coherence and the elderly audience, in a despicable display of rudeness, ignored him, stood up, and left him humiliated on stage. I had a lunch appointment with Paul the last time I saw him. I met him at his Riverside Drive apartment.

"Be sure to make sure you bring him back here," Ina insisted. "Do not leave him in the hall!" We walked slowly to the luncheonette below Columbia on Broadway, the same one they feature in the Seinfeld TV show. But there was nothing amusing as we sat at our table. Paul no longer was able to remember what he needed to say, so he wrote things down on a sheet of note pad. Unfortunately, he let the paper slip, and he dove in a panic under the table to retrieve it. For the one and only time, I paid the bill. I could see Ina in the street peering through the restaurant window. She had followed us discreetly.

I regret one part of my behavior toward Paul. He spoke often of his desire to visit his boyhood home in Brooklyn with me and he grew insistent toward the end. C'mon, we are Jewish boys from the city. We're the same age. You'll enjoy it, he coaxed. He felt a need to show me the soil of his youth—although he knew the neighborhood had devolved into a neglected ghetto. I was all for it. But other things kept getting in the way. And it was a schlep from the Upper West Side to central Brooklyn. Time seemed so plentiful. So I put him off—with the intention of "someday."

# 63

# THE GRANDCHILDREN

A famous man famously said God does not play dice. Granted he was referring to quantum physics and using God as a metaphor, but I do not agree with him when it comes to the creation of a human being. There is such a thing as luck. We are all the result of the almost infinite possibilities afforded by the mixing of our parents' DNA. And then there are the chance events that affect us in the womb and on the way to being born. You know there are physical causes of your child's misfortune, just as you know the laws of gravity and momentum determine how the dice land, but that in no way explains why misfortune must happen to your child. All of this is by way of nonexplanation of the fact that most of my parents' grandchildren were not born lucky.

Jessica, my wife, gave birth to three children:

Gregory was born in 1961. He was declared autistic before that became fashionable; he was also declared schizophrenic and has taken anti-hallucinogens his entire adult life. "Autistic" and "schizophrenic" are words to comfort the examiners. No one knows precisely what is wrong with Gregory, nor does it matter much. What matters is that he cannot function independently.

Alexander was born in 1965 and lived about one week. Jessica was holding him in her arms when he turned blue. The police emergency unit rushed him to the hospital, but it would have made little difference if we had arrived sooner. He had contracted a virulent strain of pneumonia in the birth canal and was doomed from the moment he experienced the light of day.

Of Esther and Sam's four grandchildren only Stephanie, our youngest, was born with the handicaps of the "normal." She is a successful mother and writer today.

Abe's wife, Hadassah, gave birth to one child, Rochelle.

The umbilical cord wrapped around Rochelle's neck during her difficult birth. This cut off the flow of oxygen to her brain. The "medical experts" said her condition was hopeless; she would grow up a vegetable. Put her away someplace, forget her, and go on with your life, they urged Hadassah. Hadassah would have none of that. She and Abe devoted their every breath to their daughter. Hadassah especially served as confidante, fierce defender, and, when occasion demanded, fierce taskmaster to Rochelle.

"Yes, you can button your blouse!"

"Yes, you will play with the physically normal children as well as those that are not!"

"Yes, you will be realistic about your condition, but you will not make a crutch out of it!"

No one is perfect and as the years went on it was Hadassah herself who indeed used Rochelle's handicap as a crutch, the better to beat Abe over the head. That is, to turn every decision, every disagreement, into a referendum on his devotion to Rochelle. Guilt is an excellent manipulative, if anger-generating, mechanism.

Rochelle has had to deal with cerebral palsy her entire life. And her entire life has been a quiet profile in courage. Her torso is misaligned. Her body is bent forward in a decidedly palsied gait. Her speech is difficult to adjust to. But she has given in to none of that. She is the recipient of two Master's degrees from the University of Chicago: in English and American Literature, her first love, and in Library Science, a practical back up. The Admission's Officer was gracious to Abe upon notifying him of the scholarship she received: "You know, your daughter scored one hundred percent on the symbolic reasoning section of the Graduate Record Examination (GRE). Nobody does that! She earned the scholarship on the straightforward merits of performance."

Rochelle has worked as an editor for a variety of publishers. She writes poetry, short stories, and essays. There was not a dry eye among the ladies at Rochelle's wedding as she stood up to take her marriage vows. Some of the men's eyes were a bit moist, too. To continue in this maudlin vein, the wedding took place in 1998 and Sam and Esther were many years' dead by then. How many years would Mother have shortened her life to have been there?

Rochelle remembers my parents lovingly, but she was born in Houston, Texas and has lived most of her life in Chicago. So their day-to-day attention was focused on Gregory. And Mother, absorbing his need, entered into a kind of mental and emotional symbiosis with his imaginative world. The boundary between his mind and hers seemed not to exist. It was an immense pleasure for this stout seventy-year-old woman to play on the living room floor with him, and somehow to let this child—who scarcely spoke a word and who referred to himself as "he" until the age of six—know that her devotion to him was limitless.

Gregory, as you can envision, had a rough time growing up. No school would accept him for a time and when we finally found those "special" schools that would, the students in those schools, overjoyed they finally found someone they could oppress, made his daily life a misery. He was huge, towering above the other children in height and weight, but he was uncoordinated and he spoke slowly in a loud, slow, and childish intonation, and they were merciless. He'd arrive home with his eyes blackened, his lip swollen, his watch stolen, one shoe missing. They knew, big as he was, he was not capable of fighting back.

Or so they thought. I will go off message and tell you of a rare moment of triumph. One of his therapists, noting that Gregory lacked coordination, suggested he learn judo. Not to be competitive but to learn balance and body sense and a degree of confidence. Well, it was such a good idea I signed up with Gregory! But there was a hitch. Gregory was enrolled in the children's group—and his fellow students, the offspring of upper-middle class to wealthy West Siders—the children of doctors, professors, lawyers, successful musicians, and the like—set upon Gregory with sadism that was something to behold. It was Gulliver among the Lilliputians in the tiny locker room. They tied his shoe laces in knots, hid the belt of his *gi* (uniform), and stole things from him. But their verbal savagery was the worst of it. From outside the room you could hear their laughter and the names they called him—reaching a state of glee. Week after week this went on.

Finally, I had enough. "Gregory," I said, "you are learning judo. Pick one of them up and throw him against the wall!" Which he did, full force. You could hear the metal locker shake. Shocked silence and from that moment on Gregory changed his clothes in peace. Next class, I told my fellow judo colleagues—an educated lot—of the incident and they were appalled. "You are teaching your son to resort to violence! That is not an acceptable way to resolve disputes!" and so on. But there was one fellow who took it all in quietly.

"Don't listen to them," he said when were alone. "I'm a PhD in child psychology. Those little bastards are committing psychic brutality against your son. They know exactly what they are doing. If your son cannot fight them verbally then he must fight them the way he can, physically." And he shook my hand.

From this and many similar incidents—and from my days growing up in the slums of the Lower East Side and Brooklyn—I doubt the belief that some of my comrades share in *The Inherent Goodness of the Child*.

Mother was Gregory's safe haven. From his infancy to his young adulthood he could not wait to return to her company—and to Sam as well, but in a different way. He adored Mother.

But there was a price Jessica paid for Mother's devotion to Gregory: an emotionally expensive one. You see, Gregory was born a normal child in Mother's eyes. Jessica was the reason for his problems. She did not love him enough. She was a rejecting mother. Mother said that to me privately at first, and when she saw my reaction, she no longer said it directly, but implied as much by intonation and innuendo, which was worse. At last, she backed off from that approach, though the whiff of it lingered in the air. She insisted, however, that he was "normal" in the sense that there was nothing physically wrong with him, that all he needed was love and more love.

You see, Mother had a difficult time accepting misfortune. I'm convinced this thinking went back to her childhood and biblical Father Abraham and her belief in the perfectibility of the human being. Someone had to bear the blame. There was no denying that Rochelle's problems were physical—and there was a certain covert martyrdom in Mother's of course genuine love and support of Hadassah's selfless devotion. But Gregory appeared normal at first glance. Never mind that when eighteen years old he was taken into custody several times for babbling in the streets, that he'd eat food from vacant lots, that he'd pull his pants down and shit in the street if he got caught short far from home. He was normal and Jessica did not love him enough!

Need I mention that Mother's attitude toward Jessica was cruel? Jessica and I decided to educate her, to include her in Gregory's treatments. She accompanied us to the stable of internists, psychiatrists, psychologists, psychiatric social workers, plain old social workers, recreational therapists—whom have I left out?—that we acquired over the years. Every damn one of them informed Mother that Gregory had organic brain damage, although they disagreed on details. They explained to her his problems had either a genetic base or perhaps something occurred in the womb or at birth. Love and tender care were of course beneficial, but one could not expect that to cure Gregory. Mother was flattered we took her to these people and she did not want to appear unscientific. So she would nod in agreement and add a few cogent points to the discussion. However, all that good will and agreement vanished as soon as she got home. It was Jessica's fault.

It was an obsession Sam could not fathom. "What's a matter with you? She's a young woman!" Sam admonished her! And yet I am convinced Mother cared for Jessica on many levels.

Medications helped Gregory to the extent he was able to function on a simple level. But not so in New York. A street guy put a knife to his chest and emptied his pockets of his four dollars. Others preyed on him other ways. Though basically nonviolent, he'd strike Jessica in frustration. And there was Stephanie, five years younger, to consider. Living in the same apartment with Gregory was not doing her any good. Nevertheless, taking all things into account, his story has a relatively happy ending. He is fifty-two years old and has lived the past thirty years or so in Augusta, Maine. He is semi-autonomous, looked after but independent. He calls Jessica, Stephanie, and me twice or three times a day. We visit him two or three times a year and he comes to New York where he splits his time with Jessica and me.

Gregory seldom initiates conversation. You can sit next to him for hours in silence. When I ask him if he misses Mother, his face lights up, his eyes shine, and he smiles sadly.

"Very much," he says.

# 64
## GOOD TIMES

Despite the unlucky condition of Gregory and Rochelle, and all factors considered, my parents evolved seamlessly into a satisfying old age. They remained relevant, that was the main thing. Steve Kellerman is a "lifer" Wobbly and anarchist who, after a stay in New York, has lived in Boston many years. He and his wife Nancy were close to my parents, and he has shared with me vibrant accounts of Sam and Esther in their seventies and early eighties when infirmity had yet to take its toll. His stories convey well the spirit of the time:

> Shortly after Franco's death the CNT came back to life in Spain and a bunch of North American supporters arranged a fund-raising tour for Augustine Souchy who had been the secretary general of the IWA (AIT) during the Spanish Revolution. In Boston Souchy was scheduled to speak at Faneuil Hall, the "Cradle of Liberty" of pre-Revolutionary fame. On the same program were Murray Bookchin and Will Watson, a liberal MIT history professor. Sam and Esther accompanied Souchy and Bookchin to Boston from New York where they had spoken previously.
>
> After the talks the floor was opened for Q&A. In Boston at that time there was a branch of the Spartacus League, a left-wing Trotskyite splinter, which had developed the remarkable tactic of being rude to everyone and, especially, of attending other organizations' programs and rising during the Q&A period to recite at great length their sect's correct line on whatever was the subject under discussion. They were especially venomous toward other Trotskyite sects, but in a pinch would make do with other communists, anarchists, yellow socialists, single taxers. So they did that evening and, after about five minutes of this Sam, who was in the audience got up and shouted, "Why don't you sit down and shut up. This is the same Trotskyite shit

we were hearing in 1937!" Bedlam ensued and there's still an anarchist in town who hates Sam for it. Most of the rest of the audience thought it was great.

At the conclusion of the program, Nancy and I were the last to leave the hall as we were taking down the IWW lit table. When we got down to street level in front of Faneuil Hall a fabulous scene was unfolding. There, in the middle of a good-size crowd of onlookers, were Murray Bookchin and a woman Spartacist nose-to-nose yelling, "You're a fucking liar!" "No, you're a fucking liar!," "No, you're a fucking liar!" and on and on in that vein. Well, they never resolved which one was the fucking liar but I had my money on the Spart.

On another occasion in Boston, Sam had traveled north to give a talk on Karl Marx at the Community Church of Boston which, at that time, says Steve, drew hundreds to its weekly programs: "At the time Sam spoke the majority of the Church membership were old CPers and SWPers with a sprinkling of sectarians and liberals. Ordinarily they all got along and listened peaceably to speakers they agreed with. Sam was something different. He really lambasted Marx. He tore into him for preferring the tyrant Gessler to William Tell, for always preferring centralized states to all other alternatives, for rooting for Prussia in the Franco-Prussian War, for favoring concentration of capitalist industry and finance, for his high-handed actions in the 1st International, and all the rest. Finally, a member of the audience leapt to his feet sputtering and shouting, 'The only reason you're free to say this shit is because the Red Army saved your ass from Hitler.' Sam leaned over the podium, pointed at him, and said, 'Why don't you go to hell.' Things continued along those lines for a while and then Sam, Esther, Nancy, and I left. A Wobbly friend of ours stayed behind and reported that, after Sam departed the Bolsheviks and Trotskyites (as he put it) fell out among themselves. It seems that Sam had exposed the latent fault lines between them. Sorry we missed that."

Steve also remembers the way my parents remained relevant and respected within the movement, well into old age. "It's funny to think about it, but when we first lined up with the IWW, in addition to Sam and Esther, Minnie Corder was the only old-timer who showed up regularly. Others would come out for some programs or socials but they never appeared to be in good standing nor did the younger folks get to know them." But Sam always made time for them.

One time in the late 1970s a couple of pretty young Wobblies from Maine, Dick Reilly and T. J. Simpson, were on the road and had arranged to call on Sam and Esther, who they'd never met, when they got to New York. When they arrived at 208 East Broadway they looked around the lobby, found the Dolgoffs on the directory, and started toward the appropriate elevator. They took no notice of the old duffer who'd been lounging around and who had gotten on the same elevator as them. When it started up he asked, "Say, what are those buttons you boys are wearing?" They gave him a quick exposition of Industrial Unionism and he asked, "Do you really think that would work?" They assured him it would. When the elevator stopped he got off on the same floor and as they were reading the door numbers to find the Dolgoffs' apartment, he was walking ahead of them and as they approached the apartment he got out his key and opened the door. They were astonished....

Before Nancy and I moved to Boston in the early 1970s we were active in the old New York IWW branch. We were fortunate to be in attendance at the branch meeting at 339 Lafayette Place, where we met at the time, when the Living Theatre joined the IWW as a group. Sam gave a very impressive welcoming speech in which he described who we are, what we've done, and what we propose to do. Julian Beck gave an equally eloquent response and Judith Malina also spoke for the Living Theatre....

Sam and Esther once came up to Boston for Sam to speak for the IWW. After the program we had a social at some members' house. On the way back to our house where the Dolgoffs were staying we were all pretty well lubricated and crammed into a car. A guy with a small tape recorder asked Sam to sing "Hallelujah,

I'm a Bum." He did an absolutely hysterical rendition of it which we valued for years on tape until some jerk recorded over it.

Good times! And I again thank Steve Kellerman for sharing them with us. However, since his account is about lively doings in Boston and New York, I fear the venerated figure of Augustin Souchy is barely mentioned, and I cannot let that go by.

"My goal is the establishment of a social order free of force, to replace organized compulsion and violence," Souchy writes in his autobiography *Beware! Anarchist!* The title is in fact a quotation from his arrest warrant, issued by German authorities for his opposition to WWI—a warrant that sent him into exile and hiding. In the course of his incredible life, the man knew Kropotkin, Landauer, Rocker, and Lenin personally. And Alexander Berkman. And Emma Goldman. And Buenaventura Durruti, whom he hid under his bed when the man was on the lam from the Berlin police. He was a founder of the anarcho-syndicalist International Workers Association. All this before the Spanish Revolution.

In Spain (with Sam's old friend Abe Bluestein), he was in charge of international press relations for the CNT-FAI; observed first-hand both the formation and later destruction of the anarchist communes; was the primary eyewitness source on the May 1937 uprising in Barcelona.

Building on his experiences in Spain, Souchy became an acknowledged authority on agricultural collectives the world over: Israel, Mexico, and Cuba. He had too much intelligence and integrity to buy into the Castro crap and barely escaped the "great" man's clutches after visiting Cuba and criticizing his totalitarian regimentation of the "collectives." This lifetime war resister, anarchist, and hell-raiser, author of myriad books and pamphlets, stayed with my parents whenever he came to New York. Their association extended way back to the 1930s, when Souchy reported on events in Spain for *Vanguard*.

I can tell you of his love affair with Sam. They would sit on the old couch together holding hands! They made an interesting couple: the stocky thick-shouldered Sam, in undershirt and suspenders holding up the pants that ended at his bare feet, his torso swollen with emphysema, thick glasses, smiling in delight. And the rail thin, blond but graying Souchy, impeccably neat. Two very old men holding hands, delighted in each other's company. And Mother sitting on the chair opposite, smiles all around.

I did not know Souchy well. The few times he was in and out of New York in the 1970s and early '80s our schedules did not mesh. But I do remember that last time. It was on a weekday morning that I stopped by on the way to work to check on my parents. I opened the door and the lovebirds were holding hands on the couch.

"Durruti's name sake," Sam reminds Souchy by way of reintroducing me. They exchange glances. Should I, Souchy's expression seems to ask? Sam nods approvingly. Thereupon Souchy springs off the couch, approaches me, crouches, and proceeds to do a perfect handstand—upside down, vertical to the parquet floor, arms fully extended, straight as a rod. He holds position for about ten seconds and dismounts. Can you do that, his satisfied expression asks. No, I could not.

The year was 1983. Souchy was ninety years old.

The Living Theatre? It was the leading avant-garde company of its day, breaking new ground. They were also a commune of radical actors. They were known for many experimental and expressionist productions, but they could also put on brutally realistic work. I remember Sam became unnerved when he attended a performance of *The Connection* as the guest of Judith Malina and Julian Beck. Seems a street junkie put the bite on him outside the theater and would not take no for an answer. He followed Sam inside, annoying and menacing at the same time. Sam did not like being intimidated and the incident threatened to get out of hand until the play began and Sam finally realized the "junkie" was an actor—*The Connection* being about druggies.

How they came to know my parents I am not sure, but the mutual respect was long lasting and deep. Sam spoke movingly at Julian's huge memorial service at the Joyce Theater in 1985. He sent the condolences of the New York branch of the IWW, of which Julian had been a member. The audience of the packed theater was restless. Most had never heard of the IWW. Many years later, in 2013, I was invited to a performance of a play by Judith Malina at the Living Theatre on Clinton Street, not far from my apartment. It turned out to be her last production. She was a very old lady. The Theatre, founded by Judith in 1947, closed soon after. The play was a sort of summing up of the themes of her life, her beliefs. Sam was a major character, an obvious symbol of courage and idealism. Unfortunately, Judith mistakenly emphasized that Sam had fought in Spain, when in fact, as I have mentioned, he did not go to Spain. The production was sparsely attended, and I had not the heart to correct her.

Sam acquired a degree of celebrity in his seventies and eighties. It amuses me that some of the younger comrades took seriously (albeit affectionately) his seemingly high self-regard and crusty personality. Those qualities were on public display to be sure, but it should have been obvious to anyone with the least bit of insight that they were external to the man and as thick as the fresh paint that he had applied to so many crumbling walls. Beneath that thin coat of self-protection he remained humble to the point that it was painful for me to witness.

I remember bringing him to my college shortly after mother died in 1989. It was the first time he had expressed a desire to see me at work. My "campus" without a tree consisted of a twenty-five-year-old Brooklyn office building. What most impressed Sam was the cafeteria to the side of the elevator bank in the lobby: a grimy place, really, but there were chairs and tables and a counter to get hamburgers and a soda machine.

"Look, the students are eating lunch!" he exclaimed.

"It's nothing," I said. "It is a dump."

"Dump? I never could eat like that," my eighty-eight-year-old father said. "I ate out of a paper bag." A simple remark and yet so sad.

He spoke at scores of college campuses throughout his long life, especially the last twenty years or so, and he had debated idiot lawyers, professors, authors of every stripe. Yet he never lost his awe of those who wore the formal trappings of a higher education.

"She's a college graduate, you know!" he'd say of some *pishika* who had heard of his name somewhere and come to pick his brain. I've seen him grow excited over people like that and hand them rare books and articles that they had not the capacity to appreciate. He went beyond generosity. It was almost as if he did not feel worthy of owning anything of value.

This man who wrote so cogently about capitalism and exploitation was almost childlike in his concept of money. He was shocked the day Angus Cameron of Knopf handed him three thousand dollars (or was it eighteen hundred? I forget) for the rights to *Bakunin on Anarchy*. Three thousand dollars! People were actually willing to pay him for what he wrote? He later bragged to friends that a Spanish publisher, who had in reality simply pirated the book, finally paid him five-hundred dollars. Sam thought that was a lot of money! A comrade had taken Sam to the publisher's office in Barcelona and embarrassed the man. You see, Sam saw Bakunin displayed up and down the Ramblas of Barcelona, and that is all he gave a damn about. *The Anarchist Collectives* turned a small profit. Sam promptly returned his royalty to the young publisher, Chuck Hamilton, saying "Here! Publish unpopular books!"

To people of quality the quality of the man came through. I recall now an incident in Sam's life so trivial that I am sure he'd scarcely remember. It concerns a brief meeting Sam had with a fellow I knew fairly well in the mid-1970s. I'll call him Abid. I had met Abid in judo class, which I continued to attend after Gregory dropped out. He was an Iranian doctor finishing his residency in pulmonary medicine at a local hospital. And a terrific person. The favored son of an influential Muslim family during the rule of the Shah, he became a rebel in the most uncomplicated and direct way: he worked at a clinic in Tehran. A poor woman brought her infant child to him. The child had an ordinary bronchial infection for which he prescribed a common antibiotic: cost, less than one dollar. Then he promptly forgot about the case until he encountered the woman three weeks later in the street.

"How is your child," he asked perfunctorily.

"He died."

Shocked, Abid asked, "But why? Didn't you give him the medicine I prescribed?"

The woman shook her head in grief. "I did not have the money."

"I began for the first time to take a good look at the world around me," Abid said. He joined the anti-Shah underground, at great risk:

named his son after a close friend captured and tortured to death. But Abid had joined a Marxist-Leninist underground sect and was a firm believer in its ideology. The two of us would argue politics over beers at the local bar after judo class as fervently as we had tried to throw each other during class. Naturally I told him about my anarchist parents. Abid jumped at the chance to meet them. I invited Abid and his wife, as dedicated as he, to visit my parents.

When they arrive, Sam is in the bedroom putting on his plaid shirt and suspender upholstered pants. He needs a shave. He walks out barefoot and sits at the end of our long living room table. I am at the other end. Abid and wife are seated at the center. Abid and Sam shake hands, exchange pleasantries. Finally Sam says, "What is it you'd like to discuss?"

And then this small startling thing: Abid, the aristocratic, well-educated, self-regarding doctor rises to his feet and faces barefoot Sam. Erect. Hands clasped behind his back. A schoolboy reciting his lessons to his headmaster, he proceeds to present the Marxist-Leninist theory of the State. Sam listens respectfully and they agree to disagree.

The dialogue left me faintly embarrassed. "Abid, no one expects you to stand like that," I said to him when Sam was out of earshot.

Abid disagreed. "No, No. To a man like your father, I must!"

"But Abid, how do you know? You have just met."

"You know!"

Abid is the only person I saw stand before Sam like that, but there was something my father projected unconsciously—I call it the quality of his being—that people deeply respected. Twenty-five years after his death there are comrades who speak of his life as if it were yesterday. My dear friend Herb Miller, a professor of literature and philosophy—dead many years now—loved to visit Sam, called him the most impressive man he'd ever met. "What is so impressive about him," I asked? "His soul," Herb said. "The man's soul." Not that there was anything saintly about him! Sam was gruff and vinegary as hell when pissed off, as I hope I've amply demonstrated.

# 65

## CITIZEN SAM

I say again that the '70s and early '80s were good times for my parents. Sam had retired. Abe and I were long grown and gainfully employed. They had saved a tiny bit of money, enough for them to travel for a bit. So they decided on a trip to Europe: to visit comrades mainly. There was a problem, however. They needed passports and Sam was not a citizen. Preposterous, you may think. How could a person who came to America at the age of three, in 1905, not be a citizen in 1975? But it was true and there were plausible reasons from Sam's perspective.

The fact he was born in White Russia meant he was not automatically a citizen. To become one, he had to "declare himself," that is, apply for papers at age eighteen or twenty one, I forget which. But Sam was a confirmed revolutionist by then and we are in America's most fascistic and reactionary period: World War I and its immediate aftermath. It was the time of the Espionage Act and the persecution of the Wobblies and socialists; of the Palmer raids and the summary deportation of anarchist aliens, of whom Goldman and Berkman were merely the best known. It was a time of Red Scare xenophobia. Sauerkraut was "liberty cabbage" and even that portion of the electromagnetic spectrum our brain identifies as "red" became suspect. Sam recalled those times to me with bitter humor. And then there was the little episode he did not like to talk about, when he and cousin Izzy deserted the stables of the U.S. Cavalry in New Mexico. So Sam decided to stay clear of the Immigration and Naturalization Service.

He remained in that frame of mind many years. In the early 1950s, perhaps seeking protection or perhaps wanting to travel, he consulted his friend Roland Watts, an attorney for the Workers Defense League. This was the time of the Second Red Scare, better known as the McCarthy Era. The IWW had been placed on the Attorney General's list of Subversive Organizations—those charged with trying to overthrow the government by "unconstitutional means," whatever that meant. And Sam was of course a long-time active member of the IWW. And an anarchist. So Watts advised him to let sleeping dogs lie.

But it is the 1970s now and Sam wanted to travel. His lawyer scoffed at his fears and got him his citizenship in short order. Seems his birth record had been destroyed in a great Cleveland hospital fire! Who knew?

Bob and Phyllis Calese served as the needed "two credible witnesses," about which Bob had misgivings because all four of them (Mother included) were lying, and there could have been consequences. Bob was also sensitive to the fact that "as a foreign-born anarchist, Sam was risking deportation every time he opened his mouth or wrote a single word. Had he been sent back to Russia he knew full well he wouldn't last three weeks." How likely was that? Who is to say! And who was to defend Sam if it did happen? He'd seen many people deported in his youth. I'm sure Sam did not think about deportation each time he "opened his mouth or wrote a single word." But the threat weighed in the back of his mind. Of that I am equally sure. And it shows me it took a rare form of courage to live the life he led.

I know of several occasions growing up when "inquiries" were made about Mother and Sam. And there was the occasion Sam was accosted on the street and "invited" into a car by two FBI agents. They wanted to know about a Japanese artist comrade: where he lived, what he did, etc. Sam pretended to know nothing and demanded out of the car. They obliged, but as he left one said sarcastically, "Regards to Mr. Weiner," his pen name.

Abe and I have speculated many times on the reason, or reasons, Sam was not imprisoned or overtly harassed; we will never know for sure. We have, however, agreed on several plausible explanations. The first is that "the authorities" considered him a harmless crackpot, who had after all violated no laws. Let him say what he wants to the handful of people who listened. He was not worth the effort. The second, is that he was fervently anti-communist, albeit for different reasons than the government, and hence was marginally useful to them during the Cold War. The third is that, whereas the Wobblies and anarchists had proven troublesome in the past, they had no power, nor were they likely to gain any. So why bother Sam at this point? The more effective approach was to keep an eye on him. Sam was sure his Wobbly and Libertarian League activities were monitored by the Red Squad.

Mother and citizen Sam made three trips in the mid- to late 1970s: First to Israel, then to Spain, and later, to England. I will not subject you to a travelogue. Sight-seeing was secondary to them with one exception. They visited the mountaintop stronghold of Masada, where, according to Josephus but not archeology, a community of Jews held off the Roman Legion for two years and then committed mass suicide rather than surrender. Sam became so emotional that, rather than ride to the top of the mesa, he insisted on hiking the steep ramp to get there. In the hot sun. With his emphysema and bad heart. Mother feared he would drop dead on the way, a belated self-inflicted casualty of that ancient conflict. But no, he made it, chest heaving.

Sam describes their travels in *Fragments* and other publications. I think his observations were astute; especially the comments on Israeli society, which still seem relevant after forty years. There is one person, however, that Sam met in Spain whom he inexplicably neglects to mention, although he admired him: the great historian of the Spanish Revolution, Diego Camacho, who wrote under the name Abel Paz. It was Sam's regard for Diego that motivated me to go to Barcelona the summer following Sam's death. I was newly remarried. Izolda and I had driven from Zürich to Barcelona in the company of our Swiss comrades, Dieter Gebauer and Ruedi Naef. You could define our trip a semi-honeymoon, if you believe in such things. In Barcelona, we were joined by Salvador Gurruchari—an anarchist whose ebullience and charm reminded me of Anthony Quinn in *Zorba*—and his son Felix. Our entire tribe called on Diego where he lived in the working-class Gràcia quarter.

The first lesson I learned from Diego was diplomacy, for before he allowed us to sit together in the Gràcia plaza, he first took us on a tour of the restaurants that encircled the plaza. To each one Diego offers a friendly greeting to the owner and staff; there follows a short conversation and wave toward us. I do not speak Catalan, nor does Diego speak English, so Salvador explained. "You see, we're going to eat over there later," he said, pointing to a place at the far end. "Diego doesn't want any of the others to be offended." It was obvious Diego was a neighborhood fixture—a warmly regarded elder statesmen.

However, Diego's diplomacy did not extend to Izolda. No sooner had we crowded around the small table in the plaza, then Diego, directly across from Izolda, leans forward and says something confidential/intimate to her in Spanish. Izolda stiffens in response and utters not a word to Diego for the next three hours. Now Izolda is from Brazil, speaks Portuguese, but she also knows Spanish very well. What the hell did he say to her? Not until late that night, when we were alone, could I get it out of her. Seems he said, "It's a hot night," which was true. "My shirt is open so you can see my chest." Also true. Then he added, "Why don't open your shirt so I can see your chest." By which he clearly meant her tits. Izolda is not a prude and she understood that Diego was joking. Nor was it the first time she's heard such a request. But she disliked his tone. Who was this fellow and why did he think he had a right to say that to her, a total stranger?

I learned later that Diego was famous for speaking directly, which could be refreshing but also hurtful at times. And if he did not like or respect you—watch out. A comrade who knew Diego well compared being under verbal attack from him to having stones flung at you full force. That said, and perhaps because I had spent a lifetime in the company of crusty anarchists, it took me less than ten seconds to know that Diego was a very kind man. I knew little of Diego's life, however, which took him four volumes to recount; the man was in many ways a walking embodiment of the history of Spanish anarchism. All I knew was that he was born into poverty of illiterate parents; that he went on to write books translated into fourteen languages; that he had fought on the front lines against Franco and behind the lines against the Stalinists; that he was interned in a French concentration camp following the fall of Spain; that he was conscripted into slave-labor by the Nazis, constructing the Atlantic Wall; that he managed to join the anti-Nazi underground; that he returned to Spain as a key figure in the anti-Franco underground; that he was captured and spent eleven years in harsh Franco prisons.

That night in Barcelona, Diego said to me without the faintest pretense or self-importance: "Prison was good for me. It made me a better man!"

Upon his release, Diego returned to France and in the 1960s he started writing his epic biography of Buenaventura Durruti as well as other historical books. The man was incredibly productive. In 1977 he returned to Spain after Franco's death. He lived in poverty on a minuscule government pension. None of his books sold well; they were not taken up by commercial publishers. Academic histori-ans ignored him except to plagiarize him. The man was not "objec-tive"; never mind his documentation was voluminous. He lacked academic credentials; never mind he lived through the events he described. And wouldn't it be better had the anarchists not existed?

Because he is modest, my close friend Dieter Gebauer will not be pleased when I say he was instrumental in introducing Diego to a wide audience. Dieter, now retired, was a professor in Switzerland at ETH Zürich. Hardly a rich man, he supported Diego, arranged for the translation and publication of his books into German and other languages, and drove Diego on speaking tours that he scheduled throughout Europe. Dieter did this out of the special affection he holds for the old Spanish anarchists, though he adds Sam as an honorary member of his list.

He also visited Federico Arcos regularly, flying each year to Windsor, Ontario, from Zürich. As I did, but usually by car or short flight from New York. Federico and Diego grew up together in the medieval El Clot district of Barcelona. There are photographs of them striding side by side in the streets. They fought Franco together, fought the Stalinists together, and fought in underground Spain together. They were close as brothers, but, unfortunately, like brothers who cannot stand each other and nevertheless love each other grudgingly and better at a distance. Their temperaments simply did not mesh. Federico was clean: clean living, sober, watched his diet, and was unfailingly polite. As I have mentioned, his wife, Pura, who has passed away, was an active member of the Spanish feminist organization Mujeres Libres. He was deeply attached to his daughter and only child. I loved Federico, but he did have a puritanical streak, which by the way, he shared with a number of old-time anarchists.

And Diego? I'll simply share Federico's reaction to my suggestion that he accompany Diego by car on his speaking tours; they would be a huge success, Dieter assured me.

"Ride next to him in the car! He drinks, he smokes, he farts! No way." And then Federico adds in an angry hiss, "The man does not respect women!"

I suppose the incident I described earlier would bear that out. But later that evening Diego invited us back to his tiny book-lined apartment on the top floor of the ancient Calle Verdi 109. The rooms were packed with young men and women; all kinds, coming and going. They clearly loved and looked after him. After the last one left, Diego gave Izolda and me his bed. We declined at first, but he insisted. By this time Izolda was over her pique.

In the morning Diego accompanied us to the door. Then, staring directly into my eyes, he uttered one intense, passionate sentence in Catalan as he let me go.

"What did he say?" I asked Izolda on the street.

"He said, 'Your father was a man who did more on this earth than eat and sleep.'"

# MOTHER AND SAM COME HOME

While in Spain my parents met the English anarchist Albert Meltzer, who, to mention a single instance in a lifetime of militancy, had worked tirelessly in the late 1960s to free Stuart Christie from a Spanish prison after his attempted assassination of Franco. He was an "old-timer" of immense reputation and had returned to Madrid in order to see what he could do to help revive the CNT in the post-Franco era. The three hit it off so well that Meltzer invited my parents to spend a few weeks in England as his guest. They were delighted to take him up on it; they had friends in common and had been reading each other's articles for years. The visit started well, but unfortunately had to be cut short.

Mother suffered a rapid sequence of minor strokes. My parents returned to New York.

Although not bedridden or obviously impaired, she never fully recovered. Her speech slowed. She lacked "force." She listed slightly to one side. She became repetitive, telling the same stories over again in the exact words; as if her mind was stuck on a track she was powerless to change. Less sure of herself physically, and sensing she was not mentally as sharp, she became possessive of Sam, refusing to let him out of her sight if she could help it—even to let him be alone with me, for fear we "would talk about her." Fortunately, she was not always this way. She had her good days as well as her bad days. But it pains me that many younger comrades who came to my parents in their old age did not get to know Mother in her prime: when she was feisty, incisive, and witty.

Looking back, I can see that Mother's strokes marked an inflection point, beyond which my parents began a long decline: gradual at first, but accelerated toward the end. Sam's emphysema was catching up to him. He walked slower, his breath came shorter, and he was confined to an ever-tightening circle of a block or two around their apartment. His voice grew hoarser and more croaking. He slept on the couch in the daytime. What is more significant, because it cut him off from the world, he was growing deaf; indeed was almost totally deaf by the time he died.

His deafness—or more precisely, his reaction to it—drove me mad. Ninety percent of the time he refused to wear his hearing aid, claiming that he took it off because too many people insisted on telling him the truth! He taunted me with his deafness, making me shout and repeat the simplest words. It was a kind of power he seemed to relish; the power of the child over the adult—a role reversal I did not sign up for. Mother, in her complete understanding and compassion for him, had a different interpretation of his behavior: "Can't you see? The hearing aid doesn't work and he is embarrassed he can't hear, so he puts on an act."

Only Abe knew how to tame him when he came to New York. I remember one day in the mid-1980s. Abe, Hadassah, and Rochelle were visiting; other people as well. We had a lively discussion going; the subject I do not remember. Sam sat at the end of the long living room table closest to his bedroom. He refused to wear his hearing aid and insisted we speak louder, louder, louder! I found myself shouting at him from my end of the table, as were we all. Finally, Abe said to us simply, "Speak to him in a normal tone." This we did and Sam grew furious.

"If you do this I'm going into the bedroom!" he proclaimed.

"Good! And close the door after yourself," Abe said.

Sam proceeded to go to the bedroom. He closed the door after himself. A few minutes later, he came back, sat down at his old seat, and put on his hearing aid. The discussion proceeded calmly in normal voice. Abe motioned me to say nothing to Sam about it. I have always envied that he was able to "handle" Sam in a way I could not.

He kept writing and speaking and raising hell through it all. You had to know him intimately to see the changes; he had the ability to pull himself together "in company." He and his pal Abe Bluestein founded *News from Libertarian Spain* (later renamed *Anarchist News*) in 1976 and kept it going until 1982. They published information not generally available in English. Ultimately they had to close it down for lack of funds. He remained active in the IWW, especially with young Wobblies of anarchistic bent: Mimi and Jeff Stein, Jon Bekken, Mike Hargis, Nancy and Steve Kellerman, and Richard Christopher. They were at home with Sam; age made no difference except in the constructive sense that he was a link back to the great IWW and anarchist traditions. Jeff Stein reminds me that in 1986 Sam spoke at a conference of revolutionary syndicalists in Champaign, Illinois, hosted by the IWW, and attended by members of SAC (Sweden), Solidarity (Poland), Workers Solidarity Movement (Japan), and SAAWU (South Africa).

With Jeff, Jon, Mike, and Richard, Sam founded the *Libertarian Labor Review* (*LLR*) as a forum for the "constructive discussion of anarcho-syndicalist theory and practice." They chose May 1, 1986, the Haymarket centennial, as the date of the first issue. Sam was eighty-four years old, and it was exactly fifty years since he had shared the platform with Lucy Parsons and addressed the crowd gathered in front of the windswept monument to her husband and the other martyrs at Waldheim Cemetery, Chicago. An occasion for reflection? A celebration of consistency?

Sam's inaugural article was entitled "Modern Technology and Anarchism." It was a theme he had been developing since the late 1950s: that contrary to the commonly held view that anarchism is impractical and utopian, our advanced cybernetic civilization is evolving toward anarchistic forms of organization. Sam envisioned society as a vast self-organizing, self-regulating network. Centralized, top-down structures, whether a government or a large capitalist enterprise, grow inefficient and uncompetitive in this environment; they are dinosaurs. The digital revolution had the potential to render the state and the capitalist system functionally irrelevant, although Sam was acutely aware that this same revolution provides the state with the capacity to exert control over the individual beyond anything George Orwell imagined. So the struggle against hierarchal authority continues albeit in different form. Sam was not rigid and did not live in the past, even if the very suggestion of exchanging his ancient typewriter for a computer caused him to throw up his hands in fright.

It is a minor annoyance of mine that some comrades still think Sam was wedded to the past. I encourage them to read John Duda's essay "Cybernetics, Anarchism, and Self-Organization" in *Anarchist Studies* (2013). He regards Sam's contributions of seminal importance to the reinvention of anarchism in the late-twentieth century. The misconception that he was unduly rigid stems from the fact that he refused to abandon the concept of the class struggle, and from his belief that democratic, revolutionary unions are the best instruments for confronting the capitalist system and the state. I'll not get into the thick of the debate, except to say that I think many of Sam's critics were college educated and middle class and lived in a period of rising opportunity for people like them. The nature of work had largely changed, they insisted: the class struggle and unions were obsolete.

Sam's view? Out of sight, out of mind! There are billions of people on this earth, most of whom are invisible to the educated classes of advanced nations such as the United States. Had the nature of work changed for the vast majority of the world's population? For the billions in poverty in Latin America, India, Asia, and the crumbling Soviet Union? Were the principles of anarcho-syndicalism and the IWW wrong for them? The striking Gdansk shipyard workers brought down the totalitarian regime of Poland, Sam pointed out. Or was that an optical illusion? The masses of the poor nations support the minority of the world that lives in the cybernetic age. How many Chinese wage slaves to make an iPhone? How many Bangladeshis to make our clothing? Capitalism remains a predatory system because, at its core, human beings are raw materials, commodities. That can never change and it holds as well for the privileged nations. Ask the rank and file intellectual employees of Silicon Valley how well they are treated. Yes, work is evolving, but the power relations remain unchanged.

Sam died seventeen years before the Great Recession of 2007, before those especially hard times, and before the destruction of pensions, mass unemployment, and reduced wages eviscerated the American middle class. He would not have been surprised. He felt the prosperity of the middle class was fragile and temporary. "They'll have to learn the same lessons all over again," he said to me many times, meaning the lessons of the class struggle. He would have welcomed Occupy Wall Street; it was within walking distance of his home.

Sam continued to write for and coedited the *LLR*. What I find most impressive is the depth and breadth of his interests, written while Mother was in serious decline and his every breath a struggle. Taken together, you might say the late articles, which I mention in no hierarchal order, can stand as a summary of his life-long concerns: The Spanish Revolution; Israeli Zionism; Misconceptions of Anarchism; the Evolution of Anarcho-Syndicalism; Nicaragua and the Sandinista Counter-Revolution; Business Unionism and the Suicidal Decline of the American Labor Movement; Revolutionary Unionism in Brazil. We can add to this the old standbys of low opinion: a critique of the influence of Marxism on the International Labor Movement; Third World Nationalism; and Castro's Cuba, of course. The Soviet Union was in a state of collapse at the time and that naturally held his attention. So he wrote an interesting take on Lenin and Gorbachev. Ever hopeful, his last article, "The Revolutionary Revival in Eastern Europe," appeared in the Summer 1990 issue, a few months before he died.

The name of the *LLR* was changed to the *Anarcho-Syndicalist Review* (*ASR*) a few years later so as not to confuse it with the reactionary pro-capitalist libertarians. I was gratified that, in November 2002, the comrades devoted an entire issue to Sam in recognition of the hundredth anniversary of his birth: The quality of the contributions is outstanding.

*ASR* is still publishing.

I have mentioned, of course, Sam's other books, all of them written in the 1970s and 1980s after he stopped slinging the brush. The last of them was *Fragments*, his notes toward an autobiography, as I put it. Paul Avrich insisted he write about his life as he was eighty-three years old. But Sam did not want to write about himself. He was tired. He did not enjoy introspection. He needed to devote his diminishing energy to Mother, whose health was failing. So he wrote rapidly and off the cuff and it shows in places. Abe tells me he got some facts and incidents wrong. Many of the events he describes are not dated clearly. He left important people out. He padded the text with his articles toward the end because he grew weary. He says nothing of himself beyond his involvement with the Movement: nothing of Abe and I and Mother and his personal life and his likes and dislikes. And he could have replaced all the people he mentions in *Fragments* with others he knew! That said, however, it remains an important document.

I wish *Fragments* were a different book, which is one reason I am writing this one. I wish he had "opened the windows" and let in the wider world. The book is insular. However, he was not that way with me. I dropped by one day when he was in his late eighties to find him sheepish and shaken, as if a survivor of an outer body experience. He had been watching a TV documentary on the Sacco and Vanzetti case and on the screen, for a split second, there flashed the grainy image of an outdoor mass meeting somewhere: Union Square? Boston? High on the platform a tiny speaker was haranguing the crowd. And it was Sam!

"It was me! Sixty years ago! My life, where did it go? So many years! A different person, but me! What should I say to that person if I met him now? Would he know me? Am I anyone he expected to be?"

He fell despondent. "I'm a fossil, a living fossil."

He had devoted his life to the shrinking world of the IWW and the anarchist movement, while the wider world expanded. He had dealt with this reality like an unrepentant warrior forced to give an opponent his due. Example: We are walking together in front of our building; his steps and his breath short. Three teenagers approach and pass: six feet, husky, a spring to their stride.

Sam smiles at them, says to me ruefully, "They grow 'em big under capitalism, don't they?"

Marxist, anarchist, whomever—the radicals of the nineteenth and early twentieth centuries underestimated Capitalism, Sam said when in an analytical mood. Conditions were so horrible, the contradictions so glaring, the capitalists so stupid it seemed obvious the system was on its last legs. "We all thought it was going to collapse. A matter of time. We underestimated the capacity of the system to make adjustments. We gave little thought to the middle class, how it stabilized things. And we did not understand the workers! We thought that if they learned the value of solidarity they'd become more militant, overthrow the system. Instead they became less militant. So long as they got enough. That one man lives in luxury while another man breaks his back for him they do not see as an injustice! They view it as the accidents of life!" At this Sam would turn away in disgust.

His life! Where did it go? He spoke only to me of the sadness that washed over him at times.

# 69
## SAM GOES HOLLYWOOD

So now I'll tell you of an incident where I took advantage of him. The phone rings at my parents' apartment. The voice on the other end says he is a publicist.

He represents Chumley's Bar on Barrow Street in Greenwich Village. Chumley's was a speakeasy when it opened in the 1920s. It was a favorite of poets, novelists, playwrights, bohemians, and revolutionists. Willa Cather, E. E. Cummings, Theodore Dreiser, Eugene O'Neill, John Dos Passos, Ring Lardner, Edna St Vincent Millay, and John Steinbeck—they all drank at Chumley's at one time or another. And, of course the seemingly ubiquitous Dylan Thomas.

Is there a decrepit place he was not purported to have gotten drunk, I ask? It reminded me of the sign I saw hanging in an out-of-the-way Key West bar: HEMINGWAY DID NOT DRINK HERE.

The publicist laughs. Anyway, Chumley's has been refurbished. New owners want to relaunch the place. Big party. A hundred literary celebrities. The jacket covers of their books are to be pasted to the walls, like in the old days. Your Dad is invited. He can paste Bakunin there. We want your dad there because he is an old-time Wobbly and a throw-back to the glory days of Chumley's.

I call to Sam who is at his typewriter in the bedroom. Big deal! No, he did not want to go, he says. He'd had unpleasant experiences with publicists, promoters, people like that! To hell with the new owners of Chumley's! Turns out the original Chumley had also been a Wobbly and died in 1935. Sam had known him fairly well and indeed had drunk at his bar on occasion.

And here is where I took advantage of him. I want you there! You are an author, you belong there, I said. I want you to meet these people. You'll enjoy it! Finally he agreed. Mother told me later he did not wish to disappoint his son.

I took advantage of Sam because between marriages I had a girl-friend who I wanted to impress. She was fond of bohemia, the literary whirl, the theater. In street parlance, Catherine "ate that shit up!" Chumley's made for a perfect Sunday afternoon!

So, we drove Sam to Chumley's: a colorful place with side exits, trap doors, and stairs leading to nowhere. Something medieval about it. And indeed the cover to Bakunin had been pasted to a wall where it blended with famous, not so famous, and forgotten colleagues. The publicist immediately ensconced the three of us into one of the refurbished wooden booths. I must say he was polite and treated us well. We watched the crowd mill about us fifteen minutes or so and then came a subtle parting of the waves as the publicist led royalty toward our booth: that is, a star of Broadway and film. Jack Gilford. Stage credits? *A Funny Thing Happened on the Way to the Forum, Cabaret, Romanoff and Juliet, The Diary of Anne Frank, Sunshine Boys.* Film? *Cocoon, Seize the Tiger,* and a million other movies. Also? The rubber-faced guy in the Cracker Jacks commercials. Not a first-rank leading man, but a major actor nonetheless. Mainly, but not exclusively comedic roles: Tony and Oscar nominations, a distinguished career. He is elegantly dressed but, for all that, looks like the person he was at heart: Jacob Aaron Gellman, an elderly Jewish gentleman from the Lower East Side.

"A Wobbly! A Wobbly! I always wanted to meet a genuine Wobbly!" he exclaims.

He slides in next to Sam on the bench, turns his body a certain way, puts an arm around Sam and smiles with professional aplomb at the clicking camera. Sam sits impassively. His bulldog, lined face needing a shave faces the other way. He is wearing his usual plaid flannel shirt and suspenders. His emphysema enhanced body is twice the thickness of Gilford's. He looks like he doesn't belong in the picture. He has no idea who Gilford is.

"See, I told you!" the publicist says to Gilford, like a man reminding him he pays his debts. The photographer leaves, the crowd disperses. It is quiet.

"So?" Sam says. "How old are you?"

"Eighty!"

"I'm eighty-five! You're a pup!" And the two old geezers smile affectionately at one another. Each had three more years of life.

I found Gilford to be a *very* nice man. Like so many performers from the Lower East Side, he had scraped and clawed his way up from poverty. Nor was he a man to forget that. He and his wife Madeline were blacklisted for alleged communist sympathies during the McCarthy Era and we had a long conversation about how they survived. The humiliation, the performing under assumed names in obscure places, the scrounging for crummy parts, the people who took advantage, the friends who lent them money: it was not easy.

Still, he had come to meet "his Wobbly." And I am convinced that is why Sam was invited. To lure Jack Gilford to Chumley's. I understood. Call me sentimental. But tears welled up in my eyes after Gilford left Sam in that booth and I vowed I would never subject him to anything like that again.

# 70

# MOTHER'S LAST DAYS

Our parents were long dead before Abe decided to tell me of a late night conversation between Mother and Sam during their last visit to Chicago. It was two in the morning. Abe and Hadassah were trying to sleep. Mother and Sam were in the adjoining bedroom. The wall between them was no match for Sam's booming voice in the dark. You were compelled to listen.

"I know I can't do it anymore. Let me put it up against you," he growls to Mother like a tender alligator. He was eighty-six, she eighty-two.

Sam loved Mother passionately and with a sense of gratitude that never wavered. She had anchored the life of an itinerate rebel: made a home for him, bore him sons, stuck by him when he lay drunk and an object of derision, and never regretted a day. She was responsible for the man he had become. Late in their life together he behaved irascibly and at times was abusive toward her as she developed a kind of old age paranoia and possessiveness that drove him to distraction and in truth would melt the patience of a sphinx. His outbursts could appall casual visitors and even friends. But those who really knew them well understood his rants were emotional cloud bursts. That is how Mother took them. She was certainly not intimidated.

Dr. Inkles had informed Sam—and me—that Mother's condition was hopeless. Her heart was failing. Her carotid arteries were clogged and that constricted oxygen supply to the brain. It was the cause of the series of small strokes she experienced in the mid-1970s. Now it was the late 1980s and she was slowly dying. And Dr. Inkles informed me in private that, although Sam appeared stronger than Mother, he was dying, too. His emphysema had taken its toll and his heart was weak. They had a year or two, or maybe three.

Sam took charge of Mother's remaining life. He refused car service to see Dr. Inkles. He insisted on pushing her by wheelchair the three long blocks to his clinic instead. And home. It did not matter to him that each step of his own was a struggle and the journey torturously slow. During the fall and winter months the wind would kick up from the East River something fierce and grit and paper would skip from the street into their faces. Sam did not care. He was going to take Mother to the doctor himself. I'd rush from Brooklyn after class and find them midway: this little old man pushing his aged wife down the wide, windswept street, the two of them alone on a long journey. I was the only one Sam would turn Mother over to and the three of us made our way.

At first it was Mother that had to be rushed by ambulance to New York Hospital where she'd stay a day or two in the heart unit. Later it was Sam, although he was released the same day. On one occasion it was the two of them together. I'll not forget the young doctor who approached them as they sat gnarled and wrinkled and, yes, frightened, in the Emergency Room.

"Eighty-seven and eighty-three?" he asked tenderly. "We have two old trees! Don't worry Mother. Don't worry Father. We'll take care of you. You won't die today."

Sam became impossible. Not only did he refuse car service, he refused the hospital bed sent to our apartment for Mother by the cardiac unit. He said no and slammed the door in the face of the delivery men! Are you crazy, I asked? But he was adamant that Mother was going to sleep and—though he left it unspoken—die in her own bed.

He was just as impossible concerning his own behavior. He became incontinent. Wherever he stopped while in the street he left a puddle of piss. His groin was perpetually soiled. He began to stink. The corner druggist, who said his father had given him the same trouble, sold me a package of adult diapers. I brought them upstairs to Sam, who growled and promptly threw them out the window, just as he had over the years thrown out Kipling, and the *New York Times*, and the *Daily Worker*, and Marx and everything else he hated.

"But you piss your pants!" I yelled at him. "You can't walk around like that!"

"I'm not wearing diapers!"

"What about me?"

"You'll just have to put up with it!"

I've thought about Sam's negativity toward the end of his life and am convinced it stemmed from the sense that he was losing the power to control his life. Doctors and death were in control now—in the guise of logical, rational decisions. But Sam had one power left—or the illusion of one power left. He could say "NO!" And he did all the time.

Fortunately, I did not have to put up with Sam alone, though the home-care people the hospital sent us were not much help. They saw an old man and an old lady and an easy payday. They cooked simple meals, cleaned a little and that was it. There were exceptions, however. A large, black nurse insisted it was time Sam took a bath. Sam ran into the living room wearing nothing but a delighted expression and whispered to me, "She's giving me a bath! She washes my back!"

My parents made no claim to special status and expected no deference because of their age and experience in the radical movement. They simply expected to be treated as comrades. But, of course, that is not how the young people that found their way to them felt. That object of Murray Bookchin's fury, Ulrike Heider, paints a loving portrait of Mother in her last year: "Embracing me, Esther greeted me as her 'young comrade.' The eighty-three-year-old, white-haired anarchist was wearing a brightly coloured house dress and the black and red badge of the CNT (Confederacion National de Trabajo), the Spanish anarchist union, on her collar. Her spontaneous friendliness, unconventional appearance, and profound humanity made all the elegant old ladies of the Upper East Side, whose appearance had fascinated me, pale in comparison."

That CNT button she wore was not entirely ceremonial, as Spanish anarchist Maria Gil learned. "When I left Madrid in my late teens the year after Franco died I asked the CNT—the Anarchist Labor Union of which I had been a member from before it came up from the underground after his death—for an anarchist U.S. contact and they gave me...Sam and Esther's phone number. And they more or less 'adopted' me from the get-go. We hit it off from the start.... They were a true gift to me on many levels."

Maria encouraged Mother to be more assertive. She felt Mother was too much in Sam's shadow. So she arranged for her to address a group of radical-liberal students at Vassar College in upstate Poughkeepsie, New York—a bit risky considering her bad heart. I was not present; it was an all-women thing. But I gather Mother's speech could have gone better. She had grown hesitant speaking in public since her stroke and perhaps the room full of young self-assured females with faculty looking on intimidated her. However, Mother sprung to life when an insistent student kept hammering away at her anarchism. She invariably prefaced her remarks with "Marx says this" and "according to Marx"—as if that clinched the argument. Finally, Mother had enough.

"Marx, Marx!" she interrupted, with a wave of the hand. "Who was Marx? He was a man who lived in the nineteenth century. He was a brilliant man, for sure. Some of the things he said are of value today; others not so much. Why do you feel the need to refer to him always? Why don't you stand up, think for yourself, and say what it is you want to say?" She received enthusiastic applause!

My close friend Marten Pine organized an around-the-clock task force to help me care for my parents: himself, Denise Waters, Maria Gil, Bob and Phyllis Calese, Ed Mitchell's daughter, Amelia, others. Their vigil lasted three years, and it was never "I'm going to do these things for you." No, it was "I was just dropping by, and while I am here, I'll do this and that." And the "this and that" amounted to cooking, cleaning, bathing, and caring for my parents in all ways: emotional and physical. I'll not forget their kindness, though now, twenty-five years after the fact, some barely remember or shrug it off.

The heart attacks and small strokes intensified the last year of Mother's life. The emergency crew would arrive with the stretcher and wheelchair and lift her into the ambulance waiting in the street. I rode with her at times, but more often followed with my enfeebled father by taxi to New York Hospital, where they checked her in to the cardiac unit. Her situation was hopeless and Mother was aware of this fact. Sam's brother, Uncle Tommy, died suddenly of a stroke while she lay in the hospital. With typical tact Sam gave it to her straight: "Esther, guess what? Tommy died." I could have shot him that instant! But Esther and Tommy—they had grown to adulthood together. They knew each other sixty years. Death is what it is. Mother said simply, "Tommy died quickly. I have to suffer first!"

"Oh no, you are not dying," I insisted inanely. But Mother knew better and smiled a private smile.

In those final days her mind turned upside down: the dead of night became day. She wandered the aisles of the heart ward, speaking aloud of many things—long-ago conversations that were never finished. This infuriated the other patients whom she kept awake. All except one unlucky fellow who, the day before, had been rushed in from the airport minutes before his plane was to take off; to the contrary, he did not mind her late night conversations at all.

"Your mother is remarkable," he said. "Her speech is biblical. The imagery, the beauty of her language! She has a remarkable soul!"

This graceful man, whose name I do not know and whom I never saw again, was professor of German Literature at Cornell University. Mother had that affect on people. The nurses took to her, flocked around her. She worried they worked too hard as she lay dying and was upset they were paid too low. It was the sweetness of her nature that drew them. Several had tears in their eyes when I came to take her home for those ever-briefer periods.

Her remarkable soul. Ulrike Heider goes on to say my parents' apartment "was furnished in a sober, modern style and bore witness to a craftsman's talent for improvisation. The furniture was of the type one might find on the street on a lucky day."

All true. But Heider does not mention the hundred photographs Mother had spread all over, all of them the infant offspring of comrades and friends; she knew each infant by name. Nor does Heider mention the forest of plants that Mother tended, up to and including the final day of her life. She fretted over them as if they were people. Even a mouse that skittered across the kitchen linoleum to the garbage bag fell within the purview of her compassion. She sent for the exterminator, yes, but with the sad, guilty comment, "Poor thing, all it is trying to do is survive in this world."

The day came when Mother was no longer able to survive in this world. She died at home in her own bed, the way Sam felt she should: November 11, 1989. She was eighty-four years old.

Mother would have been pleased by a number of things at her memorial service: That her old friends and comrades, people Abe and I grew up knowing, attended; that her surviving brothers, Daniel and Martin, traveled from Pittsfield, Massachusetts and Washington, DC to be there, although Aunt Sarah could not find it in her heart to do this last thing for her sister. I am sure Mother would have been pleased by the remarks Abe and I made, and most of all by the surprising way Gregory sprung to the front of the room and addressed us. He was twenty-eight years old by this time, weighed three hundred pounds and wore the beard of a Maine woodsman. And he spoke slowly and well of his love for Mother and how well she understood him as a child, and how he would not forget her for a single day of his life.

And then Sam spoke. He was eloquent and unsentimental, as one might expect. But I had been listening to him a lifetime and sensed something rushed, something irritable and not right in his delivery. He cramped over in agony as soon as the last guest left, clutching his bladder. We rushed him to New York Hospital where they drained what looked like gallons of piss from him through a catheter. Seems he had been unable to urinate for the thirty-six hours leading up to Mother's service, and had addressed us in a state of torture. Dr. Inkles stood beside his bed, exasperated.

"Your father does not listen!" he explained. "I've been after him about his prostate for years! I could have prevented this."

Several days later Sam had his prostate removed. It was one of those old-fashioned roto-rooter jobs that left him in pain and leaking blood for weeks.

"Your mother no longer exists," Sam said cleanly, upon her death and cremation. The operation was over and he was back in the apartment.

"She was a good woman," I added. Resorting to cliché helped to suppress grief.

"Good? You have no idea!" was all he would add, as if she were still in the room and nodding at some deep secret between them.

Then Sam did something I would never have thought he had in him. He curled up on the bed he had shared with Mother these many years and whimpered like a wounded animal. "What is to become of me? Who will take care of me?" he sobbed.

"I'll take care of you," I promised. Sam took my comment new and he sprung from the bed with a totally different demeanor. "Let's get some lunch!" he said. We crossed the street to the hole-in-the-wall Chinese restaurant that had recently replaced the old Jewish bakery in a sign of changing times.

His way of confronting oncoming death was to deflect it with a kind of grim humor that was not funny. "They're gonna plant me soon," he'd say too often without provocation and with a smile that was no smile at all.

"The days of my youth are fast receding," was another catch-phrase, and he'd enjoy the recognition on the part of the listener that indeed this was no youth but a very old man speaking.

True, he no longer drank much and did not smoke, but he still took rotten care of himself. Each morning he'd take the elevator the ten floors to the lobby and make his glacial way to the bodega around the corner and back—returning with a slab of unsliced bacon or fatty pork or beef. Vegetables, healthy salads were not his thing. He'd fry the meat in a tiny pan, grease splattering the kitchen and smoke choking the room, in a reprise of his cooking days in the hobo jungles. Then he'd pour the fat in the pan back onto the meat:

"How the hell can you eat like that?" I'd shout at him.

His answer was mock surprise: "More tender that way!"

"The cholesterol!" I'd snap.

"What's cholesterol?" He of course knew full well what it was. "What? So I won't live to be ninety-seven?"

It was funny, but there was a message to it.

At other times he met the subject of his death head on. A home-care attendant left a copy of the *Daily News* behind at the foot of Sam's bed. Sam motioned me to hand it to him. He turned to the back pages, to the cemetery ads. He found the one he wanted: Cremations $132, the cheapest price on the page. He tore it out, handed it to me. "That's the one! That's what I want. I don't want you to spend money on me!"

I've mentioned that other comrades helped me take care of my parents. But Sam reached the point that he needed someone to be around often and sleep in the apartment with him. I lived in Brooklyn and was freshly married. I felt that although living with us would be a comfort to him—and me—there were too many practical factors against it. How would I get him to Dr. Inkles? What of the support system Marten Pine developed? The familiarity of his home, his bed, his library, his desk and typewriter? His sense of independence? The option of his moving in with us became moot in any case, because Sam was adamant that he did not want to. At this juncture Roger O'Neill stepped in and did something noble. Roger was a long-time activist with the Catholic Worker and a close associate of Dorothy Day. He was also a widower and an old friend of my parents and he volunteered to move in and live with Sam. "To do right by Sam which I didn't do with my father," he said at the time.

I'd visit Sam daily. Mostly he'd snooze on the couch. If I brought a friend the old boy pulled himself together, adjusted his hearing aid, and shed twenty years for an hour or so. But he was tired.

I marvel at the contradictions of the human mind, which are revealed when the wiring goes bad. I refer specifically to two events that occurred on the same day. Event one: I pick Sam up in the morning for a visit to the Eye, Ear, Nose, and Throat clinic on Fourteenth Street. It is a simple trip on the westbound crosstown bus; the stop is across from us on the north side of Grand Street. Sam insists, no, the stop is on our side of the street—which is where the eastbound buses stop. He is clearly wrong. If we do as he suggests, we'll only make it three stops to the bus terminal. Now, the man has lived on the Lower East Side his entire life and taken the crosstown bus perhaps five-hundred times. But no, he insists, and shouts at me on the street, stamps his foot like a child—not that anyone gives a damn, it is New York. Finally, I get him to cross the street reluctantly and against his better judgment and onto the correct bus.

I am worried; Sam is losing it.

Then Roger recounts the second event to me the next morning: "Big meeting at the Libertarian Book Club last night. Your father was in great form! Spoke two hours off the cuff on Proudhon. The place went silent. Three profs from City University. They couldn't believe it!"

Neither could I. "Did you take the bus home?" I asked.

I am convinced now that Sam feared his mental powers were declining. But he dealt with the subject so obliquely at the time that I missed his cues. Out of nowhere, with no prompting, he'd say something to this effect: "You know, I hear So and So—and he'd name a famous French historian—has lost his memory! Can you imagine anything more tragic for an historian than to lose your memory?" And then he'd pause, as if he did not want to explore the subject any further. The term Alzheimer's disease was not common in 1990, although I am sure now that is what he meant. I simply avoided thinking about Sam that way. After all, he was turning out articles, and good ones, in the final months of his life.

A heavy sadness crept in between us. It was as if I were mourning his death while he was still alive, and he seemed to understand this. We'd sit alone in the dim Motherless apartment while Roger was away. He'd say nothing for hours and then break the silence with remarks that came from deep within.

"You know, the hardest thing in life is to stand facing the wind. That's what we tried to do, that's what we did." —And he was speaking of course of the Wobblies and the anarchists and of Mother and himself. Then he'd rise, as if facing that wind, or perhaps an invisible audience, and he'd shout, his voice hoarse and his face purple from the effort: "The whole thing is a crime, a vast crime, and I'll fight it to my dying breath."

At other times, old memories of a long-ago family slight would surface: "They said to your Mother, 'Don't marry him, he's a bum!' Well, bum that I was, she never had to work a day in her life!" And that rueful smile came over him. I could see in his eyes the pride that he had proven them wrong along with the hurt that would never be erased.

There were bright spots to his last days. The old boy would light up whenever I brought Izolda to visit. He loved women—women of all kinds—and he could eye-drool over her openly now that he needn't glance furtively over Mother's shoulder. And Izolda would turn on the Brazilian feminine charm for his benefit. He was happy to see me happy and in a way I am happy that he did not have to see me unhappy in the marriage a few years later. And there were visitors of every stripe from all over the world to break the quiet of the lonely living room.

Paul Berman dropped by one memorable day. I remember vividly the surprise knock on the door, which I opened, and Paul brushing by me excitedly to get to Sam who was seated at the far end of the long living room table. It was late afternoon and the apartment semi-dark. Paul was a young man then—we were all younger—full of energy and drive, and at the start of what has proven to be a notable career as a journalist and political writer.

"Here, Sam, this is for you," and he tossed a copy of the *Village Voice* on the table in front of him. In those days, the *Voice* was considered a far more influential paper than it is today and across the front page, in banner headline was Paul's article on the situation in Nicaragua: all about how the so-called "common people," both in Nicaragua and working abroad in the U.S. and Europe, banded together and practiced mutual aid to combat starvation and to resist the oppression of the Sandinistas and the Contras. Paul's criticism of the Sandinistas did not sit well with the liberal left—as ignorant of history as it was all-knowing—and he caught abuse for it. But he stuck to his guns. He said he owed the thrust of his article, his perspective on events, to Sam.

Paul had been gracious toward Sam when Sam was alive and has remained so in the many years since his death. They had known each other since 1972 when the seventy-year-old Sam greeted him in his *vakokta* undershorts, which caught Paul off guard. Paul came to know Sam well. I think that of the many people Sam influenced he best expresses the essence of the man. I quote from him a bit.

"Sam Dolgoff had many great traits, but the greatest of all was a nobility of character—a human sympathy that made him side with the downtrodden not just now and then, when he was feeling kindly, but consistently in nearly everything he did and said." Paul acknowledges that their political paths diverged, but he goes on to say, "And yet, though old and ailing, he had the energy and spunk to lend me support and encouragement when my critics were throwing rocks. What a generous man he was! I used to love hearing that gruff old voice on the phone. No one had a gruffer voice than Sam Dolgoff. Pure gravel."

"He taught me how to look at the world," Paul said, "through eyes that are not the same as the official eyes of the state and the big establishment and the ideologues. He taught me how to stand on my own two feet."

Our last political discussion took place in the run-up to the first Gulf War. Sam had entered his irreversible decline. His breath had grown short, his steps very slow, although his mind remained sharp despite the lapses I have described. The media spectacle, the patriotic drumbeat, disgusted him. But not the hole in the wall, South American restaurant I took him to. Steak, rice and beans, his kind of place. We played our old game: I the straight man Devil's advocate, Sam the pontificator.

"What do you think of the Iraq business?"

"Bloody bastard George Bush. He wants the war. He won't stop till he has one. He wants blood, blood. Its all about blood and oil and power."

"But Hussein is a dictator and a vicious tyrant. He invaded Kuwait, no?"

"So what? Granted, but is he any worse than the Syrians, the Saudis, Kuwaitis, Iranians? There is nothing to distinguish him from the friends of the Americans or from the other bastards there. In fact he was a friend of the U.S. a few months ago."

"Bush called Hussein 'Hitler.'"

"He gets out of Kuwait. The oil starts to flow and all will be forgiven, and we will make friends with Hitler again."

As events played out the old man's prediction was not accurate and in the decades that followed the disaster spiraled out of control in a way he could not have foreseen. Yet I think that he was accurate in the essentials nevertheless.

# 71
## SAM'S END

The inevitable call interrupted my lecture in front of forty students. "It's your father," Maria, my assistant said. "You had better leave now."

"My breath is running fast. I can't stop it," Sam said on the phone.

"Call Dr. Inkles, and then call emergency," I said.

I rushed to the hospital. Dr. Inkles was by his bed and very sad. He came from the Lower East Side and his roots were with old socialists and anarchists and the plain poor people who lived there. He had special affection for my parents; told me so each time I brought them to his clinic. The doctors had stabilized Sam's breathing, but in those days—1990—they felt there was nothing much else they were able to do for him. If he were younger they may have been able to operate, but at his age his skin and tissue would literally disintegrate at the touch of the knife. So he lay in a room on the fourth floor of the hospital along with three other fellows. I was too numb or stupid to realize this was the death room, the room of disposal. The patients brought to this room would either die there, or, if luckier, would be taken home for the short time left to them.

Sam stayed a week or so before they deemed him well enough to travel. I visited him each day, surrounded by others waiting to die: an old ultra-orthodox Jew who slept fitfully on his side, face down, taking non-stop short breaths, his son in religious garb, suspenders and long sleeves, his face against his father's, remaining in that pose hours on end; a Dominican fellow, not so old, seemingly healthy except for a grotesquely swollen stomach, alone, who seemed to take a great interest in Sam; a third bed, with much coming and going: an elderly black man; an Irish-looking guy with a florid face; others wheeled in and out.

I mentioned earlier that Abe arrived from Chicago and I took advantage of him by taking a day off. I also mentioned that he and Sam sang some of the old Wobbly songs together. I did not mention that Sam clutched his hand as they sang. The Dominican fellow seemed impressed when I came for Sam the next day and I asked him if maybe he was moved that some of the melodies to the old songs, such as "Preacher and the Slave" and "Dump the Bosses of Your Back," were religious hymns. But, no, he was taken by Sam's spirit.

"Your father is ok!" he said to me with feeling. "He thinks of the other people."

"My son has come to take me home!" Sam said joyfully, and as his arms reached out to me from the bed, I saw how shrunken and weak his body was, hidden behind that massive bulldog head.

And so, I took him home by medical van, put him to bed, and brought him the phone so that he could call his dear friend Federico Arcos to say goodbye.

Dr. Inkles said it was entirely possible he would rally once he got home; he gave him another month or three. I was surprised Roger called me late that very night that I'd better hurry. I ran to Sam feverishly. But I knew I had arrived too late as the emergency squad brushed by me on the way out the door. They nodded, "Sorry, we tried," and no doubt they were sincere, though it was all in a day's work for them. Sam lay motionless in the early light.

Paul Berman fought to have his eulogy of Sam published in the *Village Voice*; the editor objected vehemently, but at last gave in to one page. Paul got the attention of the *New York Times*. It ran three paragraphs on Sam in the Obituary section, mostly to the effect that he was one the last surviving members of the IWW. "Be proud. Your father was quite a Man," the female reporter said graciously upon checking a few facts with me on the phone. That was the extent to which the mainstream world took note of his death. Coverage was a bit different within the small anarchist world, however. *Freedom* published a thoughtful, respectful piece and the *Libertarian Labor Review* devoted an entire issue to Mother and Sam. There were a few other articles. The night of Sam's death Paul Avrich came to the apartment and put me on the phone with Murray Bookchin, who spoke kindly and gently of my father.

And, so the time arrived when Sam—who had spoken so eloquently at the memorials to Ben Fletcher and Herbert Mahler and Carlo Tresca and Russell Blackwell and Albert Parsons—was finally granted an occasion of his own. Paul Berman, with the help of Arieh Lebowitz of the Jewish Labor Committee, and others, made the arrangements. I was no help at all. Paul Avrich officiated. Some one-hundred people attended, the surviving cross section of his life: old people, young people, people I had not seen since my childhood. This was an anarchist memorial; the service was ever so loosely structured. There was a long line of speakers, most of them speaking spontaneously, moved by the moment. My cousin, Anne Price, is a folk singer and has a clear ringing voice similar to Joan Baez. She sang Ralph Chaplin's "Solidarity Forever" to close out the service. The audience joined in; probably most had not sung or even heard that wonderful song for decades. It brought back memories of youth and struggle and what were probably the best parts of them. They left the hall feeling uplifted in celebration of a life, rather than mourning a death.

I have a single crabby regret. Time constraints made it impossible for Anne to sing Sam's favorite: Ralph Chaplin's "The Common Wealth of Toil." You can get it on *YouTube*: It has an infectious melody and the lyric comes across powerfully when sung. The chorus goes like this:

> But we have a glowing dream
> Of how fair the world will seem
> When each man can live his life secure and free;
> When the earth is owned by labor
> And there's joy and peace for all
> In the Commonwealth of Toil that is to be.

Abe and I saw our parents die barely one year apart. Consider it a right of passage. "Nobody is in front. If there is anything you want to do, do it now," Abe said to me after the memorial.

He and Hadassah accompanied me back to Esther and Sam's apartment. Sorting out their tangled papers and belongings was beyond the scope of his patience. He was anxious to get back to Chicago. We decided to let Roger stay in the apartment. All he had to do was pay the $200 monthly maintenance, a small amount even then.

He stayed ten years. He was not pleased when at last I needed the apartment for my own use following my long overdue divorce from Izolda and asked him to move out. Never mind Sam had left me the apartment, which he acquired through his union membership and not through wealth. Never mind Roger owned another apartment elsewhere. Never mind I offered to pay Roger his moving expenses and then some. Never mind. I was an upper-middle-class gentrifier. He seemed oblivious to the fact that I had no place to live. What would my anarchist parents think, exploiting him like a capitalist, he implied. Let no good deed go unpunished, I guess.

I've lived in my parent's apartment since 2000. I've fixed it up a bit, but some of the furniture remains. The pieces comfort me as do the prints of the anarchists in combat during the Spanish Revolution and the water color of men laboring on a Kibbutz, stark against a simplified country side, painted by Sam and Esther's old friend Rohr, who lived in Israel.

I am seventy-nine years old. Sam and Esther are dead twenty-five years. Except for them, I doubt there is much to my life you would find interesting. In many respects, I have been fortunate. I retired from New York City College of Technology—a branch of City University—in 1998, having taught there since 1961, most of that time as a tenured Associate Professor. You might call me a hard-working academic dray-horse: Class after class, night school, summer school, meager publications. I dislike the academic world of research grants and professional organizations and all the other success paraphernalia. I much preferred my students. That they were working class and poor and immigrant and mostly ill-prepared was fine with me. I also liked the steady paycheck that came to me from, of all places considering my background, the state. The job suited me despite its drawbacks. I'm convinced no one else would have me. I have continued teaching as an Adjunct Professor at Pratt Institute since my retirement: hired not because of ability so much as through networking. My students complain in evaluations that I talk about my parents too much, proof to them that I am over the hill and growing senile. I leave it for you to decide.

I have been twice married and divorced. I remain on excellent terms with first wife Jessica. As a matter of fact, I am writing this passage on the bourgeois holiday, Thanksgiving, and will have dinner with her and my son Gregory later today. As for Izolda, I've paid a hefty ransom to be free of her and shall continue to maintain our nonrelationship. Mundane stuff!

Jessica and I have two children, much grown of course. Stephanie is a talented editor and writer, has held responsible positions in the women's magazine niche: *Glamour*, *Cosmopolitan*, *Self*, *Woman's Day*. She has also served as a reporter, authored a book, did many things. She and husband Paul have brought forth my two grandchildren, sweet girls, nearly twelve years old now.

One instinctively speaks simply to Gregory as if he were much younger—say a ten-year-old. So there is a subtle complexity that creeps into our conversation. He lives in Augusta, Maine, in a perfectly adequate room, looked after by social workers, and supported by Social Security and his parents. "Warehoused" is the proper word; he is alone, separated from others by his autism and other disabilities, unable to work. He takes his anti-hallucinogens religiously, which allow him to roam free, but they add weight. He is 350 pounds—not only from the pills but also from a horrific diet. Jessica and I cannot supervise him from a four-hundred-mile distance and he is not equipped to survive in New York. My nightmare is that after I am dead he'll lose his legs from diabetes or something awful like that. Or maybe my nightmare is that he may lose them while I am alive. In any case, I visit him in Maine several times a year and he comes to New York to stay a bit with Jessica and then me. Each time he leaves, I cry interior tears. He calls me three, four times a day. Always it is the same conversation. "You okay? How's the weather?" "I'm fine." That's it. Every three weeks he adds "I need money." Conversation is not his purpose. His purpose is to hear my voice, to find reassurance that he is not alone in this wide, cold world.

But what the hell! Everyone has got something. I'm healthy, though I have apparently inherited Sam's bad prostate and my pecker does not work the way it did when I was young.

So, again, it has been twenty-five years since the death of my parents: a quarter of a century. These last ten years I've fallen victim to a strange compulsion. I cannot get Sam—and to lesser extent,

Mother—out of my head. Not they alone, but their world, and all the stuff of my youth, which I have absorbed through a kind of emotional osmosis. As you have seen, I have become a prolix relater of anecdotes, a fountain that won't turn off!

Marianne Enckell of the International Center for Research on Anarchism (CIRA) in Lausanne knows this affliction well: "Shadows, shadows, ghosts," this charming woman said to me with a knowing smile over coffee along the peaceful shore of Lake Geneva. "That is what anarchists leave their children. Tales. Of things that happened, may have happened, maybe not! The ghosts of memory!"

Dieter Gebauer, Ronald Creagh, Marten Pine, my dear friends Federico Arcos and Herb Miller, now gone—they have urged me to put my ghosts and shadows down on paper. And so I have. I leave behind a record of my parents' life and through them a history of sorts, the history of a culture, and of a chapter of American radicalism that few people know about. It is an incomplete and inadequate record, no doubt. Sam joined the IWW in 1922. For five years before that he was a member of the socialist party (YPSL). That is over seventy years of activism and, excepting Mother, I knew him better than perhaps anyone.

We are nearing the end of my story. Since you have come this far with me I'd like to present you with a souvenir, a memento of sorts: two incidents that distill for me the essence of Mother and Sam's characters. Nothing outwardly dramatic happened in Mother's case, more so in Sam's.

Mother. In the mid-1970s the distinguished French historian Ronald Creagh, and his beloved Kirsten, visited my parents on their second trip to the United States. Their first trip, several years earlier, had been joyful. Ronald and Kirsten were newly married and were touring the country as he researched his important exploration of nineteenth-century North American anarchism. Ronald had long discussions with Sam that influenced his decision later to become one. Their second visit however marked a sad occasion. As Ronald said to me, Kirsten's "health was already quite a disaster." They were as yet unaware this young and beautiful woman had contracted leukemia but it was clear she was in dire straits, and this was her farewell. Ronald has said to me many times that Mother's sympathy and understanding of Kirsten was a thing he would never forget. It went beyond compassion to another depth. Mother had that capacity—to go to another depth.

Sam? Let me tell you of the night he was awarded his Nobel Prize. The ceremony took place in a dim, cavernous Irish bar in New York's Meat Packing District at the far end of West Fourteenth Street, hard against the Hudson River. Today the Meat Packing District is a theme park for upper-middle-class tourists, the quaint nineteenth-century structures and cobbled streets a pleasant stage set. Every old city has that kind of place. But in 1985, the year of Sam's Nobel Prize, they still packed meat in the Meat Packing District. It was a coarse, working-class neighborhood, a remnant of the old days: winos and dingbats and truck drivers and meat packers, rather than the chic people.

Early 1985 would come to mark a sad occasion for the union movement. Margaret Thatcher had finally broken the two-year strike of the British coal miners. "The enemy within," she had called them and claimed they were "a mob" that did not share the values of other British people.

On May 29, 1984, five-thousand pickets clashed violently with police. Arthur Scargill, the president of the National Union of Coal Miners, described the battle this way: "We've had riot shields, we've had riot gear, we've had police on horseback charging into our people, we've had people hit with truncheons and people kicked to the ground. The intimidation and the brutality that has been displayed are something reminiscent of a Latin American state." (As if violence is contrary to British tradition!)

And so, to the huzzahs of the British and American conservatives, Thatcher broke the strike and obliterated a working-class culture, and consigned thousands of proud men and their families to poverty.

I do not know the details, but Sam was asked to address a delegation of Welsh coal miners who, in desperation, had come to the United States in search of funds and support. Sam still got around reasonably well but his step was shaky and his breath short and so Marten Pine and I brought him to the cavernous Irish bar on

Fourteenth Street. The regulars up front let their turned heads follow us as we made our way to the back room.

I was a bit startled by what I saw. The room was larger than I expected and so was the crowd. Perhaps one-hundred people, it was hard for me to tell, but certainly not the twenty or so on a good night that I remember about the old IWW meetings. And the men were seated silently and expectantly in waiting; we were a bit late.

As Sam put it later, what was there to say? My father stood before these roughly dressed miners, with their gnarled faces—even the younger among them—and big hands. Years ago, I had seen the John Ford classic *How Green Was My Valley*, about Welsh miners, but no actor is capable of capturing the expressions of these men, their eyes, and their sadness. Perhaps Sam saw before him the Wobbly miners, gandy dancers, seamen, and lumberjacks of his youth. I wonder what the Welsh miners must have thought at the sight of the old man facing them: thick shouldered, wild hair, emphysema stout—the Jewish face, the checkered shirt, the suspenders, the white socks showing beneath the cuffs of his wrinkled pants. As it turned out none of that stuff mattered.

What was there to say? The strike was lost. Words were insufficient. A long pause as Sam stood before them. If there was nothing to say, why say it? Without a plan, in the moment, Sam raised his right arm high in a fist. And then he sang-croaked in his gravel baritone the old English strike song he was sure the men knew:

Hold the fort for we are coming
Union men be strong....

It was a Wobbly favorite.

The room exploded! Martin said later he never saw anything like it. I certainly hadn't, this release of emotion, the entire room thundering *Hold the fort for we are coming/ union men be strong/ side by side we'll battle onward/ victory is ours.*

Finally the room went quiet and Sam said simply that no strike is really lost. The men had stood up for their rights, their dignity, and that is something never lost.

And now, at last, Sam's Nobel Prize. The men of the dark, crowded bar out front had heard the explosion, the songs, and Sam's short speech. They fell silent as Martin and I helped Sam navigate past them to the street.

"You kin drink here any time you like!" the bartender called out to Sam in Irish tribute.

I wish I had words to describe to you Sam's face: Pride, self-deprecating humor, irony, a complete understanding of the human condition:

"You know," he said solemnly, "that's the highest compliment!"

THE END

# CHAPTER NOTES

15     "In the broader sense." Walter C. Smith, *The Everett Massacre* (Chicago: IWW Publishing Bureau, 1917), 183.

18–19  All quotes about Durruti from Peter E. Newell, *Fighting the Revolution*, no. 1 (London: Freedom Press, 1971).

24     "Through the many years." Sam Dolgoff, *Fragments*: A Memoir (London: Refract Publications, 1986), 2.

26     "Upon our arrival…" Ibid, 2–3.

26     "Despite the horrible…" Ibid, 3–4.

36     "The hair-splitting quarrels…" Ibid, 6.

37     "The anti-war World War I…" Ibid.

38     "A few months after its St. Louis…" Ibid, 7.

45     "We were heartile welcomes…" Ibid, 8.

54     "I became a migratory worker…" Ibid, 37.

54     "But the working hobo…" Ibid.

56     "There was no discrimination…" George S. Schuyler, *The Messenger* (July 1923).

56     "I remember shipping…" *Fragments*, 38.

58     "Of the 46 on bond…" Fred W. Thompson and Jon Bekken, *The Industrial Workers of the World: Its First 100 Years* (Cincinnati: IWW, 2006), 130–131.

60     "The Communist Party official mouth-piece…" *Fragments*, 50.

62     "The Unemployed Union at 2005 West Harrison…" *Fragments*, 53.

67     "Maximoff's pre-eminent place…" Sam Dolgoff, "Gregory Petrovich Maximoff," in Gregory Petrovich Maximoff, *The Guillotine At Work, Vol. 1: The Leninist Counter-Revolution* (London: Cienfuegos Press, 1979), xvi.

69     "Lenin, according to Maximoff…" Bill Nowlin, "Introduction," in Gregory Petrovich Maximoff, *The Guillotine At Work, Vol. 1: The Leninist Counter-Revolution* (London: Cienfuegos Press, 1979), vi.

117    "Aunty was strong willed…" Paul Avrich, *The Modern School Movement: Anarchism and Education in the United States* (Oakland: AK Press, 2005), 270–271. Quoted in *Fragments*, 58–59.

119    "Numerous attempts conclusively demonstrate…" *Fragments*, 66.

120    "Lilly Sarnoff…" *Fragments*, 61.

120    "Harry Gordon…" Paul Avrich, *Anarchist Voices: An Oral History of Anarchism In America* (Oakland: AK Press, 2005), 273. Interview with Lydia Miller.

122      "I was so overcome by the sight…" Paul Avrich and Karen Avrich, *Sasha and Emma: The Anarchist Odyssey of Alexander Berkman and Emma Goldman* (Cambridge, MA: Harvard University Press, 2012), 133, 134.

125–126 "Did you know Emma Goldman…" Interview with Sam and Esther Dolgoff, June 1972, Oral History Project in Labor History, Roosevelt University. Available at http://www.roosevelt.edu/Library/Locations/UniversityArchives/OralHistory.aspx128. "There is no horror…" Michael Bakunin, *Federalism, Socialism, Anti-Theologism* (1867). Quoted in Sam Dolgoff (ed), *Bakunin on Anarchy: Selected Works by the Activist-Founder of World Anarchism* (New York: Vintage Books, 1971), 134.

130      "his first speech…" Nunzio Pernicone, *Carlo Tresca: Portrait of a Rebel* (Oakland: AK Press, 2010), 13

131      "Tresca recalls that Mussolini…" *Fragments*, 28.

133      "A photograph of a handsome…" *Carlo Tresca*, 37.

133      "Typically, after a long day…" *Carlo Tresca*, 26.

134      "With his comrades…" Gerald Meyer, "Carlo Tresca: The Dilemma of an Anti-Communist Radical," *Political Affairs* (November 3, 2009)

137      "After the meeting…" *Fragments*, 142.

137–138 "The whole building…" *Fragments*, 133.

139      "Ninety-four was also…" Ibid.

143      "Galleani rejected all forms of organization…" *Carlo Tresca*, 53.

143      "The anarchist movement and the labor movement…" Luigi Galleani, quoted in Ibid.

143–144 "Such activities…" Paul Avrich, *Sacco and Vanzetti: The Anarchist Background* (Princeton: Princeton University Press, 1991), 57.

145      "The cities are the new front line…" *Fragments*, 102.

147      "Within a week…" *Carlo Tresca*, 267.

151      "the ideas of Bakunin and Kropotkin…" *Anarchist Voices*, 424.

152      "Both the CIO and the AFL…" *Fragments*, 12.

153      "My husband was born Wong Chay-tin…" *Anarchist Voices*, 411.

153      "Yat Tone travelled…" Ibid, 424.

158      "Rocker, although a gentile…" *Anarchist Voices*, 7.

161      "There was a certain selfishness…" *Anarchist Voices*, 456.

167      "In Spain during almost three years…" Gaston Leval, quoted in Sam Dolgoff (ed), *The Anarchist Collectives: Workers' Self-Management in the Spanish Revolution 1936–1939* (New York: Free Life Editions, 1974), 6.

169      Russell Blackwell, "Introduction," in *Spanish Revolution: A Bulletin Published by the United Libertarian Organizations*, Vols 1–2,

1936–38 (New York: Greenwood Press, 1968).

169    "According to the US State Department..." *Fragments*, 17–19.

171    Fenner Brockway "The CNT as I Saw It," *Spain and the World* (July 1937).

173    "Russian policy at that time..." Russell Blackwell, "The Spanish Revolution Revisited," *New Politics*, vol. 7, no. 3 (Summer 1968).

173    "They entrenched themselves..." *Spanish Revolution* Blackwell's Introduction is available at https://libcom.org/library/spanish-revolution-newspaper.

174    "[T]he editors of the paper..." Ibid.

174    "Upon taking power..." "The Spanish Revolution Revisited."

178    "The daily experiences..." Charlatan Stew, "The Spanish Revolution: A Brief Introduction," Kate Sharpley Library, http://www.katesharpleylibrary.net/wpzj42.

181    "Captain Raymond Dronne..." Anonymous, "Forgotten Heroes: Spanish Resistance in France, 1939–1945," *Fighting Talk*, no. 15 (November 1996): 23.

187    One of the IWW's most innovative..." Franklin Rosemont, *Joe Hill: The IWW and the Making of a Revolutionary Working-Class Counterculture* (Chicago: Charles H. Kerr, 2002), 277

187    "The deepest taint..." Jane Street, quoted in Meredith Tax, *The Rising of the Women: Feminist Solidarity and Class Conflict, 1880–1917* (Chicago: University of Illinois Press, 2001), 134.

187    "don't believe in mistresses..." Ibid, 134–135.

188    "One cold morning..." William Haywood, *The Autobiography of Big Bill Haywood* (New York: International Publishers, 1929), 249.

191    "Local 8 was a black-led..." Peter Cole, *Wobblies on the Waterfront: Interracial Unionism in Progressive-Era Philadelphia* (Chicago: University of Illinois Press, 2007).

194    "On one of my organizing..." Matilda Robbins in *Industrial Worker* (November 2, 1960), 2. Quoted in Peter Cole (ed), *Ben Fletcher: The Life and Times of a Black Wobbly* (Chicago: Charles H. Kerr, 2007), 132.

199    "These hundred and one are outdoor men..." John Reed, *The Education of John Reed: Selected Writings* (New York: International Publishers, 1955), 177.

203    "Fletcher was punished..." Stephen M. Kohn, *American Political Prisoners: Prosecutions Under the Espionage and Sedition Acts* (Westport, CT: Praeger, 1994), 99.

214    "Now the logger..." Commission on Industrial Relations, *Industrial Relations, Final report and Testimony Submitted to Congress by the Commission on Industrial Relations*, Vol 5 (1916): 4236.

217     "Herbert Mahler has been dead…" *Fragments*, 136.

234     "The disintegration of the MTW…" *Fragments*, 145.

235     "was from early morning…" Ibid, 141.

235     "The MTW fought…" Ibid, 142.

235     "Maritime workers…" Ibid, 139.

237     "The MTW as an organization…" Ibid, 145.

244     "Sam looked like he combed…" *Anarchist Voices*, 472.

246     "Tuli was a true American…" Richard Gehr, "Tuli Kupferberg, 1923-2010: The Fine Art of Whittling It All Away to Nothing," *Village Voice*, July 13, 2010.

248     "She has always insisted…" Dwight MacDonald, "The Foolish Things of the World," *New Yorker*, October 4, 1952.

251     "For only his close connections…" *Fragments*, 86.

251     "Thomas took an active part…" Ibid, 87.

265     "working on his PhD…" William Bryk, "The Jesus de Galindez Case," *New York Press*, August 21, 2001.

266     "When Bayard Rustin…" William Flamm, "The Original Long, Hot Summer: The Legacy of the 1964 Harlem Riot," *New York Times*, July 15, 2014.

273     "was among the thirteen…" Wikipedia entry on Dave Van Ronk.

277     "At one of our meetings…" *Fragments*, 100.

282     "One of the most vociferous…" quoted in *Fragments*, 176–177.

283     "The members who built…" *Fragments*, 177.

284     "All over the world the submerged peoples…" Sam Dolgoff, "The South's Negroes are in Motion," *Views and Comments*, February 1956.

289     "Behold!…" Sam Dolgoff, "Ghana—Birth of a State," *Views and Comments*, February 1958.

295     "without doubt…" Frank Fernandez, *Cuban Anarchism: The History of a Movement* (Tucson: See Sharp Press, 2001).

296     "from Cuba after the May Day…" Ibid, 72.

296     "The first lengthy installment…" Sam Dolgoff, "Cuba: Dellinger Returns from Animal Farm," *Views and Comments*, Summer 1964.

321     "A capitalist democracy…" Sam Dolgoff, *The Labor Party Illusion* (New York: Libertarian League, 1961), 3–4.

325     "Bakunin asserted…" Mark Leier, *Bakunin: The Creative Passion* (New York: Thomas Dunne Books, 2006), 248.

326     "remarks make up…" Ibid, 249.

328     "I helped him prepare…" Murray Bookchin, "A Meditation on Anarchist Ethics," *The Raven: Anarchist Quarterly*, vol. 7, no. 4 (Winter 1994): 343.

329     "After three or four days…" Ibid, 328.

330    "One may reasonably wonder..." Ibid, 343.

331    "Thus it was not because..." Ibid, 346.

351    "as a foreign-born anarchist..." *Anarchist Voices*, 245.

369    "Embracing me..." Ulrike Heider, *Anarchism: Left, Right, and Green* (San Francisco: City Lights, 1994).

377    "He taught me how..." Paul Berman, "Sam Dolgoff" *Anarcho-Syndicalist Review*, 35/36, Fall 2002.

AK Press is small, in terms of staff and resources, but we also manage to be one of the world's most productive anarchist publishing houses. We publish close to twenty books every year, and distribute thousands of other titles published by like-minded independent presses and projects from around the globe. We're entirely worker-run and democratically managed. We operate without a corporate structure—no boss, no managers, no bullshit.

The Friends of AK program is a way you can directly contribute to the continued existence of AK Press, and ensure that we're able to keep publishing books like this one! Friends pay $25 a month directly into our publishing account ($30 for Canada, $35 for international), and receive a copy of every book AK Press publishes for the duration of their membership! Friends also receive a discount on anything they order from our website or buy at a table: 50% on AK titles, and 20% on everything else. We have a Friends of AK ebook program as well: $15 a month gets you an electronic copy of every book we publish for the duration of your membership. You can even sponsor a very discounted membership for someone in prison.

Email friendsofak@akpress.org for more info, or visit the Friends of AK Press website: https://www.akpress.org/friends.html

There are always great book projects in the works—so sign up now to become a Friend of AK Press, and let the presses roll!